FOREWARD

For Freya, Isabelle, William, Niamh my b..i-
ent children, I'm so proud of you all in (.... 's
follow your dreams and fly high despit...n
through. Love you, Mum x

For Maria, Jacky, Scott, Julie, Chloe and Deb aka The Secretary, Nurse, Alpha women, The Stage manager, The Nanny and The Work coach.

For Miss A who is now part of my family and Tam if you're out there and this reaches Korea, you're also welcome for supper anytime in my home with your sisters.

For Suzanne, to whom I'm sorry for any hurt I caused you, but how happy you are to be free and happily married to your Tony, thank you for your ongoing support.

And for J my first husband, whose choices and behaviour that came with all these consequences, that sent me on this journey to arrive at where I am now. I will be forever grateful for the depth of love you did show me, I felt, and you showed our three children. Also, for your incredible hands-on parenting and how important you made me feel in the children's lives before you went f**king mental, thank you.

This book is all I have learnt in 13 years and how I've kept swimming. If my experiences, random ramblings helps just one person, I'll be pleased, because no one needs to be single for a year, take a warm bath and learn Yoga, F**k Yoga!

To all those who read my ramblings, enjoy!

Sarah x-x

I'M NOT A REHABILITATION CENTRE FOR POORLY RASIED MEN

(a.k.a I attract narcissists (deadbeats) and then can't get away from them)

Wow I pick em'! At 19 I fell in deeply in love with let's face it an omnipotent twat, not that I realised at the time. A fairy-tale wedding (thanks dad), three beautiful children, a gorgeous home, a hands-on dad, doting husband, provider. His faults? … not great at DIY! But there was always a friend to fix a shelf or mend a tap. But what was behind my rose-tinted glasses was an adulterer and a 'smoke and mirrors con-artist' where money was concerned, husband. This guy tested my anxiety to new levels with his lies, crimes and life mission to try and remove all my rights as a mother and to make it is mission at all costs, including those of our children to seek revenge on a broken marriage that he created known amongst my friends and family as AT1.

What followed was anxiety, worry, upset, heartbreak and three very young children to raise and shape through the abuse that then followed, due to allowing myself to be preyed upon.

Cue twat number two, a widowed man I'd known since I was 15, he didn't have to work very hard, we had history. Love bombing came easy for him, false promises and mirroring all I loved to hook me in, and I jumped into his arms blindly in love thinking all our problems had been solved. What followed was his revolting self-promotion over the death of his wife who would know doubt be disgusted at his behaviour and how he used his grief to worm his way out of crimes and various behaviours turns my stomach. 13 years on and another beautiful daughter to add to my two girls and a boy, I've learnt he used all the same routines to hook the women in his life since 2007... The cooking breakfast routine, check. Telling each women Lyme Regis was their special place or anywhere by the sea, check. We all had to call him Mr B, check. I note as I write this the current 'supply' is being spoilt to all the above. When she's ready there's a place in our club for her and we have the t-shirt ready! This guy (AT2 as we call him) has under his belt a secret daughter, affair, frauds and lies, so many lies he doesn't know where the truth begins. My nan and wise friend Maria always said, 'oh what a tangled web we weave if at first we deceive'. Christ, when his lips move it's usually lies. If he ever said (and he did on a regular weekly basis) "Believe what you want" then he had done exactly what I or any of us were accusing him of.

Why do I or any of the other women 'hooked' by these two narcissists and attract men like this? Because we all have the same attributes in common, we are kind, thoughtful, good listeners, home makers and we the most common denominator, we like to help fix people. But these kinds of partners can't be fixed, your just their 'primary fuel' for a period (some last longer than others) and already they have the 'next fuel supply' lined up unknowingly to the current fuel supply. I've already spotted the next 'supply' for one of them.

So, two decades, my 20's and my 30's given to two men, poorly raised and with a master plan to follow only their own narratives, gains, wants, wishes and needs.... 2 wankers, 4 beautiful anchors. How have I survived? I don't really know... I just know that this short book is full of all the ways I have, the things I've implemented, the antics I got up to, ways I coped and how life has changed, but I've just gone with it. What's next? Who knows, but I do know that I will never ever, ever ignore red flags, or hold onto someone who doesn't value my worth as a women, mother or human being.

DID YOUR MUM EVER TELL YOU; HOW IMPORTANT FRIENDS ARE?

(a.k.a The Secretary, Nurse, Nanny, Stage manager, Alpha women and the Work coach)

Did she? Or perhaps someone else in your family? How true it is! I'm really blessed to have lots of friends, but the small crew mentioned above have been the A-team right from 2009, The Avengers you might call them.

Without these men and women at the end of my phone, email or using up my T-bag supply, I wouldn't be where I was at this stage, penning this all down.

Three of the above 'my legal team' friends who helped me construct emails to Judges, sloppy solicitors, Cafcass officers and text messages to AT1 and 2. Oh the messages we've thrown about the room on a Friday evening over wine or on conference video calls. Vicarious living through my life at its best.

Friends are invaluable in these situations, they are not family, they can remove the emotion from correspondence. We also tended to write 'f**k off and f**k you' emails, alternative content for the things you really want to say, but just can't! So, cathartic. Use the notes app on your phone and write them there, just bash those keys and say it, but DO NOT send them.

I have so many 'f**k you' drafted emails, texts and letters stored, which make me laugh when I read them back. Cause if you don't laugh through these processes, how the hell do you make it through and come out the other side. Laughter has been and is my biggest tool.

Then there's your friends who will make your exes into photo shopped memes (those kinds of friends), my all-time favourite being 'the bin man' and 'one grave, two spades'. If I ever died in these subsequent years, Deb please get hold of my phone and delete all the saved photos, thank you.

Surround yourself with those that can help you fire back but, see a positive and laugh out loud at the same time.

Fill your time with a small group of your friends who can support you with different aspects of what you're dealing with. Everyone's got friends with different skills and careers. Knowledge is amour and knowledge is power. A different prospective can work wonders on a day if you're feeling a bit bitter (yeah, we all have those days)

That prospective of the outsider really helps you clarify your actions, processes and sometimes it's just too much for a new partner to onboard. Their emotional support can be invaluable but, not always is there space, in your new relationship to lay everything on them. Although, there have been times when I have laughed when I've received messages or email that have clearly been written by the 'new supply' because they contained commas in all the right places and 'gentle' words. It made the reading more fun. Laugh at it, that some new sucker, is the old you.

Remember this…. "THEY ARE NOT BETTER THAN YOU, THEY JUST HAVE LOWER STANDARDS!"

I promised my friends a big party to celebrate when this chapter in my life is over, I didn't realise I'd have to reassemble The Avengers 7 years later to 'go again' but, this time we had experience to draw on and a leopard never changes his spots, so predictions came easy. We were almost able to bet on behaviours heading my way and boy were we right.

You can't put a price on friendship, ever!

BEING MY OWN BLOODY BARRISTER AND DEALING WITH SLOPPY SOLICITORS

(a.k.a Pretend you're a cast member of suits and watch lots of CSI, they are not all good at their jobs)

A degree in law and time 'at the Bar' doesn't mean you're great at your job, just like anyone else in any other profession. Ex footballers don't often make great football managers. Never in my life did I think I'd deal with a barrister who refused to negotiate with me in family court. Surely top of their CV/Resume it says

Skill set:

Represent and Negotiate

But I did. I held my own, her refusal to negotiate pre court hearing or in the ten-minute recess given by the judge meant my ex got less child contact time, less of what he wanted, what would have been better for our daughter, and we then had to return to court, I do hope he got a bloody big discount, hah. It does happen.

Being your own barrister in family law proceedings, isn't that scary, once you do it for the first time. The court must make allowances for you being litigant in person. Sometimes it's incredibly frustrating to have a barrister, because they don't always say what you desperately want to blurt out. They can't mind read and there's only so many times they can lean over and whisper to you during proceedings before they can't concentrate.

If you do decide to be your own barrister, make good notes, rehearse it through with a friend, although all the rehearsing in the world can't prepare you for what the judge will say. Always negotiate before a hearing, if possible if the other party has representation that will! I would never advocate negotiating with a narcissist. Many a time, I've just rocked up to a hearing not an hour before, because I had no intention of negotiating with AT1 or AT2 and waited to be before a judge. The judicial system in family law is there to assist your children and help you make decisions best for them, you haven't committed a crime. It goes back to children being frightened of the Police due to stories read to them and what they are taught, they are there if they need help.

When you get to the court building, find out which number court your listed in (there are many, usually floors worth) then sit as far away as you can from that court number in your own space, just make sure you've told the court clerk where you are. Take a friend if you're representing yourself. You can take a friend or family member into the court hearing under a ruling called 'Mc Kenzie's friend' Someone just to sit with you and write your notes for you. They can't speak up, but they can be a God send of support if you're nervous. I always go to the court with one of my sisters, we decided that she would wait outside. She finds it incredibly emotive to be in the hearing and watch. Always take someone who is objective, that friend who will look 'outside the box' and play 'devil's advocate'.

Body language is key, don't throw off a 'resting bitch face' or raise your eyebrows in a 'you said what now?" you know the one's that give you those '11' deep wrinkles between your eyebrows and cost you an arm and a leg in Botox down the line?

I always write in a notepad in court when an ex is talking, usually a food shopping list or some song lyrics, it stops you throwing your best 'wtf' face and the judge can't gage your reaction or opinion through a facial expression.

Dealing with a solicitor on the other side....

Make them your new pen pal, write and write and write so that they must read and read and read and then speak to their client and they must respond and respond and respond. Unless you end up with a solicitor like I did that only responded to things she knew she'd get money out of her client for. Not child led at all, oh there out there, believe me. Each town in the UK has at least two firms that are renowned for being poor and money orientated in family law.

I've come across two on this journey and I'm still dealing with one, her skills are incredible as to what and what she won't reply too, her correspondence is funny, the grammar and spelling are incredible for a legal firm. I hope she sees this. I'd want a refund if I'd have instructed her or the next letter free.

Remember this.... You don't have to respond to anything they send you if you don't want to. Some legal firms will try and frightened you by saying 'We advise you to get some legal advice due to the contents of this letter' after a while you get to know what you need to and don't need to respond to. There are some situations where you do need to instruct a solicitor, but in my experience, unless it's for divorce and financial remedy, there's no need to. Depends on if your ex-partner is particularly litigious, AT1 enjoys the whole experience and it's like a hobby to him.

There are times when you do need to instruct a solicitor in family proceedings, but overall you can reply and apply yourself. In financial remedy applications you need a solicitor. Ask around with friends, someone whose had experience of a firm.

If you're dealing with a solicitor, does your anxiety soar, when a letter from their solicitor comes in, a correspondence from Cafcass or maybe a court hearing listing? Ask that the representatives don't send anything via email, it's your right to request this. I also don't allow any legal letters to be sent to me on a Friday electronically and the odd one's that do arrive on a Friday I don't open until the following week, so not to cause me anxiety at the weekend, when I am with my children and want to focus on them.

Tit for Tat' get into a habit of not responding to 'tit for tat' solicitor emails. I think my favourites this year have been a letter asking me "Why I felt it appropriate to document the moment?" as in take a picture of my own son, ha, ha, ha! Closely followed by a script, yes, a script of what I can and cannot say to my children when I see them. Not a request as to topics to steer off (which is also laughable and incredibly controlling) but an actual line for line of things I can and cannot say. This is an extension of domestic abuse through authorities and a brilliant exhibit of controlling behaviour for court. Scan that and get it e-filed to the court if in proceedings.

You don't need to reply to those kinds of emails, there's not point, just take great satisfaction that they spent money to get someone to write 'flannel' letters that mean absolutely nothing if you are in proceedings, Judges aren't interested in them. It's different if they wrote you a letter about a concern about a child they had or some information that was needed.

Other than that, mudslinging satisfaction for them it isn't needed and is just a huge waste of money on their part... "Powder your nose dry and have a little chuckle to yourself.

THE BAT PHONE
OR THE BURNER

(a.k.a How to give yourself a quiet life, anxiety free until you're ready)

Get yourself a phone that is just for an ex-husband/partner or co -parent, oh the silence this brings to yourself is bloody fabulous. Best thing I did.

The 'Bat phone' or 'The burner' as my friends and family call it, I put this device in a drawer when my children aren't with their father. Then I chose when I want to look at, when I am ready to read the emails or respond to texts. You don't need to be at their beck and call or respond when they want you too, you probably did that when you were with them.

Also, if you have the type of personality that needs to feel like you've got 'the upper hand' or 'have the last word' say what you want to and then switch it off and pop it in a drawer! So, satisfying, if not a little childish, but who cares, your time is YOURS.

DON'T FEEL OPRESSED! For so long, I'd try to take the 'higher ground' or 'be the better person' sometimes that's just not possible, say it! Have you heard that saying 'get it off your chest' DO IT! Just say what you want, if it's not a threat or something that one of these deadbeat exes can use in court in financial or family proceedings, then go for it!

Nothing worse than someone who is still living in their married 2.2 Instagram perfect family to tell you 'Do not to retaliate' or 'Be the better person' GET LOST! What do you know? Has this happened to you? No! so thank you for your advice, but I won't be practicing it, on this occasion. Be gracious, but bloody go for it, as eloquently as you can. In my experience it's a bit like being a first-time mum and all in sundry giving you advice, take what you want but, ultimately do your on thing and own it.

One of the children's dads (AT2) used to tell me to never do the right thing where AT1 was and is concerned in replying to messages, so thank you, I'm now rolling that advice out to your ridiculously messages and emails. What goes around, comes around.

However, there is one exception to this rule for me taught to me by one of 'The Avengers' sometimes known as 'Cagney' when we've had to go on reconnaissance missions in the back of cars to collect evidence... don't ask! She would tell me to "Powder my nose dry" when court hearings were approaching and not to "engage" in those situations she is still correct. Don't let the other 'party' know how you're feeling, stay factual in those times.

The best answer to deal with a narcissist or deadbeat ex on a text message is always "OK", it's my favourite 'one liner' because it means absolutely nothing. Practice replying "ok" in those times when you can't unleash the rath of what you really what to say.

For example: (one of my favourites)

"I would have thought as you are her teacher and her Mum it isn't too difficult to catch her up. I've planned things this side of Christmas, as it's the only time I get with her"

"Ok"

"What? What do you mean Ok?"

"Ok"

Keep up that Ok, shiz', for as long as you need to, until you get silence.... Heaven! And what I call a minor victory, fist pump time!

Then prepare yourself for probably a response from their new supply, with much calmer tones and commas in all the right places where they think they can appease the situation for their new partner. After all, don't forget He/she has told them you are crazy, controlling and probably if there's children involved, that you keep their children from them, oh and probably that you spent all their money. Sound familiar? Geeze. Wait until someone else is writing the messages to them in the future and take great satisfaction in that.

TAKE A WARM BATH AND A MOMENT TO YOURSELF. NO THANKS, LIKE THAT EVER BLOODY WORKED

(a.k.a Useless advice given by professionals, do your own thing, you do you),

"Light some candles, draw a bath and spend a moment alone" worst advice ever and I've heard spoken so many times over by professionals, like that bloody ever worked said no one experiencing divorce, separation or family court.

What the hell does a warm bath do? It makes none of it go away or momentarily make you feel any better? Drown the other party in the bath maybe or add itching salts (are bath salts still a thing, am I showing my age?)

"You do, you" learn what it is that helps you cope with high moments of anxiety, aggravation from the 'other' party or just stress from the journey that can catch you up. For some it's a trip to the gym, a walk or watch a film, for me it was to jump a train for supper with a friend, or grab a coffee with a friend at Costa (other brands available, but not as good in my opinion) or organise another date/gathering to distract me. With more forward planning, I've been on spa days, all day bottomless brunches and exploring in the forests where my parents live. For me, it was to remove myself form home, where things would irritate me or remind me of all that is currently going on.

Therapy, however, can be amazing and finding the right psychotherapist can be a God send, a weekly session where you fire fight or set you up to get you through the next week, as long as they don't prescribe a bath. It can be to gain new strategies on how to get through it all.

My advice would be to find a quick 'go to' that you can 'go to' at any time you need it and a more planned activity that you can factor in when you are leading up to court hearings, mediation or a difficult stretch, like maybe a holiday season. I have a close friend in similar circumstances to mine and we just do 'fly by cuppa's' sometimes we just call in for a cuppa at each other's and all times of the day and night.

You find your thing, it doesn't have to be what the self-help books say or what friends who haven't been through this think, do your own thing, for you. We are all different there is no formula to deal with what you're going through, just don't do it alone.

LEARNING TO BE IN YOUR OWN COMPANY

(a.k.a thinking you'll be like Rachel from F.r.i.e.n.d.s and spend your time with wine, naked in your home)

I'm not particularly great at being in my own company, my dad isn't either. It's because my jobs are very social, I teach, and direct Musical theatre and I've also qualified as a coach and mentor. People everywhere, always.

But there is something (once you master it) to being on your own and doing as you please that can be brilliant. I never thought I'd say that sentence, ever.

I always find that after I've had to exert massive amounts of strength, fight back and courage that I'd get a low day. But it's not a low day it just a day to gather that energy you lost ready to go again. I won't ever be a victim again. So down or low days for me, is my body telling me to recharge because in a few days we are going again to fight with even more conviction.

On weekends where my children have been at their dad's house, I always had plans to catch up with friends and family and go out for supper. It's the only bonus about co-parenting, you get time to recharge your batteries and adult without a gaggle of children. For 5 years I had 4 children under my roof with no co-parenting (and a man child, who was absolutely no use) and now I look back it was a manic time in our lives from the moment I woke to the moment I closed my eyes, with bathing, clothes, cooking, clubs, school runs, but I wouldn't change that for the world because all 4 of my children are resilient, beautiful, intelligent, well rounded children and

3 of them blossoming young teens and adults.

Looking back at photographs in the past 10 years, I look haggard, tired, harassed, worn down. Breaking free of being with an abuser has taken 8 years off me at least, as I approach 44, people think I'm 35 (I'll take it) When I asked my sister about how terrible I looked, she said we had just thought you were tired from having 4 children *cough, cough, 5 children to look after!

But it's my eyes, when I look back at photo's, there's no light behind them, it's amazing when being free of being told you're not attractive every day and negativity, does for you.

Even my skin is better, but then I'm taking time to look after myself more, those things that I'd run out of time to 'fit in' because I was exhausted from the constant chipping away at my personality and I'd started to believe that no one liked me, so I'd just given up.

Now there's something awesome about having an hour or two to myself and looking at how far I've come and what I have accomplished through adversity.

THEY ONLY TEACH YOU AT SCHOOL HOW NOT TO GET PREGNANT

(a.k.a No one teaches you divorce, separation, heart ache, co-parenting or budgeting!)

Am I right? 12 years of schooling in the British education system, GSCE's and A 'Levels in Maths, History, Sciences and Technology, but not one sodding lesson in dealing with difficult relationships, practical parenting or just plain old how to seek help, resources, just back to the TAKE A BLOODY WARM BATH and use a condom.

Why aren't we educating these senior school aged kids to learn where to get help, look for red flags in potential partners and to value themselves?

I mean I would have really benefited from a lesson in reminding me that life is not a Disney relationship (I love Disney by the way) and that Prince charming in my case, as I am very straight, isn't going to swing by on a horse and take me to live in a huge castle. I was raised in a very traditional relationship and although my mum had carved her own very successful career, she gave up work to be a mother and a housewife to me and my two sisters.

Us Brits think the American's are bonkers for accessing therapy so regularly as if it's part of their adult life, but there's something to be said from having a qualified adult to talk to or at, and just listen and suggest. I mean at school I think the only support we had was a 'careers' advisor and in 1994 she asked me (because I was a girl) did I want to be a nurse or a teacher?!?! I wish they'd normalise accessing help in schools from a young age. There are so many great charities and therapists out there to help us gain perspective.

I was lucky enough to attend good schools, in a nice area of Bristol, UK where pastoral care was good, particularly in my primary school which was a church school. Already in my youngest daughter's school I can see that pastoral care is lacking or over stretched.

This morning I was a speaker at a gathering of women to talk about my experience of domestic abuse and one of the questions when I opened the floor was "Why do I think schools still normalise and romanticise family lives through written texts and our curriculum that could lead to women and men being open to potential relationship abuse?" I wish I'd had more time to answer the question. Yes, this woman was right, how? And why? I certainly, being slightly dramatic (ok, very dramatic but, come on it's my job) had a fairy-tale vision of how my adult life in relationships would be, which was built upon during school years. I guess my answer for my own children is to not be frightened of confrontation and how to deal with it and to ask for help even if they feel it is for the smallest issue they are facing. I certainly teach them how to spot 'red flags' and 'not okay behaviour', to question everything and not be swept up with a popular opinion

COMING OUT OF A BREAKUP, WOMEN BE LIKE "I'VE GOT A SCHOLARSHIP TO OXFORD, NEW CAR, POD CAST SERIES COMING OUT AND A TAN TO DIE FOR

(a.k.a We can turn our lives around and become successful while you dive into a new version of me with lower standards)

Women in my experience be like 2 weeks post break up," I've got a new Personal Trainer, made over my wardrobe, a have scholarship to Oxford and a brand-new car on my drive". We thrive on being successful in helping us get over a breakup.

This was a bit tricky for me in my last break up as it was just before the Pandemic hit us in 2020, but nevertheless, I picked back up my open university degree, completed a level 7 course in Coaching and Mentoring and dyed my hair back to a colour I love, I'm such a cliché. But am I happy? yes, I am.

Achieving goals helps me move forward and being successful for my family, work life and plans for my new home life move me further away from the abuse I and my 4 children have suffered and endured.

You don't have to have ambitious plans, but a few tweaks here and there can-do wonders for your confidence and boost you forwards. Blood, sweat and tears maybe required, but what a distraction from the other circus going on around you. Let them continue with their circus recruiting 'flying monkeys' and carry out smear campaigns, usually on social media about you. Focus your time on improving the already high value you, even more.

You don't have to pass a course or learn to sky dive, it can be something like, choosing a new hair style or reading again (I know the more children I have, the less I have read books, what even are they?) Something that really 'got my goat' was when people said "be on your own for a year and learn yoga" honestly, I can't think of anything worse. What's sexy about doing Yoga on your own for a year? I suppose there's no one around should you not be able to hold flatulence in, in those all-important poses. Other than that? I'm always trying to look for a positive in everything that I do or happens to me...

You do you, you do what YOU need to do, to get you through 'those days' it doesn't matter how crazy that might look to someone else, who cares! Dance like no one's watching.

YOU KNOW YOU'VE HAD A LUCKY ESCAPE WHEN TWO OTHER WOMEN CONTACT YOU AND WHY LAUGHTER IS IMPORTANT

(a.k.a how we formed the club and I became the chairwomen, first hand support at its best)

In 2018 a women contacted me with a picture of my partner and her with a baby that was born in 2016, yeah, I fainted in a well-known coffee shop in a blind panic.

My daughter suddenly had a half-sister. He told some truth but, failed to omit that it had been a 7-year affair on and off. This woman bared all the text messages between them, as well as emails. It made for quite the fictional novel. I still have them in a folder on my phone called 's**t I've been sent' Sometimes I look at them to bring it back to reality and not what feels like an episode of 'EastEnders'. Because just every now and again I find myself slipping back to make excuses for his behaviour and I stop myself by looking at the messages.

What's worse is when I entered a relationship with this man, he was in a marriage and seeing the women above who he went on later to have a baby with! Yes, it's not just EastEnders, maybe a little Dynasty thrown in there too.

These two women and I are now friends, we've met and laughed, oh how we laugh and laugh, we can all recount the same things this man did to 'hook' us in. The same routines, cooking breakfast for us, saying Lyme Regis was our special place, making us call him Mr B. The same pattern repeating itself over 14 years to date.

But STRENGTH COMES IN NUMBERS and for us sharing gin and laughing together, we've reserved a chair ready for the next supply, but we suspect this one may hang in' for a lot longer due to her kind nature and calming personality, oh and because she is an SEN teaching assistant who knows how to process everything, EVERY LITTLE HELPS and all that jazz.

But what helps meeting with these women is that I was not alone in what I and my children had endured, I was just stupid enough to put up with the crumbs and lies for the longest to date. It's so cathartic to have a meeting of what he probably no doubt calls 'The coven or The Cronies', but strength comes in numbers, all our children share a lovely relationship and for me I've felt I've been able to put right a wrong with the women I stole him from! She will laugh at this when she reads it. The one thing, however that always comes up (or not very often as the case was for us all) is the push pop. Thank you, ladies, for your support and ongoing friendship.

But seriously, find people who understand to talk to, I'm lucky enough to have actual 'victims' of this man's covert Narcissism and oh boy it helps to meet up with them. But find a friend, a new friend who can really understand each other's situations. Those that haven't been through it, can give advice, but they don't truly feel how it is to want to go back to an abuser, which we all do.

The three of us just hope that 'the new supply' is free of it soon and she sees through the mirroring, projection and lies before it's stolen her boy's best years and they are grown up, she knows really what she's dealing with it, cuppa waiting for you lady cakes.

With AT1 I didn't have the luxury of another women to compare notes with. Mainly because I never have and never will give the supply, he ran off with the satisfaction of ever being able to have a conversation with me. And oh, she tries some 13 years on. Emails, DM's or PM's "Is this still your email address, would it be ok to contact you here" ummmm NO! never will I ever dignify her with a drop of oxygen for a conversation after what you did to my children to fracture their lives and futures. So, keep them coming, they are a great source of amusement to us all and old friends.

Not everyone will have the luxury of this experience and meeting other 'victims' I feel incredibly honoured that these women were able to speak with me and just validate what I really already knew.

If we learnt one thing from the experience of all talking together, it's this.

"If someone says, "believe what you want"" (and he did anytime any of us accused him of anything) THEY DID EXACTLY WHAT YOU'RE ACCUSING THEM OF. Trust your gut instinct always.

IS IT PETTY OR IS IT A SMALL MINOR "JOG ON" VICTORY IN THE FACE OF STATISFACTION?

(a.k.a being petty can sometimes give awesome satisfaction, if only short lived)

Being petty can sometimes be pathetic behaviour but, can also bring a large woosh of satisfaction in the form of a what I call a 'Royal Wave' (two fingers up)

These little 'boosters' on your journey can help immensely and they don't have to be obvious to anyone else or can even be a little inside joke that you can get satisfaction out of.

For example, one of my exes never in 5 years of my daughter being at school never ever read her schoolbooks until now (Funny the latest supply is a teaching assistant) not only that he's never read a schoolbook with the daughter he's never bothered with either. But suddenly and as a side note, I'm pleased for my daughter that he's reading with her but...... The notes he makes in the reading record are a weekly source of amusement and are that of a middle aged passive aggressive peri-menopausal women. But then... oh, you reply down there at their standard because it is funny and well, because you can!

For example, he wrote:

"Great reading, very proud of you as always"

So, what do I do? I screen shot it and send it off to a WhatsApp group with a laughing emoji. But they don't laugh back, one better, they send what I should reply in the reading record the very next day. And so, I reply this....

"No one is prouder of you than me, I see how hard you try every day" hah!

So childish, but so satisfying. It caught the reading assistants' eye and she emailed to say how funny it was, did I stop there? Well for a while, then I started it again on a day where I needed a pickup. I feel like I should finish this paragraph with an evil laugh mwu-hahahaha. So childish, Sarah, so childish, but to hell with it.

Another little victory, I love to do, is a patronising comma in the beginning of my messages, it will go straight over one of their heads, I suspect.

"Being the bigger person" really means shrink and silence yourself in the face of mistreatment. In healing may you learn to honour yourself and take up space with your voice!" and for me that meant small moments of pettiness, sorry, not sorry!

WHEN THEY RECRUIT FLYING MONKEYS AS A SMALL ARMY TO DISCREDIT YOU IN THEIR CIRCUS

(a.k.a grown adults who feed on lies and drama and love to passively aggressively smear campaign you, but have no idea they are just puppets in the plan)

Flying monkeys recruited by a Narc' can usually come in the form of people you thought were friends (or probably still are friends, but haven't seen through the deception to date) In my experience they come in the form of middle aged women who feel sorry for them, not quite enough to be the next supply due to not being their type, but, probably 'like a project' enough to want to help but, this applies to them…

"Thank goodness, social media is out there so you can resolve personal issues by making general passive aggressive posts. I'm sure we'll never know what you're doing"

You know the types I mean, the posts where they think they are cryptic, yet poetically passive aggressive enough to not actually say what they mean. It's honestly made some of my days and I've never laughed so much in my life. The baseline is, what on earth have they been told for them to post something like that and are they really that stupid to believe it? Oh, yes. The funniest thing is, they will be saying to the other party, if she/he wanted support it, of course we would be there for them too. Whatever!

Flying monkeys can sometimes be family members too! Particularly if you have immediate family that have a belief that there's two sides to every story, rather than immediately jumping to support family. 'Blood is thicker than water' and all that.

Social media can be a blessing and a curse during a breakup, separation or divorce.

For me initially when my marriage broke up, it was soul destroying, the women in question would post pictures of their new home, bed and where my children would eventually sleep. It was like a drug, I didn't want to look, but I did.

More recently it is a source of great amusement, because I look at the current supply and think 'poor cow' (sorry mum I said 'cow, to be honest I've said f**k a few times while writing this too, but I'm not surprised given what I've been through)

Sometimes I've been on the most fabulous dates at my favourite restaurants or being treated to a date at the beach for a sunset BBQ (how Mills and Boon) and received a screen shot of an ex's social media and thinking I wouldn't swap this in the world right now for your garden BBQ sat on an office chair with a bottle of Lidl's finest tropical crush, hah.

Another favourite of mine was while I was giving a talk about being a victim of domestic abuse for a women's refuge charity and a screen shot came moments before I was due to stand up to address 100 women in a community church. It was a picture of the latest supply out celebrating his success for passing an exam, so the new supply had been led to believe, but a multiple choice 20 question paper, hah. Oh, how I wanted to scream at her, look at this and run for the hills. But she'll have to make her own mistakes like the rest of us in 'the club (with t-shirts) did.

Whilst sometimes I laugh at things, I'm sent there are other times they make me sad, not because I feel hurt or jealousy, but I feel sad for my children at the choices they made over spending time with the kids or money on them. My first husband came off social media entirely around about the time he was incarcerated, funny that!

My experience and therefore my advice concerning social media... I have had moments where I've suspended various platforms for a while to give myself a break just to concentrate on other projects, or my children and then I've come back to them. You do, you, but don't let these flying monkeys knock your confidence, they are just having a foolish momentary lapse in their lives.

REALISTICALLY HOW LONG DID IT TAKE ME TO GET OVER MY FIRST MARRIAGE

(a.k.a yeah not 6 days, like some of these bitches out here, who can just move on)

It's a marathon not a sprint and if you saw my physique, you'd see that I do not run marathons, more I only get choices in clothes shops that carry awful t-shirts with slogans "Naughty or nice" hah and therefore to cross the finish line took me about 6 years. At least 5 years of those were spent in a new relationship where I felt worthless. Being told no one liked me for those years and the following 4 became wearing.

These men/women who can just move on aren't telling the truth, they just deal with it differently.

I was so trauma bonded to my first husband, all these promises he'd made to me and our 3 children and then was like someone I didn't recognise, he'd been a reflection of myself "mirroring" and it's why I fell for him so deeply. All the things I loved in 'one package' handsome and chivalrous too, kaboom!

Anyone who jumps into a new relationship straight from their last is just looking for what they had with you in someone else. If they haven't taken the time to 'just be' and (I hate this word) but heal then it's doomed from the start and will eventually never last.

Always, implement (for me) a 'Man ban' stir clear of relationships for a while, I have to be honest a 'man ban' has led me into the most trouble in my 40's and a series of dates. It's like buses "Not one for ages, then they all come along at once" enjoy that! Value yourself and take pride in the fact people like you for you and your glorious personality.

So annoying when your friends say "Just be on your own" they are right, but it's ok to think "I don't want to be on my bloody own" me and my friend Deb aka The work coach often say this to each other.

How did I get over the heart break of divorce? Am I still over the heart break of it?

What I did that follows is not for everyone, what did I do? Not take my own bloody advice is what I did!

I allowed myself to be vulnerable and was then predatory meat for the next relationship. I undervalued myself and decided that HALF A STALE LOAF was better than NO LOAF AT ALL! And God it was worse than half a stale loaf for over a decade of my life, it was like crumbs under the table. My family wanted me out and I stuck it out, because of my sheer bloody determination and pride.

Am I over the heart break of my first husband having an extra marital affair with my best friend? (double whammy) Not really, but it's like grief you learn to live with it. His choices have steered the entire course of my life for 13 years and I allowed that for which I get annoyed at myself and that's ok.

So, I'm still running this marathon, this omnipotent overt narcissist is still at large and although I thought when he committed arson, yes arson and went to prison he'd calmed his tits, boy was I wrong. That time incarcerated gave him time to plan this new chapter he's currently putting me through. Covid-19 gave him the opportunity and he swooped in, premeditated and decide to keep hold of our twins, our eldest being off at university and over 18. A year later in court and he's still driving my beautiful, smart, resilient twins 154 miles every day to attend school where they lived with me from his home. Just stuck his fingers up to any authority and the law and has exercised Parental Rights and keep them at his home. It's fractured my family and in particular my youngest daughter's family home life, but it hasn't stopped us having a life and adventures. You may have stolen our children AT1, but you haven't stolen our lives. We continue to have adventures and holidays and learn new skills and make memories.

Think of Ex's like a blue bottle fly, they sometimes fly into your face and annoy you, just get out your racket and bat them off for a bit, sure they'll come buzzing back in your face again, but just bat them away. Don't let the stress and anxiety they bring take over your life, they are like energy sucking vampires. Karma will come for them it always does; I'm fairly convinced they've got people down there warming up their places ready for when their time comes.

MUSIC – IT'S A BLOODY CURSE OR SOMETIMES IT BRINGS SO MUCH LAUGHTER

(a.k.a Having to leave shops or restaurants because a certain song comes on or laughing about the time when…)

Have you heard that saying? "When you're happy you just hear the melody, but when your upset or in trauma you really hear the lyrics and their meanings in songs?"

There's the obvious 'our song' you know the one that belonged to us or maybe a first dance from your wedding, the song your child was born too or maybe even a song that was playing on a first date, that was maybe your last date too. Whatever the tune, I put those songs onto a playlist, my playlist is called 'Survival Sarah' on my phone. There are moments when I like to listen to those songs or times when they feel too much.

It doesn't help that at our wedding, my husband read out lyrics to a song as part of his wedding speech, but later put a twist on them when he left, like this one that always sticks in my throat… "For me it's waking up beside you, to watch the sunlight on your face, to know that I can say I love you, in any given time or place. It's the little things that only I know, those are the things that make you mine" CRINGE! Or maybe I should have paid attention to this one "Cause, whose to know, which one you let go, could have made you complete" moving swiftly on.

Music is so good for the soul, it literally increases dopamine levels naturally, make a play list and dance to that, play it loud in your car or on a smart speaker at home, dance like no one's watching. I particularly feel it when I'm teaching dance with my youth theatre school, I'm immediately happier after classes, even if rehearsals for a production don't go particularly well.

Find new songs that make you smile or go right back to your youth; you know those school disco days and search out those songs that stir memories of first loves or those class mates you had a secret crush on.

Reignite your soul with sounds, on days when I just 'wanted out' I'd go for long drives and turn up the tunes. We've all got those tunes we'd never admit to anyone else we listen to, guilty pleasures, whack those up and sing like no one else can hear.

HOW TV ADVERTS OR FILMS CAN ANNOY YOU WHILST ON THIS JOURNEY

(a.k.a laugh instead at couples arguing on the beach or in the supermarket over cheese)

When your dating, separating, divorcing or single tv adverts can be so nauseous and films for that matter.

I found films particularly nauseous when I was in my last long-term relationship, particularly those where there were fabulous romantic sex scenes, you know the ones with romance and tenderness. I used to sit there and think...why am I still letting you be part of my life, I used to have this with my first husband, and I've settled for this.

Or TV adverts, one that particularly used to get under my skin is my 'McCain's potato products, advocating that families come in all shapes and sizes and yes, they do through tragedy but, not by choices made by d**kheads and that were actually deadbeat fathers in disguise.

I was on a date recently where we went to the supermarket to grab some pasta and wine for our supper and we saw at least 4 miserable men and women, dragging each other around the supermarket, bickering about what they wanted and why they were there.

Remember those times? Aggggggghhhhhhh

AT2 used to always moan that I'd take him to the supermarket with him, but it was sometimes the only time we'd get together in a weeknight, date night? hah

Instead of seeing those adverts as a negative, think in the future I'll be in a better situation to maybe look at those adverts and laugh at the time they used to annoy me.

THINGS PEOPLE SAY THAT THEY THINK ARE HELPFUL, BUT SEND YOU INTO A SPIN

(a.k.a I don't need to get over it, no I don't have a picture of the new supply)

People intentions are usually in the right place, but, sometimes when they don't come from a great place and can affect you…. Any of these familiar?

"Times a healer?" "How long ago did you break up? You should be over it by now"

"It was obvious you two were never meant to be together"

"You just need to meet someone else, quickly"

"What does it matter if he's seeing someone else, you're not together?" Thanks for reminding me.

"Can I see a picture of his or her new partner?"

"Guess what your ex is doing?" NO, thanks, I had to do that while we were together!

Wow, right? But sometimes it's just because you are so highly emotional going through this trauma that it triggers you. It is literally like someone fires a gun on your emotions and you spiral or sends you into 'flight mode' And what people don't realise is that you will dwell on what they've said probably most of the day and certainly up until you fall asleep.

It's that age old saying 'be careful what you say, you can't take your words back'

Two of my long-standing beautiful friend's sons died this year at the age of 21years and I know in their experience with grief that people often say, 'times a healer' and it cuts deep or this one 'at least he wasn't married and had children' is it?

It's the same in separation, divorce and break ups, people think they are saying helpful things to get you through, and they can just stick in your throat like shards of glass.

Equally an ex can say things that stick with you for a long time.

One of my is my first husband texting me (and I can still visualise the text on my black berry, yes, I'm that old) it simply said, "Get my children ready, I will see them in an hour" The disrespect alone in that message stuck with me for years. My beautiful children aren't objects, they are fantastic individuals that don't deserve to be spoken about like that. I still have the text printed out from a screen shot and from time to time when I feel myself feeling sorry for him or swaying to be lenient on him, I glance at it and think 'pull yourself together girl, never look behind you because you're not going there'

Friends that also just agree with you aren't helpful in this situation, empathic maybe, but, sometimes for them to say be objective is a massive asset to your team, go Avengers!

YOU SAID WHAT NOW? TO WHOM?

(a.k.a Nothing either of 'The boys' ever do shocks me in the slightest)

Nothing AT1 or 2 do ever shocks me, even now, I may raise my beautifully micro bladed eyebrows, if Botox allows to an extreme behaviour by AT1, but other than that nothing and I mean nothing is a great shocker. In fact, it was AT2 that always taught me AT1 would not stop and is relentless to submission.

One is intelligent but, has zero common sense and the other is thick as two short planks, but has some street smarts from a life of ducking and diving to survive and not get caught.

If I get a call from some authority, company or committee the poor caller is usually apprehensive to begin the conversation and after the first sentence I usually reply with "this was predicted and bet upon by many at my end, I'm surprised you haven't called sooner" then I usually follow it with "please be aware I am formally recording this conversation due to the circumstances".

If one isn't playing up the other generally is as a rule of thumb or occasionally and rather foolishly (as there is always repercussions) they join forces and align themselves together like something out of a Star Wars movie to try to discredit me. It's like two of the highest order flying monkey's joining together for a jolly escapade or like that terrible political coalition we suffered in the UK in 2010. The funny thing is AT2 doesn't see that AT1 is manipulate him for his own agenda, everyone just laughs at them, it's not unusual for my friends and family to take a sweepstake on who will do what next.

Strategy for when feeling under attack, laugh, the tears of laughter I have shed at their behaviours far out ways any tears of sorrow. Gather 'The Avengers' get a pot of tea brewing and just look at how stupid they look. I mean one of them said once that the reason he didn't see his illegitimate secret child when we were together was because I locked him in an understairs cupboard. One: This guy is a very large unit even for me to hustle into a cupboard and Two: have you seen the cupboard under my stairs there's 10 years of 6 people's shoes and coats in there, it's affectionately known as 'Narnia' to my friends.

As a final note in this short but serious chapter, I want to add that I need Botox due to me having to pull a 'what the f**k frown' for some years now at this pair of fools.

WHAT WERE MY BIGGEST FEARS ALONG THE JOURNEY IN SEPARATION AND DATING?

(a.k.a Yes, they really do run alongside each other, one forms the other in a theme)

A close friend of mine in a similar situation to me (yes, part of The Avengers) once described her initial worst fear of a separation that the new supply was taking her place and that they can fix your ex and she couldn't. Not true! In reality no one and I mean no one can, as they are unfixable. History will repeat itself, sometimes it takes a little longer than anticipated but, it always happens.

My first husbands supply came and went from their various house (4 in total I think, always on the run) several times for months at a time and eventually he dis-guarded the supply. HAH! #minifist-bump yes, petty moment (see a previous chapter) I hope she was worth the therapy my precious children now need and the heart-ache she caused us all by you making the choice you did.

"You can make all the choices you want in life but, you must remember they come with consequences, and you must live with those consequences"

For some people their biggest separation fears come in finances or security, but for those who have been emotionally abused it comes it spoken words and what ifs'.

So how did this apply to dating for me? When you've suffered emotional abuse, when you date it's hard to value yourself and have confidence in yourself to meet new people, particularly when they could be potential relationships. You automatically think they will like someone else better than you? You immediately assume the worse or you do not invest int hem, so that when it doesn't work out you can get over the breakup quickly. I know I still find it hard to take compliments, that comes from 10 years of being told by my ex that no one liked me and people only pretended to be my friends. Constant chipping away at my looks and my personality made me numb to high value compliments. I'm getting better at receiving them.

Recently a guy friend cooked me some supper, after a particularly difficult day dealing with AT1 and he stopped me mid conversation because another guy sent me a voice note, which we listened too. It just simply said "Sarah, do you have any idea what an incredibly f**king beautiful women you are, I look at you and all you've achieved, and I see an attractive, intelligent women" I laughed, and he told me off (I'm not great at being told off) So what am I fearful of? Thing's people say and why? Goodness knows, because it really doesn't matter whatsoever, it's words. My mum would always say to us as kids "Sticks and stones may break your bones, but words will never hurt you" but for me what people thought of me really affected my daily life and my confidence. Now... well now, I think bollocks to everyone, I've reached an age where I'll throw those sticks and stones right back at you or take a shovel to your face. But learning to take those compliments, I still need to work harder at.

A PICTURE BY THE URINALS, HOLDING A FISH OR WHICH ONE IN THE GROUP ARE YOU?

(a.k.a Dating in my 40's and navigating Sleepy, California, Warwickshire, Cornwall, The MP and The Vicar)

Dating in your 40's basically consists of answering a series of questions that I wish I had printed on a T-shirt that I could reveal at that beginning of each first date that say this….

My favourite colour is Blue

I like Italian Food

I have 4 children

I work in the theatre and as a divorce/separation coach

I have 2 sisters and I grew up in Bristol

It's like being on repeat, but still trying to sound very enthusiastic with a forced smile about it at the same time. I felt very similar when our twins were born, and people would stop me in the local shopping centre and want to know the same information repeatedly.

My best dating advice, for an actual date…. meet for a coffee, if you hit it off then progress to get some food and continue the date, don't get stuck at a 5-course sitting at 'The Ivy' where you can't escape for the next 4 hours like me... honestly the guy must have thought I had a weak bladder the number of times I went to the toilet to text my friends.... Help code: get me out of here. Still the food was nice.

Funniest dates I've been on....

I had one guy over covid – 19 pandemic fall asleep on my sofa while I was sat eating our Chinese take away. RUDE! I like to say to myself he, was just comfortable in my presence, not that I bored him to death. Needless to say', we are great friends.

Then there's the 'Vicar' amazing date, full of laughter and antics, he arrived to meet me at the train station on an electric scooter, that he then had to go and park up in a designated area, some 9 minutes later I thought he'd done a runner. I was about to catch a train back home and he came running back round the corner, full of apologies and even more apologies because he's American. What followed was a lovely yet hilarious date and when I asked him "why this town in England, he'd settled in" his reply "I came here to be a pastor" What followed was my friends asking "Was it a long sermon?" and "Did he drink from the Holy cup?" and was there any "pre service confessions?" ha, ha, ha.

I'll be forever grateful for your friendship, love, laughter, cooking, and carpool blue tooth karaoke Josh, thank you, oh and how you're my best date stories and continue to be.

If you're going to 'throw your hat into the ring' of dating in your 30's and 40's definitely develop a thick skin, you need it (Like armour!) Not every potential date is your next long-term relation-ship, have fun...pick and mix. How they act after the first date is not a reflection on you, ever! Everyone has a different agenda when dating and everyone comes from very different places in their previous relationships and some people just don't have man-ners or a moral compass.

The hardest thing about 'dating' is the maintenance, the waxing (not just my moustache) tanning, hair treatments, outfits and babysitters! Phew! Makes me exhausted thinking about it.

But I've been spoilt, I've had the best times and met some lovely men, had beach BBQ dates, high tea, cinema dates, autumnal walks, fire work nights and having some really lovely food cooked for me. And all those dates have helped me to value myself and be more confident in who I am, what I like and value my own worth.

Self-imposed 'man bans' have brought dates like buses, they all come along at once. I often get bought drinks in coffee shops, yes, not bars, I'm 43. Then I worry I give off a 'single aura' 'come on over and by me a skinny latte face'? maybe...

I'm always courteous as I know it may have taken that guy some courage to come over and speak or maybe they are a player, oh the players, they are out there. There are ways to spot them, red flags or sometimes banners.

Women are cruel you know. We talk about our dates in details and sometimes go as far to demonstrate moves or bad chat up lines used for the other women, yeah, we really do that, and we don't need a drink on board, to go into heavy detail.

We give dates nicknames, so that we can refer to you in later conversations or for comparison, oh and we are like FBI agents. We find out all your details even go as far to look at your 'LinkedIn' and check companies house to see what you've been up to in business, yes, we go that far. We look at your social media and anyone with the same surname as you, so we can look at your family!!! Sometimes we open Google earth to get a street view of your property, any women who say they don't look or has a friend who looks, is lying.

In the times when I was 'dating' I would date for a few months then impose a 'man ban'. One bad date can put you off, but I can assure you, it's not a reflection on you.

My second biggest dating advice in my 40's would be, meet within

4-5 days of talking, otherwise you can end up with a pen pal and you don't need one of those.

As well as teaching musical theatre, I coach dating as well as divorce and separation, I love coaching dating, most of my dating coaching clients are middle aged men. I think I'm the most useful to them, because I've been on the other side of equation and have experience.

Enjoy this time, if you find yourself a long-term relationship then look back on this time as a fun part of your life. Just because you're a little older it doesn't mean you can't have the same fun you had in your early 20's. Enjoy making new connections and sharing your life with someone new, if if you are repeating the same answers to questions

I HOPE THIS IS USEFUL FOR SOME

(a.k.a This is just a little of my journey, the fiction book is in progress)

I hope all I 'spilled' just helps one person, then I'll be pleased.

I've been writing a book about what's happened to me for some time now, it's not quite ready as there is a current chapter to close and so much to pen down.

I didn't write this little book to make money or for self-promotion, it has been a cathartic journey for me to pen some of my experience down and boy have I laughed along the way.

I know lots of my friends and family want me to write the 'nitty gritty' and I am, and I will, but writing that side of my journey is so emotional and there are days when I write and I have to put it aside for a while and come back to it.

So where does this leave me? Happy, spending so much time now with Niamh who is 8 and developing into a sassy young tween. What's next? Who knows? I'm sure though 'the boys' will make the next 5-10 years eventful, but I'm ready for whatever they try and throw at us as a family, because I am surrounded by amazing support, family, friendship and a love that will never be afforded to them.

THANK FOR LISTENING I'm OFF FOR A WARM BATH! Like hell am I!

SARAH HAWORTH

SARAH x-x

Printed in Great Britain
by Amazon

72479775R00031

Ethnicity, Exclusion and the Workplace

Ethnicity, Exclusion and the Workplace

John Carter
Oxford Brookes University

First published 2003 by
PALGRAVE MACMILLAN
Houndmills, Basingstoke, Hampshire RG21 6XS and
175 Fifth Avenue, New York, N.Y. 10010
Companies and representatives throughout the world

PALGRAVE MACMILLAN is the global academic imprint of the Palgrave
Macmillan division of St. Martin's Press, LLC and of Palgrave Macmillan Ltd.
Macmillan® is a registered trademark in the United States, United Kingdom
and other countries. Palgrave is a registered trademark in the European
Union and other countries.

ISBN 0–333–92922–5 hardback

This book is printed on paper suitable for recycling and made from fully
managed and sustained forest sources.

A catalogue record for this book is available from the British Library.

Library of Congress Cataloging-in-Publication Data
Carter, John, 1962–
    Ethnicity, exclusion, and the workplace / John Carter.
        p.   cm.
    Includes bibliographical references and index.
    ISBN 0–333–92922–5
    1. Discrimination in employment—Great Britain.   2. Race
discrimination—Great Britain.   3. Sex discrimination in employment—Great
Britain.   4. Minorities—Employment—Great Britain.   I. Title.

HD4903.5.G7 C37 2003
331.13′3′0941—dc21
                                                                2002042817

10   9   8   7   6   5   4   3   2   1
12   11   10   09   08   07   06   05   04   03

Printed and bound in Great Britain by
Antony Rowe Ltd, Chippenham and Eastbourne

For Marian Carter

Contents

Acknowledgements		ix
List of Tables		x
Introduction		1
1	Ethnicity, Employment and Exclusion	9
2	Equity, Policy and Outcomes	31
3	Strategies of Social Closure and Professional Cultures	64
4	The Racialization of Nursing	84
5	Ethnicity, Segregation and the National Health Service	118
6	The Policy in Practice at Unicorn Trust	131
7	Racism, Institutional and Otherwise	160
8	Conclusions	176
References		184
Index		193

Acknowledgements

There are several people who have helped greatly in the writing of this book. They include Jackie Bee, whose laughter is infectious, Rohit Barot for supervision during the early part of my PhD, and Harriet Bradley and Steve Fenton for agreeing to supervise my work and helping it to a successful conclusion. John Bird also made helpful and sensible comments on the text.

Many of my friends and colleagues have helped by encouraging me during some very slow (and painful) periods of writing. I would particularly like to thank Richard Adams and Julie Higgs. Others friends who deserve a mention for keeping me going are Hilary Snaden, Pete Snaden and Simon Philips.

I am also very grateful to my editor, Jo Campling, for saint-like patience.

All the errors, however, are my responsibility.

Most of all I am grateful to Marian Carter to whom this book is dedicated. She will be almost as relieved as I am at the completion of this project.

List of Tables

1.1 Unemployment by sex and ethnic group (1984) 17
1.2 Rate of male unemployment by highest
     British qualification 18
1.3 Rate of female unemployment by highest
     British qualification 18
5.1 Ethnicity and number of applications for promotion,
     hospital B 124
5.2 Ethnicity and number of promotions, hospital B 125
5.3 Ethnicity and current job grade, hospital B 125
5.4 Ethnicity and education 126
5.5 Ethnicity and length of time acting up, hospital B 126
5.6 Ethnicity and training, hospital B 127
7.1 Academic staff by ethnic national group 165
7.2 Total academic staff by ethnic group 165
7.3 Ethnic groups as a percentage of all minorities 166
7.4 Age by ethnic national origin 166
7.5 Minority academic staff by higher education sector 168
7.6 Academic staff by ethnicity/nationality group
     and higher education sector 168
7.7 Mean ages of gender and ethnic groups 168
7.8 Staff holding PhD qualification by
     ethnicity/nationality group 169
7.9 Grade by ethnic national group 169
7.10 High/low grade posts by ethnic national group 170
7.11 Contract status by ethnic national group 170
7.12 Males and females by high/low grades
     and ethnic national groups, HESA dataset 172
7.13 Primary employment function by gender,
     HESA dataset 173

Introduction

This book is an attempt to describe and analyse the monopolization of privileged occupational positions by different social groups. It focuses in particular on the position and experience of ethnic minority groups within professions. The social group that I will mainly, though not exclusively, focus on is African-Caribbean women. My interest in this area may seem strange to some, as I am a white man. However, more than anything, this book is an exploration and discussion of how the notion of ethnic difference is articulated theoretically and practically in the world of work. It is the way in which difference and otherness is constructed that forms the basis for exclusion, both between and within professions. In the wake of the attacks on the World Trade Center in New York, notions of difference that are based on Islamic and Arabic identities are likely to take on a new and greater political significance within the United States, with profound consequences for the definitions of 'others' who are different and regarded as a potential threat to security. To characterize this as an esoteric debate that has no relevance to 'real people' is to miss the point. In both the UK and the US, ethnic minority groups live with the realities of discrimination and the consequences of that discrimination, be it a lack of promotion prospects, poorer pay than their peers or outright rejection from a particular occupational sphere because they are not 'one of us'. My aim is to scrutinize and explain the strategies used by dominant social groups to exclude subordinate social groups from prestigious occupational spheres and to evaluate the success of policies such as equal opportunities and affirmative action policies that have sought to redress discriminatory behaviour.

Those occupational areas defined as professions have, until relatively recently, remained exempt from sociological analysis. This in part reflects the ability with which professionals have been able to protect themselves from external scrutiny. One of the principal claims I will

1

make in this book is that the upper echelons of professions have been, and remain, predominantly white, male and middle-class. Thus, despite the increasing occupational mobility of women and ethnic minorities, those who occupy senior positions in professions have largely been able to insulate themselves from broader social changes. That is not to say that women and ethnic minorities have not been able to enter professions; rather, that they have been allowed limited access to professions and often only to the less desirable parts of a professional sphere.

We live in a world where labour markets change rapidly. One only has to think of the decline in the UK and the US of mining, steel-making, shipbuilding and textiles to know that both the type of work people do and the way they work have changed considerably over the last 30–40 years. As heavy smokestack industries have declined, there has been a corresponding rise of sunrise industries and more flexible ways of working. The impact of these changes has not been lost on ethnic minority groups in both the UK and the US. One of the key debates that is taking place within the sociology of work is the extent to which traditional skill, class, gender and ethnic boundaries are starting to break down or change.

For professional groups that have traditionally been dominated by white, middle-class men, the growth in educational and occupational opportunities for social groups that have until relatively recently been excluded formally or informally from senior positions and professional occupations means that things have started to change. The change has been a result of legislation that has made discrimination in employment illegal, as well as greater aspirations on the part of women and ethnic minorities. The ability of white, middle-class males to monopolize certain professions has become a matter of some sociological significance. Given the rise of the discourse of equal opportunities in the UK and affirmative action in the US one might be forgiven for thinking that ethnic minority job-seekers are now applying for jobs in a climate where discrimination on the grounds of ethnicity is a thing of the past. There is growing empirical evidence to suggest that this is not the case.

There are, of course, two sides to this debate: the demand side and the supply side. Before we consider what sort of employees employers want to hire, we should also consider that people make judgements about where they are likely to be successful when they apply for jobs. If we assume that ethnic minority groups wish to enter the professions and the existing empirical evidence suggests that they have been unsuccessful in doing so, we might also assume that certain dominant social groups have been correspondingly successful in restricting entry to these professions. Leaving aside what constitutes a profession, there is evidence, in the UK at least, that in some occupational areas, such as the police, the fire service, the universities and the nursing profession, ethnic minority employees are likely to fare less well than their white peers. Indeed, the recent Macpherson Report (1999) into the murder of Stephen Lawrence has highlighted the extent to which racist assumptions are embedded in many of the major UK institutions. The response to the Macpherson Report has been muted; however, the empirical evidence to which I shall refer in this book suggests that racism and racist assumptions are indeed part and parcel of several professional cultures.

The exclusion of ethnic minority groups from desirable occupational areas and niches has attracted considerable attention from policy-makers. So much so, that a discourse of equal opportunities and affirmative action has developed. Indeed, it may be possible to argue that the growth of feminist ideology after 1945 has been one the most significant causes of social change in Western European societies. Feminist notions of equality and social justice have been among the most important driving forces behind the development and implementation of equal opportunities and affirmative action. It may be possible to think of not one coherent and cohesive equal opportunities discourse, but several, each focusing on an aspect of social identity, such as gender, ethnic origin, disability or sexual orientation. Although (as I will point out later in the book) the trend within the personnel profession is towards the promotion of a 'diversity' policy that encompasses all these aspects of social identity, this brings with it certain challenges for those who implement such policies. One of the implicit themes within the discussion of equality and affirmative action policies is the extent to which competing claims of different social groups, such as women and ethnic minorities, may sometimes cut across one another. So, when Walby (1986) talks about professions that are 'gendered', there is a tendency to neglect the fact that professions may also be racialized; in other words, the topography of discrimination is not one-dimensional but multi-dimensional and is a terrain which is, by its very nature, controversial and politicized.

The aims of equal opportunities and affirmative action policies are many and varied. Some argue that they have a symbolic significance and are little more than 'lip service' on the part of employers. Others argue that they represent a vehicle for social change and the promotion of social justice and equality, although, as I will point out later, what notions of equality actually mean in practice are far from clear-cut.

Equal opportunities and affirmative action policies may also attempt to increase the representation of certain social groups (most frequently women and/or ethnic minorities, although the disabled and homosexuals and lesbians may also be included in the scope of such policies) in areas of the workplace where they are under-represented. These policies represent a response to the perceived and actual inequality experienced by these groups. However, a number of writers have been highly critical about the impact of equality policies. Jenkins (1986), for example, argues that recruiters are able to circumvent formal equality policies and justify discriminatory selection decisions on the basis that minority candidates 'do not fit in'. Jenkins' thesis shifts the weight of discrimination towards individual recruiters, suggesting that their ethnocentric ideas and assumptions influence selection outcomes. However, what Jenkins neglects to address is the issue of labour market structures in which certain areas or niches become so closely identified with a particular social group that it is the structure of the labour market that determines the final destination of certain social groups as much as the individual acts of discrimination that are perpetrated by recruiters. Moreover, labour market structures are dynamic and the position of social groups may shift, as has been the case with some ethnic minority groups in the UK. This may be as much a result of the desire on the part of excluded social groups to try to gain access to another occupational area as it is a result of the success of dominant social groups in closing a particular niche.

Throughout this book I will refer to a major piece of research that I undertook between 1993 and 1997, which examined the position and experience of ethnic minority nurses within the National Health Service. The research also sought to evaluate the impact of equal opportunities policies in the NHS and to explore the experience of those ethnic minority nurses currently working in the NHS and also of retired nurses who migrated to the UK during the 1950s and 1960s.

The second major piece of research that I will refer to is a research project jointly undertaken by Professor Steve Fenton, Professor Tariq Modood and myself on the experience of ethnic minority academics in the UK university system. This was published in 1999 and became known as *Ethnicity and Employment in Higher Education*. These two pieces of research provide empirical data about two different professions and the experience of ethnic minority staff within them. Both studies attempt to evaluate and measure the impact of equal opportunities policies on the progress of ethnic minorities through their respective career hierarchies.

In terms of understanding what a profession is, I will use a Weberian ideal-type model. Thus we can understand a profession as an occupation which possesses some or all of the following features. First, specific skills or formal educational qualifications are required of those seeking to enter. That is, there is a basic qualificational aspect to a profession and often the acquisition of these skills or qualifications is marked by a ceremonial rite of passage. An unusual example of this is coopers who, when they have completed their apprenticeship, are made to sit inside a barrel filled with tar and wood shavings and then rolled around the workshop floor. (Thankfully, most other occupational rites of passage are rather less messy.) Second, entry into a professional sphere is closely monitored by bodies that are nominally independent, though it is important to acknowledge that the composition of these bodies is usually a good approximate guide to the type of person who is recruited. In other words, entry is not entirely dependent upon the acquisition of formal qualifications; the possession of certain *social* characteristics may also be a crucial determinant of the success or failure of the person seeking entry into a professional sphere. Third, the regulating professional body retains a monopoly over the distribution and dissemination of the skills and qualifications that are required to enter professional spheres. Fourth, there is a clearly defined hierarchy, with power, prestige and privilege distributed in a way that is directly related to a person's position within that hierarchy. Fifth, those who work in professional spheres are thought to possess greater autonomy over how and when they perform their work task than, say, those in routine, nonmanual or manual jobs, although it is important to note that the ability of 'professional' people to determine when and how they perform their work is increasingly being eroded. Sixth, many professional positions are thought to involve some notion of public service, altruism and a sense that the chosen profession is a vocation.

There have been changes within the professions. Perhaps the most important is that the term 'profession' is not as exclusive as it once was. Many occupational groups have sought to have the label 'professional' attached to their work, even if the acquisition of the term does not bring with it greater material gain in the shape of increased pay. Rather, it is thought to lend a certain amount of cachet and status. Thus it should be of no real surprise that more and more occupational groups describe themselves as 'professionals'.

Where ethnic minority groups have been able to penetrate professional occupational spheres they often become professions within professions, occupying positions within professions that are, at best, marginal. While there has been extended debate about the position of women (see Walby 1986; Witz 1992) within professional spheres and the extent to which they rarely break through the 'glass ceiling', little has been made of the position of ethnic minority groups within professional areas.

Before going any further I should clarify some of the terminology used in the text. Students of ethnicity will know that terminology in this area is complicated and at times controversial. As Fenton (1999) notes, 'ethnicity' and 'race' seem to have lost precision, if they ever had any, and are often used by academics and others in a very confused way. Thus to use the term 'Black' to describe people who were born in Pakistan or Bangladesh may not only be inappropriate but lacks analytical clarity since the experiences of Africans, African-Caribbeans and those from the Indian subcontinent are very different. The use of the term race is equally contested. As a scientific concept it has long since lost credence, although overhearing conversations during my frequent bus and train journeys suggests to me that while scientists, both natural and social, have abandoned the concept of race, real people have not! Within the social sciences the notion of 'race' has been written about extensively by Banton (1977, 1987, 1988), Miles (1989) and Jenkins (1996). The use of the term 'race' is now controversial because of the connotations of inferiority and superiority that are said to be associated with it. To acknowledge the sensitivity of the term some writers prefer to use it in inverted commas, and while there is a debate about this practice (see e.g. Fenton 1996) it is one I will be adopting throughout the text. The additional complicating factor is that both 'race' and ethnicity are often used interchangeably although they mean different things. During the writing of this book I have found it impossible not to do this, partly because of the ways in which the people who have taken part in empirical research have expressed themselves and partly because other writers in the area have used different terminology at different times. The resulting overlap, while unhelpful, is unavoidable.

A succession of controversial events in both the US and the UK have kept 'race' or ethnic origin at the forefront of public debates over equality of treatment. For example, in 1991 the videotaped beating of the motorist Rodney King by Los Angeles police officers and the subsequent riots in the wake of the trials relating to the so-called King Affair have made the question of 'race' and ethnicity highly sensitive. Similarly, the openly racist conduct of Detective Mark Furhmann during the trial of O.J. Simpson raised a number of serious questions about the relationship between the police and the ethnic minority communities in the US. The questions about racism and the police force raised by the King trial have recently resurfaced with two videotaped incidents of police officers apparently using undue force to subdue ethnic minority suspects. On the basis of the evidence from these incidents, it would seem that very little has been learnt by the police from the King Affair. Equally, there have been a number of high-profile cases in the UK. These have included the murder of Stephen Lawrence which has ensured that 'race' remains publicized, politicized and controversial. Indeed, the debate around 'race' and equity of treatment could hardly be more sensitive given the sporadic outbursts of civil disorder (often dubbed 'race riots') which took place in major British cities during the 1980s. The disturbances that took place in London, Liverpool and Bristol are frequently described as 'race' riots in much the same way that the disturbances that took place in a number of towns in the north-west of England during 2001 are referred to as 'race' riots.

In the case of the disturbances during the 1980s there were a number of contributory factors that helped to explain them, including high unemployment, a profound sense of alienation and exclusion among the communities where the disturbances took place, a history of tension between those communities and the police force, as well as a lack of dialogue between police and community. It is indisputable that in the communities where the disturbances took place, the majority of the population were members of ethnic minority groups. None the less, the fact remains that White members of these communities were also an integral part of the disturbances. There are disturbing parallels between the disturbances of the 1980s and the more recent disturbances in the north-west of England in 2001. These riots occurred in cities and towns where there is an established Asian community. Those who are said to have taken part are reported to have been overwhelmingly young Pakistani and Bangladeshi men. Like the earlier disturbances of the 1980s, the context of these more recent disturbances is the poor labour market position of these two groups, coupled with poorer educational performance (in comparison to other ethnic groups) and a history of exclusion from broader society. Add to this a tense relationship with the police and the conditions that prevailed at the time of the 1980s disturbances are reproduced in a different geographical location. The response to this mix of discrimination and disadvantage, combined with a resurgence in the political fortunes of the New Right, should not be surprising. The response of central government to the underlying causes of discontent, disenfranchisement and alienation among Asian communities within the UK is awaited with anticipation.

The principal contribution of this book towards the debate about the salience of ethnic origin in the labour market is that the forms of racism and discrimination that members of ethnic minorities experience differ depending on the type of occupational and professional culture in which they find themselves. Theories of social closure, such as those proposed by Witz (1992), have argued that professions are characterized by forms of social closure that have systematically excluded women from the most powerful and prestigious positions. But because the primary focus of Witz's work is gender there is no real acknowledgement of the importance of 'race' or ethnic origin in the examination of professions and social closure. The purpose of this book is to demonstrate that professional strategies of social closure are not only gendered but also racialized. I am not proposing a monolithic, overarching concept of race and racialization within professions that should always be the primary focus of theories of social closure, rather than any analysis of social closure within occupational and professional areas should take into account not only gender but race as well. To do so requires an understanding of the social conditions that prevail in any occupational area and, equally importantly, an understanding of the history of each occupational area, particularly in the case of occupational areas into which large numbers of migrants have been recruited. Thus, to understand how race or ethnic origin, gender, age and class might combine in a specific occupational area requires an acknowledgement that there can be no single theoretical approach that explains the experience or position of ethnic minority labour.

1
Ethnicity, Employment and Exclusion

Introduction

The labour market position of ethnic groups in the UK and the US has been the subject of much debate (Daniel 1968; Smith 1977; Brown 1984; Marable 1995; Modood 1998). Questions about the extent to which the working lives of ethnic minorities have been shaped by discrimination and racism, or whether they have received preferential treatment, have rumbled on for some years, intermittently erupting when cases of unfair treatment are publicized in the media. The role of employment practices and discrimination has featured prominently in national debates about social justice, equity and inclusion. The sphere of employment is central to the discussion of inclusion and exclusion since it is through work that we earn money and gain status and any sense of job satisfaction. Indeed, employment can be said to be a crucial part of integration into wider society. Throughout this chapter I shall chart the employment fortunes of ethnic minority groups in the UK and US in order to assess the extent to which they can be said to be upwardly socially mobile.

In the case of the UK, people from New Commonwealth countries were recruited to work in areas where the postwar labour shortage was most acute: for example, textiles, transport, metalworking and the newly established National Health Service. What marked the incorporation of New Commonwealth migrants into the British labour market was a tendency for them to be recruited to the lowest levels of the various occupational spheres that they entered. At the same time, the indigenous White population remained in positions of relative superiority. This was partly a result of the fact that where labour shortages existed, they tended to be at the lower levels of occupations, that is work that had come to be defined by the indigenous population as undesirable. Thus migrants were simultaneously included in certain spheres of work but also, and crucially for them, excluded from the upper echelons of those occupational spheres.

To assume that there is a natural division of labour which results in ethnic minorities being concentrated in specific labour market locations (often those characterized by the worst pay and conditions) ignores what is a complex set of social processes that have led to the exclusion of ethnic minority workers and their confinement to such areas. I intend to concentrate on the historical period immediately after the Second World War, though that is not to deny that ethnic minority groups had a significant presence in the UK and the US prior to that period. In the case of the UK, however, the process of recruitment and migration of people from the New Commonwealth during the immediate postwar period marked an important point in labour and 'race' relations. The patterns of employment that were established were to have long-term social and historical effects, which have shaped the labour market experience of ethnic minorities. It should be noted that the experience of the indigenous White population in the UK and the US of ethnic minorities prior to this is likely to have been crucial in determining attitudes towards 'others'. In both countries slavery had been an all too grim reality for many Africans, while British colonial expansion contributed towards notions of White superiority.

The ascription of negative characteristics to ethnic minorities and migrants is a well-documented social phenomenon. The discrimination experienced by ethnic minorities has had myriad effects in housing, health, policing and, crucially, employment. Early studies of race relations in the UK, such as Patterson's *Dark Strangers* (1963) and Rex and Tomlinson's *Colonial Immigrants in an English City* (1979), show how the different forms of disadvantage and discrimination coalesced in ways that severely limited the social and occupational mobility of migrants. As we are now some forty years on from these early studies it is timely to ask pertinent questions about the extent to which ethnic minority groups have been either integrated into or excluded from labour markets and more generally from the social life of the countries to which they migrated. Within the sociology of 'race' relations there has, until relatively recently, been a tendency to describe the effects of discrimination and racism in a monolithic way which suggests that its manifestations and effects are uniform. This book demonstrates how different work cultures have excluded and/or incorporated ethnic minorities, arguing that while there *are* some important similarities in the experiences of ethnic minorities, there are also some very significant differences.

A useful sociological concept which can be applied to the experience of minorities in the labour market is the Weberian concept of social closure. Again, rather than applying the concept in a uniform way to the experience of ethnic minorities it is more accurate to suggest that there is a variety of different forms of social closure which are employed by powerful social groups to exclude less powerful social groups. These processes are both conscious and unconscious. It is precisely these mechanisms of exclusion and closure that require scrutiny if there is to be a systematic understanding of the position of ethnic minorities in the labour market.

The position of ethnic minority workers in the American economy has also been the subject of heated debate. The debate has been intensified by the development and implementation of affirmative action policies, which have sought to overcome discrimination. One piece of academic work that has led to a radical reassessment of the position of ethnic minority workers in the US is W. Julius Wilson's *The Declining Significance of Race* (1980). Wilson argues that while 'race' certainly *was* a key determinant of success in the labour market, it is now less significant than socio-economic class. That is, class has become more important than 'race', at least in labour market terms. As a result, it is possible to talk of the declining significance of 'race', particularly with the development of a Black middle class in America. Wilson's argument is not without critics as we shall see; however, one key aspect of the debate about the success of ethnic minority groups in the American labour market that has been underplayed is the impact of Mexican, Cuban and Haitian migrants to the US. The essence of Wilson's argument is that the civil rights campaigns of the 1960s resulted in concerted government action to tackle racial inequality; and along with the improvement in civil rights there has been a corresponding dismantling of barriers in education and employment, which has opened up new avenues of social mobility for ethnic minority Americans. For Wilson inequality based on 'race' has not been eradicated; it remains a real part of the lives of Black Americans. However, what is increasingly affecting the social and occupational mobility of Black Americans is their class or socio-economic position, or as Thomas and Hughes (1986) state:

> disadvantage continues for members of a growing Black lower class, racial discrimination is not the primary determinant of their economic situation; past discrimination created the large black lower class which continues today primarily because of economic and social structural reasons.

Wilson's argument has been hotly contested by other academics in America, who argue that far from declining in significance, 'race' is becoming increasingly important in determining the social and occupational position of ethnic minority Americans. However, what Wilson and Manning Marable, among others, emphasize is the importance of affirmative action programmes as a way of opening up areas of American society to minority groups. This is theme to which I return in chapter 2.

While writers such as Thomas and Hughes, and Marable tend to assert the primacy of socio-economic class over ethnic identity it should also be made clear that ethnicity can cut across socio-economic class. In other words, ethnic minorities' sense of identity and their life-chances are not only shaped by their membership of a social class, they are also shaped by the fact that they are of a different ethnic origin from the majority of the population in the UK and the US. Racism and discrimination are experienced by those ethnic minorities who have been economically successful as well as by those who remain trapped in poorly paid employment or even in the hotly contested underclass that is said to exist in both the US and Britain. Thus while socio-economic class as defined principally in relation to economic factors (such as income and property ownership) is one of the central aspects of stratification within the US and the UK, ethnic origin is a different and distinct aspect of stratification, which nevertheless influences the experiences of ethnic minority groups. In Weberian terms ethnic minorities are a negatively privileged status group. The use of strategies of social closure to exclude ethnic minority groups from prestigious spheres and strata of employment, as well as from other desirable life-chances, reinforces a Weberian notion of ethnic minority groups as negatively privileged status groups. Or to put it another way, racism runs from the shop floor to the boardroom. What this suggests is that racism cannot be subsumed into a Marxist model of class relations since aspects of ethnic identity assume a primacy in all sorts of occupational niches and spheres. To reduce questions of racism and ethnic identity to class misses the fundamental point that in order for racism to occur, there has to be some recognition, however tacit, of ethnic differences between groups as well as an assumed ethnic hierarchy. As the empirical material that I will be referring to later in the book suggests, racism does not exist in factories and offices only; it also exists in universities and other professions such as law and medicine.

Although the study of ethnicity and the labour market is an area that has become increasingly part of the sociological mainstream in both the UK and US there have been relatively few detailed case studies which have sought to examine the role of ethnic minority labour. The best known include Dennis Brooks' *Race and Labour in London Transport* (1975) and Richard Jenkins' groundbreaking *Racism and Recruitment* (1986). Both studies tended to focus on what could be described as blue-collar employment, the first focusing on workers in London Transport, the second on workers in a car assembly plant. There has been little attention paid to the role of ethnic minorities in white-collar professions or professions that have are largely feminized, such as nursing. Undoubtedly Jenkins' contribution to the debate has been crucial and his development of the notions of acceptability and suitability criteria remains a powerful analytical tool for understanding discrimination in the workplace and the ways in which the labour market position of ethnic minority workers are determined. However, the relative dearth of contemporary empirical material relating to ethnicity and the labour market is surprising in light of the continuing salience of ethnic origin and its impact on labour market location.

While Jenkins' analysis of the labour market position of ethnic minority workers focuses more on the meanings attached by actors to social markers such as ethnicity, there is a tendency to overlook more structural determinants of the labour market position of ethnic minority workers. This book has two central themes: first, that while the sort of approach adopted by Jenkins to the closure of occupational areas is useful, to understand fully occupational segregation requires a socio-historical dimension which helps to explain the structural aspects of disadvantage, discrimination and exclusion; second, that different work cultures affect ethnic minority workers in different ways. Thus it is important to acknowledge that the articulation or the nature and shape of racism differs depending on the work culture it is part of.

Ethnicity and the labour market

No simple pattern of disadvantage emerges when examining the position of ethnic minorities in the labour market; rather, there are trends which reflect the overall position of minority groups, but with significant exceptions. This reinforces the fact that ethnicity is not an either/or dichotomy. There have been real differences in the employment position of Asian groups and African-Caribbean groups. More recent employment surveys have highlighted that within the groups categorized as Asian there are pronounced differences with, for example, Bangladeshi groups performing much less well than, say, Indian groups. There are also important gender differences that further complicate the analysis of the labour market position of ethnic groups. Moreover, there appear to be equally important differences in the labour market experience of those ethnic minorities who migrated to the UK and the US in the 1950s and 1960s and those subsequently born in the countries in which their families settled.

While there are differences, there are also similarities. As outlined earlier, many of the migrants who came to the UK entered occupational areas in which there was a severe shortage of labour. However, no systematic examination of the position and experience of ethnic minorities took place until the 1968 Political and Economic Planning Report, which contained limited references to employment practices. The later (1977) Political and Economic Planning Report was a much more detailed examination of the labour market position. In an attempt to assess the extent of discrimination, actor testing was used in both written and verbal job applications. (It is worth bearing in mind that researchers who employed a similar approach in 1995 to assess the extent of discrimination in medical schools in the UK were arrested by the police for making fraudulent applications; see Esmail and Everington 1995.) The researchers found considerable disparities between White and ethnic minority applicants. The 1977 report confirmed findings from earlier work that discrimination on the grounds of 'race' or ethnicity was common. One of the principal conclusions of the 1977 report was that minority groups – particularly Asians and West Indians – were concentrated in certain types of work, principally in manufacturing industry as semi-skilled or unskilled labour.

During the restructuring of the labour market in UK during the late 1970s and early 1980s manufacturing industries began to shed jobs rapidly in a bid to streamline and rationalize their productive processes. This process had lasting effects for ethnic minority workers. Evidence from subsequent labour force surveys shows that ethnic minority employees are particularly susceptible to unemployment. Thus in periods of economic contraction, the ethnic minority unemployment rate rises faster than that of White people, and during periods of expansion it takes longer to recover. Moreover, fluctuations in unemployment do not affect ethnic minorities evenly – young ethnic minorities are disproportionately likely to experience unemployment. As more and more employers have tended to operate a 'last in, first out' policy, this may explain the sensitivity of ethnic minorities to unemployment. Other possible explanations that have been explored include English being a second language for some ethnic minority groups (see Gray et al., 1993). It should be noted, however, that Modood et al.'s (1997) analysis shows that there are marked differences in fluency in English and that critical factors affecting fluency include sex, age on arrival in the UK and the proportion of one's own ethnic group in one's neighbourhood. Another possible explanation of the comparatively poorer position of ethnic minority groups in the labour market revolves around a discussion about a lack of formal educational qualifications. While there are very real differences in the educational achievement of different ethnic groups, much of the evidence from studies by Smith (1977), Brown (1984), Jones (1993) and Modood et al. (1997) suggests that when qualifications are controlled for, ethnic minority groups still fare worse than their White counterparts. Moreover, there are some ethnic groups in the UK who outperform the White population in the education system.

The other factor that explains the relatively poor position of ethnic minority workers is discrimination. Michael Banton's work (1988, 1994) does much to illuminate discussions of discrimination. At its simplest, discrimination amounts to selection of someone or something on the basis of a set of beliefs. Thus a person might prefer one brand of soap to another because of beliefs about the properties and superiority of a particular brand. This notion of choice and selection underlies Banton's notion of a 'taste for discrimination' (1994, p. 13), though it should be pointed out that selection for entry into a school or university, or for employment, is a qualitatively different process when compared to the selection of consumer durables. None the less both are informed by personal and/or institutional preferences based on assumptions (whether grounded in reality or not) about why one type of product or person is better than another. In the case of employment there is a long-standing literature (Daniel 1968; Smith 1977; Brown 1984; Jones 1993; Modood et al. 1997) that suggests that choices made by recruiters in the UK labour market are informed by racist assumptions about ethnic minority groups. Indeed, it may be argued that many of the nineteenth-century ideas of 'race' discussed by Banton (1977, 1987, 1988), Miles (1989) and Van den Berghe (1981), among others, still inform common-sense thought and ideology in terms of the hierarchy of 'racial' groups. No matter how flawed such assumptions are analytically, hierarchical notions of race remain pervasive among the population at large.

Discrimination based on stereotypical assumptions about different ethnic groups has been a constant feature of the experience of ethnic minority groups in both the UK and the US. What is interesting about the way in which discrimination has been articulated is that it is not simply a question of employers refusing to employ people from ethnic minority groups because of their prejudicial beliefs about the alleged inferiority of ethnic minorities. There is also evidence that employers might be reluctant to employ ethnic minority workers for fear of antagonizing a mainly White workforce (see Smith 1977). This justification of discriminatory behaviour could be described as a 'the boys on the shop floor won't stand it' model of discrimination, though the extent to which employers justify discriminatory decisions may be a convenient way for them to attribute blame for discrimination elsewhere. The existence of grass-roots racism at the shop-floor level implied in Smith's analysis suggests that race was, and remains, a highly sensitive issue within the workplace. The justification of discrimination against ethnic minority applicants on the basis of shop floor racism is a controversial issue to which I shall return in later chapters.

In 1984 the PSI Report *Black and White Britain* noted that it was no longer accurate to talk of an 'immigrant' population, as over 40 per cent of the ethnic minority population were British-born. This was the first time a large-scale study of this nature had made this distinction. The report examined individual examples of discrimination affecting the ethnic minority population. This approach reflected the distinction made by the 1976 Race Relations Act between direct and indirect discrimination. According the Race Relations Act, s. 1(1)(a) there are three types of discrimination:

1. *Direct discrimination* involves less favourable treatment on the grounds of colour, race, nationality or ethnic or national origins.
2. *Indirect discrimination* in which a condition or requirement is applied which is such that the proportion of persons of a particular colour, race or ethnic or national origins able to comply with it is considerably smaller than the proportion of other persons able to do so, which works to the detriment of the complainant, and which is not shown by the alleged discriminator to be justifiable on non racial grounds.
3. *Victimization* of those who, among other things, bring proceedings under the Act, or give evidence of information in connection with the Act.

Black and White Britain was in many ways 'an end of term report' on how well the 1976 Race Relations Act had worked. A gap of seven years between the two Reports might not be thought of as a long enough to make an assessment of whether the Race Relations Act had worked, though it is arguable that there should be some tentative, early indications as to how the Act had affected patterns of employment. However, the economic recession of the early 1980s, and subsequent fairly dramatic waves of redundancy, had a marked effect on those sectors of employment where many ethnic minority workers were located. More broadly speaking, many of the employment patterns identified by the 1977 study had continued as ethnic minority workers remained located predominantly in unskilled and semi-skilled labour in manufacturing industry. The concentration of non-white workers in traditional areas such as textiles and manufacturing made them more vulnerable to fluctuations in unemployment as it is these areas that have undergone the most marked changes in employment patterns through the processes of restructuring and rationalization. The effect of the shake-out from such industries is shown in the much higher rates of unemployment for ethnic minority workers, which the Report reveals. Indeed, unemployment had risen much faster for ethnic minority groups in comparison to the White group. The comparative rates of unemployment for the different ethnic groups are shown in Table 1.1.

As Table 1.1 shows, there are considerable differences between ethnic groups. If we look at the position of White women during this period, 10 per cent of White women compared to that 52 per cent of Bangladeshi women were unemployed. Similarly, the comparison between White men (13 per cent) and Pakistani and Bangladeshi men (29 per cent) suggests very real differences in the extent of unemployment. A comparison between Table 1.1 and two of the tables from the Modood et al. (1997) suggest that there are some very interesting aspects of both change and continuity in the ethnic minority experience of unemployment.

While different ethnic categories have been employed in each of the Reports, some patterns nevertheless emerge. The most notable of these

Table 1.1: Unemployment by sex and ethnic group (1984)

	Men %	Women %
White	13	10
West Indian	25	16
Asian	20	20
Indian	14	18
Pakistani	29	28
Bangladeshi	29	52
African/Asian	17	21

Source: C. Brown (1984) *Black and White Britain*, PSI, p. 189.

Table 1.2:   Rate of male unemployment by highest British qualification

	White %	Caribbean %	Indian/African Asian %	Pakistani/ Bangladeshi %
All ages				
No qualification	19	42	20	46
O level or equivalent	11	31	20	36
A level or equivalent	12	23	12	17

Table 1.3:   Rate of female unemployment by highest British qualification

	White %	Caribbean %	Indian/African Asian %	Pakistani/ Bangladeshi %
All ages				
No qualification	13	19	13	54
O level or equivalent	10	16	10	42
A level or equivalent	7	16	12	18

Source: T. Modood et al. (1997) *Ethnic Minorities in Britain*, PSI, pp. 91–2.

is the consistently higher levels of unemployment in the Pakistani and Bangladeshi groups. Bearing in mind that 13 years elapsed between the publication of the two Reports, the persistently worse position of the Pakistani and Bangladeshi groups should be a cause for concern. Similarly the group that Brown's (1984) survey refers to as West Indian and Modood et al. (1997) refer to as Caribbean fare consistently less well than their White counterparts. Explaining these differences requires an understanding of forms of inequality that are embedded and transmitted from generation to generation. The cumulative effect of poor housing, low educational achievement and poor health constitutes a complex mesh of social, economic and political factors that combine in ways that constrain and exclude ethnic minority groups. The crucial additional factor to this explanation of labour market disadvantage is that of discrimination by employers against ethnic minority applicants. The very nature and invisibility of discrimination makes it hard to establish empirically the effect it has had on patterns of employment and unemployment amongst ethnic minority groups. While most writers acknowledge that measures of discrimination are problematic, references to the persistence of discrimination against ethnic minority job-seekers has been a constant theme in empirical research on 'race' or ethnic origin and employment. All the research from the earlier studies, such as that by Daniel (1968), to the most recent analysis of ethnic origins and the labour market by Modood et al. (1997), acknowledges the impact of discrimination on ethnic minority job-seekers.

The discussions about those ethnic groups that fare poorly in the labour market reveal a great deal about the transmission of accumulated disadvantage in terms of poor health, inadequate housing, lack of cultural capital and low educational attainment, although it should be noted that one of the key findings in the 4th National Survey is that there is a major commitment on the part of all ethnic minority groups towards education, particularly post-16 education. There has, however, been a notable lack of analysis and discussion as to what has contributed to the success of ethnic groups such as the Chinese and the African-Asian group. Modood et al. (1997) have identified these two groups as having a labour market position that is directly comparable to that of the White population, in as much African-Asian and Chinese men are as likely as White men to be professionals, managers or employers. The increasing influence of educational qualifications and the acquisition of such qualifications by these groups partly explain their success in the labour market. It is also possible to identify a growing trend towards self-employment among some ethnic groups, which appears to be one way of side-stepping discrimination in the labour market more generally, though it would unwise to overstate how effective this is as a strategy. None the less to explain fully why and how these groups have been successful while others have been unsuccessful requires a much more detailed analysis. A key question would be to try to ask whether or not discrimination and racism have affected the ethnic groups that have either achieved parity with or overtaken the White population in the same way that discrimination and racism have affected those groups that have fared poorly in the labour market. Put another way, have the successful groups experienced more or less discrimination and racism than those groups that have been unsuccessful, or is there some other factor that explains their success?

None the less, having formal qualifications does not guarantee a labour market experience free from discrimination. Research suggests that ethnic minority graduates experience much greater difficulty than their White peers in obtaining employment (Brennan and McGeevor 1990).

The UK, with its tradition of empirical research on 'race' and employment, has allowed regular snapshots to be taken of the position of ethnic minority groups in the labour market. This has meant that it has been possible to chart the fortunes of different ethnic groups over a period from the first survey in 1968 to the most recent 4th National Survey in 1997. These reports highlight a range of different aspects of life for the ethnic minority population in the UK, and the impact of racism and discrimination on the lives of the ethnic minority population in the UK remains a depressing and constant thread throughout these reports. The influence of racism and discrimination on the choices that members of the ethnic minority population make when entering the labour market is made clear in Smith's Second Report (1977), where reference is made to a 'snowball effect', or what Banton (1989) calls the chill factor.

> Asians and West Indians will tend not to apply for work at a plant which is known to have refused minority applications in the past... they will tend to apply instead to plants where some of their friends are employed. This will lead to a snowball effect. Plants with many Asian and West Indian employees will receive many more applicants and will increase their minority workforce still further. (Smith, D.J. 1977, p. 101)

The impact that discrimination and racism have on occupational choice would therefore appear to be a crucial factor in deciding what sort of job ethnic minority employees will apply for. After all, why apply for a job when there is a very strong likelihood that your application will be rejected? Surely it is better to apply for a job in an office, factory or store that already has employees who are members of ethnic minority groups?

Understanding how these choices are made and the notions that underlie such choices is a vital part of understanding why some occupational spaces within labour markets become populated principally by ethnic minority employees. This colonization of a space within a labour market also helps us to understand why segments of the labour market become imbued with a racial or ethnic significance. One example of this, identified by Fevre (1984), is the concentration of men of Pakistani origin who choose to work in the textile industry in the north-west of England. The patterns of employment that Fevre refers to show that Pakistani men opted to work the night shift in textile mills. What makes this choice particularly interesting are the ideas that inform their choice. The starting point in the process of 'choice' is to find out where vacancies exist. In this and many other cases, vacancies existed in segments of the labour market which indigenous White labour had abandoned because the pay or conditions were thought to be bad. By colonizing these spaces ethnic minority employees were less likely to experience racism, discrimination and confrontation with White employees precisely because these areas had been abandoned by White labour. Additionally, for those ethnic minority employees whose grasp of the English language is partial, they would be able to communicate effectively with other employees.

What matters when gaining access to an occupational sphere is whether or not it is defended; or, in Weberian terminology, is an occupational area socially closed or socially open? Different social groups can and do defend occupational areas. The most obvious of these are trade unions and professional associations (which to all intents and purposes are middle-class trade unions). Different forms of social closure are used to restrict entry into occupational areas, the most common of which is to impose a barrier based on skills, apprenticeship or the acquisition of formal qualifications. These apparently 'objective' and 'colour-blind' barriers may not always be as objective as they seem. The extent to which strategies of social closure are informed by assumptions about 'race', gender and a range of other characteristics will be discussed in more detail later in the book. It is, none the less, important to establish that it is the very possession of some essentially social characteristics that is the foundation of strategies of social closure. These strategies are exclusive; that is, they actively seek to exclude some groups and include others. They are as closely tied up with social boundary markers (such as gender, age and ethnic origin) as they are with the more 'objective' elements (such as skill and qualifications).

The fact that some parts of the labour market come to be seen as the province of one social group rather than another in turn influences the ways in which recruiters think about their applicants. There is, therefore, a two-way process at work in terms of employers making assumptions about the type of worker they want for particular types of work and applicants making judgements about the types of employers likely to employ them. The tendency of ethnic minority workers to apply to employers who they know employ other ethnic minority workers produces a self-sustaining and self-fulfilling prophecy. This is as important for those who are applying for employment as for those who are responsible for recruitment. While the existence of the chill factor helps to explain how certain occupational niches become imbued with a racialized significance, it is less helpful in explaining how employment patterns change. That is, how do areas of the labour market other than those traditionally associated with ethnic minorities become socially open? Equally, it does not help to explain how and why those areas that become colonized by Black labour tend to possess undesirable characteristics such as instability, low pay and poor working conditions. This is not a coincidental or a 'natural' process. Rather, it is a socially determined process that reflects attitudes towards race and ethnicity and the power of successful occupational groups to secure their own occupational areas while abandoning other less desirable forms of employment.

Notwithstanding the sorts of employment patterns that have been established for ethnic minority groups in the US and the UK, there have been shifts in terms of the aspirations and the amount of upward occupational mobility of some ethnic minority groups. These changes can be partly explained by certain trends in the labour market. First, a pronounced shift away from manual work towards non-manual work; this has become more significant as the impact of information technology has made itself felt around the globe. Second, a recognition on the part of governments in the US and UK of the problems and discontent that racism and discrimination cause, and the subsequent enacting of equality legislation in the shape of Race Relations Act 1976 and the Race Relations Amendment Act 2000. Third, a recognition on the part of employers themselves that there are legal and social penalties associated with discrimination; that is, there is a cost related to discrimination.

The question of what constitutes a cost and what constitutes a benefit in the pursuit of equality has very important consequences within organizations. If the pursuit of equality is regarded as an expensive, bolt-on extra it is likely to be relegated to the bottom of management agendas. A recent example of this is the Ford Motor Company. In the late 1990s an advertising campaign for Ford cars in the UK which was based on large posters on billboards showed a group of workers who were responsible for the production of their most recent model. When it subsequently came to light that ethnic minority workers who had originally been a part of the poster had been airbrushed out, the resulting furore attracted considerable adverse publicity. Allegations of racism at the Ford plant in Dagenham added weight to the belief that Ford actively discriminated against ethnic minority employees. It should be noted that since then Ford have invested a considerable amount of time and money in vigorously pursuing an equalities policy.

Fourth, an acknowledgement on the part of ethnic minority groups that educational achievement is the key to occupational success. This is reflected in the increasing numbers of ethnic minorities entering higher education (in the UK at least).

The changes that have taken place in the labour market should not necessarily be taken as a sign of increasing equality and that problems of racism and discrimination have been eradicated or have somehow disappeared. It is more appropriate to think of ethnic minority groups who have been excluded from particular employment opportunities and parts of the labour market as reacting in a dynamic way to racism and discrimination. Some of the key questions that we should ask ourselves are these: How successful have ethnic minority groups been in entering areas that have been socially closed to them? To what extent have affirmative action and equal opportunity policies aided the occupational mobility of ethnic minority groups?

Restructuring and ethnic minority workers

The process of restructuring in the US and the UK economies has had a profound effect on the fortunes of their respective ethnic minority populations. As heavy or smokestack industries have declined and the increasingly international division of labour that is a central part of the global village has become a reality, the fortunes of those workers who formerly worked in these areas have declined as well. It is in these very areas of the economy that many ethnic minority workers were employed. As restructuring has had such momentous effects on labour markets it is worth examining briefly the impact of economic changes on the ethnic minority population. Both the US and UK economies have undergone periods of recession in which large companies have rapidly shed labour and rationalized their workforce. The trend towards rationalization and the drive to produce more for less are now regarded by most employers as an integral part of management practice and orthodoxy. The days of labour-intensive industries with rigid demarcation lines have gone and lean production is a reality that is unlikely to go away.

Restructuring became an increasingly common phenomenon during the 1980s and the early 1990s. It is a process through which jobs are reorganized in order to maximize labour productivity. The process of restructuring often has two principal aspects. First, the shedding of labour. In many cases this amounts to a simple numerical reduction in the size of workforce. It may, for example, occur as a result of a drop in demand or the relocation of jobs overseas. The second aspect is the reorganization of the actual work process. With a leaner workforce those who remain are often expected to increase their productivity to compensate for the reduction in the number of workers. Ethnic minority groups have tended to be located in the most unstable areas of the labour market and have been susceptible to restructuring and compulsory redundancy. Research in 1995 by the Department of Employment suggests that ethnic minority workers are particularly vulnerable to redundancy. This raises questions about the extent to which firing as well as hiring are processes in which racist assumptions inform the decisions employers make. There is anecdotal evidence to suggest that ethnic minority workers are selected for redundancy on the basis of their 'race' and some more systematic research in this area would be welcome. It appears that employers often use restructuring as a way of shedding those whom they regard as 'difficult' or expendable. Stereotypical judgements about workers from ethnic minorities mean that they are frequently singled out for redundancy during restructuring.

Restructuring allows managers and employers to exercise discretion over who is, and who is not, made redundant. In a situation where there is surplus labour it seems likely that their decision will be informed by judgements about a whole range of factors including productivity and whether or not particular workers 'fit in' with the workforce as a whole, as well as presenting an opportunity to get rid of workers they simply dislike for whatever reason.

Ethnicity and exclusion in the labour market

The empirical data of the PSI and PEP surveys suggest a labour market in which ethnicity and gender are key determinants of labour market position. The knock-on effects of labour market position on other life-chances such as housing, health and citizenship are profound. Indeed, labour market position might be regarded as crucial to understanding the overall position of different social groups within broader hierarchies of status and income. Rather than referring to exclusion as a simple either/or concept that suggests that people are either excluded or not excluded, it is more useful to think of exclusion on a sliding scale which may change over time.

While there are differences within and between ethnic groups, typically, ethnic minorities occupy positions in the labour market that are inferior to those of their White peers. The pattern in the UK between 1950 and 1980 has been one of exclusion and segregation within the labour market, with minorities confined to certain areas. However, more recent analysis of the labour market position of ethnic groups suggests a pattern in which differences between ethnic groups are becoming more pronounced, with some groups outperforming White workers.

The extent to which ethnic differences are cross-cut by gender differences is, of course, of very real importance. Thus there are some very different rates of economic activity for women within ethnic groups. Labour Force Survey data (2000) show that African-Caribbean women (76 per cent economically active) are more likely to be economically active compared to, say, Pakistani and Bangladeshi (both 23 per cent economically active) women. While the Indian and Chinese groups have been relatively successful over the past twenty or so years they are also more likely to be self-employed than White people. The economic changes of the 1970s and 1980s have also affected the occupational position of many members of ethnic minority communities in the UK. During the 1980s particularly a prolonged economic recession affected areas of manufacturing such as textiles and metal working in which ethnic minorities were concentrated. There has been a corresponding rise in unemployment for those ethnic groups who were recruited to work in these areas. This partly explains the much worse position of ethnic groups such as the Pakistanis and Bangladeshis. There has, however, been change in the position of ethnic minority groups in the labour market. The most recent indications suggest patterns of diversity in the labour market rather than a simple division between White and New Commonwealth migrants which characterized early studies of 'race' or ethnic origin and employment. There are also signs in the UK that some ethnic minority groups have begun to enter the professions.

The most recent, and by far the most comprehensive, study of the labour market position of ethnic minority groups in the UK was undertaken by Modood et al. (1997). Perhaps the most refreshing aspect of Modood's analysis is his willingness to challenge long-held assumptions about ethnic disadvantage in the labour market. The findings of the 4th National Survey present a picture of very real difference both within and between ethnic minority groups and between ethnic minorities and their White peers. There are indications that some ethnic groups are experiencing real upward mobility in the labour market, with the Indian and Chinese groups more likely to reach the top employment categories than Bangladeshis and Pakistanis, who appear to be experiencing a degree of downward mobility and are more likely than other ethnic groups and their White peers to be unemployed. This may be at least partly explained by the growth in self-employment and the increasing likelihood that members of the Indian, African-Asian and Chinese groups will have degrees or be professionally qualified. The most telling aspect of Modood's analysis of employment and labour market position is that:

> It is sometimes asserted that migrants 'have tended to be from the poorest and most underprivileged groups of their countries of origin' (Anthias and Yuval Davis 1992, 77). This is almost certainly not the case. (Modood et al. 1997, p. 141)

Indeed, what Modood suggests is that some New Commonwealth migrants to the UK were often from higher socio-economic classes and, on reaching Britain, experienced rapid downward social and occupational mobility. As such, the recent trend for some ethnic groups represents a reversal of the initial trend.

As I have noted earlier, there are also some very different patterns between males and females within ethnic groups. The 4th National Survey confirms the low economic activity rates of Pakistani and Bangladeshi women and the persistence of high levels of economic activity for Caribbean women. It is, perhaps, worth reiterating some of the key points from Modood's discussion of 'ethnic penalties' in the labour market. Bearing in mind the consistent levels of discrimination reported in the 4th National Survey and the continuing work of the Commission for Racial Equality in the field of employment, it is clear that discrimination continues to shape the employment experience of ethnic minority groups profoundly. Modood refers to the use of the notion of an ethnic penalty, described as 'all sources of disadvantage that might lead an ethnic group to fare less well in the labour market than do similarly qualified whites' (Heath and McMahon 1995, p. 1, cited in Modood et al. 1997). Using the ethnic penalty as a way of understanding the success of different ethnic groups in the labour market helps to shed light on what is a very complex picture. There are those such as Heath and McMahon who argue that:

> For non-white groups, being born in this country is not associated with any improvement in competitive chance for the second generation experienced the same pattern and magnitude of ethnic penalties in the British labour market as the first generation did. (Heath and McMahon 1995, p. 29)

Others, such as Iganski and Payne (1996), argue that the labour market is increasingly open and meritocratic. Indeed the data from the 4th National Survey do show that some ethnic groups have experienced real upward social and occupational mobility. Modood acknowledges that the labour market may have become more socially open but that:

> It may still be the case that even the over-achieving groups are being under rewarded, that is to say, that typically, for the more competitive posts Ethnic minority individuals have got to be not just as good but better than their white competitors in order to get the job. (Modood et al. 1997, p. 145)

The idea among ethnic groups, particularly in professional occupations, that to be successful requires extra effort, qualifications or experience was frequently reported in *Ethnicity, Employment and Higher Education* (Carter et al. 1999) and reinforces the notion that racism and discrimination are not confined to manual work, though discrimination in professional occupations is qualitatively different from that of the typical factory floor.

The simple assumption that ethnic minorities will fare worse in the labour market than their White peers is one that has to be treated with a degree of caution. However, the impact of racism and discrimination in employment remains a very real phenomenon for many ethnic minorities.

The 4th National Survey proposes a threefold division for ethnic groups in the labour market: 1) the Chinese and African-Asians performing well compared to their White peers though still experiencing disadvantage within top positions in the labour market; 2) the Indian and Caribbean groups experiencing relative disadvantage; 3) the Pakistanis and Bangladeshis experiencing severe disadvantage. Thus the position of ethnic minority groups within the labour market is a complex one. The experience of ethnic minorities is not homogeneous. Rather, it is heterogeneous, with some groups, notably the Chinese and Indians, occupying positions similar to or better than those of White people, and other ethnic minority groups, such as the Pakistanis and Bangladeshis, occupying much worse positions than White people. The position of ethnic minority groups is further complicated by the different position of women, with some ethnic minority women more likely to be economically active than others. There is, however, one aspect of the ethnic minority experience in the labour market that remains constant for all ethnic groups whether male or female: the persistence of different forms of social closure, which render certain occupational areas off limits.

Conclusions

There are aspects of change and continuity in the experience of ethnic minorities in the UK labour market, though the extent to which their employment experience has been shaped by the initial patterns of migration that took place in the 1950s and 1960s should not be underestimated. The recruitment of people from the Caribbean and the Indian subcontinent to work in labour-intensive areas of the economy meant that when these areas began to experience contraction during the 1970s and 1980s they experienced a disproportionate amount of unemployment. The impact of restructuring, or downsizing, has had a marked impact on the sensitivity of ethnic minority groups to broader economic changes.

For some ethnic groups their position has not radically changed since their entry into the labour market. Indeed, as we have seen, the Bangladeshi and Pakistani groups have remained at the bottom of the occupational ladder. Figures from the Department of Employment for the year 2000 show that the unemployment rate for Bangladeshi men was 20.4 per cent, compared to 6.9 per cent of White men. For women the difference is equally stark. Bangladeshi and Pakistani women have unemployment rates of 23.9 per cent compared to 4.7 per cent of White women. Similarly, one of the most successful ethnic groups in terms of their employment experience, the Indian group, have the lowest unemployment rate of any ethnic minority group in the UK: 7.2 per cent. Overall the unemployment rate for White men is 6.9 per cent while the rate for all ethnic minorities is 13.0 per cent. In itself the unemployment rate cannot be interpreted as an indicator of discrimination. Rather, there is a set of interrelated aspects of inequality and exclusion that have disproportionately affected some ethnic groups in comparison to others. That is not to say that discrimination is unimportant or inconsequential when it comes to shaping the experiences of ethnic minority groups in the labour market.

What makes the case of the US particularly interesting in relation to the experiences of ethnic minority groups in the labour market is that there is increasing evidence of an emerging 'Black' middle class. At the same time there are ethnic minority groups whose position in the labour market remains poor. The polarization of ethnic groups within the labour market between those who are successful and those who remained located in unstable, poorly paid employment has taken place against a backdrop of affirmative action policies that have sought to make the labour market more open and meritocratic.

In the UK, data from the Department of Employment show that ethnic minority men are likely to be better qualified than their White peers, yet ethnic minority men experience higher levels of unemployment. This is in a context in which the Commission for Racial Equality continues to report that levels of discrimination in the labour market remain disturbingly high. These aspects of the employment experience of ethnic minority groups in the UK suggest that the impact of equal opportunity policies has been at best limited. Indeed the impact of the 1976 Race Relations Act to combat discrimination in employment might be questioned given the current position of ethnic minority groups within the UK labour market. The extent to which the Race Relations Amendment Act 2000 gives equality a much needed shot in the arm remains to be seen.

In terms of understanding the combination of different aspects of socially constructed identity such as gender, ethnic identity or social class, the notions of double or triple discrimination have largely been abandoned as they fail to take into account the fact that aspects of social identity cut across one another and that different aspects of social identity may assume prominence in different social situations and contexts.

Whatever the merits of more contemporary ideas about stratification are, there is a great deal of Weberian sociology that allows us to get a firmer analytical grip on the position of ethnic minority groups in the labour market and in society at large. As I will argue in chapters 2 and 3, there is increasing evidence to show that forms of social closure are used in a variety of occupational spheres to ensure that ethnic minorities remain firmly situated outside the most prestigious parts of occupations and professions. Thus racism and discrimination affect middle-class ethnic minority groups as well as working-class ethnic groups. While the nature of the racism that they experience may be qualitatively different, what determines their relative position in an occupational hierarchy is ethnic origin rather than ownership or non-ownership of the means of production. There is a strong case for arguing that ethnic minority groups constitute status groups that have symbolic and real boundaries that are defined from without by White racism and from within by a sense of collectivity and belonging. Different forms of social closure facilitate the differential distribution of not only material rewards and life-chances but also the differential distribution of status, which in turn reinforces existing ethnic boundaries within the labour market.

The contemporary context in which ethnic minority groups pursue employment opportunities is one in which contradictory social forces are at work. Legislative programmes in the US and the UK have sought to reduce discrimination and make access to employment more open and fair, and there can be no doubt that over the last thirty years attitudes towards discrimination have changed. This should not diminish the impact that discrimination had and continues to have on employment. The impact of feminism and the ways that the debate on gender equality have affected employment practices have been real and considerable. However, there is a lingering doubt about the extent to which employment practices which have sought to address 'race' discrimination have achieved the sort of success that advocates of gender equality have achieved. Indeed evidence about the gap in earnings between White and ethnic minority employees suggests that there is a considerable gap between White and ethnic minority employees:

> Ethnic minorities do not appear to face a level playing field in the UK labour market and their relative position does not appear to have improved since the 1970s. Native ethnic minorities also appear to be faring little better than their parents...ethnic differences in the labour market remuneration cannot be explained [in terms] of poor qualifications, and an unfavourable regional and industrial distribution...generalisations about the attributes of ethnic minority populations can reinforce stereotyping, which may result in these populations being excluded for the most remunerative jobs. (Blackaby et al. 2000, p. 28)

The notion of 'equality' appears to have become part of mainstream management vocabulary. Of course, equality for one person may mean inequality for another, and the very definition of equality is contingent upon a wide range of factors. These are key terms, which I will discuss in the following chapter. At the same time that 'equality' is becoming an established part of employment practice there is a growing group of disaffected ethnic minorities whose opportunities are very limited and whose confidence in the sort of equality expressed by employers is minimal. It is not too dramatic to talk of ethnic groups within the UK and US who are profoundly alienated from mainstream society precisely because they are unable to get a job. It is the construction of equality and affirmative action policies, as well as the impact they have on the employment opportunities of ethnic minority job seekers, to which I will turn next.

2
Equity, Policy and Outcomes

Introduction

To understand the impact of equality and affirmative action policies it is necessary to understand some of the key concepts that underpin the translation of intentions and ideas into action. It may be useful to try to draw a distinction between equal opportunities policies and affirmative action policies. There are no hard-and-fast definitions of either, although affirmative action is often thought of as being an American version of equal opportunities. One of the major differences between equal opportunities policies and affirmative action policies is that affirmative action policies are generally thought of as being backed by some element of compulsion. For example, employers are compelled by law to employ a specified percentage of people from ethnic minorities, or a specified percentage of women. Equal opportunities policies, on the other hand, tend to rely much more on employers acting without formal legal compulsion, though it should be noted that in the US the use of law to compel employers to enforce equity is not as common as people may imagine. A useful definition of affirmative action policies suggests that:

> Affirmative action is a generic term for programmes which take some kind of initiative either voluntarily or under compulsion of law, to increase, maintain, or rearrange the number or status of certain group members usually defined by race or gender. (Johnson 1990, p. 77)

Bacchi (1996) makes the point that affirmative action programmes are in essence proactive and forward-looking rather than simply waiting for discrimination to occur and to react to it. Bacchi correctly notes the difficulty in the use of terminology relating to affirmative action and equal opportunities. Questions of whether or not affirmative action constitutes reverse discrimination have proved highly controversial in the US as reverse discrimination suggests the conferring of some special privilege on under-represented groups. Bacchi's most useful contribution to the debate about affirmative action policies is her distinction between soft affirmative action and hard affirmative action. Soft action is seen as legitimate while hard affirmative action is seen as illegitimate. What this suggests is a spectrum of policy with hard affirmative action at one end and soft affirmative action at the other, with lots of spaces in between for forms of affirmative action that fall between these two extremes.

The debate around affirmative action that is taking place in the US seems to suggest that it is typically more vigorous and proactive than the corresponding equal opportunities policies in the UK and Europe. In the UK equality policies have been a part of the lexicon of employers since the early 1980s, but without the sort of impetus or urgency that has been apparent in the US. Many employers in the UK have tended to regard equality issues as a bolt-on extra, to use management terminology; indeed, much of the debate in contemporary equality management is about mainstreaming diversity and equality issues.

It is important to stress that the very concept of equality is one that is highly contested: what is equal treatment for one person may not necessarily be equal treatment for another. Of all the policies aimed at the sphere of employment, affirmative action and equal opportunity polices are among those that have attracted the most controversy. During the late 1970s and 1980s in both the US and Europe employers started to adopt polices that sought to level the playing field for different disadvantaged groups. It is significant that the first attempts to deal with inequality and discrimination in employment were aimed at ethnic groups.

Given that the history of ethnic relations in the US and the UK during the 1950s and 1960s was one punctuated by urban unrest (in the US the Watts riots; in the UK the Notting Hill riots) and conflict the early attempts of employers and governments to encourage and engender an ethos of equality within the workplace should not come as a surprise. The political undertones that are associated with attempts to introduce equality and affirmative action policies should, therefore, be seen in this context. Some have sought to characterize such policies as a form of political correctness that interferes with the natural working of the marketplace, while others have argued that affirmative action and equal opportunity policies are too little, too late. Indeed, opinions in America about the impact of affirmative action policies tend to be highly polarized. The Centre Right in America have argued that the mechanisms of the marketplace are being interfered with, indeed that affirmative action policies have reversed the shift of power from White Americans to Black and Hispanic Americans. Others in the US have argued that the backlash towards affirmative action from the Centre Right is evidence that such policies are achieving their aims. The debate in America about affirmative action concerns the legitimacy of quotas and 'racial' preferences. In universities and colleges throughout America affirmative action policies have been employed in an attempt to overcome disadvantage. The resulting controversy over their use and effects has led to calls for such practices and policies to be made illegal. However, it is clear that whatever the controversy surrounding affirmative action, it has had a very real and marked effect on the career trajectories of many Black and Hispanic Americans.

It should also be remembered that when references are made to affirmative action in the US, what is being referred to is a raft of different policy initiatives, some government-sponsored, others a part of normal business practice. Certainly early attempts to make access to education and employment more open and less discriminatory were part of a Federal Government response to segregation in the southern States. These policy initiatives included the 'Philadelphia Plan' under which federal contractors were set targets for hiring ethnic minority employees, and which resulted in an increase from 1 per cent of building workers being of ethnic minority origin to 12 per cent. What is notable about the approach of the US government is how much more aggressively it has sought to promote the employment of ethnic groups through the use of government machinery, particularly through the use of contract compliance. Successive British governments have, by contrast, shied away from such direct intervention and sought to educate and encourage employers to adopt more open and accessible employment policies rather than compelling them to do so. It is, however, true to say that US government initiatives on affirmative action tended to wither during the Reagan years. In addition much of the hyperbole surrounding affirmative action policies tended to emphasize the (erroneous) notion that White people were losing jobs as a result of such practices. As Marable (1995) notes, the White backlash against affirmative action is reflected in opinion polls during the 1990s. Greater numbers of White people are expressing a lack of support for affirmative action policies than in the 1980s with the rejection of affirmative action being more pronounced among White women than White men. This despite the fact that many White women have been the direct beneficiaries of affirmative action policies aimed at reducing gender discrimination. Crucially, Marable presents evidence of persistent disadvantage and discrimination against Black and Hispanic workers in the US labour market, notably that census data reveal that average earnings for African-Americans are almost 33 per cent lower than for White Americans. Marable also refers to research that suggests that Black workers are more likely than White workers to be fired. Thus the debate around affirmative action remains highly contested and polarized. It is clear that affirmative action has made some areas of the US economy more socially open, none the less there is evidence that Black and Hispanic Americans remain under-represented in professions. Evidence from Darity and Mason (1998) and Borgas (1992) also suggests that affirmative action and anti-discrimination policies have played a significant role in making the labour market more open. The election of a Republican president in 2001 is also likely to influence the development and impact of affirmative action, as historically the Republican Party has been much less sympathetic to it than the Democrats.

The question of equity has always been a controversial and sensitive subject in the UK and the US. How to achieve it? Is equity intrinsically desirable or not? What is meant by the words equity and equality? All have been the subject of a debate that is rarely rational and frequently sensational. As the boundaries of equality and affirmative action policies have expanded to take in questions of disability, sexual orientation and age, as well as gender and ethnic origin, the debates have only intensified. The increasingly controversial nature of the debate about equality in recruitment and the workplace should alert the reader to the fact that the very terms of the debate are not neutral or objective. I will examine what is meant by 'equal' in both theoretical and practical terms and the implications that different interpretations of it have for the formulation and implementation of policies directed at overcoming inequalities in employment. The use of different definitions of equality have real effects on the measurement of the success of equality/affirmative action policies. Thus to be able to measure the success of such policies is highly dependent upon on how the term 'equal' is employed by those social actors within the policy process.

Policy implementation is a process that is not always straightforward or easy to understand. It may be inextricably linked to organizational political agendas as well as broader political agendas. As a result, the process of policy implementation can be highly politicized. One very obvious example is the series of events that have been set in motion as a result of the Macpherson Report. The Report investigated the conduct of the Metropolitan Police during the investigation that took place when a teenager, Stephen Lawrence, was murdered. One of the central conclusions was that the Metropolitan Police are institutionally racist. Reactions from senior police officers have varied from acceptance of the basic premise and an acknowledgement of racism to outright rejection. Indeed many rank-and-file police officers regard the Report as unhelpful and damaging to their reputation. The subsequent attempts of police forces throughout the UK to attract more ethnic minority recruits have been public, sensational and controversial.

Much of the literature in this area emphasizes the difference between the formally stated policy at an organizational level and informal policy in terms of what actually happens within an organization on a day-to-day basis. Indeed the ability of different groups within an occupational sphere to resist the implementation of equality policies is a crucial determinant of the success or failure of a policy. The whole question of bottom-up resistance to top-down policy initiatives is one that figures prominently in the debate on equality policies. Given the increasing tendency within organizations to devolve recruitment practices to line managers, their ability to circumvent formal policy and substitute it with policy based on 'gut feeling' (Collinson et al. 1990; Jenkins 1986) is of central importance to the implementation of policy. It is the very relationship between what is determined at a higher level within an organization and what happens at the sharp end that throws into relief the discussion about what constitutes a policy and the issue of policy implementation.

In the UK at least notions of equality, positive action and positive discrimination have all been shaped by the Sex Discrimination Act 1975, the Race Relations Act 1976 and the Race Relations Amendment Act 2000. In order to understand how and why the discourse of equality has developed it is helpful to have some understanding of the logic underlying these key pieces of legislation which have sought to promote equality of opportunity.

Equality legislation in the UK

The impact of legislation on the discourse of equality within the UK was profound inasmuch as the Race Relations Act 1976 not only made discrimination in employment illegal, it also drew a distinction between direct and indirect discrimination. While it would be difficult to prove beyond any reasonable doubt that the Act was responsible for breathing life into equality policies, it seems highly likely that the two phenomena are related. One of the reasons for employers starting to develop and implement equal opportunity policies is the possibility of being found guilty of indirect discrimination rather than direct discrimination. It is important to bear in mind the social and historical context in which the Race Relations Act 1976 was developed: worsening industrial relations with a focus specifically on areas of employment where large numbers of migrants from Pakistan, India and Bangladesh were employed, notably the Grunwick dispute. In addition, the rise of the Far Right in the early and mid-1970s in the shape of the National Front and the British National Party meant that ethnic relations, particularly in the sphere of employment, became highly politically sensitive.

The Race Relations Act 1976 should be considered in the same light as the Sex Discrimination Act 1975. Indeed the notion of indirect discrimination which has proved both problematic to define and instrumental in the development of equality policies is most clearly defined in the Sex Discrimination Act 1975. Indirect discrimination is a crucial part of the discrimination legislation because underlying it is the notion that discrimination that is the result of unintended consequences is as important as discrimination based on prejudicial judgements about different social groups. The notion of indirect discrimination is a tacit admission that there are structures and procedures that are a part of organizations and employers' practices that place some social groups at a disadvantage. So in some ways it is a signpost to the findings of the Macpherson Report and the notion of institutional racism which can be both conscious and unconscious and, more importantly, built into the fabric of organizations.

Under the terms and conditions of the Sex Discrimination Act 1975 in order to prove indirect discrimination a woman must:

> Show the existence of a requirement or condition which applies equally to both men and women. If a considerably smaller proportion of women as compared with men can comply with that condition and, irrespective of sex, there is no justification for imposing it, then, providing the complainant cannot to her detriment, comply with it, there is discrimination. (Morris and Nott 1991, p. 82)

Having first established that a requirement or condition exists, the complainant has to demonstrate that it is applied equally to men and women and, crucially, that the proportion of women who can comply with it is smaller than the proportion of men who can comply with it. For example, in *Price* v *Civil Service Commission* candidates for the post of executive officer had to be at least 17 and under 28 years of age. Figures show that between these ages women may withdraw from the labour market to raise their families. Price successfully claimed in this case that proportionately fewer women than men can comply with the condition and that it therefore amounts to indirect discrimination.

Thus while the notion of indirect discrimination is a potentially powerful legislative weapon to combat racism and discrimination, establishing that it has taken place, even using the lower standard of proof required at industrial tribunals ('on the balance of probabilities' rather than 'beyond reasonable doubt' as in criminal cases), is extremely difficult. Moreover the fact that different tribunals have interpreted it in different ways leads to further uncertainty and inconsistency in the way the law is applied. An examination of case law on the Home Office web-site, which cites cases of indirect discrimination, shows just how difficult establishing whether or not indirect discrimination has actually taken place. Some of the decisions made by Industrial Tribunals about what constitutes indirect discrimination suggest that there is no certainty about the way in which the concept of indirect discrimination is translated into legal practice and decision making.

The provisions of the Race Relations Act 1976

Like the Sex Discrimination Act 1975 the Race Relations Act 1976 prohibits direct and indirect discrimination. According to section 1(1)(a) of the Act there are three types of discrimination:

1. *Direct discrimination* involves less favourable treatment on the grounds of colour, race, nationality or ethnic or national origins.
2. *Indirect discrimination*, in which a condition or requirement is applied which is such that the proportion of persons of a particular colour, race or ethnic or national origins able to comply with it is considerably smaller than the proportion of other persons able to do so, which works to the detriment of the complainant, and which is not shown by the alleged discriminator to be justifiable on non-racial grounds.

3. *Victimization* of those who, among other things, bring proceedings under the Act, or give evidence of information in connection with the Act.

Like the Sex Discrimination Act the Race Relations Act is theoretically not interested in the motivations of an employer, simply the actions. It is only if the effects of the employer's actions are that members of other ethnic groups are treated less favourably that it constitute direct discrimination. An interesting case in point is *Din* v *Carrington Viyella*, in which a Pakistani employee was not re-employed after a long trip to Pakistan. Before he had left for Pakistan there had been some trouble between the applicant and a foreman. The industrial tribunal found that the reason for not re-employing the applicant was the employer's desire to avoid a repetition of the industrial unrest that occurred previously. The Employment Appeals Tribunal found that:

> To seek to resolve actual or potential unrest by removing an employee against whom racial discrimination had been shown may itself be a discriminatory act, even if the employer acts from good motives. (Bourn and Whitmore 1993, p. 49)

The provisions of the Race Relations Act have been significantly extended by the Race Relations Amendment Act 2000. Though the impact of the Amendment Act is as yet unclear, the major provisions of the Act are that it:

1. *outlaws race discrimination* (direct, indirect and victimization) in public authority functions *not* covered by the Race Relations Act 1976;
2. *defines 'public authority' widely* for the purpose of outlawing race discrimination, so that it includes public functions carried out by private sector organizations and has only limited exemptions;
3. places a *general duty* on specified public authorities to *promote race equality*;
4. empowers the Home Secretary to *extend the list of public bodies* in the Act that are subject to the general duty to promote race equality to include other bodies exercising public functions;
5. empowers the Home Secretary (or Scottish ministers where appropriate) to impose *specific duties* on public bodies which are subject to the general duty to promote race equality to ensure their better performance of the general duty;

6. gives the Commission for Racial Equality (CRE) *powers to enforce specific duties* imposed on public authorities;
7. gives the CRE *powers to issue codes of practice* to provide practical guidance to public bodies on how to fulfil their general and specific duties to promote race equality;
8. allows race discrimination *claims to be brought against educational bodies direct to a county or sheriff court* without, as now, a two-month 'cooling-off' period of notification to central government;
9. makes *chief officers of police vicariously liable* for acts of discrimination carried out by officers under their direction and control and provides for compensation, costs or expenses awarded as a result of a claim to be paid out of police funds;
10. removes the power for a minister to issue conclusive certificates in race claims to the effect that an act of race discrimination was done for the purposes of *national security* and was therefore not unlawful.

What is particularly significant about the Amendment Act is the requirement that public bodies such as local government should 'promote race equality'. For many statutory organizations there will be considerable debate as to what constitutes race equality and what practical steps can be taken to promote it.

The other major feature of the Amendment Act is the increased scope. It covers the following areas:

- *Law enforcement*: for example, criminal investigations, arrest, bail, detention and stop and search by police officers and officers with similar powers, such as those in Customs & Excise. Also enforcement action by tax officers, Environmental Health Officers, Trading Standards Officers and the Health & Safety Executive.
- *Licensing*: for example, the issuing of street trading licences, gaming licences, liquor licences, etc.
- Public appointments *and the conferment of dignities and honours made on the recommendation of Ministers and the arrangements regarding all public appointments*: for example, Crown appointments and the conferment of dignities (e.g. peerages) and honours.
- The core functions of the *Immigration and Nationality Directorate* of the Home Office: specifically, where discrimination is not provided for in statute or expressly required or authorized by ministers on the grounds of nationality, ethnic or national origin, plus any discrimination by immigration and entry clearance officials on the grounds of race or colour.

- The core functions of the *Prison Service*: for example, prison allocation, discipline, punishment and the searching of visitors.
- The core functions of the *Probation Service*: for example, the preparation of pre-sentencing reports and the revocation of community sentences.
- Certain compulsory detention under the *Mental Health Act*.

One of the most obvious ways in which public bodies may 'promote race equality' is through the use of positive action. What constitutes positive action (in the UK at least) is relatively well defined by the Commission for Racial Equality, who state that:

> The Race Relations Act does not allow positive discrimination or affirmative action – in other words, an employer cannot try to change the balance of the workforce by selecting someone mainly because she or he is from a particular racial group. This would be discrimination on racial grounds, and unlawful.
>
> However, employers and others can take positive action to prevent discrimination, or to overcome past discrimination. Where over the previous twelve months no one from a particular racial group, or only very few persons from that racial group, have been doing a certain type of work then it is lawful to offer training only for people from that racial group or to encourage people from that racial group to apply.
>
> For example, an employer with no black supervisors but a high proportion of black assembly line workers, can arrange training for black workers seeking promotion, encourage black workers to apply for vacancies at that grade when advertising vacancies, or print leaflets in relevant minority languages to encourage them to apply.
>
> The aim of positive action is to ensure that people from previously excluded ethnic minority groups can compete on equal terms with other applicants. It is intended to make up for the accumulated effects of past discrimination. Selection itself must be based on merit and treat all applicants equally. The law does not compel employers to take positive action, but it allows them to do so. (Commission for Racial Equality 2002: http://www.cre.gov.uk/legaladv/rra.action.html)

The language that is used here suggests that, as far as the CRE are concerned, positive discrimination is the same as affirmative action. This is very different from Johnson's (1990) definition. In essence the distinction that the CRE are trying to draw is between what they call positive discrimination – that is, appointing people because they are members of under-represented groups – and positive action – that is, encouraging applicants from under-represented groups to apply for posts they might not otherwise apply for.

The confusion over what the terms mean has not always been helped by the media, who have sought to portray laws and programmes whose underlying aim is greater equity as either misplaced or simply wrong. The whole jumble of terms – equal opportunity, affirmative action, positive action and positive discrimination – has been used interchangeably, which does not make an analytical distinction between them easy. In interviews with NHS professionals, Iganski and Mason (2002) noted that positive action policies within the NHS have been hampered by a confusion over the difference between positive action and positive discrimination, with some managers believing that positive action (which really amounts only to encouraging applications from ethnic minorities) is in fact the same as positive discrimination, which, as I have noted, is illegal under the terms of the 1976 Race Relations Act.

Conceptions of equality

Many of the terms used in the debate over equality of opportunity are highly value-laden. It is difficult to use the term equal opportunity in a non-partisan way. The discourse of equal opportunity is a contested terrain in which there are multiple meanings attached to terms and concepts. The use of the word equality is frequently used and abused by the media, politicians, employers, trade unions, labour organizations and social actors without any agreement about what it means. Indeed, the very term 'equal opportunities' is often associated with some of the more radical policies adopted by some local authorities in the immediate aftermath of the race riots of the early 1980s. Reactions to the policy initiatives among the general public range from scepticism to outright hostility – feelings often fuelled by unsympathetic coverage of such issues in the tabloid press. The debate about the impact, scope and ethos of equality policies has led to debates over the nature of the inequality such policies seek to overcome and whether this is either desirable or even possible. Undoubtedly, the waters surrounding this debate have been muddied by unscrupulous individuals who have sought to manipulate such policies to their own ends.

One central axis of debate is between those who advocate *liberal* equality policies and those who advocate *radical* equality positions. The radical approach concerns itself principally with the *outcomes* of policies while the liberal approach seeks to ensure equity within the *process* of appointment, even if the outcome is that members of disadvantaged groups are not appointed. A popular analogy for the competition for jobs is that of a race. Thus the liberal position is less concerned with the relative starting points of the different contestants within the race and more concerned to see that the race is run fairly. The liberal model is closely related to an ideal type of meritocracy – that is, a society in which individual attributes and skills determine the relative success or failure of people in their attempts to obtain scarce resources, most usually jobs. The best example of this model is that proposed by Davis and Moore (1967). It presupposes that if individuals possess the requisite ability and talent, then their rise to high occupational status is assured, regardless of gender or skin colour. In such a model there are no barriers to occupational mobility other than the ability of the individual.

The emphasis on the ability of the individual fails to recognize that employers have preferences for different types of employee, as well as the fact that different social groups have very different experiences of broader social structural disadvantages. Similarly the notion of merit is far from neutral. However, the most significant criticism of such a model is, put simply, that it fails to take into account the fact that different people start from different places in the race for high occupational status. That is, there are sections of the population who experience considerable economic, educational and social disadvantage and who may possess the merit to rise to the top but do not have the opportunity. Indeed, the persistence of elite self-recruitment or, as it is more popularly referred to, the old boy network, remains a very serious constraint on those seeking to enter senior occupational positions which are effectively socially closed.

By contrast, the radical view of equal opportunity is concerned with the position of groups of disadvantaged people and the outcomes of policies designed to improve their position in society. Radicals point out that however equal the competition for scarce resources is, tinkering with the mechanism is pointless. Since disadvantage is so entrenched in society, some groups will inevitably be more successful than others however equal the process of competition is. To put it another way, it is hard to ensure equitable selection outcomes in an inequitable society. Thus, the radical position is less concerned with the way the race is run and more concerned with the nature and outcome of the race. For advocates of the radical position it is the membership of a social group that is disadvantaged that is of key importance. The very membership of a subordinated social group is the central factor that shapes the identity and life experience of individuals within it. Thus, for radicals, equality is a matter of ensuring that sufficient members of such groups are able to reach the occupational positions that have been closed to them, regardless of the process.

Radical equality policies or hard affirmative action has been controversial as the *raison d'être* for such policy is to increase the numbers of people from disadvantaged groups in areas of employment where they are either absent or under-represented. If the most important criteria for appointment is that the candidate is a member of a disadvantaged social group – for example, a woman or an ethnic minority – rather than skills and qualifications that are appropriate for the job, then there are a number of consequences. For example, the possibility exists that people who are appointed on the basis that they are members of a disadvantaged group may be regarded by existing workers not only as having being appointed using a different set of criteria but they may also be regarded as tokens. In ethnic terms this White backlash can be manifested in a variety of ways, not least of which is the canteen culture referred to in the Macpherson Report. That is, an atmosphere in which people from different backgrounds from the majority of the workforce are made to feel uncomfortable through a variety of strategies, including verbal intimidation and allocation of the least desirable types of work within the workplace.

The radical position recognizes that different groups of people start the race from different positions and seeks to make winning the race for scarce resources easier for the disadvantaged by removing barriers to their success. Both radical and liberal proponents of equality implicitly accept the nature of the hierarchy of rewards that are attached to different occupational positions. Both try to alter the way in which such rewards are allocated, but without changing the structures of inequality which underlie the hierarchy. That is, proponents of equal opportunity have to accept that there is an unequal distribution of rewards and life chances.

New Right thinkers, who emphasize the primacy of the market and are antipathetic to state intervention, regard attempts to alter what is a natural market with considerable suspicion. State intervention to promote equality of opportunity is, from such a perspective, fundamentally wrong because it interferes with individual liberty and the mechanisms of the market. Moreover, since the distribution of talent and ability is *not* equal, there is little point trying to interfere with the workings of the market to try to ensure that people are treated equally. From a neo-conservative position, the intrusion of the state into the workings of the market can only be seen as negative and pointless. The intervention of the state will inhibit the equality of the market in which the able and competent rise to positions of seniority. Thus any attempts to level the playing field will be doomed to failure because, in the long run, the law of the market must prevail and attempts to do so are nothing more than bad social theory leading to bad social engineering. The birth of New Right-style politics in the UK with the election of the Conservative Party under Mrs Thatcher in 1979 and in the US with the election of Ronald Reagan in 1981 marked a very real shift in attitudes to ethnic minority groups. A major plank of New Right policies was in the words of Smith (1994) to re-code racism in a way that meant that references to physical difference and inferiority disappeared and references to cultural differences started to appear. This new racism, as Smith (1994) puts it, is in many ways more insidious than old racism.

> The new racism therefore transforms racist immigration policies into an entirely natural humanism. It re-codes intolerance as a legitimate expression of natural beliefs; it liberates the racially intolerant from their post colonial condition of guilt. Above all the new racism promotes contradictory political identifications around racial intolerance. Within the new racism it is perfectly consistent to state that a quite blatantly racist immigration law has nothing to do with racial intolerance and. Indeed, ought to be passed in the interests of racial minorities themselves, for greater restrictions on racial immigration will by definition prepare the way for better race relations. (Smith 1994, p. 56)

So in effect notions of New Right thinking combine aggressive reformations of national identity that exclude others who are different, a primacy for the workings of the market at all levels, a desire to restrict the growth of state intervention at all levels with a pronounced antipathy to notions of equality that are based on the premise of intervention either by the state or by organizations. For New Right thinkers equity can be achieved only through the cut and thrust of the market where the strong survive and the weak fall by the wayside. Attempts to interfere with the workings of the market can and will fail, so to try to achieve equity for disadvantaged groups is not only impossible, it is a waste of time and effort.

The extent to which New Right political thought has fundamentally shifted the political centre of gravity in the UK and US should not be underestimated. The legacy of the Thatcher and Reagan years lives on in successive administrations that have sought to reduce the role of the state in the lives of ordinary citizens. Notions of equity as well as the means of achieving it have been reconsidered and redefined in ways that differ considerably from the tone of the debate that took place in the 1960s and 1970s. One thing is certain: the state has become increasingly reluctant to engage in attempts to reduce ethnic inequalities particularly in the field of employment.

Conceptions of opportunity

In its broadest sense opportunity is a set of circumstances that enable something to happen: that is, circumstances that are permissive. In the case of equal opportunity the question of *how* permissive circumstances should be tends to be a product of values about how best to advance the cause of a disadvantaged group. The question of what constitutes an opportunity could be reformulated as: What is a fair chance? The measurement has proved highly problematic precisely because of the competing notions of what fair means in practice.

The term equal depends upon the political stance of those who use it. Access to information *is* opportunity. It is impossible to divorce the question of power from the issue of information, that is, that people in positions of power within organizations define who sees an internal job bulletin. Indeed, in some cases those in power pursue a particular person for a particular post. For some types of job the practice of head-hunting is prevalent, although this is an extreme version of defining the parameters of who has access to information about vacancies. So, for example, in some organizations internal job bulletins are distributed to limited groups or individuals, thus restricting opportunity to acquire information about jobs. The question of what opportunity is should take into account not only selection and promotion, but also the power to negotiate for different working conditions and pay, as well as defining the skill levels of different jobs. That is, some types of work that are usually referred to as unskilled or semi-skilled have tacit skills which are not acknowledged simply because groups lack the power to define themselves as skilled.

Notions of opportunity are defined, redefined, formed and transformed within a context of the pursuit of profit and/or efficiency. In the case of equality policies or affirmative action policies employers rarely develop and implement an equal opportunities policy because of the inherent goodness of equality. It should be remembered that developing an affirmative action policy or an equalities policy may be a symbolic act, rather than a sincere commitment to social change. Almost every major employer in both the US and the UK has a statement attached to their job advertisements that states that they are an 'equal opportunities employer'. This is not in itself a guarantee of equality, though the fact the employers feel compelled to make a public statement about their espousal of equality and affirmative action policies does represent a considerable shift in attitude. There may be other very real reasons why employers have equality policies – for example, the threat of legal action from an aggrieved employee or applicant, pressure from local or central government, or even the possibility of positive or negative press and media coverage. The decision-making process in relation to equality policies is one in which there is a very careful evaluation of costs and benefits about whether, why and how to pursue equality. The question of what constitutes a cost and what constitutes a benefit is one to which I shall return later.

If defining the term opportunity is a difficult intellectual and conceptual task, operationalizing it is even more difficult. In common-sense terms, the question of what constitutes an opportunity, particularly an equal opportunity, may depend on a number of factors. There is a range of factors which may affect the definition. These include the political, moral, practical and economic. Thus the cost of implementing an equality policy will always be weighed against the benefit. However, definitions of cost and benefit tend to be rather elastic. The notion that equality costs money is a central part of the equation that determines whether or not employers develop and implement an equality or affirmative action policy. Indeed, one of the most striking aspects of my empirical research in this area is that both personnel managers and line managers in the National Health Service believed that the pursuit of equality is a cost in terms of time and/or money.

The fact that the debate is framed in such a way that it is always about what the opportunity costs of equality and affirmative action policies are, obscures the fact that there are real opportunity benefits. It is the social construction of what constitutes a cost and a benefit that is crucial to the understanding why so many equality and affirmative action policies fail. This is a theme to which I will return.

Defining policy

The process of policy-making and policy implementation are not discrete areas; one clearly affects the other. Those who develop policy do not do so in a vacuum, they are part of the organizations, and indeed the societies, in which they live and work. In most organizations there are conflicting interest groups jockeying for position, that is, there is a political process in which policy-makers are often bound up. The question of what constitutes policy has been the subject of much academic debate, but little consensus.

Rather than conceiving of policy as something clearly defined, it is more helpful to think of it as a complex nexus of decisions that are involved in producing and influencing action. Policy is rarely expressed in a single decision and there can often be contradictory aspects of policy, which further complicate its definition. There may also be shifts of emphasis on different parts of the same policy as well as changes of policy. The fact that defining what policy is, is so difficult makes it hard to agree on what appropriate measures of its success or failure are. Policy has been defined as:

- a course of action or inaction rather than specific decisions or actions;
- a web of decisions and actions that allocate values;
- a set of interrelated decisions concerning the selection of goals and the means of achieving them within a specified situation;
- more broadly: 'a stance which once articulated contributes to the context within which a succession of future decisions will be made' (Ham and Hill 1984, p. 11).

Defining the term policy depends on the perception of issues of agency and structure. Those who believe that structure dominates over agency may feel that a 'top-down' policy model in which there is a clear relationship between intentions and outcomes is needed. In such a model, it is, theoretically at least, easy to make judgements about cause and effect in an empirical and demonstrable way. However, those who argue that the meanings and interpretations of different groups of social actors throughout a hierarchy or organization are of paramount importance to understanding the development and implementation of policy lower down the hierarchy and have an important impact upon the way in which policy is delivered, are closer to a 'bottom-up' definition. In fact, the definition of policy should reflect the fact that it is a complex combination of both the 'top-down' and the 'bottom-up' approach. Thus the following definition takes into account both social structures which prescribe forms of policy and the agency of social actors who interpret it: *A set of interrelated decisions concerning the selection of goals and the means of achieving them within a specified situation* (Ham and Hill 1984, p. 11). It is, however, important to bear in mind that although decisions may be made with particular goals in mind, those goals may not necessarily be achieved.

Policy implementation 'top-down' and 'bottom-up'

The relationship between policy and outcomes is often assumed to be straightforward. So if a policy is adopted with certain intentions in mind, there will be a number of intended (and measurable) consequences. Thus, policy is based on the assumption that there is a clear and obvious relationship between cause (the policy) and effect (the outcome). Studies of policy implementation suggest that the relationship between policy and outcome are not at all straightforward; indeed the question of unintended consequences that result from policy initiatives is an area of interest that is of growing importance in sociology.

There are two broad approaches to understanding the implementation of policy: the top-down model and the bottom-up model. When policy-makers attempt to change or modify the behaviour and actions of people within an organization it is often through the use of the top-down model. There are a number of assumptions underlying the top-down model, for example, that there are enough resources available for the policy to be implemented; and that the policy itself is administratively possible – that is, that all actions are coordinated in the desired direction. There may also be external circumstances that may impose severe constraints on the policy. These, broadly speaking, might be regarded as structural problems. There are other factors which affect the implementation of policy which are more closely related to the agency of individual social actors, most notable of these is that key actors, such as managers, within the hierarchy fully *understand* what the policy is about and how it is to be implemented. Of course, what is vital to the success of policy implementation is that there is no resistance to the policy from within or without the organization.

Policy, however, is never developed or implemented in a political vacuum. Particular groups within any given hierarchy may have vested interests in ensuring that certain policies fail or succeed. Such groups often exercise a considerable degree of discretion over how a policy is implemented. The opposition of groups is a crucial determinant of the success or failure of a policy, and nowhere is this more obvious than in the case of an equal opportunities policy. In cases where there is a culture of opposition it is possible that the letter of the law is observed, but not the spirit.

One of the main criticisms of a top-down model is that it is not always possible to isolate clearly policy-making and policy implementation. Indeed, it is rare that all the preconditions set out above are met, and it is perhaps more useful to think of a model which allows for the interpretation and agency of social actors lower down the hierarchy who actually implement policy. Their actions and interpretations are crucial to the successful implementation of policy. A bottom-up model takes into account the fact that some forms of policy are necessarily dynamic or flexible when they are being implemented. Some form of change or modification becomes desirable if the stated goal is to be achieved. Thus, it is argued, it is necessary to consider implementation as a policy–action continuum in which an interactive process is taking place over time between those seeking to put policy into effect and those upon whom action depends.

It is precisely this debate about how policy is understood and implemented that has such profound implications for the success or failure of equal opportunity and affirmative action policies. One of the most frequent criticisms of such policies is that there is a lack of commitment from the top of organizations. The evidence to support such claims is contradictory. Indeed, it is often senior managers who are among the first to make a public commitment to equality. None the less it remains a fact that in many organizations affirmative action or equal opportunities is often regarded as both a bolt-on extra and an expense that cannot be afforded. Assuming that senior managers are committed enough to the underlying principles of such policies that they accord them a high organizational priority, there remains the important issue of resistance from managers lower down the hierarchy and the extent to which the entire culture of a workplace is able to accommodate this type of change. Bradley (1999) argues that middle and line managers are often resistant to equality policies because they disrupt established employment practices and norms. She might also have added that equality policies often indirectly threaten the power of line managers to control the recruitment process in ways that reflect their professional, personal and political agendas.

Equal opportunities: affirmative action or diversity

There is no single, all-encompassing definition of equal opportunity or affirmative action. Indeed, as I mentioned at the start of this chapter, there is a range of competing definitions which have an important influence on the ways in which a policy is understood, implemented and evaluated. In the most general terms it is possible to say that equal opportunities and affirmative action policies seek to reduce discrimination in employment on the grounds of race, gender, age, religious affiliation, sexual orientation, nationality and a range of other socially constructed aspects of identity. To do this, policies are aimed at changing practices that either directly or indirectly discriminate against disadvantaged groups. In the UK it is important to remember that employers may set targets for the recruitment of different ethnic groups but that the use of quotas is illegal. It is worth pointing out that many of the most vocal critics of equality policies have deliberately tried to confuse the use of targets with the use of quotas.

In the US the history of affirmative action has been characterized by the use of policies that are more forceful and directive than equality policies in the UK. For example, America's best universities and colleges have introduced ethnic-sensitive admissions policies in order to increase the number of minority students. These policies have been in place for thirty years and have only recently been reviewed as a result of a Supreme Court decision making them illegal. It is worth pausing here to make a brief comparison between the attitudes of elite universities in the UK and the US. It is mind-boggling even to imagine that members of the Russell Group of elite universities in the UK (which include Oxford, Cambridge, Warwick, Imperial College and a number of others) would even consider a strategy that made it easier for ethnic minority students to enter as undergraduates. Of course, the history of affirmative action policies in US universities has not been without problems or controversy. However, they have displayed the sort of boldness in tackling ethnic inequality that is noticeably absent from many UK universities whose undergraduate intake is dominated by white, middle-class students, some of whom have been educated in fee-paying schools. While there have been some very modest policy initiatives to widen access to higher education, the position (at elite universities at least) appears to be to maintain the existing arrangements.

The programme of ethnic-sensitive admissions policies in American universities has been severely criticized by conservatives, who argue that it has lowered educational standards by admitting students with lower qualifications than other (White) students. Conservative critics have also argued that such policies have exacerbated rather than relieved racial tension. Indeed, in 1995 the University of California declared that 'race' could no longer be taken into account in admissions decisions at any branches of that university. Other American universities have followed suit and the wider legislative attempts to revoke or dilute affirmative action in America are starting to have an impact. What is clear from the literature in this area (Bacchi 1996; Williams 1997; Dworkin 2000) is that affirmative action policies have had a very marked impact. In the case of American universities success has been in terms of increased earnings for minority graduates, greater tolerance and understanding within and between ethnic groups, and an increase in minority graduates reaching senior occupational positions. One of the most interesting aspects of the discussion of affirmative action in elite universities cited by Dworkin is that:

> While graduation from a selective college hardly guarantees a successful career, it may open doors, help Black matriculants overcome any negative stereotypes that may still be held by employers and create opportunities not otherwise available. (Dworkin 2000, p. 394)

Thus it seems that graduating from a selective college enables minority graduates to get past the first hurdle in applying for jobs. The reversal of programmes designed to give minority applicants to universities and colleges greater equity in access can only have a deleterious effect on the wider social and occupational mobility of ethnic minority groups in the US.

The fact that American universities have been able to apply differential standards to ethnic minority students in order to increase their representation speaks volumes about the differences between the UK and the US. If, for example, it was proposed that ethnic minority applicants to UK universities should be allowed to gain entry with a points score below that of White students, the opposition and controversy that would inevitably result would be headline news.

Recent developments in the UK and US suggest that equality and affirmative action policies are being replaced by diversity policies. Whether or not diversity policies are significantly different from either affirmative action or equality policies is a matter of some debate. What can be said is that the umbrella of diversity is spread wider than either equality policies or affirmative action policies as diversity seeks to manage the experiences and expectations of diverse social groups. These include men and women, White and ethnic minority groups, young and old, straight and gay. Whether or not diversity will succeed where equality and affirmative action have failed is a question I shall take up in the latter part of the book.

Hard and soft equality or gendered and racialized labour markets?

Policies aimed at achieving equity vary from those that can be described as proactively pursuing equitable outcomes, or what can be called hard equality to those that are more reactive and can be described as soft equality. Jewson and Mason's (1987) liberal/radical dichotomy fits closely with this hard/soft division. Thus, their liberal model is an ideal-type meritocratic recruitment model in which the emphasis is on process and not outcome. Employers should seek to ensure that the recruitment process is scrupulously fair. Thus people are appointed on the basis of their skills and merit rather than on the basis of whether or not they fit in. Meritocratic ideology is central to this model whose aim is to remove obstacles within the process that might prevent a fair race from being run. To continue with the sporting analogy, the employer takes on the role of a referee and ensures that all the competitors are treated equally and that the race is fairly run. The most obvious flaw with the liberal model is that it fails to recognize that not everybody starts from the same point. In other words, it ignores the structural sources of inequality. Critics of the liberal model argue that procedures and policies may be operated in a way that is, or at least appears to be, fair but that it fails to deliver in terms of outcomes. Liberal policies may very well ensure that the process is fair but the actual numbers of people from disadvantaged groups who are employed may remain small.

By contrast the radical model ignores the issue of process and concentrates mainly on outcome. Unless there is equitable representation that reflects the population at large, the only possible explanation is the existence of discrimination. Within the radical model the process of appointment should be one that is overtly politicized and takes a moral stance that seeks to appoint candidates on the basis of membership of a disadvantaged group. It should be noted that to pursue such a policy publicly in the UK would be of highly dubious legality. Some local councils have sought to apply a radical equal opportunities policy. Lambeth, Haringey and Brent, for example, have employed a radical equal opportunities policies and have been derided in the media as being part of the loony left who are obsessed with political correctness. It is clear that there have been abuses of such policies within local authorities by people who have sought to manipulate them for their own ends. None the less the fact that equality and affirmative action policies have been labelled examples of excessive political correctness suggests that some groups feel threatened by their existence.

Radicals tend to assert that most jobs can be done by most people and, as such, skills and qualifications are artificially imposed barriers used to exclude from jobs some people who are perfectly able to do them. Thus talent and skill are not neutral terms. They reflect the values of a dominant class which is mainly male, White and middle-class. Moreover within the radical model it is argued that the skills that are associated with jobs are largely irrelevant since all jobs are increasingly deskilled. So for the radical model criteria such as educational qualifications are relatively unimportant. The criteria that guide selection are based on political and social judgements about what is morally right and wrong. In brief, the radical agenda is little short of a crusade that attempts to redress previous wrongs by appointing on the basis that members of disadvantaged (mainly ethnic minority) groups should be appointed over other (usually White groups) precisely because of their membership of that disadvantaged group.

While Jewson and Mason's work frames much of the debate on equal opportunities the simple bifurcation of liberal and radical positions they propose is in some ways unhelpful. Participants in the recruitment and promotion process do not always easily fall into one of the two categories. It is more realistic to think of equal opportunities as a sliding scale, with radical at one end and liberal at the other. At different times and for different reasons participants will move from one position to another depending on broader conflicts between interest groups within organizations. If also fails to take into account those organizations that remain outside the equal opportunities/affirmative action discourse whose recruitment policies rely on a wide range of formal and informal recruitment methods. The debate on equal opportunities and affirmative action always seems to overlook those at the top of organizations. Appointments as managing director or chief executive officer appear to take place in a world where considerations of equity remain firmly in the background and much of the appointments process remains as mysterious and surrounded in secrecy as the election of the pope.

The major contradiction surrounding equality affirmative action policies is that while the majority of employers in the US and the UK have adopted such policies there appears to have been little in the way of progress of ethnic minority groups in the labour market. Equally, ethnic minority groups appear to remain sceptical about affirmative action/equal opportunity policies. If employers are developing such policies without any underlying commitment to genuine change, and ethnic minority groups harbour suspicions about the motives of employers, the question arises why have employers bothered at all. The answer is not straightforward. It is partly due to central government implementing civil rights legislation in the US, and in the anti-discrimination legislation in the UK in the 1970s. However effective, or indeed ineffective, such legislation has been, it sent a signal to employers and others that discrimination and racism were problems that required the attention of government. The impact of civil unrest or riots should not be underestimated. While there is no simple cause-and-effect relationship between, say, laws prohibiting discrimination or riots and the development of equality and affirmative action policies, all of these things could be said to contribute to an atmosphere in which equality, racism and discrimination were put on the political agenda.

Cockburn's argument that the typology of equal opportunities proposed by Jewson and Mason is something of a straitjacket raises important issues. The substance of her argument is that liberal EO policy is little more than a cosmetic exercise to clean up recruitment policy. Evidently one of the principal motivations for developing and implementing equality policies is that it represents a form of insurance in the event of an industrial tribunal case. In the case of radical equality policy Cockburn argues that giving disadvantaged groups a leg up the occupational hierarchy fails to address the underlying source of inequality itself, namely the very structure of the hierarchy, which remains unchanged.

Cockburn's alternative to the liberal/radical dichotomy is the short and long agenda of equal opportunities. She argues that genuine equality of opportunity is achieved through a critical and comprehensive examination of the way in which power is distributed throughout organizations and then reorganized in ways that allow disadvantaged groups access and opportunity. Her long agenda is a change not in procedure but in culture. Cockburn (1989, p. 218) refers to a project of transformation in which organizations and institutions shifts power away from those social groups that have historically monopolized it towards disadvantaged groups. It should be emphasized that this sort of transformation is envisaged as being a long-term project. Bradley (1999) argues that there are signs that there has been a gradual shift in power within organizations, at least for women. The evidence that equality/affirmative action policies have had the same effect for different ethnic groups is less clear-cut. The sort of long-term transformation that Cockburn envisages is unlikely to occur in the UK without a radical shift in policy. The types of policy that have been successful in the US in increasing ethnic minority representation in both the public and private sectors, and which are now coming under attack from the conservative Right, have undoubtedly had a greater effect on US institutions than equality policies have had in the UK. Whether or not there is a government in the UK that has the political will to promote ethnic equality in such an aggressive and proactive way is open to debate.

Cockburn's analysis of equal opportunities is convincing, in so far as she recognizes that the *raison d'être* of commercial organizations is profit. She also recognizes that the aims of profit-making, efficiency and achieving equity are often a source of conflict for managers. The principal strength of Cockburn's arguments about projects of transformation is that it forces a reconsideration of the hard/soft division because it focuses on the structural determinants of inequality within and without organizations. The notion of a project of transformation suggests that change will be gradual and incremental rather than sudden and revolutionary, and it is perhaps optimistic to imagine that managers and organizations will radically alter the way they think about equality/affirmative action policies in the short term.

Webb and Liff (1988) also argue that analysis of equal opportunities policies must be extended. They suggest that the division into liberal and radical policies overlooks the fact that jobs are defined in ways that rule out potentially competent women (and, by implication, Black workers). Thus what has to be examined is the way in which terms such as skills and abilities are constituted. The question of what sort of social qualities are embedded within particular jobs is key to understanding how and why some work is seen as women's work and other work as men's work – an argument that can be extended to Black work and White work. The fact that these qualities are ascribed is what matters. Since the ascription can be understood as a social process, it should also be remembered that categorization of work is a dynamic not a static process. The implementation of a long agenda is one that is likely to face considerable difficulties. Developing and implementing equal opportunities/affirmative action may be an important step on the way to achieving broader cultural change, but for organizations to become more egalitarian and socially open can only be a long-term goal.

What is clear from my research is that certain types of work are categorized, understood and defined as the province of particular social groups. For example, certain parts of the nursing profession as well as certain work tasks have come to be seen as almost exclusively performed by African-Caribbean women. It is this process of ascription of social characteristics to particular types of work and labour market niches that helps to determine patterns of labour market participation and the range and level of occupational mobility.

Any radical transformation in attitudes and culture alluded to by Cockburn, Webb and Liff, and others is unlikely to occur in the UK, without the weight of government behind it. Unless there is a concerted political effort to promote equality of opportunity more aggressively, the sort of ad hoc, gradual and inconsistent development of equality policies will either splutter to a halt or be allowed simply to atrophy. It should not be forgotten that those who are able to transform the culture of organizations are usually nearer the top of the organizational hierarchies than the bottom. They therefore stand to gain very little from such transformations. That is not to preclude change from the bottom; indeed, it is undeniable that the position of women in paid employment has changed dramatically over the past forty years. In both the US and the UK women now constitute a vital part of the workforce and it is no longer unusual to see female chief executives. While there have been positive changes it is also true that gender discrimination persists and that forms of patriarchy are powerful determinants of the occupational position of women. The type of transformation that Cockburn discusses appears to have started for women; however, for ethnic minority groups there is much less ground for optimism. Racism and discrimination continue to be a major part of the experience of ethnic minorities in the US and the UK.

While there has been a real expansion in the number of employers who have adopted affirmative action and equal opportunities policies, the effects of such policies are unclear. There is evidence from case studies that formal methods of recruitment and promotion that seek to promote equality often coexist with informal methods that are either explicitly or implicitly discriminatory. Critics of the discourse of affirmative action and equality policies suggest that such policies have a symbolic, rather than a practical function. That is, they pay little more than lip service to equality.

The fact that personnel managers have colonized the area of affirmative action or equal opportunity policies as a way of reasserting their authority over organizations without necessarily having any genuine commitment to equality has lent weight to such accusations. In such situations there are inevitably accusations of bad faith from disadvantaged groups. Bad faith may result from disadvantaged groups having their expectations of affirmative action/equality policies being artificially inflated and then not being met. In cases where the outcomes of policies do match the expectations of the groups who are their intended beneficiaries, tensions about the nature of the policy will ensue. The tensions between the personnel function and policies designed to promote equality of opportunity have been a fruitful area for analysis. I discuss this next.

The personnel function and equal opportunities

Responsibility for the implementation of affirmative action and equal opportunities policies has tended to be part of the personnel function. The fact that affirmative action/equality policies have become associated with personnel officers assumes greater significance when the cull of middle managers that took place in many organizations during the 1980s is taken into account. What was left at the end of this process were management structures in which line managers assumed more power and responsibility, coupled with a greater stress on results and productivity. At the same time as part of the devolving of power to the lower levels of management, the personnel function found itself with less and less responsibility for interviewing and recruitment. Thus affirmative action and equality policies represented a sphere of influence in which personnel officers were able to reassert their authority. As Dale and Liff (1994) note, it also meant that personnel officers had the ability to define what was good, and what was bad, practice. The implementation of affirmative action/equality policies has increasingly taken on the characteristics of a contest between line managers and personnel officers, with line managers arguing that they are in possession of all the relevant information about the way their department works. Thus, attempts by personnel officers to exert an influence over the recruitment and promotion process are viewed as an unwelcome incursion by those whose knowledge of the operational boundaries of the organization is strictly limited – a point supported by Collinson (1988) and others.

In this respect affirmative action and equality policies are closely related to power and by extension power struggles within the workplace. Whether or not racism and discrimination are the product of a few prejudiced individuals within organizations or whether racism is, in fact, an integral part of the fabric and structure of organizations is a question that has become topical in the UK. The publication of the Macpherson Report highlighted the role of institutional racism within the Metropolitan Police and other public institutions at the heart of British society. The ensuing debate about the extent and nature of racism has been both emotive and controversial. In the immediate aftermath of the publication of the Report, questions of equity and how to achieve it assumed an urgency and prominence which had been notable by its absence, until that point.

Personnel managers have used equal opportunities as part of a professionalizing rhetoric. When attempting to implement equality policies, personnel managers use two justifying ideologies, which Jenkins (1986) calls a technical rationale and moral rationale. The technical rationale refers to the idea of best practice, that is, that the best possible candidates are selected and therefore it is the best possible use of resources. The moral rationale refers to the notion that fairness in itself is desirable. Examples of the moral rationale periodically appear in personnel journals such as *Equal Opportunities Review*:

Our business should adopt equal opportunities practice because we believe in treating everyone fairly. After all if we were in the position of being a different gender, a different ethnicity, older, younger, disabled, we would wish to be treated with respect. What is more, by treating all employees fairly and ensuring their human dignity at work we also ensure that they feel happy, secure and confident and produce quality work. (Rennie 1993)

Thus the use of equality issues as a way of increasing the power of personnel officers can be justified either as a legal requirement in order to avoid having legal action taken against employers, or as moral issue in which employers have a moral duty to promote what is fair and right. The two knit together in a way that gives personnel specialists the maximum amount of leverage to promote equality of opportunity. The threat of legal action represents the stick, and the knowledge that doing what is right represents the carrot. This is not to say that the work of personnel or equality officers is in any way easy!

In many large organizations personnel departments have created the post of equalities officer or diversity officer. Typically, such officers are pulled in two directions. On the one hand, they face scepticism from managers elsewhere in the organization who attempt to resist what they see as unnecessary interference. On the other hand, the expectations of ethnic minority workers within the organization are often high and if these not met the equalities specialist is seen as a failure. Given the weight of expectations of all the participants in the recruitment and selection process it is hardly surprising that it has become such a contested terrain.

Policy implementation

The discussion of conflicts over implementation suggests that equalities policies are complex and riddled with contradictions. There may often be a large gap between the stated intentions of an organization and the actual behaviour of individuals and groups within it. Among the factors that militate against the successful implementation of an equal opportunities policy are:

1. The devolvement of the recruitment process to line managers and the corresponding weakness of the personnel function within many organizations. Personnel officers are frequently marginalized within organizations, partly because they do not make any tangible

contribution to an organization in the way that others may do. The corollary of this is that they lack institutional power which is vital if changes to policy are to be made.

2. The question of top-down pressure from senior management which is vital for success. This commitment manifests itself in one of two specific strategies; either to assign responsibility for equal opportunities to a departmental head or to assign responsibility to line management. Underlying such strategies is a view which fails to recognize the complexity of issues related to equal opportunities. The prevailing assumption in many organizations seems to be that equality issues are easy enough to manage if good practice is identified and is clearly linked to targets and objectives that are part of the management mainstream. There are, however, in any organization groups who have specific objectives and interests that may not necessarily coincide with those of personnel managers seeking to implement an equality policy. That is there are cliques, cabals and interest groups with their own agenda, and it is quite possible that sabotaging an equality policy may be one of their prime objectives, if only to preserve their position of relative strength within the organization.

3. The persistence of informal recruitment practices alongside more formal ones. It is important to distinguish between individual discrimination and disadvantage:

individual discrimination results in unequal starting points in the race...recruitment by means of the old boy network is an obvious example. Inequalities in pay and conditions and in access to training for career progression are other examples.... Disadvantage is due to factors external to the organisation and this helps give credence to the classic explanation for poor progress on equal treatment strategies, i.e. that no women, or ethnic minority people applied for the job or those that did apply lacked experience. (Wilkinson 1992, p. 27)

The significance of elite self recruitment or the old boy network should not be underestimated in relation to the successful implementation of equal opportunities policies. The existence of the old boy network leads to discrimination which:

results in hurdles for some groups. Some of these are fairly straightforward, e.g. the networks that men establish in the pub or on the golf course, or in the mens toilet! Others are more subtle, and are concerned with the type of person who is valued by the organisation and other issues linked to the culture of the organisation. (ibid., p. 28)

Although there are many different problems attached to implementation which are specific to particular organizations some are common to most organizations. They include the relative weakness of the personnel function to impose formal equality policies and practices over line managers. Related to this is the autonomy of line managers who often jealously guard their powers of appointment and appoint on the basis of intuition. Moreover, it is argued that in many organizations highly informal methods of recruitment persist alongside more formal ones so that the informal methods tend to cancel out more formal ones. The extent to which formality in the recruitment process can be said to ensure equality of opportunity is thus highly contested.

There is an assumption that formality should be preferred to informality in the recruitment process. Underlying this is the notion that there is a direct relationship between formality, efficiency and equity. Of course, the assumption that a formal policy which states clearly what is and what is not legitimate practice makes it easier to determine whether or not rules have been broken. In other words, it might be logical to assume that a formal framework for recruitment is going to make it more difficult for those who wish to discriminate on the grounds of ethnic origin to do so. The reverse is also true. As Jenkins (1986) argues, informality in the recruitment process creates a space for discrimination to develop and flourish. It is however important to say that formality in itself does not automatically eradicate discrimination. In discussions about the implementation of policy there is one very simple axiom that should be remembered: people do not always do what they are supposed to. This makes the work of personnel officers seeking to implement an equalities or affirmative action policy doubly difficult. Thus any supposed cause-and-effect relationship between formal equality policies and equitable outcomes should be seen in this context.

While personnel managers argue that formality is an essential aspect of successful policy, if only because it means the policy is given some credence, it does not always ensure success (however that is measured). In Jewson and Mason's (1986a) research formality and informality frequently coexisted and in some cases cancelled each other out. For example, the process of interviewing may be specifically related to an equal opportunities policy, but the advertisement for the post may have been informal, e.g. by word of mouth. Throughout the 1990s there has been a shift towards decentralization of management and this gives rise to a lack of uniformity within the recruitment process. Thus recruitment practice is now more closely guided by the employer's instinct about applicants. The implication is that selection decisions may consciously or unconsciously be informed by negative stereotypes about ethnic minority applicants. The possibility that an affirmative action or equal opportunities policy will be flexible enough to tackle all the different forms of discrimination that may occur in the recruitment process is extremely unlikely given the variation in practice that has resulted from a decentralized management structure. In other words, there is no single process or policy that will always result in equality of opportunity.

As I noted earlier, affirmative action and equal opportunities policies have been a vehicle that personnel managers have used to reassert their legitimacy within organizations. While it is unlikely that the interest of personnel officers in equality is altruistic and may have something to do with an instinct for self-preservation, none the less it has meant that issues relating to equality have assumed a higher profile than they might otherwise have done. While formality in the recruitment process is preferable to informality, the evidence that formality has had the effect that was intended is unclear. The shift of decision-making towards the lower end of the managerial hierarchy has meant that managers have been given more scope to make selection decisions. This has led to more variation in recruitment practice and more scope for discrimination. The justification of selection decisions is rarely couched in terms that are overtly racist since this would be contrary to the stated policy of equality or affirmative action. None the less selection decisions are made that either directly or indirectly discriminate because they can be made in ways that favour established groups and further perpetuate the disadvantage of ethnic minorities.

One of the most controversial elements of the radical approach to affirmative action or equal opportunities is race-awareness training. The purpose of 'race'-awareness training ostensibly is to make people aware of their prejudices in a way that will make them re-evaluate their perceptions of, for example, women and or ethnic minorities in a more positive light. Thus racism and sexism are thought to be less likely to occur once people are made aware of their own pre-judgements. Such training runs the risk of becoming acrimonious, heated and counter-productive. For many White workers, race-awareness training is perceived as coercive. In my own work the atmosphere of such training has been likened by respondents to a witch-hunt.

As such it has hardened attitudes rather than softened them, a point reinforced by Wainwright:

> A lot of people are processed through training which they don't want, don't see as relevant and quickly forget back in their job away from the training course...in the worst case, race awareness training can make racism a conscious and explicit behaviour whereas before people had not really thought out their assumptions. (Wainwright 1983, p. 9)

In organizations where an affirmative action or equal opportunities policy has been implemented and the procedures are seen to be open and fair, the question of whether or not the outcomes are seen as fair and equal inevitably causes tension between disadvantaged groups and those managers attempting to implement the policy. If the policy fails to deliver, at least in terms of the groups who are the intended beneficiaries, there is pressure on managers to adopt more radical measure to ensure the success of the policy. In such situations there are two competing groups employing different measures of success. Any attempt by managers to revise or alter the policy may be interpreted as a sign that the policy has been a failure. It is the competing concepts of success for the two different groups that cause confusion and bad faith. Indeed, employers adopting a liberal policy may feel forced to adopt a more radical approach if, despite a scrupulously fair recruitment process, members of disadvantaged group remain in subordinate positions within the workforce. In such situations an equal opportunities policy may be seen as a sign of bad faith. Workers of minority origin may view the policy with suspicion and treat it as no more than a paper commitment to equality of opportunity. Consequently, some appointments may be made regardless of ability in order to prove that there is no discrimination. This in turn may lead to accusations of tokenism. If, however, there is persistent discrimination in conjunction with an equal opportunities policy this is likely to lead to disillusionment and disenchantment. For example, if informal networks circumvent equal opportunities policies this may lead to suspicion about the nature of equal opportunities. My own work shows how line managers bypass formal policies and how highly subjective criteria are used in the recruitment process.

Conclusions

Two key points arise as a result of the analysis of formalization and fairness. First, that a highly formalized and bureaucratized procedure may help in the successful implementation of an equal opportunities policy, but formalization does not guarantee equality of outcome. Second, that if individuals are determined to discriminate, then this is possible through the manipulation and circumvention of rules.

In short the adoption of a formal equal opportunities policy should not be treated as a panacea for the ills of discrimination. Evidence suggests that in organizations where people are opposed to such policies informal networks are as important as formal ones, if not more so. Informal networks which are predominantly patronage-based allow for a far greater possibility of discrimination. The people who make appointments are far more likely to choose someone who is 'one of us'.

> Formal policies will not ensure equal opportunity if they are at variance with the informal norms and values of the organisation. For example there might be a well managed policy, indeed a system for evaluating job performance and promoting on merit. Parallel to that, however, it is quite possible for an organisation to have a shadow system which depends on a network of contacts to assess suitability for the job. The formal system operates but the reality is that if you want promotion you need to work the informal system. (Wainwright 1983, p. 5)

For policies aimed at achieving greater equity in both process and outcome, the greatest difficulty is that there are likely to be social groups within organizations who have a vested interest not only in maintaining existing arrangements but also in opposing any changes to them. Specific occupational groups have developed complex strategies for maintaining their dominance. Usually the occupational areas that are the hardest to gain access to are those that have the greatest material rewards attached to them. That is not to say that other occupational areas remain socially open. There are hierarchies both within occupations and between occupations, and the strategies that are employed by dominant social groups to include some and exclude others can work in many different ways. It is to these forms of social closure that I will turn next.

3
Strategies of Social Closure and Professional Cultures

Introduction

The question of how some social groups are able to monopolize scarce resources such as desirable, well-paid and secure jobs is one sociologists have attempted to explain in a variety of ways. The contribution of Max Weber to this debate has been of central importance. The Weberian concept of social closure can be used to understand the mechanisms and strategies socially dominant groups employ in order to maintain their position of dominance.

Specific aspects of social identity such as gender, ethnic origin and age are used to differentiate between social groups. Indeed, it is the identification of 'difference' that is the axis around which social closure rotates. Thus there are commonly held conceptions about what men's work and what women's work are (see Bradley 1989); equally, there are tacit assumptions made about the types of work that ethnic minorities are concentrated in. The corollary is that it is possible to talk about Black work and White work. Of course, to characterize the debate in these terms is an oversimplification. Recent evidence in the UK shows the labour market profile of different ethnic groups diverging considerably. For example, the Chinese and Indian groups occupy labour market positions comparable to those of their White peers, or even, outperform them. Other ethnic groups have fared poorly. None the less, there is evidence to suggest that even in occupations that have become increasingly socially open to ethnic minority groups they remain at low or intermediate levels. Or to borrow some feminist terminology, ethnic minority groups have not yet broken through the glass ceiling. In fact, there are some professions and occupations in which the position and experience of ethnic minority groups seems to have scarcely changed since the 1950s. In the case of the fire service the recent 'Equality and Fairness in the Fire Service' report (Home Office 1999) suggests a culture in which discrimination is embedded within the structure of the organisation itself and equal opportunity is regarded as a marginal management issue.

The work of Weber on social closure has been extended and developed by Parkin (1974), Murphy (1984) and Witz (1992), among others. Social closure as a concept is central to the understanding of gendered divisions in the workplace and labour market position. The use of the concept of social closure in understanding workplace divisions based on ethnic identity has been less common. There is a variety of different forms of social closure and the following section examines how these can be applied to the workings of the labour market, with particular reference to ethnicity as a social marker. A useful starting point is Parkin's definition of social closure:

> The process by which social groups seek to maximise rewards by restricting access to rewards and opportunities to a limited circle of people. This entails singling out of certain identifiable social or physical attributes as the...basis of exclusion. Weber suggests that virtually any group attribute (such as) race, language, social origin, descent may be seized upon for the monopolization of specific, usually economic, opportunities. This monopolisation is directed against competitors who share some positive or negative characteristics; its purpose is always the closure of social and economic opportunities to *outsiders*. (Parkin 1974, p. 3)

Social closure can be successful only if it possible to identify outsiders and insiders. That is, there has to be some notion of how, why and who is excluded and who included. Boundary markers such as gender, ethnic origin, age, or even the school or university a person has gone to are all part of the social identity kit that allows status groups to form and to start to exclude others who do not share the same background and social origins. Thus the notion of difference is crucial to understanding the operation of social closure. Difference is a fluid concept and can be interpreted in a number of ways. Skin colour, gender, language and culture have all been cited as evidence of difference and used to identify distinct social groups. It is the social construction of this difference that is of central importance if we are seeking to understand how and why some social groups are excluded from occupational areas while others are included.

There are three strategies of social closure that merit particular attention; credentialism, sponsorship and patronage and the use of informal networks. I will examine the consequences of these strategies and refer to some examples of professions (nursing and universities in the UK) in which different forms of social closure have effectively excluded different social groups.

Credentialism

An important form of social closure is credentialism. Credentialism, as a strategy of social closure, imposes educational requirements upon candidates before they can be considered for certain jobs. Thus, in order to drive a bus, the possession of a driving licence is a key qualification or credential.

There are, however, many cases where the requirements imposed for jobs are less clearly defined. There is often thought to be a clear relationship between the formal qualifications required for a job and its desirability, status and pay. Thus the more qualifications that are required the more desirable the job. What this suggests is that access to desirable jobs is restricted by imposing educational requirements. Or to express the same idea in a different way, the most desirable jobs are those that are the most exclusive. Equally those jobs that are not generally regarded as high status, for example a refuse collector, have few educational requirements. Thus credentialism and other forms of social closure are closely related to ideas about the hierarchy both between and within occupations. Different forms of social closure are used to protect or defend areas of professions that possess status, high pay and good working conditions. Thus it is possible to think of the labour market as a terrain in which some spaces are fiercely defended and others are poorly defended, if at all.

Historically, many professions have been dominated by White middle-class males. Thus the law, medicine, science, academia and many other occupational spheres are characterized by forms of social closure that have effectively excluded groups such as ethnic minorities and women. The use of credentialism as a form of social closure is particularly common. The use of credentialism is closely related to Jenkins' arguments about the use of suitability criteria and acceptability criteria in interviews. Suitability criteria refer to 'objective' qualifications, experience and skill; acceptability criteria refer to the much more nebulous ability to 'fit in' with existing workers. Jenkins concludes, quite rightly, that discriminatory selection decisions are justified on the basis that ethnic minority candidates will not fit in. In other words, alongside formal criteria for selection there coexists a set of informal criteria that are shot through with ethnocentric assumptions about ethnic minority job-seekers.

What Jenkins underplays is the extent to which acceptability and suitability criteria merge and cut across each other. What shapes the way in which suitability and acceptability merge is the external structure of the labour market. Thus certain occupational niches become predominantly populated by different ethnic groups. For example, the night shift in textile factories in the UK has tended to be an area where Asian workers are concentrated for a variety of reasons, including the desire of certain ethnic groups to remain together as they are less likely to experience hostility and racism from others who share their ethnic identity and, of course, simple racist discrimination. Whatever the reason, once an occupational niche becomes identified with a specific ethnic group, recruiters tend to reinforce these divisions by placing other ethnic minority applicants in the areas where they are already concentrated (see chapter 1 for discussion of the chill factor). These occupational divisions become self-perpetuating, as in the case of ethnic minority nurses in the UK. During the 1950s and 1960s psychiatric and geriatric nursing were areas into which migrants from the New Commonwealth, principally the Caribbean, were recruited. The result of this is that these areas became identified by White recruiters as being those areas where there was already a concentration of ethnic minority staff so new ethnic minority applicants were channelled into these types of nursing. In such cases the job itself becomes imbued with particular social characteristics. Thus one of the key suitability criteria is that candidates are members of ethnic minority groups, though this is rarely, if ever, explicitly stated. In addition, workers and applicants themselves make rational judgements about what sort of job to apply for. If a Black applicant knows that an employer already employs other Black people then it is more likely (though not inevitable) that they will be offered a job.

Forms of social closure can be used to protect particular occupational areas and ensure that wages and working conditions are kept at a relatively high level. An example of this is the newspaper industry. Newspaper production in the UK was strongly unionized and predominantly male. As part of a campaign on the part of managers to break the power of print unions, new micro-technology was introduced. Prior to the introduction of new technology the productive process was dominated by a labour-intensive, highly skilled form of newspaper production known as 'hot metal'. The skills required to operate this specialized machinery were passed from father to son. As a result any person wishing to enter the world of hot metal would be excluded if they were female and were not part of a 'print' family (Cockburn 1991).

Organized groups of workers can legitimately demand high wages for scarce skills if they are able to maintain their monopoly over an occupational area. The consequence of such forms of social closure is that certain occupational areas come to be dominated by particular social groups, either male or female, black or white. As particular spaces within a labour market become colonized by specific social groups there is a likelihood that the self-fulfilling prophecy I have described will affect both employers and potential employees and their perceptions of what sort of work is appropriate for different social groups. It should be emphasized that division within the labour market is not so rigid that it cannot change. If no opportunities for upward occupational mobility occur, or the experience of discrimination within a specific occupational space is so pronounced, then, historically, there has been a tendency on the part of ethnic minority groups to move to other occupational areas where the perceived opportunities for promotion are greater or the pay and conditions are better. Certainly in the case of nursing in the UK, there is increasing evidence to suggest that the ethnic minorities in nursing are rapidly approaching retirement with little sign that British-born ethnic minority people replacing them. Among many reasons to account for this shift are that young, British-born ethnic minorities are not attracted to working in a profession characterized by poor pay and working conditions and that is believed to discriminate against them. My research with ethnic minority nurses who are close to retirement or who have retired suggests that they have actively discouraged their children from entering nursing and encouraged them to acquire as many formal qualifications as possible to widen their career choices.

Walby (1987) cites the example of the engineering industry in the UK and argues that the reason why it remains male-dominated is that trade unions were able to organize in ways that resisted the introduction of female labour. During the Second World War women were recruited to work in engineering to overcome the shortage of labour caused by conscription. At the end of the war engineering unions were able to secure the agreement of the government to remove women from the engineering industry. Walby argues that this demonstrates the ability of trade unions to mobilize state power on their own behalf. By contrast, clerical work, which was once the exclusive preserve of men, became increasingly feminized as the clerical sphere expanded. In this case there was no tradition of union organization or militancy. Thus clerical work could be regarded as a 'soft spot', or an occupational area which was and is poorly defended or wholly undefended.

It is important to acknowledge the impact of the state on the social closure of particular occupational areas. Both Walby and Bradley have alluded to the way in which the state tacitly and occasionally overtly supports the existing social and political divisions within the labour market. Indeed governments and civil servants are not neutral players in the process. As I will describe in later chapters, the impact of the British government on the type of work 'colonial girls' were regarded as suitable for was work that allowed for little upward mobility. Official government documents suggest that senior civil servants acknowledged both the need for cheap labour in the NHS and the necessity of ensuring that White nursing labour retained a position of relative superiority and fully endorsed this.

Are credentials neutral?

Credentials such as educational or professional qualifications are often thought to be objective indicators of ability that have no relation to the identity of the person who acquires them. However, there are indications that qualifications from countries other than the UK are regarded by some employers as inherently inferior to those gained within the UK. Equally, a degree from an old university in the UK compared to a degree from a new university tends to possess greater prestige. Smith's study (*Overseas Doctors in the National Health Service*, 1980) found that qualifications gained outside the British university system count for less than qualifications gained within the British university system. This has resulted in overseas doctors, particularly those from the New Commonwealth countries, being located in less desirable specialities of the medical profession. Indeed, research by the King's Fund concluded that:

> Country of qualification and ethnic group are regarded as an indicator of competence, they influence doctors' judgement of their colleagues and are used quite openly for selection criteria. (Coker 2001, cited in the *Guardian* 19 June 2001)

One of the most remarkable findings in the King's Fund report *Racism in Medicine* (Coker 2001) is that White candidates with lower A level grades were more likely to be accepted to study medicine than ethnic minority candidates. This is consistent with the response of ethnic minority academics who took part in qualitative research for the *Ethnicity and Employment in Higher Education* study (Carter et al. 1999), who argued that to be successful in an academic context meant that ethnic minority teachers and lecturers in higher education had to be twice as well qualified as their White peers.

Similarly with British universities there is a certain cachet attached to qualifications from Oxford or Cambridge and other old universities. In the *Ethnicity and Employment in Higher Education* study (Carter et al. 1999) ethnic minority respondents reported that if their qualifications were from an overseas university they felt that they were treated less favourably compared to those whose qualifications were from a British university. In America there is some evidence that qualifications from Ivy League universities command the same sort of status (Dworkin 2000).

In the case of women from the Caribbean who came to the UK to work in nursing in the 1950s and 1960s many of them possessed only a basic education. The minimum requirement of five 'O' levels to become a State Registered Nurse was therefore one to which they were unable to aspire. Even in cases where women from the Caribbean did have the required qualifications they were directed into training for State Enrolled Nurse, the less prestigious and less well paid counterpart. The application of credentialism to women from the Caribbean proved to be a rigid form of social closure. As Parkin notes:

> In modern industrial societies closure is effected by the use of exam-
> inations that are ostensibly open and fair to all...the education
> system is an especially refined instrument for guarding and control-
> ling entry to the charmed circles. (Parkin 1982, p. 100)

The use of educational criteria to exclude certain social groups from occupational areas is principally a method of screening, in which the possession of qualifications rather than their content is used as a basis for selection. The fact that many ethnic minority nurses appear routinely to perform work that is the province of a higher grade of nurses was recognized in the 1995 PSI study:

> There are many enrolled nurses with basic additional qualifications,
> such as those with post basic certificates or those who supervise other
> staff. (Beishon et al. 1995, p. 9)

The acquisition of certain credentials and qualifications has less to do with the content of those credentials and more with ensuring that some social groups are excluded from certain occupational areas while others are able to retain a monopoly over entry to it. Indeed, to assume that forms of credentialism are somehow neutral ignores the fact that those from the lower socio-economic classes do less well than those from the higher socio-economic classes in the education system. This may be a result of material deprivation, a lack of cultural capital, low parental expectations or a complex combination of these and many other factors. To impose educational requirements on a job automatically imbues that job with a specific class identity. What credentialism as a form of social closure cannot explain is how and why groups such as ethnic minorities and women are excluded from desirable forms of employment when they possess the same qualifications as others. In the UK the increasingly international profile of those recruited to work in nursing includes substantial numbers of women from the Philippines. There is some anecdotal evidence that their qualifications are regarded as inferior to qualifications acquired by UK nurses and that this is used as a justification for directing these recent migrants into the lower grades of the profession and into the less desirable areas.

Notions of social closure are inextricably tied up with the way in which professional knowledge is produced and legitimized. Embedded in bodies of professional knowledge are assumptions about who has access to it and who is able to reproduce it. It is also important to acknowledge the role of professional associations in intervening to make access to professional bodies of knowledge more or less difficult and redefining the criteria for entry and access to the knowledge that allows entry to a professional sphere.

To understand how different forms of social closure knit together to exclude particular social groups requires an analysis that goes beyond credentialism. There may be a more complex web of social closure that combines elements of credentialism with other forms of closure such as patronage and sponsorship. It is to these forms of social closure I will turn next.

Sponsorship and patronage

Evidence from the medical profession suggests that sponsorship from senior doctors is vital for young doctors seeking to advance their career. Sponsorship can take different forms. It may be by encouraging people to apply for certain jobs; it may take the shape of offering advice or guidance about where to apply; it may also include providing formal written references as well as informal recommendations.

For those seeking upward occupational mobility, a powerful sponsor is vital. The sort of sponsorship described by Smith (1980) also applies to the academic world. Evidence from the 1999 study *Ethnicity and Employment in Higher Education* suggests that sponsorship is a key determinant of academic success and occupational mobility. In cases where candidates have similar qualifications, skills and experience, the backing of a powerful sponsor may prove to be the deciding factor. The difference between sponsored and contest mobility as described by Turner (1971) suggests a dichotomy between an open social system in which all participants compete in a contest with clearly defined rules and a closed social system in which only those participants with powerful sponsors are successful. In fact, evidence from the academic system and the medical profession suggests that these two forms of mobility reinforce one another. Thus to be a successful academic requires a certain number of formal qualifications, but once within the academic hierarchy it is necessary to acquire the sponsorship of a senior academic to gain access to opportunities for research funding, career opportunities and book contracts. Thus much of the evidence suggests that forms of sponsorship tend to reinforce existing social divisions as sponsors rarely act as a patron to someone from a different social background. As Smith (1980) suggests:

> The 1981 qualifiers were overtly critical of the system, and women in particular were concerned about what they say as the old boy network, in some cases based, they felt, on too many old boys wielding power and creating a closed shop. As this woman SHO said about patronage: 'It's the most important thing. You get tipped for the top if you are male, white, Oxbridge or London. Female or coloured, forget it!... The reasons behind sponsorship aren't always good. You succeed in getting sponsors if you are a good toe the line sycophant, so the right people don't reach the top. Consultants work together – their own private empire. If you're not among the chosen you can't break in. You're on the outside and that's that.' (Smith, D.J. 1980, p. 159)

To acquire a sponsor requires access to a powerful and socially closed group of professionals within a profession. Access to sponsors may take place in a formal work-related setting or an informal setting. Indeed, it may be that because certain social groups socialize in particular ways outside of work, informal contacts are made through playing sport. Informal settings such as these tend to be ones from which women and ethnic minority groups are excluded.

What is implicit, and sometimes explicit, is the recognition that to enter this socially closed group it is vital that incomers have the same social identity as those already in powerful positions. Thus patronage and sponsorship are self-perpetuating forms of mobility in which there is little possibility of a change in the composition of particular professional groups. To allow outsiders access to a social and occupational group who have a clearly defined social identity immediately makes such a group less exclusive. In other words, 'the old boy network' is one in which only other old boys are deemed suitable for recruitment to desirable positions within an occupational hierarchy. Of equal importance is the absence of alternative sponsorship mechanisms for ethnic minority groups or women.

The use of sponsorship is an interesting example of a strategy of social closure. Successful candidates are successful because of their membership of a social group rather than because of any objective merit. The way in which forms of sponsorship operate force us to reconsider what credentialism means. In the case of medicine White, middle-class males continue to dominate because they select others to succeed them who share their social background. Thus when we think of credentialism as a strategy of social closure it is important to take into account the social identity of the applicant. So if all the candidates possess all the requisite formal qualifications the way in which selection outcomes are determined is through the possession of social characteristics such as ethnicity, gender and class, which then take on as much significance as formal qualifications. When Jenkins talks about acceptability criteria being the space within which discriminatory decisions are made, he is referring to a situation where all the candidates for a job appear equal on paper but the deciding factor is the extent to which they fit in with the existing workforce or the prevailing ethos of the employer. Systems of job allocation based on sponsorship differ from this because there is an element of acceptability that is a central part of the suitability criteria. That is even to be considered for a post one of the key qualifications is the possession of certain social characteristics. These may include having been to a certain school or university.

It is difficult to imagine a system or mechanism for the allocation of jobs which is more contrary to the spirit of equality of opportunity. The system of patronage relies on an invisible, often unaccountable, process, which cannot be monitored. It is permeated with assumptions which, at best, could be regarded as problematic and at worst as overtly discriminatory. None the less, the patronage system is real, powerful and has real effects and is unlikely to change, at least in the short term. As Smith notes:

> There was no evidence of anyone seriously contemplating challenging it, either in the open or more specifically in the courts. There was a strong feeling that any challenge would effectively mean the end of a career in the profession which accepted this method of promotion...the main inhibition in challenging the system was that it was so deeply ingrained in the custom and practice of the medical profession. Anyone challenging that would be seen to be taking on a very powerful structure. (Smith, D.J. 1980, p. 159)

Dominant social groups are able to monopolize desirable occupational niches because of their ability to close those spaces within the labour market. While it would be foolish to deny that some social changes have taken place and the representation of groups such as women and ethnic minorities in the upper strata of occupations (police, fire service, armed forces, education) has improved, they remain in large part on the outside looking in. What is remarkable about systems of patronage and sponsorship that persist in professional spheres is not how much they have changed, but how much they have remained the same.

Informal networks

The use of informal networks to secure work is also an important form of social closure. Informal networks may only be open to specific social groups. If recruitment is restricted to within an organization, that is a post is not advertised externally, informal networks and recommendations that come via informal networks carry very considerable weight. If recruitment takes place within organizations, the necessity to stick rigidly to formal appointment procedures is less apparent, so alongside the formal procedure there often exists an informal procedure that relies on informal networks, or word-of-mouth recommendations, which are of course totally counter to the spirit of equality policies. In my research in the National Health Service it was clear that many managers preferred appointing people via informal networks because it allowed greater scope for personal judgements about individual candidates to influence selection outcomes. It should be stressed that many of the judgements made about potential candidates are both ethnocentric and impressionistic.

One of the major implications of the extension of informal networks is that the essence of what discrimination *is* changes. Selection outcomes are justified in ways that are not overtly racist – how could they be if there has been no formal, rigorous, transparent selection procedure, but instead a person has been approached because of a recommendation from another manager within the organization? In other words, discrimination is no longer direct and overt; it is indirect and covert.

Those first-generation migrants who entered the profession in the 1950s and 1960s who took part in my research frequently reported overtly discriminatory behaviour and justification of selection decisions, while younger ethnic minority staff reported structures within organizations that discriminated against them and militated against their upward occupational mobility.

Resisting exclusion: strategies of usurpation

While certain social groups are excluded from parts of professions that are often the most secure and best rewarded, it is important to emphasize the agency of these people. Those excluded rarely passively accept their 'fate' and instead often attempt to resist forms of social closure that effectively limit their career choices. Analytically those forms of resistance to social closure are referred to as a usurpationary strategy. Murphy defines a usurpationary struggle as:

> A struggle by the excluded group to become included... This inclusionary form of usurpation involves the struggle for equality of opportunity and for the shift from collectivist to individualist criteria of exclusion. (Murphy 1984, p. 560)

Thus, in Murphy's terms, groups who are excluded on the basis that they share certain social characteristics seek to be treated as individuals to be judged on their own merits rather than as members of a specific social group. The most obvious way to undermine or usurp strategies of social closure which are based on credentialism is to acquire further qualifications and/or training. For ethnic minority nurses who were directed to State Enrolled Nurse training this required a conversion course. However, as the Equal Opportunities Commission has noted:

> Fewer training opportunities were available to Black nurses. A high proportion of Black nurses are SENs, a grade which is being phased out and the availability of conversion courses for registered practitioner

grade is therefore crucial if Black nurses are not to be downgraded to the role of nursing auxiliaries. However, many Black enrolled nurses are mature women with children and virtually no conversion courses from SEN to SRN are available on a part time basis (EOC 1991, p. 11)

What makes the lack of provision of training courses to allow ethnic minority nurses to convert their qualifications particularly interesting is that this would appear to be a very clear example of positive action (as discussed in chapter 2) that would increase minority representation in specific parts of the nursing profession. So why there is a lack of such courses remains a mystery. It would be a very cynical analysis that suggests that personnel officers have avoided actively developing courses that would give ethnic minority nurses a chance of promotion and greater autonomy at work at the expense of developing equality policies that have had little chance of success precisely because they have aspects of credentialism built into them.

Despite attempts to resist exclusion from the more desirable niches of the profession it appears that the position of ethnic minority nurses has largely remained unchanged. The 1995 PSI report *Working in a Multi-ethnic NHS* suggests that many ethnic minority nurses remain in the lowest grades and in the least desirable areas. In theoretical terms the strategies of usurpation that ethnic minority nurses have adopted have been unsuccessful. It seems possible that the current demographic trend within the NHS, namely that 9 per cent of nurses within the NHS are of minority origin, but less than 1 per cent of these are under 25 (Department of Health 1998), is a response to perceived discrimination and lack of promotion prospects.

In the case of the nursing profession in the UK there is evidence to suggest that the whole issue of equality and the ability of certain social groups to close occupational areas is a highly contested terrain. The current situation within the nursing profession is complicated by the fact that the profession is currently experiencing a serious problem in recruiting sufficient numbers to replace those leaving the profession. This has led to the recruitment of nurses from as far away as Australia, Italy, Switzerland and the Philippines. Indeed there is anecdotal evidence to suggest that nurses recruited from the Philippines are regarded by ward managers as obedient and docile. This recruitment drive is taking place at the same time as New Commonwealth migrants who entered the NHS in the 1950s and 1960s are retiring and there is little evidence that the sons and daughters of these first-generation migrants are in a rush to enter the nursing profession. The evidence from my research (which took place in 1997) with retired New Commonwealth nurses suggests that they have actively discouraged their sons and daughters from entering the profession as a direct result of their own experiences.

When thinking of attempts to resist exclusion within a particular labour market context, it is obvious from the example of nursing that the strategy of usurpation or resistance employed by ethnic minority nurses, namely their attempts to overcome credentialism by attempting to acquire more qualifications, has been a failure. There is no hard evidence that ethnic minority nurses have moved out of the parts of the profession traditionally regarded as less desirable or that they have moved up the occupational hierarchy within these areas. While Witz (1992) refers to strategies of usurpation as a way of resisting labour market exclusion, she neglects to mention that they racialized, and that White female strategies of usurpation have been partially successful, while Black female strategies of usurpation have been largely unsuccessful.

Dual closure and inclusion

Witz (1992) argues that to understand the different process of social closure and exclusion it is necessary to understand not only exclusion but inclusion as well. Witz cites the experience of women in the medical profession. She suggests that their campaign for inclusion was only partially successful. After a campaign of agitation to be allowed entry into the medical profession women were allowed to enter some areas of the medical profession characterized by low prestige. The partial encroachment of women into what was a traditionally male terrain has essentially bought off the opposition of women to male domination in medicine. In female areas of medicine women have sought to close that particular occupational area off from below (other women) and above (men) by using what Witz calls dual closure strategies. One of Witz's most interesting assertions is that:

> Exclusion on the grounds of race and gender is an informal element of credentialing... and this case study demonstrates, gendered exclusionary mechanisms were embedded in the formal credentialing process. (Witz 1992, p. 195)

This assumes considerable significance when combined with Jenkins' concept of suitability and acceptability criteria in that it becomes apparent that one of the central aspects of suitability is being male or female. There has, however, been a real failure to extend this argument to ethnicity. There has been a marked reluctance to discuss the question of why some jobs are regarded as Black jobs as opposed to White jobs in the way that gender theorists such as Curran (1988) have examined the gendering of jobs. Thus, while Witz makes an important contribution to the development of closure theory, it is done with little reference to ethnicity. Instead Witz refers to the way in which strategies of social closure restrict *women* in the labour market, without acknowledging that women of ethnic minority origin may have very different employment experiences from those of White women. Thus she is able to assert that:

> Women are typically hedged into low-paying, low status jobs with little autonomy which invariably stand in a subordinate relation to male occupations. It is precisely this vertical, hierarchical dimension of sexually segregated occupations that is generated by gendered strategies of demarcationary closure. (Witz 1992, p. 77)

While Witz correctly identifies exclusionary practices as those that are mechanisms of intra-occupational control and demarcation practices as mechanisms of inter-occupational control, she does not acknowledge that within these strategies women of ethnic minority origin have a distinctly different experience. Thus in the case of nursing, ethnic minority women historically have been confined not only to the lowest grades, but have been allocated the least desirable tasks, are less likely to be occupationally mobile and more likely to be working on the least desirable shifts. Similarly in the UK academic profession evidence from the 1999 *Ethnicity and Employment in Higher Education* study shows that women generally are located at lower grades than men, but that women of ethnic minority origin are located at lower grades that their white peers.

The notion of dual closure and inclusion is a useful analytical framework to apply to the experience of ethnic minority groups within professions. Put simply, groups who were excluded from professional spheres have been allowed entry but only at the periphery. That is, socially dominant groups still retain positions of power within professional groups but are able to point to the fact that previously excluded groups have been allowed entry. The fact remains that excluded groups are marginalized within professions; in other words, they are professions within professions.

Social closure and the professional project

Clearly, there are a variety of different forms of social closure which restrict social groups to specific positions within hierarchies. A useful concept which aids analysis of social closure is that of the 'professional project' which is described thus:

> [we should] conceptualise these projects as strategies of occupational closure, which aim for an occupational monopoly over the provision of certain skills and competencies in a market for services. (Witz 1992, p. 5)

What is notable about the nursing profession is that White nursing labour has been able to monopolize the most desirable parts of the profession through a variety of forms of closure. It is important to consider that the inclusion of migrant labour took place in the context of a severe labour shortage and a position within the NHS that meant that the less prestigious parts of the profession had been abandoned by White nursing labour. The process of recruitment from the New Commonwealth was one in which closure was an integral part so that young women from the Caribbean were channelled into the parts of the profession that had been left undefended. White nursing labour was able to close off the more desirable areas through a range of strategies. During the initial period of migration forms of credentialism were used to direct young female migrants towards areas of the nursing profession which were characterized by a lack of upward occupational mobility and poor working conditions. When these forms of closure were resisted, White nursing labour was able to employ a different form of social closure which, during the 1950s and the early 1960s, was based on overt forms of discrimination. Indeed accounts of women from my data show the way in which overt forms of discrimination restricted the progress of Caribbean women. Although overt discrimination on the grounds of 'race' became illegal in the UK, the use of informal networks has allowed discrimination to persist. The result of the way in which nursing has been constructed as a professional project is that the sons and daughters of the women who migrated in the 1950s and 1960s have not entered the profession in the same numbers as their parents. As a result the NHS, once an area in which migrants from the New Commonwealth were relatively common, is now one in which their numbers are declining so rapidly that it seems possible that once the 'first-generation' migrants have retired there will be only a tiny number of British-born African-Caribbeans in the NHS.

To summarize: nursing in the UK was originally constructed as a female rather than a male professional project, then reconstructed in ways that tacitly and explicitly exploited the labour of colonial migrants. Unlike other professions a particular set of economic and historical circumstances allowed for the reconstruction of nursing in a way that racialized labour from the Caribbean. So Caribbean women were drawn into a specific part of an occupational sphere from which there was little chance of upward mobility. In the terms of social closure, White nursing labour employed a strategy of dual closure, or what I prefer to call partial encroachment, in that it allowed 'Black' labour into the profession, but in such a way that it was restricted to those parts of the nursing profession that were not desirable or prestigious and also to grades of the profession from which mobility (under the old grading system) was virtually impossible without retraining. Historically, then, different strategies of social closure have been used at different historical points to ensure the subordination of 'Black' labour, in the immediate postwar period, and forms of credentialism were used to socially close certain parts of the nursing profession. In addition, there is evidence that Caribbean women were channelled by the state recruitment machinery into nursing grades for which they were overqualified. The latter can only be described as state racism which took place with the tacit acceptance of the White nursing establishment. Were this to take place in the current social and political climate it would almost certainly be described as institutional racism. As the 1950s, 1960s and 1970s progressed the attempts of Caribbean women to escape from the occupational ghettos in which they found themselves were, by and large, unsuccessful. Since the occupational segregation which Caribbean nurses experienced was based on credentialism, the most important strategy of usurpation used by Caribbean nurses was to retrain to acquire new and more relevant qualifications which would allow them upward mobility.

It is important to emphasize that there may be age differences between women who migrated to the UK in the 1950s and 1960s and those ethnic minority women born in the UK who have entered nursing. One of the difficulties for older ethnic minority nurses who came to work in the NHS in the 1950s is the problem of converting their qualifications. As a strategy of usurpation the attempts of Black nurses to retrain to overcome forms of credentialism have been largely unsuccessful, as training courses for converting an SEN to SRN have been hard to access. However, it seems likely that even if training courses had been available, the strategy would have been unsuccessful as recruiters tended to perceive Caribbean nurses as ideally suited to work in the very areas that they were trying to get out of.

The fact that mainly White recruiters tend to allocate ethnic minority nurses to the sorts of jobs where they think they will 'fit in' the best reinforces the very inequalities that Black Caribbean nurses experienced in the early days of their incorporation into the labour market.

By contrast the construction of academia as a professional project was one that was more overtly related to a class-based culture. Indeed, it is only in the last 50 years that women have begun to make significant inroads into universities as teachers and researchers. The university sphere would be one in which it would be possible to apply Witz's theory of dual closure in relation to women. As with medicine, women agitated to enter universities and were partially successful. However, senior positions in UK universities remain dominated by men. For ethnic minorities the position is markedly different from that of women. To understand the position of ethnic minority academics in UK universities requires an appreciation of British colonial history which has traditionally regarded universities in the colonies as inferior to those in the UK. What distinguishes ethnic minority academics in the UK university system is instability, as ethnic minority academics are more likely to be on short-term contracts than their White peers; and their concentration in the lower rungs of the profession, though this may be a result of the length of time they have spent in the system. They are also more likely to be in short-term research posts rather than in the more prestigious tenured teaching and research categories.

Conclusions

In many ways the question that should be answered when examining equality and affirmative action policies is thus: have they made a difference to the employment chances of ethnic minority groups and the practices of employers? The answer must be yes. How much of a difference they have made is much harder to answer. It is a fact that the majority of employers now have some form of affirmative action, equality or diversity policy, which must at some level suggest that there has been a shift in attitude away from the overt racism and discrimination of earlier years towards some tacit acknowledgement that this kind of behaviour is socially sanctioned and/or unacceptable. However, it is clear that racism and discrimination persist in spite of these policies, so their effects should not be overestimated. One of the central themes of much of the literature in this area is that the adoption of an equality or affirmative action policy does not necessarily ensure equal treatment or equal results in terms of selection outcomes.

What is often missing from the analysis of equality and affirmative action policies is that for many they represent either an implicit or explicit attempt fundamentally to shift the distribution of power within organizations. Nowhere is this more apparent than in the professions. For many years recruitment to the professions has been through patronage and sponsorship which have allowed socially dominant groups to maintain their monopoly over privileged occupational positions. It is only as concern about equity has assumed a greater political prominence that professions have been urged and compelled to become more open and transparent in the ways that they appoint.

As I have pointed out elsewhere in this book, those social groups who already possess power, and who are able to dominate prestigious occupational spheres, are unlikely to embrace the notion of equality or affirmative action without reservation because they have something to lose. Indeed those social groups who stand to lose something from making a profession more socially open are likely to become part of a culture of opposition. Others who contribute to the culture of opposition include line managers who resent the encroachment of personnel specialists into what they see as their personal domain. The culture of opposition to equality policies has far-reaching consequences. In cases where line managers persist with a recruitment and promotion policy based on gut feeling, nepotism or overt discrimination, it is inevitable that an informal structure will emerge alongside the formal one. Since line managers are reluctant to admit to discriminating on the grounds of race or sex, selection decisions are frequently justified on other grounds. Informal structures are hard to eradicate and are often tacitly acknowledged by senior power-holders. The effect is that policy can also be defined as what actually happens as a result of the decisions of line managers lower down the hierarchy, in spite of, not because of, the equal opportunities policy.

There is a variety of manifestations of the culture of opposition. One of the most common is the notion of political correctness. There can be little doubt that many of the programmes and policies aimed at increasing equity and making occupational spheres more open have been labelled by their opponents as politically correct. This term has rapidly become one of abuse. Policies and programmes described as politically correct are held up for ridicule as being counter to common sense and often regarded as at best unbalanced and at worst verging on lunacy. The use of the term political correctness is clearly a part of the culture of opposition and is used to deflect attention away from long-standing issues of inequality and discrimination.

In the UK at least the types of programmes and policies that could be described as hard affirmative action or radical equal opportunities have declined in number and importance. What is interesting is the way in which the notion of equality has been simultaneously incorporated into mainstream management practice and also located at the periphery of management agendas. The radical school of equality has quite clearly been marginalized while softer, more liberal notions of equality and diversity management have gained real hegemonic ascendancy. The sort of transformation and shift in power that Cockburn argues is necessary for genuine equality of opportunity to flourish seems highly unlikely given the prevailing social and political climate. Moreover in organizations where efficiency, cost-cutting and lean production are priorities, equality and diversity are often sidelined and regarded as an unjustifiable expense.

Underlying both affirmative action and equal opportunities policies there is a human dimension in that at some point in the decision-making process a power-holder has to make a subjective decision about the merit of each candidate. The notion that merit is somehow neutral and objectively measurable remains a central plank of many recruitment policies. Merit, however, is by no means as neutral and objective as it appears. In the final analysis it must be recognized that selection decisions are suffused with a range of different notions of merit. These may be influenced not only by the internal culture of the organization seeking to recruit, but also the attitudes of the person recruiting, and by broader attitudes within society towards ethnic identity, gender and age. When advocates of equal opportunities argue that what such policies do is make sure that employers get the best person for the job, this fails to acknowledge that notions of merit and who is the best person might be shaped by assumptions about the candidates who are applying for the job and the nature of the job that is on offer.

4
The Racialization of Nursing

Introduction

This first half of this chapter is based on interviews conducted with ethnic minority nurses, some still working and nearing retirement and others who have retired. The interviews provide a micro-sociological account of the processes described in the official documents of the time. The interviews show what the human experience of migration and working in the health service was like for African-Caribbean women. Some of the issues that emerged during the interviews were the causes of migration, the response of the, then, young women, to life in Britain, the 'racial' division of labour, the processes of discrimination and exclusion, and 'racial' harassment at work.

The analysis of the interview material is intended to illustrate the extent to which the professional sphere of nursing within the National Health Service was not only a gendered occupational sphere but also a racialized one, in which notions of colonial identity and racism played a key part in shaping the experiences of migrants from the New Commonwealth. The processes that are described in this chapter, such as the recruitment of New Commonwealth migrants to specific occupational niches, the allocation of the most menial tasks to these migrants, the routine harassment of ethnic minority nurses by colleagues and patients as well as the effective closure of routes out of these occupational ghettos, all contribute to the definition and redefinition of nursing as an occupational sphere in which ethnicity is used as a boundary marker to denote desirable and undesirable forms of work.

The empirical material in this chapter should be read in terms of the discussion of the labour market position of ethnic minorities and the impact of equal opportunity policies and affirmative action that precedes this chapter. That is, the material seeks to illustrate several of the key points made earlier, particularly the impact of ethnic origin on both labour market position and location within a specific occupational hierarchy. The overall purpose of this chapter is to shed light on the way in which the professional project of nursing has been constructed and reconstructed in ways that have ascribed different segments of the profession with an ethnic identity and significance, which are closely related to aspects of colonial identity as well common-sense notions of ethnicity. Put more simply: the material should describe and explain the social and historical processes that let to particular types of nursing labour becoming ethnic enclaves.

The second half of the chapter uses recently released documents from the Public Record Office to show the way in which the government reacted to the shortage of nurses in the 1950s and sought to import migrant labour with the intention of filling the vacuum at the bottom. The documents illustrate very different views of the role of labour from the Caribbean. Different departments, for example, the Colonial Office, the Ministry of Health and the Ministry of Labour, clearly disagreed over what the role of colonial migrant labour within the Health Service should be. The documents show that the principal concern at the time was not with training nurses for the colonies, or with providing a skilled workforce of nurses for British hospitals. Rather, it was to provide 'pairs of hands' for a National Health Service that was struggling to keep wards open because of a lack of staff at the bottom of the nursing hierarchy, most notably nursing auxiliaries and domestics. This gap in the labour market was filled by young women who were recruited specifically for that purpose.

What the empirical material I will be referring to demonstrates is the way in which the parts of the nursing profession that came to be occupied by New Commonwealth migrants were occupational ghettos – that is, spaces within the nursing profession abandoned by White labour and characterized by a lack of occupational mobility, poor working conditions and poor pay.

Migration to Britain in the 1950s

The pattern of migration to Britain in the post-1945 period was, in many ways, an historical anomaly. Peter Fryer (1984) correctly emphasizes the fact that there had been Black people living in Britain for many years prior to 1945. As early as the eighteenth century there were approximately 10,000 Black, Chinese and Asian people living in Britain, often employed as servants, although Fryer

notes that some entered the army. While not numerically significant, there was an established Black presence in Britain. However,
during the post-1945 period, there was a surge in migration to
Britain from its colonies.

Sociological studies of migration during the postwar period
(Patterson 1963; Hiro 1971; Lawrence 1974) describe the influx to
Britain as being a result of push-and-pull factors. Factors that pushed
migrants from the Caribbean, India and Pakistan included demographic factors, weak economies and high unemployment. In the case
of India and Pakistan, economic factors as well as the partition of the
two countries created a group of refugees which pushed people towards
life in Britain. Frank's (1976) notion of underdevelopment is a particularly useful concept to apply to many British colonies and former
British colonies that supplied labour to the UK in the postwar period.
When Frank refers to underdevelopment it is a condition in which certain nations are forced to aid the development of other nations at their
own expense. Countries that developed colonial empires, such as
France, Holland and the UK, established the relationship between
satellite colonies such as the West Indies and Britain as a relationship
of dependence in which Britain typically exploited any natural
resources in the colonies. The absorption of migrant labour from
colonies can be seen part of Frank's theory of the development of
underdevelopment.

The most significant pull factor was the acute shortage of labour in
Britain in the immediate postwar period. Demographically, Britain's
population had been reduced by the war. Thus, combined with the massive task of postwar reconstruction, as Hiro (1971) notes, it was imperative
that Britain do something to redress the problem of labour. Britain's
position at the heart of an albeit rapidly disintegrating Empire made it
a logical and for some a natural choice for many West Indians, Indians
and Pakistanis.

Within studies of postwar migration there has been considerable
debate over the relative importance of push and pull factors. Patterson
(1963, p. 70), for example, suggested that push factors were stronger
than pull factors. She cited overpopulation, economic underdevelopment, underemployment and a lack of educational opportunities as
significant push factors. Indeed, Patterson goes on to point out that
the Walter McCarran Act 1952, which effectively stopped Caribbean
migration to the US, was a further factor that pushed Caribbean
migrants towards the UK. Other writers dispute the notion that push
factors were the more significant of the two sets of factors. Walvin

(1984), for example, argues that however restricting the conditions in the Caribbean were, the key factor that determined the phenomenon of postwar migration was the shortage of labour in the UK. Clearly both push and pull factors played their part in determining the nature and scope of postwar migration and it is increasingly difficult to say whether push or pull factors were more significant. In interviews with migrants it is obvious that both factors played a part in their decision to migrate. There is however one factor that has remained underplayed in the debates about migration to the UK from the Caribbean and from other parts of the New Commonwealth: that is the impact of paternal colonial ideology. As the data from interviews with retired migrants show, the notion of the UK at the heart of an empire and as 'the mother country' remains a potent image among many of those who migrated to the UK in the 1950s and 1960s. It is also important to note that many of those who migrated to the UK during this period had UK passports and, as Commonwealth subjects, had free right of entry to the UK.

The physical and economic reconstruction of postwar Britain was an enormous task. With much of British industry readjusting to peacetime production and trying to cope with a chronic shortage of labour, the British state turned to its colonies as a plentiful supply of labour. There is some debate as to the causes of postwar migration from the New Commonwealth. The expansion of Britain's postwar economy clearly was one of the most important factors, and the role of the state in setting up machinery for recruitment should not be underestimated. Ceri Peach argues that:

> Caribbean migration to Britain was essentially powered by free market labour forces, but it had its origins in government sponsored war time recruitment. Post war direct recruitment by British Rail, London Transport and the National Health Service, although not numerically dominant, were important in shaping the movement...however these schemes were introduced after the migration had got under way. Family and island social networks were by far the most important channel of diffusing information and arranging initial footholds in Britain. (Peach 1991, p. 4)

The debate over push and pull factors has been criticized by others such as Miles for failing to take account of the structural dynamics of a capitalist economy. He argues that a debate over push and pull factors obscures what really caused the migration of the 1950s:

The British economy, in common with all other Western European economies, experienced significant shortages of labour in the context of a new phase of capital accumulation...certain economic sectors faced acute shortages of labour, and in conditions of relative full employment, these positions could not be filled from the population within Britain. Thus, structural circumstances defined a demand for labour in certain sectors of the economy, and it was these positions that Caribbean and Asian migrants filled. (Miles 1989, p. 124)

Migration from the New Commonwealth was part of a wider trend of migration to Britain. During the immediate postwar period there was considerable migration from Ireland and from Eastern Europe, through the European Volunteer Workers Scheme. Indeed it could be argued that migration from the New Commonwealth was a phenomenon that ran counter to existing trends in migration at that time. It is perhaps significant that migration from Ireland and Eastern Europe failed to resolve the shortage of manpower and led the British government to look to the colonies for a supply of manpower.

Miles' emphasis on the broader structural dynamics of migration from within a global capitalist framework is inextricably linked to his analysis of migration and race relations in which the economic assumes primacy over all other forms of explanation. While the seismic shifts within capitalism that were taking place in the immediate postwar period did shape patterns of migration, it is also true to say that there were equally important cultural factors that influenced the choice of migrants, particularly from the Caribbean and the Indian subcontinent to head for the UK. The most notable of these was the colonial culture in which Britain was seen as benevolent mother country in which migrants from colonies and former colonies would be welcomed with open arms and treated as equal to the indigenous White population. The difference between this idealized image of the UK and the actual experiences of many of those who were interviewed is particularly stark. The production of the idealized myth of the UK as the centre of civilization was clearly an integral part of the colonial mindset which sought to subjugate alien cultures and assert the primacy of White culture in comparison to the culture of the countries that were being subsumed as part of the empire. Many of the interviewees made explicit references to ideas of England being full of bowler-hatted gentlemen, notions of fair play and precisely the sorts of images that are so often mobilized by the political Right as a model of society that should be restored. Nowhere is this is more obvious than in John Major's speech in which he described a Britain of 'invincible green suburbs', 'dog lovers' and 'long shadows on county cricket grounds'.

Migrants from the New Commonwealth experienced a very different Britain from the one described by Major. They acted as a replacement population in the labour market. That is, they took on jobs that the White population were unwilling to fill. Typically, the sorts of jobs that they filled were in service industries. Such jobs, vital to the infrastructure of a capitalist economy, could not be exported to other countries where the labour was cheaper and could not be mechanized since the technology did not exist at the time. As noted earlier, the industries into which migrants from the New Commonwealth were recruited were prone to high levels of redundancy and rationalization.

There is some doubt as to whether or not migration from the New Commonwealth was ever envisaged by the British government, or indeed the migrants themselves, as permanent. The tone of government documents to which I will refer later suggests that immigration was to be a temporary solution to the shortage of labour. Similarly, in interviews with retired African-Caribbean women, the majority state that they came to Britain thinking that they would return to their country of origin after amassing a suitable amount of savings. Lawrence (1974) and Patterson (1963) suggest that most migrants did indeed come to Britain purely as temporary measure. Patterson notes:

> Most West Indians do not, at least for some years after their arrival, intend to settle permanently. And many are used to the idea of migrant work and travel. (Patterson 1963, p. 71)

Studies of the labour market position of migrants in the 1950s suggest that Caribbeans were clustered in transport and nursing, while Indians and Pakistanis were absorbed into textile manufacture in the north-west and metalwork, particularly in the West Midlands. Many New Commonwealth migrants took up positions in the labour market that the indigenous White population were not prepared to accept, a process Hiro (1971) describes as 'filling the vacuum at the bottom'. It is also important to note that some migrants were recruited to more middle-class professions. For example, it is estimated that one third of hospital doctors in the National Health Service in 1981 were born overseas (Anwar and Ali 1987) and had obtained their basic medical qualifications before coming to the UK. Most of these doctors came from New Commonwealth countries. The demand for doctors in the NHS could not be met by British medical schools. The recruitment of doctors from

parts of the New Commonwealth in many ways parallels the recruitment of nurses, in so far as there were vacancies in general practice in
areas that White doctors refused to work in, principally inner city areas
with poor health and social profiles. As these overseas doctors now
reach retirement age the NHS is finding it increasingly difficult to
attract new medical staff into these areas. In the immediate postwar
period the shortage of labour in the NHS was particularly severe. So
acute were the labour shortages within the NHS that migrants from the
New Commonwealth coming to work in the NHS were exempt from the
provisions of the 1962 Commonwealth Immigration Act.

Nursing as a gendered profession

The creation of the National Health Service in 1948 was major
milestone in the development of the British welfare system. The newly
formed NHS was to provide health care free of charge to all regardless of
their ability to pay. However, one of the major problems that the NHS
encountered in the immediate postwar period was a serious shortage of
staff. Like other areas of British industry the indigenous White population were able to become more selective about the work they performed.
As a result there was a vacuum at the bottom of the labour market
which was particularly acute in transport, textiles, the steel industry and
the new NHS.

The most severe staff shortages were in the least desirable areas of
nursing: psychiatry and geriatrics. To solve the shortage, the British government appealed directly to former colonial subjects in the New
Commonwealth, particularly the West Indies and the Indian subcontinent. In the case of London Transport recruiting offices were set up in
the West Indies. Similarly, the NHS sought to recruit young women to
work as nurses principally in the areas where the shortages of staff were
the most serious. Sheila Patterson, one of the early writers in the field of
'race relations' notes that:

> The shortage has been only partly eased by the entry of an increas-
> ing number of Southern Irish girls and made more acute by the intro-
> duction of the National Health Service. This situation, combined
> with earlier marriage, the opening up of a greater number of alterna-
> tive careers for women and perhaps a certain loss of social prestige
> for the profession, has led to some dilution and relaxation of
> educational standards, and also to the employment of an increasing
> number of Commonwealth nurses, student nurses and pupil

assistants. The process has in recent years reached a point where many smaller and more remote hospitals would be unable to function without them. (Patterson 1963, p. 156)

The British government made a conscious decision to recruit women rather than men as nurses. In the official documents references to 'colonial girls' make it clear that nursing was regarded as a female rather than a male occupation. The recruitment of women from the Caribbean particularly combines assumptions about gender and ethnic origin. These assumptions combine in ways that determined the position of New Commonwealth migrants within the specific occupational hierarchy of the nursing profession.

In the first instance it is important to understand nursing as a feminised profession. Patriarchal ideology is central to understanding the recruitment of women into nursing during the 1950s. Indeed, nursing is a good example of a profession that has been defined as almost exclusively female. Bradley argues that:

> Tending the sick is one of the six core female tasks. Certainly this task had been historically in Britain woman's work…numerous commentators have commented on the way family imagery has permeated the world of medicine. In the hospital, consultants are patriarchs, matrons matriarchs. Nurses play a variety of feminine roles, wives to doctors, mothers to patients, mistresses of the house to the ward domestics. Patients are treated as children, handled with severity by the doctor father, but given motherly if firm tenderness by nurses. (Bradley 1989, p. 192)

Indeed, there is evidence to show that gender roles are internalized by children very early on in life, and one of the professions that has been identified by researchers as one children regard as female is nursing. Nemerowicz (1979) argues that girls identify positively with the role of nurse, while boys reject it from an early age.

Bradley also observes that Asylum nursing was the only area in which male nurses were considered normal since they had to deal with potentially violent patients. Such nurses were not so much carers as warders. This sort of nursing was thus defined as not fitting in with the feminine view of women as carers (see Carpenter 1980). There is indeed a very clear gender segregation within the NHS. Davies and Rosser (1986) argue that all occupations within the NHS are characterized by an absence of women in the higher grade posts. In clerical work, women form the majority of the junior grades, while men tend to dominate the senior posts. Thus while the NHS is staffed by women it is managed by men. This segregation has a number of implications for the division of labour within the NHS. Curran (1988) argues that certain jobs are regarded as female and others male because of the skills involved in different jobs. That is, that stereotypical assumptions about men's work and women's work have an effect on the way that skills are defined:

> Since skill is a social construction it is saturated with sexual bias...recruiters explained their gender preferences in ways which suggest that they regarded the jobs themselves as gendered. The gendering of jobs is embedded in requirements and preferences about a range of personal and social qualities which are, in a circular link, themselves embedded in gender. (Curran 1988, p. 348)

It is only possible to understand the current division of labour in nursing, particularly psychiatric nursing and general nursing, by looking at the complex relationship between gender and race or ethnicity. Indeed, psychiatric and geriatric nursing have become spaces within the Health Service that were occupied almost exclusively by minority ethnic nurses. Psychiatric and geriatric nursing are examples of areas where race overlaps with gender in a way that structures both the labour market location and the work experience of Black women. Gender is central to understanding stratification within the nursing profession. As in many other 'caring' professions there is a widespread belief that women are much more likely to possess the necessary characteristics to be a successful nurse than men. Thus the spaces in the NHS during the 1950s were filled by women rather than men, and became predominantly Black spaces. The particular labour market location which these Black women came to occupy were ones from which there was little chance of upward mobility, partly as a result of many Black nurses being trained as State Enrolled Nurses and partly as a result of the social closure of the more desirable areas of nursing. These areas of nursing are ones that had been abandoned by the indigenous White population precisely because of the lack of prestige and the poor working conditions associated with them. The closure of the more prestigious grades of nursing through credentialism and the concentration of White nursing labour in areas such as general nursing instead of the Cinderella sectors of geriatrics and psychiatry may not have been consciously and explicitly racist. None the less the effect was to exclude migrants from the New Commonwealth.

Subsequent studies of demarcation within nursing suggest that the old dividing line between State Enrolled and State Registered Nurse may have been an entirely artificial one with State Enrolled Nurses performing many of the same functions as State Registered Nurses. What the interview material with retired Caribbean nurses shows is that at the same time there was a concerted effort on the part of White nursing labour to make sure that the demarcation between the types of nursing which had in effect become a racialized barrier was reinforced through the use of informal networks and through the restriction of training opportunities which would have allowed Commonwealth migrants a route out of State Enrolled Nursing.

The consequences of these patterns of recruitment are important for understanding the current segmentation within the Health Service with Black nurses still mainly confined to psychiatry and geriatrics. Moreover the predominance of Black nurses in psychiatry and geriatrics as a result of the patterns of recruitment in the 1950s indirectly helps us to understand the decline in the number of Black nurses in the NHS since both these areas of nursing have contracted considerably as a result of care in the community and the increasing privatization of geriatric care (these patterns are more fully discussed in chapter 5).

A working life in nursing: The experiences of African-Caribbean women

The empirical material included in this chapter is taken from interviews with 21 retired African- or Asian-Caribbean nurses, which were conducted between 1995 and 1997. Those who were interviewed were self-selecting as they were recruited using a snowball sampling method. There were no respondents from the Indian subcontinent or from other former UK colonies. There is documentary evidence (to which I will refer later) that women from a wide variety of countries were recruited to work as nurses in the NHS and, while this may suggest that the experiences of the respondents described in this chapter might be thought of as atypical, there is a very close fit in their description of their working lives in the NHS and many of the key themes that emerge in the 1995 Beishon et al. study of ethnicity in the NHS.

The research took place in the south-west of England. The interviews varied in length, but typically lasted between one and two hours. The intention was to let the respondents talk as freely as possible about their experiences of work, migration and discrimination with minimum intervention from the interviewer. An advert was placed in a local newspaper in order to gain access to respondents. Initially the response was poor with only three replies. However, after the first three interviews the sample snowballed through the introduction of the researcher to other retired nurses whom the first three respondents knew. Consent was gained before conducting interviews. Venues for interviews included social clubs, community centres and the homes of respondents. To preserve the anonymity of the respondents their names have been changed. All the women who were interviewed were in their sixties.

A number of themes emerged during the interviews. These included the experience of occupational segregation, a division of labour in nursing based on crude conceptions of 'race' or ethnicity and experiences of physical harassment from patients. Perhaps the most interesting aspect of these interviews are the strong notions of British colonial identity that permeate these women's accounts of their working lives.

Recruitment and migration to Britain

The accounts of the women who were interviewed suggest that both push factors, such as poor employment prospects in the Caribbean, and pull factors, for example the lure of 'steady' employment in the UK, influenced their choice. Significantly many of the women who were interviewed articulated strong notions of British identity and argued that the UK was a natural choice of destination given its position at the 'heart of the empire'. The idea of empire and 'belonging' to Britain remains very real to the women who were interviewed. One of my respondents, a woman who came to Britain to enter nursing, stated:

> There was no work in Jamaica and I thought Britain would be a good place to come and work. After all we were British subjects, we had British passports, it was only natural that we should come here, it was, and is, our country just as much as it is yours. I'm proud of being British and besides there was work here then.

The notion of Britain as the 'mother country' at the centre of the Empire was referred to in other interviews. For example, one of the nurses I interviewed, whom I will call Maureen (not her real name), spent her first night in Britain in London. Her brother who lived there took her on a short sightseeing tour:

We went to see Buckingham Palace and up and down Oxford Street. It was such a thrill to me. In Trinidad we were always taught that the mother country was England so it was wonderful to see it all.

Maureen's story shows the weakness of the economy in her island of origin (Trinidad) and the lack of opportunities for employment, both significant push factors:

My father was an indentured Indian labourer who came to work on the sugar plantation in Trinidad. He was illiterate, my Mother was Indian too. She was married at 9, it was an arranged marriage and her husband died when he was 10 so she had another arranged marriage when she was 12 that was to my father and she had my brother when she was 14...We lived in a house on the plantation...I am indebted to my mother because she always pushed us, she pushed my brothers and sisters into going to college to improve ourselves, in my sisters and my own case she actually dissuaded us from entering into arranged marriages and told us to get qualifications...By the 1940s the oil refineries had started up in Trinidad and my father went to work for one of the refineries run by Shell and he managed to get one of my brothers a job as an apprentice. With the money that my father got from his job we were able to save enough money to buy a small plot of land where we could grow vegetables and keep animals. As I said my mother was very ambitious for us. She said there was no future for us in Trinidad so she pushed us to look for jobs abroad.

Maureen's story also illustrates the importance of pull factors in the process of migration:

I saw an advert in the *Nursing Times* asking for student nurses. So I sent a number of letters to hospitals in Britain asking about a place as a student nurse and Lancaster Moor, which was a psychiatric hospital, wrote back offering me a place.

Similarly one of the nurses at the day centre said:

Back in Jamaica, in newspapers there were always adverts from British hospitals asking for nurses. That's what made me think about it in the first place.

These responses accord with information from others such as Brooks (1975), who have traced the way in which employers such as London Transport recruited labour from the Caribbean. For a labour market to function adequately there must be four distinct processes. First, employers must be aware of the availability of labour. Thus, employers must have some knowledge of what sort of labour they require – skilled or unskilled, male or female, black or white. In short, workers must inform employers of their availability for work and the skills and experience they posses. Second, workers must be informed of vacancies. That is, workers must be aware of the sort of work that is available. Third, employers must screen applicants in order to ensure that they meet all the necessary criteria for the job. This includes both suitability and acceptability criteria. Fourth, workers must screen employers. That is, they make a choice about whom to apply to for work. In the case of women who came to Britain in the 1950s to become nurses, it is clear that the employers had knowledge of the pool of labour available in the Caribbean from the government. In the case of London Transport the employment of migrant labour was facilitated by setting up a recruiting office in Barbados (see Premru 1995), which suggests that employers in the UK were specifically aiming at recruiting in a particular labour market. Since much of the work was either unskilled or of a low level it was simply a matter of employers simple filling vacant posts rather than being concerned about the skills, education and experience of work. Employers, in this case, hospitals, informed women in the Caribbean of vacancies through newspaper adverts and through official government machinery.

There is, however, documentary evidence to suggest that British hospitals did not have to go to great lengths to attract young black women. Many young women came to Britain simply to find work in hospitals without going through the official machinery which suggests that migration to the UK was a well-established phenomenon with particular employers being regarded as suitable. Given that in Caribbean islands during the 1950s there was little prospect of employment and indigenous economies were weak, it seems entirely plausible that news of work in British hospitals would spread quickly back to islands of the Caribbean. Some hospitals screened workers through the Colonial Office prior to their coming to Britain to train. In the case of women who came to work as domestics or auxiliaries, no screening was necessary since the real requirement was that workers were able-bodied and willing. For the workers from the Caribbean, screening employers was a futile gesture since the lack of work in the islands meant that any employment would be regarded as desirable.

The New Commonwealth migrant as a 'stranger'

In much of the early 'race relations' literature there are frequent references to the notion of the New Commonwealth migrant as a 'stranger'. The indigenous White population reacted to New Commonwealth migrants as strangers. Several of the interviewees referred to this during their description of their early years in the UK:

> I remember not long after I got to England I started courting with Derek, my husband, and as we were walking through the streets we got spat at, and Derek was called a nigger lover. For white people in the '50s it was very strange to see Black people. They did not know anything about us, so I suppose it was the way they were brought up.
>
> I remember getting on the bus in Birmingham where I used to work and it often used to happen that White people, men and women, would just get up and go and sit somewhere else on the bus. Sometimes people made comments about me when they thought I couldn't hear. What they were saying, it was awful. But things were very different then. Black people were strange to White people and they did not know what to make of them.

The culture shock experienced by migrants during their transition from the Caribbean to the UK was obviously genuine and heart-felt. Understanding and becoming part of a new and different culture, living in a different physical geographical and social environment were difficult processes. The transition from one to the other constitutes a considerable leap and for some of the women I interviewed migrating to Britain was a very real culture shock:

> I remember having to get up to go to work in the winter, when there was snow. It was so cold, I mean snow! I had never even seen it until I came here.

Others were slightly better adjusted to some aspects of British life. Maureen describes her journey to Britain and her first impressions thus:

> On the boat to Britain there were a lot of young girls who were going into nursing. In fact it was very common for young girls from Trinidad to go to Britain to enter nursing. I suppose there were between 20 and 30 young girls on the boat I was on, most of them were heading for London or Birmingham. The boat docked in Southampton on the 5th of January 1965, it was freezing when we got here and all I had was a short fluffy coat. You must remember that I had come from Trinidad which has a tropical climate; it was so cold. At the time I really did not know very much about Britain at all except, of course, all the things about the Queen and the royal family being at the heart of the Empire.

Another retired nurse describes her first impressions of the UK:

> I came here in 1956 from Barbados. In the '50s there was a lot of unemployment at home, and there were jobs here. I trained here as a nurse. I remember arriving at Victoria Station. It was horrible, there was the smog, the buildings, the weather, everything was just so very, very different to the place I had known. I had come from the country out in Barbados and when I got here I was totally bewildered. Even the way people spoke was strange. Where I lived in Barbados was a tropical paradise. Everything was different, the climate, the people, everything. Although I knew about Britain, when I actually got here everything seemed so alien to me. During the first few months I was very homesick.

Several of the women I interviewed made explicit references to what has become known as the myth of return. Several of the retired nurses that I interviewed at the day centre stated that, originally, they had planned to come to Britain only as a temporary measure, but for various reasons had decided to stay in this country.

> I remember my first night here in Britain, it was so cold. I thought: I cannot live here. And I decided that I was going to go back to

Jamaica the next day! But of course I could not, because there were no jobs there and I had already spent a lot of money getting here.

Another explained that:

I just planned to come for a few years, you know, earn some decent money and go back to Jamaica, but it didn't work out like that.

It is unlikely that we can ever establish whether the government of the time envisaged the migration of workers from the Caribbean and the Indian subcontinent as permanent or temporary. The concern about migrants that was evident within various government departments suggests that, at best, Britain was ill-prepared to receive large numbers of migrants. This tends to reinforce the view that the government thought only in terms of the labour shortage and pairs of hands, without taking into account the broader question of housing, health, education and other social issues.

The 'racial' division of labour in nursing: 'The dirty jobs'

In terms of the areas of nursing in which migrants were recruited to work, the nursing profession was no different from many other occupational spheres, in that the jobs and types of work that White labour had deserted were those to which migrants were recruited. The intrinsic features of many of these jobs were that they were characterized lack of promotion prospects, low pay and poor conditions. The Cinderella areas of nursing were and still are psychiatry and geriatric nursing and, in the case of many of the respondents, it was these areas into which they were recruited without being aware of the stigma attached. Within these two specialities migrants tended to be concentrated at the bottom of the grade structure and often performed the most menial tasks. There also appears to have been a crude division of labour, which appears to have been based on 'race' or ethnicity, which meant that New Commonwealth migrants were often found emptying bed pans, washing patients and making beds. The cumulative effect of these different forms of segregation meant that within the least desirable specialities, Black nurses were often to be found at the lowest grades, performing the worst kind of work on the least desirable shift.

These different forms of segregation emphasize the ability of White nursing labour to socially close the more desirable areas of nursing to outsiders. As many New Commonwealth migrants were either

SEN-trained or not trained at all, this tended to reinforce the barriers between Black and White areas of nursing. An example of the 'racial' division of labour was provided by one of the respondents in the research. She recalled her early days nursing in the West Midlands:

> It was a case of Black staff not being able to do things that the White staff were allowed to do. White nurses got shown all sorts of things, they discussed things with doctors, but all we ever did was things like cleaning out the lockers, the dirty jobs. I noticed that it went on for some time that Black staff always ended up with the worst jobs, we always did the most menial work.

When asked if she had experienced anything similar in the hospitals in the south-west of England she replied:

> In my early days at the Western Hospital, Black nurses were expected to do certain things that White nurses would not do. Rather than doing it themselves they would wait for us to do it. Western Hospital is a geriatric hospital and the patients are very dependent on the nurses and they have to have a lot of help just to get up. They need to be washed and dressed and they need to be lifted into the bath sometimes. While we did all that the White nurses just waited until we had finished and then they made the beds.

One of the retired nurses who worked in a psychiatric hospital describes poor working conditions and a rigid division of labour based on 'race':

> I worked at a mental hospital and I had a terrible time there. They had children there who were so badly handicapped some of them were bed-ridden and we had to turn them over every two hours so that they didn't get bed sores and it was always Black nurses who did the lifting and it was hard work, very hard work. All the nurses at that hospital were Black...The children were sedated a lot of the time, but there were some who used to misbehave and I remember the male nurses just pushing them into a corner and beating the hell out of them. Sometimes when the kids had soiled themselves they just used to put them in a shower cubicle and get a mop and a bucket and throw the bucket of water over them and use the mop to clean them with. They were treated like animals. For breakfast they were given porridge and it was put into a huge trough at the middle of the ward and they were fed like pigs or goats. I spent a year there and

I just could not take any more. I spent some time on a ward for old people a lot of them had fleas and I used to come home itching, I just could not bear it. At the mental hospital almost all the nurses were Black and we had to do some dirty jobs, I don't ever remember seeing the White nurses emptying commodes and changing patients. The worst thing was the lifting: we had to lift patients up and out of bed and friends of mine had a lot of back problems because of the amount of lifting they had to do, but you never saw White nurses doing anything like that.

Another of the retired nurses whom I interviewed at the day centre commented:

For most of the time I was stuck doing really nasty jobs – you know, bedpans and things like that – and I remember it was always the Black nurses who seemed to be lifting patients out of bed. In fact, I have a lot of friends who were nurses and, do you know, the one thing we all have in common is that we all have bad backs and I'm sure it's because of the lifting we did as nurses.

Respondents in the research made frequent references to backache, injuries and illness sustained as a result of working in hospitals, as well as their inferior occupational status, which limited their occupational mobility. The findings of this research corresponds to two of Fenton's (1988) key findings. First, that nearly all of the African-Caribbean women in his study were nursing auxiliaries or SEN-trained nurses and, second, nearly all of them complained of work-related illnesses, for example, back trouble, high blood pressure, leg pains and complaints of attacks by patients.

Many of the nurses who were interviewed provided detailed accounts of discriminatory practices in both recruitment and promotion. Their descriptions of their working lives and career progression show the extent to which other areas of nursing were socially closed. The exclusion of Black nurses from certain areas served to reinforce the perception of them as suitable only for work of a menial type. Exclusion was not limited to the occupational sphere. In one interview, a respondent referred to her exclusion from social functions:

It took me years before I was accepted, I was never invited to the Christmas parties. For the first few years I got quite upset about it, but after five or six years it didn't bother me any more. But if I had been White I would have been invited. I did gain the respect of some people as a professional, but not as a friend.

Any notion that discrimination is likely to recede over time as contact between host and immigrant populations becomes more frequent and 'normal' might therefore be regarded as problematic if the accounts of respondents in this research are in any way representative of the ethnic minority experience.

State Enrolled Nurse training and State Registered Nurse training: A two-tier system

There is evidence to suggest that New Commonwealth migrants were actively encouraged to undertake training as State Enrolled Nurses rather than as a State Registered Nurse. The successful closure of the State Registered Nurse grade was achieved through a form of credentialism which meant that to be eligible for training candidates had to have five 'O' levels. Many of the women who were interviewed during the course of the research had only a basic education and were therefore disqualified from SRN training. However, even in cases where migrants did have sufficient qualifications there is anecdotal evidence to suggest that they were nevertheless recommended for State Enrolled Nurse training. The way the work of the SRN has been constructed means that it has acquired an almost scientific status, for example through the administering of drugs and giving injections. However, the work of SEN and auxiliaries retains a domestic quality, as they perform tasks like bathing patients; it was widely regarded as less prestigious qualification.

One of the women interviewed for the research explained her experience of training:

> When I came to Britain and I decided to go in to nursing the matron at the hospital suggested that I should train to become a State Enrolled Nurse. I knew nothing about nursing and I did not know that it would have been much better for me to become a State Registered Nurse. It meant that it was much harder for me to get promotion.

This was a story repeated by other interviewees and suggests either a conscious or unconscious desire on the part of recruiters to channel New Commonwealth migrants towards particular areas. If this were to occur today there is no doubt that it would labelled, quite correctly, as institutional racism. In other cases migrants possessed only basic qualifications which effectively excluded them from the State Registered grade, for example:

> I was educated in Barbados and I left school with an elementary cer-
> tificate, when I came to the UK in 1960 I found that it did not count
> for anything. It meant that I could only work as a nursing auxiliary.

The use of qualifications as a barrier is central to understanding how some areas of nursing remained socially closed. To become a State Registered Nurse required five 'O' levels, and as such this requirement might be thought to be 'colour-blind' and so non-discriminatory. However, the allocation of jobs on the basis of formal qualifications is symbolic in that the intrinsic value of the qualifications is often of little relevance. Rather, the purpose of this sort of barrier is to keep some social groups out of particular areas and other social groups in, even though the work performed by the different groups may be broadly similar.

The channelling of minority nurses into SEN training has been documented by Baxter (1988). The institutional predisposition for pushing New Commonwealth migrants into SEN training suggests a structural element of discrimination, but it is also important to acknowledge the agency of social actors such as ward sisters, matrons and nursing officers whose selection decisions may have been influenced by common-sense perceptions of 'race' or ethnicity. The attitudes of senior nursing staff who acted as gatekeepers during the immediate postwar period bear examination, in interviews with retired African-Caribbean nurses they suggest that discrimination and racism was often overt.

Common-sense notions of 'race' informed the way in which ethnic minority nurses were excluded from certain types of work. Several respondents gave examples of how unskilled White labour was some-times regarded as preferable to skilled migrant labour:

> The managers made it clear that they did not think much of Black
> nurses, they treated Black nurses so badly. Remember, I was a trained
> nurse who had looked after a whole ward before. I could take the
> responsibility, but they would not let me do it – they would rather
> let a bank nurse or an agency nurse who was White and who had
> less experience than me do it... They used to undermine me all the
> time. They would start the daily report before I got there and I was
> the senior nurse! And when the sister was away they would not
> leave me in charge of the ward even though I had the qualifications

and experience. They would get someone from the bank or an agency nurse who did not know what they were doing.

Opportunities for promotion and upward mobility also appear to have been restricted, with Black nurses excluded from study days (paid days off from work that allowed nurses the chance to undertake further training). This practice no doubt had serious consequences when applying for promotion:

> We were not even allowed to go on study days. We were supposed to be entitled to go on those study days, you know, so that we could improve our chances for promotion, but they never let me or any other Black nurses go on them.

These practices are consistent with a strategy of social closure in which the possession of formal qualifications is used to justify the exclusion of 'outsiders', in this case, New Commonwealth migrants. The professional divisions based on the possession of qualifications were reinforced through the use of informal networks to secure jobs. Gatekeeper discrimination also exerted a powerful influence over the career progression of New Commonwealth migrants:

> In '55 one of the first hospitals I worked in, in London, was the Springfield hospital in Tooting. It had quite a lot of Black nurses around then, but they never seemed to get promotion. One of the other Black girls overheard the chief nursing officer saying that, as a rule, Black nurses should not be promoted, but to promote one or two just to keep them happy.

In one interview with a retired African-Caribbean nurse the impact of discrimination and how it shaped her career was made clear:

> It was not long after I left the psychiatric hospital that I went over to America for my sister's wedding and when I came back I went on a two-year course at college in catering. I got my diploma in catering and we were struggling for money at that time and I applied for a job as a catering assistant at the Maternity Hospital. The job had been advertised in the *Evening News*. I went to see the man who was in charge of catering and when I got there he told me that post was gone. I am sure that it was because of my colour. I said, 'How can it be gone? It has only been in the paper for a day.' and he got very

cross with me and told me that it was gone and that was that and would I kindly leave his office. He was nasty to me. I felt sure it was because of my colour so I got a White friend of mine to apply for the job the following day and sure enough she was told that there was a situation available in catering. The same thing happened at the Southern Infirmary. It was just so awful. I had four children at the time and we were living on social security. It was very tough. I felt it was so unfair that they would not give me a job just because I was Black. I cried my heart out that night. Things were getting so desperate that I went to the personnel office at the Maternity Hospital because I had heard that there were nursing jobs there. I went in and said, 'I want a job. Anything, any job will do.' The lady in there sat me down and asked me all about my work experience and she got in touch with a Sister who had worked with me at another hospital and she gave me a good reference and they gave me a job working nights at the Maternity Hospital.

This nurse's experience of working in the NHS appears to have been typical of many of the respondents in the research. The majority of her working life was spent in the least desirable types of nursing and on the least desirable shifts. Attempts to move out of these areas were unsuccessful largely as a result of gatekeeper discrimination and the successful closure of other, more prestigious areas of nursing.

'Racial' harassment at work

The issue of harassment at work, by patients and other staff, was a common experience for many of the nurses I interviewed. The harassment took a variety of forms, ranging from verbal abuse to physical attacks. During interviews with respondents at a day centre for the elderly the question of verbal abuse brought the following responses:

> I used to get it all the time: sambo, darkie, black bastard. I tried not to take any notice of it. Some of those patients were ill, you know, mentally ill, and they did not know what they were saying

> I had patients call me all sorts of names, black bugger, black bastard, that was pretty common, but a lot of them were ill which explained it.

While the verbal abuse was acknowledged by the nurses, they often attributed it to illness rather than any malicious intent on the part of the patients. As the recent PSI study, *Working in a Multi-Ethnic NHS*, shows, ethnic minority nurses still tend to attribute verbal abuse from patients to illness rather than to racist beliefs:

> Illness *per se* was sometimes given as a reason for racism as a nurse working in a general medical speciality suggested 'One of the patients said 'take your dirty hands off me'. You just ignore it. They are ill...after a while they come round. We never retaliate.' Hence, old age, illness, confusion, mental ill health, were all given as reasons for the racist behaviour of patients, and nurses often gave the impression that receiving such harassment was simply part of the job, explained by the vulnerable condition of many of the people they were dealing with. (Beishon et al. 1995, p. 129)

The abuse experienced by African-Caribbean nurses was not restricted to verbal abuse. One retired nurse described her early days working in the NHS:

> In the first few weeks when I was working at the Western Hospital I went to lift a male patient out of bed and he punched me in the face and said, 'Take your hands off me you black bastard.' I didn't know what to say or do. I was so shocked and upset. I used to get called things like that all the time, black bastard, black bugger, it was part of the routine. But then in those days most White people had not seen any Black people and it must have been strange to them to see Black people, so I suppose in some respects it was understandable.

This confirms what the recent PSI report suggests, namely that ethnic minority nurses are reluctant to attribute even the most blatant forms of abuse to race or racism.

Harassment of Black nurses came not only from patients but also from staff. In interviews with retired African-Caribbean nurses different forms of harassment were described. They included being referred to disciplinary proceedings for minor infringements of rules and verbal abuse from managers. One retired nurse described her experience thus:

> The ward sisters just treated Black nurses as a problem...The managers were so racist, it was just so obvious. They were not trying to discriminate and then cover it up. It was just blatant and they did not care. You were told to your face that you weren't allowed to do

certain things because you were Black...I developed hypertension. I used to come home from work and cry. It got so bad that I would cry before walking through those doors into the hospital.

Other examples of harassment nurses included intimidation and threats from managers and senior nurses:

I was ill in bed one day and the ward sister rang me up at home and said that I had been suspended because I had not come into work. I was very upset and so I rang the manager of the ward and he said that he did not know what was going on and that the sister did not have the authority to suspend me. Obviously, this was very worrying to me and I was ill anyway. I was told if I did not get back to work, that I would not have a job to go to. I don't know of any White nurses where this sort of thing happened.

At the General Hospital the discrimination was obvious. The way they treated Blacks on the psychiatric unit it was terrible...they were trying to push the Black nurses out; I felt sure that they wanted me to leave. They kept asking me if I would be interested in doing some other type of work. So I decided that I would not leave because that was what they wanted.

Nursing is a hierarchical profession in which the informal recommendations of managers can shape the future nurses at the bottom of the career ladder. In this context to complain about harassment would have been a high-risk strategy. Several of the nurses who were interviewed suggested that to complain was to run the risk of being labelled as a troublemaker. In such cases Black nurses often received poor references, which effectively restricted their occupational mobility. One of the nurses who was interviewed describes her experience:

There was one occasion when there were no trained staff on the ward and I was the senior nurse because I had the most experience, so I took over the ward until they could get some trained staff. So I had to ring the matron for the key to the office on the ward, I got the key and went into the office to look at the communications book, to find out what happened on the previous shift and to allocate jobs to nurses. In the book there were some very nasty comments about the Black nurses...You see we were not allowed in the office, so they could write what they wanted and they obviously didn't think that any of us would get to see the book. I told all the other Black nurses on the ward and they were very upset. The sister heard about it all and she was very cross about it. The next day she called all the Black nurses into the office and she told us off for going in there without her permission. I was the only one who said anything, I think all the other girls were too frightened to say anything. I told her that we had to look in the book and have access to the office if we were going to be able to do our jobs, to look after the patients. She got very cross and told me that if I didn't like it I could see the Matron. But I left it because I had my exams to pass. But then after I got my exams I found it very difficult to get a job, I had obviously got a bad reference. The only reason I got a job was because a nursing officer told me that I had good qualifications and a bad reference and he asked me to explain why I thought that was. He was the only one with enough guts to ask me about it, and he gave me the job. That was back in 1970.

Another African-Caribbean nurse, who at the time of the interview was still working in the NHS, made the point about complaining about racism and harassment very clearly:

So it happens, you get called names, you get told to do jobs that other nurses never, never do and you are made to feel very small and unimportant. But what happens if you complain? I've seen it before, other nurses have made complaints, so it goes on their file that they made a complaint about harassment and they never go anywhere, never get promotion. Sometimes the person you should be complaining to about harassment is the person who is actually harassing you! So how do you complain? I just keep my mouth shut and bide my time until I retire.

The only retired African-Caribbean nurse in my sample who reached the position of ward sister and was a State Registered Nurse describes her experiences in the NHS:

There is racism in the NHS, it goes on at all levels and runs all the way through it from the bottom to the top. Only a few people actually said things to my face, but there was always an atmosphere that made me feel uncomfortable. Some people were very hostile to me...There was one particular sister who I had trained as a nurse who came back to the hospital as a sister after I had trained her...she always treated me with a sort of coldness. Other staff made allegations about me and

I often had to defend myself against them. It made my job very difficult. Doctors and other nurses often made derogatory remarks about Black people in front of me...I don't think the NHS has changed at all, the work has changed but the atmosphere has not...When I used to sit on appointment panels, if we had Black candidates there would always be some derogatory remark about that candidate, you know phrases like 'jungle bunny', and these comments were coming from educated men. Even if there was no difference in qualifications between a Black candidate and a White candidate, it would always be the White candidate who would be appointed.

These accounts of working in the NHS suggest a form of hyper-segregation. Migrant labour was restricted to certain parts of the nursing profession which were regarded by white nursing labour as less prestigious and less desirable. Moreover, migrants were *also* restricted to the lowest grades and performed the most arduous types of work. What these accounts show is the way in which different aspects of social closure and discrimination cross-cut and mutually reinforce one another so that the possibility of upward mobility is slight.

The government response to the shortage of nurses in the 1950s: how psychiatry and geriatrics came to be gendered and racialized

What makes nursing different from other employment is the way in which civil servants, hospital administrators and others consciously pushed migrant labour from the Caribbean into specific occupational spaces. The fact that these areas of nursing came to be occupied by African-Caribbean women helped to create a self-fulfilling prophecy on the part of managers, who in turn directed more migrants into these spaces within the labour market.

Like many other major employers the NHS experienced a serious shortage of labour. Official government documents show that as early as 1946 hospitals were facing a shortage of staff:

There is an acute shortage of nurses and domestics, resulting in some places in the closing of wards. (MH55/1466 Shortage of Nurses and Domestics, Public Record Office, Kew)

The government responded by setting up official machinery to recruit young women from the colonies to work in British hospitals.

The system worked in the following way. The Ministry of Health and the Ministry of Labour estimated how many nurses were required throughout Britain to the Colonial Office. The Colonial Office then set up departments in each of the colonies to recruit women deemed suitable for training. They screened suitable candidates and placed them in British hospitals where there was a shortage of labour. The package provided by the Colonial Office included the cost of the fare (one-way) to Britain. On arrival the student nurses would be escorted by representatives of the British Council to their new place of employment. Documents suggest that one of the main reasons the Colonial Office was involved in the recruitment was to provide trained nurses for the colonies. This view was clearly at odds with that of the Ministry of Health and the Ministry of Labour, who were quite clearly interested in cheap labour to fill the gaps left by indigenous workers. The conflict of views between the Colonial Office and the Ministry of Health was apparent as early as 1955, since it was clear that the official government sponsorship machinery was not providing the volume of labour required by the hospitals in Britain and a decision was taken to relax the entry requirements for nurse training.

Official documents reveal that many of the colonies were eager to participate in schemes which alleviated the twin problems of high unemployment and a growing population. The implication of these documents is that the British government never intended labour from the Caribbean to be anything other than restricted to the lowest rungs of the profession, leaving the more desirable areas of nursing for the indigenous White population. In a telegram from the Governor of Barbados to the Secretary of State for the Colonies dated 4 August 1954 the position of the Barbadian government is clear:

As you are aware, over-population in Barbados presents a most serious problem. A possible source of some small relief appears to lie in the employment of Barbadian girls in the United Kingdom as student nurses, and later as qualified nurses, for whom there appears to be a need...these proposals envisage permanent migration of girls willing to make their career overseas. It will consequently be made clear to candidates accepted that return passages will not be provided...it is proposed that the scheme should cover employment and training as State Enrolled Nurses. *The type of work involved, and the smaller prospect of advancement would be made clear to the girls and to their parents.* (my emphasis)

Although many young women came from the Caribbean through the official sponsorship machinery, it is also clear that large numbers of West Indian women came to Britain without sponsorship with the express intention of working in the Health Service. It seems that the many of these women came to work in menial, unskilled and poorly paid parts of the nursing profession, often as nursing auxiliaries. As a nursing auxiliary with no training there was no possibility of upward mobility. These women were thus stuck in the least desirable areas of nursing. There are no official estimates of the numbers of women who came to Britain in search of work and who eventually became either auxiliaries or domestics. However, documents in the PRO reveal that the flow of candidates without sponsors was a cause for concern in the Colonial Office – so much so that the Colonial Office sought to stem the flow. On the other hand, the Ministry of Health and the Ministry of Labour were very keen to allow the flow to continue since there was still a considerable shortage of labour in jobs which, while essential to the day-to-day running of the Health Service, were unable to attract the indigenous population to fill them.

The conflict between the desire for labour and the desire for trained nurses was the subject of considerable discussion between different government departments. For example, in a circular telegram to the colonies dated 3 December 1954 it was decided to relax the entry qualifications for women from the New Commonwealth wishing to enter nursing:

A review has recently been undertaken of the existing system of selection and recommendation of candidates for nurse training In the UK, in view of the willingness of many hospitals to accept Colonial girls for nurse training and of the increasing flow of unsponsored candidates, many of whom are of good calibre. After consideration by an interdepartmental committee of representatives from the Colonial Office, the Ministry of Health and the Ministry of Labour it has been agreed to effect some relaxation in the present system as follows:

It is proposed to discontinue the present system of selection and recommendation for all candidates as from the 1st of January, 1955, and they should be instructed to make their own arrangements in future with the hospitals of their choice. The Colonial Office would be prepared to assist Matrons in checking references and arranging a medical examination in the territory if desired.

However, a year later, problems with the sponsorship machinery were emerging, as is noted in a similar telegram from the Colonial Office to all British Colonies:

> The decision to relax the system of selection and recommendation of nursing candidates who wish to apply for training while still in their territories has given rise to certain difficulties both here and in the territories. In particular Matrons have been unable to obtain speedy information about the references of candidates who are in many cases not known to this office. Overseas Governments have in some cases felt that a complete relaxation of control is undesirable and have found difficulty in replying to enquiries from authorities in the UK and in advising candidates on suitable hospitals. The whole question has been further discussed in this office. It was agreed that there seemed to be an urgent need for the continuance of some machinery in overseas territories.

The reaction of the Ministry of Health to the imposition of restrictions was predictably agitated:

> I have today had a visit from Mr Jamieson, of the Ministry of Health, who was anxious to learn the position as regards colonial student nurses. The point of view of the Ministry of Health is mainly that these nurses are a useful body of workers and they would be reluctant to restrict the flow of them.

During the mid-1950s it is clear that there was a considerable difference of opinion between the Colonial Office and the Ministry of Health. A letter from the chief nursing officer of the Colonial Office to the Permanent Secretary at the Colonial Office shows the nature of the split:

> there are *obvious* differences between the Ministry of Health and ourselves towards the training of colonial girls as nurses. Their point of view is obviously concerned with obtaining 'pairs of hands' for hospitals whereas we are concerned to provide suitable training for suitable students to the ultimate benefit of the nursing service in the colonial territories. I am beginning to feel that these two points of view are completely irreconcilable and that if the Ministry begins to join the colonial groups who are at present pressing us to relax our

sponsorship machinery we are going to be fighting a losing battle. (my emphasis)

The response of the Ministry of Health to the possible restriction on candidates for nurse training is encapsulated in this letter from the Ministry of Health to the Colonial Office dated 17 June 1954:

> Our point of view on this is, of course, rather different from yours. We gather that there are probably now three thousand or more colonials in the hospital nursing service, and this quite a significant percentage of our establishment. Hence any discouragement to Colonial girls to come to this country is, from our point of view, another difficulty in keeping up the numbers needed for staffing the hospitals. So great has been this difficulty that the ministry of labour is going to a great deal of trouble to recruit girls from the continent for nursing work. I wonder if it would not look rather odd if it came out that the Government was giving financial encouragement to foreigners to work here as nurses (we often pay their fares) on the one hand, while on the other, was taking steps to discourage British Colonial subjects from getting nursing training.

The basis for the conflict between the Ministry of Health, the Ministry of Labour and the Colonial Office appears to have been that the Colonial Office was chiefly concerned with providing a pool of skilled nursing labour, for both Britain and the colonies. The correspondence between the Ministries shows that the Colonial Office was particularly concerned with references and qualifications of candidates for nurse training. For example, a letter to the Colonial Office from a hospital Matron states that:

> The most unsuitable candidates can often provide most glowing references from plausible sounding persons and referees will state categorically that 'she is a model young lady', 'highly educated', or even 'brilliant', without much idea of the objective requirements. Again, so many Matrons have little idea of local conditions, e.g. the use of the term 'school certificate', it means a local certificate from the elementary school, or 'qualified nurse' in the Gold Coast meaning something like State Enrolled Auxiliary Nurse which will be entirely misleading.

As we have seen, much of the migration, particularly from the West Indies, was unsponsored and there are only passing references to it in official documents. Official sponsored migration through government machinery is, by contrast, relatively well documented. This presents a problem in terms of trying to measure accurately the volume of migration to Britain during the 1950s. Official government records often refer to the 'problem' of migrants from the New Commonwealth simply arriving in Britain without making prior arrangements for accommodation and employment, a fact that suggests that push factors may have been at least as significant as pull factors. The following is an extract from a telegram from the Secretary of State for the Colonies concerning nurse training. It was sent to the regional governments of Sierra Leone, the Gold Coast, Gambia, Cyprus, Jamaica, Trinidad, Barbados, British Guiana, British Honduras, Bahamas, Leeward Islands and Windward Islands. It is dated 20 August 1955:

> Some embarrassment has been caused recently by selected candidates arriving in the United Kingdom unheralded and without sufficient means to pay for their rail fare to the hospital or for their subsistence during the days which must inevitably elapse before they can be taken into the hospital. I shall be grateful if selected candidates can be encouraged, by whatever means possible to notify their travel arrangements through you to the director of Colonial Scholars in advance so that these may be notified to the British Council, and if they can be advised of the absolute necessity of equipping themselves with sufficient funds to meet their immediate needs on arrival.

Similarly, a letter from the Chief Nursing Officer of the Colonial Office to the Permanent Secretary of the Colonial Office shows comparable problems:

> See the attached note from the British Council confirming the arrival of unrecommended student nurses from the West Indies. You will see that these nurses are now arriving overland from Genoa and increasing the problem for the council...I do not see that there is much that can be done other than asking the local West Indian governments to stress through various publicity services the difficulties the students will encounter if they make their way here without going through the proper channels.

Conclusions

The first half of this chapter dealt with interviews which illustrated the individual experiences of various women who came to work in the Health Service during the 1950s and their experiences do indeed suggest that certain areas of nursing were racialised. That is, that the more prestigious areas of the nursing were socially closed by White nurses. The graphic accounts of work in hospitals provided by these women also show the extent to which there was an implicit, sometimes explicit, assumption that Black nurses were somehow inferior to White nurses. This view served as a justification for a highly inequitable division of labour, with Black nurses confined to the most routine and menial tasks, typically tasks like lifting patients out of bed, bathing them and emptying bedpans. Thus, on one level, there is evidence to suggest that there was a very straightforward and explicit attempt to make particular niches of the nursing profession Black. However, what documents from the Public Record Office show is that the process of racialization was actually much more complex than many have assumed. There is evidence of a significant split in opinion between different government ministries. The Colonial Office argued strongly for the importation of skilled labour which would temporarily fill the gaps in the Health Service and ultimately return to the colonies. Opposing this point of view was the Ministry of Health and the Ministry of Labour. It is clear from the documents I have obtained from the PRO that their agenda was one entirely concerned with obtaining labour skilled or unskilled at any cost. There is evidence that the labour shortage in British hospitals was severe and from the point of view of the Ministry of Labour, the importation of labour from the colonies was to play a very significant role in solving that problem. Indeed, there are frequent references to 'The Barbados Proposal' in the correspondence and it is frequently mentioned that Barbados had supplied a considerable number of young women to work in British hospitals. Beyond that there is nothing. However, there is a document (MH 55) in the Public Record Office entitled NHS Workers from Barbados dating from the early 1950s which is closed until 2038. Repeated requests to government departments to have access to the document have been refused on the grounds that the contents are too sensitive. Both the interviews and the documents show how colonial identity was a central force in shaping the relations between Black and White during this period. What colonial identity meant for people from the New Commonwealth was that they had free right of entry to the country that was at the centre of an empire of which they were an integral part. The interviews show how some of the women expressed a very real sense of belonging to Britain. However the term 'colonial' had very different connotations for White people in Britain in the 1950s and 1960s. In the documents from the PRO there are implicit assumptions made about the sort of work that is regarded as suitable for 'colonial girls', these were evidently imbued with racism and colonialism, and the legacy of these attitudes has undoubtedly shaped the experience of Ethnic minority women who have entered nursing.

To characterize the inferior position of Caribbean women in the NHS as simply a result of racism is a considerable oversimplification of a complex combination of social forces. Although racism did play a considerable part in determining the position of Black women in the Health Service, there was a range of other, equally significant factors which many writers in this area have neglected to refer to. To explain satisfactorily the labour market position within the Health Service which Caribbean women found themselves in sociologists must consider a specific combination of factors. The factors that determined the position of those women were first, British colonial ideology, much of which was essentially paternal in outlook; second, the crude forms of racism that women encountered from patients and other colleagues in the form of abuse both verbal and physical; third, acts of 'racial' discrimination which effectively prevented minority ethnic women from finding jobs in other occupational areas. Indeed, many of the interviews allude to the social closure of certain areas of nursing. Official records show that the role of Caribbean labour in the Health Service was a highly contested issue, with different government departments arguing for very different outcomes. For example, the Colonial Office clearly had it in mind for 'colonial girls' to be trained in Britain to alleviate the labour shortage in the NHS, but that they should return to the Colonies to the ultimate benefit of the colonies. There was clearly a complex conflict between different government departments which had very different agendas. However, the contest was an unequal one in which the Ministry of Health and Ministry of Labour were always likely to prevail, since there is little evidence that the government, at the highest levels, was concerned with anything other than alleviating the labour shortage. Concern for the well-being of the colonies was, in comparison, a very remote concern. It is only by understanding the historical processes of the migration of the 1950s that it is possible to understand segregation within the nursing profession today. It is the patterns of recruitment structured by a colonial and racist ideology in the 1950s that have subsequently gone on to affect the position of Black workers in the Health Service. Divisions between Black and White areas of nursing were crystallized in the 1950s and reinforced ever since with the result that, even today, there is a very clear concentration of Black nurses within psychiatry and geriatrics.

5
Ethnicity, Segregation and the National Health Service

Introduction

Having discussed the nature of social closure and the creation of what Feuchtwang (1982) calls occupational ghettos, I will now turn to the practices associated with promotion and recruitment in more detail. The research referred to in this chapter shows how the divisions based on common-sense notions of race which permeated the nursing profession during the 1950s and 1960s have persisted in the Health Service of today. Using empirical material from two case studies of hospitals, different aspects of ethnic disadvantage will be demonstrated. These include: inferior promotion chances and the impact of an institutional preference for selection using internal labour markets.

The research took place in large city in the west of England between 1993 and 1997 at a health trust (Unicorn Trust, not its real name) that is responsible for the running of several hospitals within the city. The research took place in two of the hospitals run by the Trust the first of which (hospital A) is a large city centre hospital which is responsible for general medicine, heart surgery, radiography and accident and emergency admissions. The second hospital (hospital B) is located on the outskirts of the city and is a psychiatric hospital. The research used quantitative and qualitative methods. Quantitative analysis took the form of a questionnaire distributed to 1,400 respondents in the directorate of medicine and the directorate of psychiatry. The questionnaire achieved a 67 per cent response rate. Qualitative analysis comprised approximately 50 open-ended, in-depth interviews with staff from different ethnic groups at different levels within the Trust. Because of the sensitivity of the issues involved in the research, all the names of the respondents have been changed to avoid identification.

Ethnicity and shift work

Aspects of institutional discrimination form an important part of the experience of ethnic minority nurses within the NHS in the UK. That is, both conscious and unconscious actions are informed by crude racist stereotypes, not least of which is the unspoken assumption on the part of many of the middle managers who were interviewed in the research that ethnic minority nurses belonged in particular types of work where other ethnic minorities were already concentrated. Ethnic minority nurses tend to be located in the least desirable forms of nursing; however, their structural location within these types of nursing is also of significance since the majority of ethnic minority respondents in the research worked on the night shift. Working night shifts has a number of advantages; these include allowing more flexible childcare patterns for women whose partners are employed to work more conventional hours, and the better rates of pay for night work. However, there are undoubtedly counterbalancing aspects that make the night shift less, rather than more, desirable. These include the disruption to sleep patterns and, in the case of nursing, less opportunity for promotion. There is already evidence from the equal opportunities commission that within the NHS ethnic minority nurses are disproportionately located on the least desirable shift of all: the night shift (Equal Opportunities Commission (1991). Agobolegbe (1984) also refers to the concentration of ethnic minority staff on the night shift. His research also revealed a disproportionate number of ethnic minority staff on geriatric wards and in psychiatric hospitals.

Data from questionnaires at hospital B show that 73 per cent of the ethnic minority sample were working on the night shift compared to 36 per cent of the White sample. This is a considerable disparity which is hard to explain away by saying that ethnic minority staff prefer to work the night shift as managers at the hospital did. There are various reasons for this. Clearly some ethnic minority staff did have a positive preference for working the night shift; however, as the quotes from interviews with ethnic minority staff show, there were many who did not make a conscious decision to work at night. Some ethnic minority staff cited different reasons, including the availability of childcare. Some suggested that the night shift was less confrontational, partly as a result of larger numbers of ethnic minority nurses who worked nights. Some also cited the higher rates of pay as an incentive. All those interviewed complained about the physical effects of the night shift, for example:

> Yes, it does affect you. My sleeping took a long while to adjust and, working nights, you don't actually get to see anybody other than my husband and the kids in the morning. I can't remember the last time we went out. (African-Caribbean nurse, hospital B)

Others stated the problems of working on the night shift more bluntly:

> Since I have been working nights I have felt permanently exhausted. (African-Caribbean nurse, hospital B)

The degree to which ethnic minority nurses actually made a conscious choice to work the night shift is problematic. A number of nurses stated that they made a conscious choice to work nights because it made childcare easier. However, in an interview with the only ethnic minority senior manager at hospital B she alluded to an unofficial policy of placing ethnic minority staff on the night shift. When I asked her why there was such a preponderance of ethnic minority workers on the night shift she replied:

> Because it is the only job they get given, you hardly ever see Black staff on days, the night shift is a Black ghetto. (African-Caribbean manager, hospital B)

During an interview with an Asian nurse who had recently finished a long period of working nights at hospital B she revealed that:

> Some of the Black people here don't like to be on days, you have to be more involved, there is more chance of confrontation [with White staff]. On nights you deal with fewer people and there tend to be less problems. I have worked nights for ten years. Don't get me wrong, it is demanding in different ways. I would never go back to it because it wrecked my sleep. The other reason people work nights is transport, if a family has one car then one person can use it during the day and the other can use it at night. (Asian nurse, hospital B)

By working nights ethnic minority workers are more likely to avoid direct contact with White racism and are also able to maximize their earnings since night work is paid at higher rates. There is, it is argued, a quid pro quo, in that by working nights the disadvantages of physical disruption and health problems are compensated for by higher rates of pay and feeling of solidarity among ethnic minority workers. The notion that ethnic minority workers choose to work the night shift was challenged by one of the respondents who said:

> What do you do when the only job they offer you is on the night shift? (African-Caribbean nurse, hospital B)

Clearly some advantages do accrue from working the night shift. However, the disadvantages are equally real and have marked effects on promotion opportunities.

Discrimination in recruitment

Recruitment within the Trust during the period of the research was at a low level. The personnel department estimated that there was an annual staff turnover of 15 per cent. The Trust has a policy of no compulsory redundancy and, in cases where wards or departments are closed, the Trust has a policy of relocating staff within the organization. An important feature that was revealed from questionnaire data was the high levels of internal recruitment within the organization.

The existence of an extended internal labour market within the Trust has consequences for how staff operationalize equality policies. In both hospitals where the research took place internal recruitment was common. Vacancies were advertised in a weekly jobs newsletter, *Employment Opportunities*. In the case of hospital A the figure is 68 per cent of the sample who found their job through the internal market while for hospital B the figure is 60 per cent. In light of the low numbers of non-White workers in the Trust the obvious consequence of the high levels of internal recruitment is that the ethnic composition of the workforce is unlikely to be substantially changed.

Like many other employers, Unicorn Trust developed an internal labour market for three main reasons. First, it reduces training and advertising costs. Second, it assists in the evaluation of candidates since their records are easily available. Third, it allows greater flexibility through the redeployment of staff from areas of contraction to areas of expansion thus reducing redundancy payments. However, the combination of an extended internal labour market, economic contraction and a small number of women and/or ethnic minority groups can only be inimical to the promotion of equality of opportunity.

Whether or not such actions constitute intentional and direct discrimination is highly debatable. However, such actions could easily be interpreted as indirect discrimination. The Commission for Racial Equality states that:

> It is unlawful to use recruitment methods which exclude or disproportionately reduce the numbers of applicants of a particular racial group and which it cannot be shown to be justifiable. It is therefore recommended that employers should not recruit solely through the following methods: a) recruitment, solely or in the first instance, through the recommendations of existing employees where the workforce is wholly or predominantly white or Black and the labour market is multiracial. (CRE Code of Employment Practice)

There may be a variety of reasons why employers may want to restrict vacancies to internal candidates. However one of the most important is that ward managers may already know of suitable candidates for a post who are already working within a particular hospital. Beishon et al. (1995) suggest that the use of internal labour markets is likely to militate against ethnic minority groups and reinforce existing inequalities. Although personnel managers within the Trust asserted that internal candidates are treated the same way as external candidates, it seems clear from interviews with staff in the two hospitals that internal candidates often have an advantage, particularly if they are known to senior members of staff. It is equally true that internal candidates who had a reputation as being difficult or a troublemaker were rarely successful. All of this suggests that the weight attached to informal recommendations from other managers can be crucial in determining the success or failure of applicants. External candidates, on the other hand, constitute a risk as little is known about them, whereas internal candidates can use both formal and informal networks to create a good impression at interview.

A range of different media are used for advertising posts at Unicorn Trust. For Professions Allied to Medicine, such as physiotherapists, dieticians and occupational therapists, posts are advertised in professional journals. Vacancies for nursing posts are advertised in a range of different places. Higher grades such as G, H and I are likely to be advertised in the *Nursing Times*; grades A–F are more likely to be advertised in the local press if they are not advertised internally. None of the ward sisters responsible for recruitment used the local Council for Racial Equality's newspaper.

Within the Trust there are stringent restrictions on advertising externally. Many of the ward sisters who were interviewed regarded this as a serious problem. One sister at hospital A said:

> It is a bit like interbreeding. We are not going to get new ideas from people who have always worked at this hospital. I wanted to advertise a Health Care Assistant post in the local newspapers and I had to fight with personnel to get it in there. They always refuse to let us advertise outside. I suppose because it costs money, but I can remember when we had about 40 D grade posts and they were all advertised internally and nobody applied for them. Eventually we got them put in the *Nursing Times*. But I am always fighting a running battle to get adverts in the local press. (Ward manager, hospital A)

Another sister at hospital A said:

> There are restrictions on where we can advertise. It takes a lot of pressure to get an advert in the local press and only very occasionally do we get to advertise in the *Nursing Times* and usually only for G grade posts. (Ward manager, hospital A)

The issue of where posts are advertised is one that is pertinent to the promotion of equal opportunities within the Trust. Senior managers have consistently argued that ethnic minority people fail to apply for jobs with them. This is not unrelated to the sorts of media that are used for advertising posts. This point was not missed by an Asian community psychiatric nurse at the inner city mental health team. The team are based in buildings some way from the city centre in an area noted for a high African-Caribbean population, with a number of serious social problems, not least of which is mental health. This member of the inner city mental health team was responsible for setting up a new Asian day centre in the city who argued that:

> We spent a lot of money on advertising the post of team leader at the new Asian day centre because we wanted an Asian person to run the centre, and we had over fifty applications from Asian people most of whom were very well qualified, so if we can do it the Trust can do it. (Asian Community Psychiatric Nurse, Inner City Mental Health Team)

The issue of how people come to hear of jobs within the Trust is of crucial importance. Much depends on how the labour market is defined. As Fevre

(1992) points out, labour markets can extend from formally defined areas such as job centres and personnel offices, to informal areas, such as bars, social clubs and, increasingly, internet sites. Labour markets are not clearly defined fixed areas. Instead, they are dynamic, shifting sites to which not everyone has equal access. For example, if I wished to become the Director General of the BBC it is most unlikely that I would be shortlisted, not simply because of my lack of appropriate skills, but because of my lack of access to the informal networks and channels that prospective candidates for this type of job have.

Discrimination in promotion

Without doubt the area where there is a large gap between ethnic minority staff and White staff at hospital B is promotion. The data from my sample show that ethnic minority workers have applied for promotion far more frequently than their White counterparts and that the patterns of promotion for White and ethnic minority workers are diametrically opposed. There is a particularly noticeable disparity between the White and Black groups in the number of promotions they have made (Table 5.1).

Table 5.1 shows that the percentage of ethnic minority and White applicants who have made one application for promotion are similar (27 per cent and 29 per cent respectively), while 12 per cent of white staff have applied for promotion twice compared to 7 per cent of ethnic minority staff. The most marked disparity is in those staff who have applied for promotion five times with less than 0.5 per cent of the White groups having applied for promotion compared to 13 per cent of ethnic minority staff. Bearing in mind the higher numbers of applications made for jobs by the ethnic minority group shown above, the data in Table 5.2, which shows the actual number of promotions, present a highly polarized picture of promotion chances for the Black and White groups within the directorate of psychiatry.

Table 5.1:   Ethnicity and number of applications for promotion, hospital B

Number of applications	1	2	3	4	5	6	8
White group	29%	12%	7%	2%	0.45%	0.45%	0.45%
Ethnic minority Group	27%	7%	7%		13%		

Table 5.2: Ethnicity and number of promotions, hospital B

	0 promotions	1–4 promotions
White group	24%	76%
Ethnic minority group	75%	25%

There may be a number of factors that may explain the gap between White staff and ethnic minority staff in the promotion process. For example, it is important to note that health care assistants have no route for promotion, unless they undergo nurse training. Nearly all of those ethnic minority health care assistants who were interviewed regarded further nurse training as a considerable potential risk with no guarantee that such investment would pay off. For example, one Mauritian-born health care assistant said:

> I could go on and do nurse training, but I would have to stop work-ing and I would have to think about the financial consequences for my family. Besides, there are a lot of trained nurses who can't find work, so I think I would rather stay here as a health care assistant. It's not great, but at least it's steady. (Mauritian health care assistant, hospital B)

Thus if the majority of ethnic minority nurses were health care assist-ants this would go some way towards explaining the differential rates of promotion. However the data show that only 18 per cent of the ethnic minority sample were in the lower grades. Table 5.3 shows the distribution of ethnic minority staff by grade:

Another factor likely to influence the promotion process is the con-centration of ethnic minority staff on the night shift. As I have men-tioned earlier, opportunities for promotion on night shift are usually fewer than for those who work on day shifts.

The questionnaire data from hospital B show that although there is a small difference, it is not enough to explain the differences in rates of

Table 5.3: Ethnicity and current job grade, hospital B

	Higher	Intermediate	Lower
White group	21%	34%	45%
Ethnic minority group	18%	64%	18%

Table 5.4:   Ethnicity and education

	Ethnic minority group	White group
No formal qualifications	16%	14%
Apprenticeship	2%	–
'O' Level	31%	36%
'A' Level	15%	14%
Diploma	16%	18%
Degree	13%	14%

promotion between white and ethnic minority groups. Of those people who had been successful in promotion 63 per cent of the night shift had been promoted compared to 75 per cent of the day shift. This figure does little to explain the difference in rates of promotion for White and ethnic minority workers shown in Tables 5.4–5.6. Indeed, ethnic minority workers have applied for work more frequently than their White counterparts and have been promoted less.

A key factor that influences promotion for the two groups is their education. The data from the sample show that there is very little difference between the two groups in terms of education. If anything, the ethnic minority group are slightly better qualified. It would, therefore, be very difficult to attribute the differences in promotion to education (see Tables 5.4 and 5.5).

At both hospitals, the practice of acting up is commonplace. It refers to temporary promotion to a higher grade while the incumbent of the post is absent, usually because of illness or maternity leave. All the privileges associated with the higher grade are accorded to the person who is acting up while they are in that position. Acting up can sometimes be a prelude to promotion if the person acting up acquits themselves well at the higher level; success while acting up is often regarded as good indicator of the suitability of a person for promotion. The data in table 5.5 reveal that the ethnic group have acted up more frequently than their White counterparts and would therefore seem to suggest that ethnic minority nurses are experienced in working at higher grades.

Table 5.5:   Ethnicity and length of time acting up, hospital B

	1–3 months	4–11 months	12–18 months
White group	36%	44%	20%
Ethnic minority group	60%	0%	40%

Table 5.6: Ethnicity and training, hospital B

	Have received training since joining Unicorn Trust	Have not received training since joining Unicorn Trust
White group	57%	43%
Ethnic minority group	73%	27%

Another factor that may affect the promotion prospects of the different groups is whether they have received training within the organization which may enhance their promotion prospects. Table 5.6 shows that more of the ethnic minority group have received training than their White counterparts, which, theoretically, should mean that they would be more likely to be promoted.

The research at Unicorn Trust suggests that discrimination, both institutional and otherwise, has a clear impact on the career trajectory of ethnic minority employees. Most ethnic minority nurses within the Trust are located in the less prestigious areas of psychiatry and geriatrics, often in grades where the opportunities for movement up or out of their existing jobs are very limited.

Social closure has affected not only the promotion prospects of ethnic minority nurses but also their recruitment. In the two hospitals where the research was carried out there is evidence to suggest the existence of an extended internal labour market. Internal labour markets can, in some cases, constitute a very real and concrete form of social closure. Fevre (1984) refers to different levels of closure within organizations, arguing that there is a series of concentric rings, with each ring representing a higher form of closure.

At Unicorn Trust it is possible to conceive of employment opportunities in a similar way. The first ring is a form of external closure: external because information about employment opportunities is restricted to those within the Trust, while job-seekers from outside are consciously excluded. The most important consequence of this external closure is that it ensures that the composition of the workforce will rarely change, with all the attendant implications for areas that are predominantly White or female.

The second ring of closure can be termed internal closure. Ethnic minority nurses are excluded from posts near the top of the nursing hierarchy through forms of credentialism. That is, many first-generation migrants who remain in the NHS lack the necessary qualifications to reach the higher nursing grades while for those who are health care assistants there is no career ladder. Assuming that such divisions apply in all areas of nursing it is possible to conceive of these forms of closure representing a vertical form of segregation. The horizontal forms of closure are bisected by horizontal forms of segregation, which relate to the traditional hierarchical divisions within nursing and medicine, which means that areas such as psychiatry and geriatrics become predominantly ethnic minority areas. Further layers of closure cut across these divisions to create a complex picture that explains and helps to determine the subordinate position of different groups within the labour market generally and certain occupational areas (such as nursing) in particular. One of the most significant of these additional layers of division and closure is the concentration of ethnic minority staff on the night shift. The way these divisions are maintained reveals the latent ideology of relations between men and women, ethnic minority and White, which are predicated on notions of inferiority and superiority as well as stereotypical concepts about what the appropriate roles of different socal groups are in the division of labour.

The issue of discipline and control was an underlying theme in interviews with ward managers. Their highest priority is the smooth and efficient running of their ward; indeed it is not hard to understand why such pressures exist given the current climate within the NHS. Employing ethnic minority staff constitutes a risk. Most ward managers are acutely aware that ethnic origin might cause a problem, either because ethnic minority workers might feel aggrieved at perceived discrimination or being passed over for promotion, or because – to use Jenkins' concept of acceptability – they do not fit in. However, the issue of discipline and control goes beyond the acceptability of a candidate. What managers want are people who are easy to manage, people who are pliable. One of the key factors that formed part of a general backdrop to the research at Unicorn Trust was that there had been a consistently higher rate of disciplinary cases involving ethnic minority workers. In a situation where the ideal candidate is one who is not going to cause trouble the consequences for ethnic minority job-seekers are considerable. Clearly, crude racial stereotypes can and do inform the selection decisions of ward managers, since there is evidence from this research that this does indeed happen. However, the issues of control and discipline are ones that have become inextricably intermingled with the construction of racial stereotypes.

There is evidence from the research of very different career patterns for the different ethnic groups within Unicorn Trust. I will go on to explain the role of the Trust's equal opportunities policy in relation to the recruitment and promotion process at the two hospitals where the research was carried out.

Conclusions

Three broad themes emerge from the empirical research. First, how the managerial structure affected the implementation of the equal opportunities policy, the key question being: Are senior managers powerful enough to enforce the equal opportunities policy? An allied question is, how autonomous ward managers are in resisting the policy. The culture of resistance from ward managers is documented in interviews and suggests that while the Trust has a formal commitment to equality, there are many middle and junior managers who are far from committed to it. Second, the competing conceptions of equal opportunity both between and within different groups within the Trust caused confusion about the aims of the policy. The third theme to emerge was the influence that external pressures such as cost-cutting and working within an occupational sphere that is financially contracting had on the development and implementation of the Trust's equal opportunities policy.

The culture of resistance within the Trust is closely related its managerial structure, in which the personnel function is marginalized and ward managers are highly autonomous. The implementation of an equal opportunities policies in a highly bureaucratic and rationalized system in a formalized way has been the subject of considerable sociological scrutiny and has been one of the dominant themes in the sociology of equal opportunities. Indeed, I would argue that the issue of power and autonomy is probably the single most important factor inhibiting the successful implementation the Trust's relatively modest equal opportunity policy. At both hospitals ward managers were responsible for recruitment and promotion. The influence of common-sense stereotypes when recruiting was hard to ignore, despite the attempt of the policy to make the process more objective. Another issue that featured prominently in interviews with ward managers was that of workplace control. It was clear that ward managers felt that the single most important quality for potential applicants was that they were compliant or, in the words of one ward manager, that they did not rock the boat. The controllability of workers was emphasized time and again as highly significant. Where ethnic minority nurses were concentrated it was clear that many ward managers believed (rightly or wrongly) that they constituted a risk. In the previous chapter I described the operation of the disciplinary policy and how ethnic minority nurses had been more frequently disciplined than their White counterparts. This had major implications for their recruitment and promotion. One of the ways in which ward managers sought to bypass the formal equal opportunities policy was through the use of word-of-mouth networks. My research suggests that there were well-established, informal, word-of-mouth recruitment networks. Such networks tend to militate against ethnic minority nurses, particularly as so few of them are in a position of any power.

It is also clear that different groups within the Trust have different conceptions of the term equal opportunities. This has led to a consider-able amount of tension, mistrust and bad faith between senior person-nel managers responsible for the implementation of the policy and a group of ethnic minority workers who have articulated a very vocal anti-racist stance through the formation of a group known as the Black Workers' Forum. There are considerable differences in the subjective understanding of the equal opportunities policy both within and between different interest groups within the Trust. The tensions between these different groups has proved to be a serious obstacle to implementing the Trust's equal opportunities policy. The following chapter will examine the dual concepts of acceptability criteria and suit-ability criteria and how these concepts influence recruitment and pro-motion at Unicorn Trust. More importantly, I will show how the two criteria merge in ways that are related to the spaces within specific labour markets. The discussion and analysis of acceptability and suit-ability necessarily raise questions about the assumptions of employers and employees about the sort of work that is regarded as appropriate for different social groups.

6
The Policy in Practice at Unicorn Trust

Introduction

The equal opportunities policy at Unicorn Trust falls into the liberal category, described by Jewson and Mason (1986b). It emphasizes the importance of the process rather than the outcome. That is, it seeks to ensure that the 'rules' of the competition are scrupulously adhered to. Personnel managers at the Trust have, for example, refused to discuss the use of targets for employing ethnic minority nurses or ancillary workers for two reasons. First, it seems likely that there will be compulsory redundancy; and second, the use of targets is regarded as a hostage to fortune. One of the senior personnel managers argued:

> If we introduce targets and we don't reach them, then it's going to look very bad for us. It will look bad from the point of view of outsiders, it will reflect poorly on personnel managers and there are a group of people in this Trust who would gain a considerable amount of political capital from a failure to reach targets of that kind and I don't want to give them that kind of ammunition.

The policy was introduced in the mid-1980s for a number of different reasons. There had been some high-profile industrial tribunals within the Trust. Although the Trust had not been found guilty of discrimination, much of the publicity surrounding the cases was highly critical. The implementation and development of the policy can be seen partly as a response to the industrial tribunals. Jewson and Mason argue that some of the following are characteristic reasons for the introduction of an equal opportunities policy: a wish to gain a reputation for good practice, 'race relations' problems, CRE investigations, concern with public image, and the possible commercial advantages of such a policy. In the case of Unicorn Trust the poor 'race relations' record within the Trust, and a concern about public image, combined with the more general trend towards equal opportunities per se. The most significant reason for the introduction of the equal opportunities policy seems to have been problems with race relations and the industrial tribunals. Thus it is possible to characterize the development of an equal opportunities policy as a reaction to the problems faced by ethnic minority workers in the recruitment and promotion process. The policy states:

> The [Equal Opportunities] policy is to ensure that fair and non-discriminatory treatment is given by management to all applicants for employment within the organisation, to all existing employees of the organisation and by those employees to each other.

The policy goes on to say:

> Unicorn Trust is committed to a policy of equality of opportunity in its recruitment and employment practices and aims to ensure that employment and progression within it are determined solely by application of objective criteria and personal merit. No applicant or employee, will be treated less favourably than another on the grounds of sex, marital status, race, nationality, ethnic or national origin, colour, creed, religion or disability. Selection procedures will be kept under review to ensure that individuals will be selected, promoted and treated on the basis of their abilities, merits and according to the requirements of the job, and will be given equal opportunity to show their ability...The Director of Personnel is the responsible officer for the Trust, and is responsible for the overall implementation, understanding and review of the policy...training courses covering the equal opportunity policy and related legislation form part of the training provided for newly appointed and existing managers who have not yet had training covering the Trust's equal opportunities policy and its implementation.

The policy was introduced in 1984 and revised on several occasions since then. There are several reasons for this. First, there has been an impetus from the Department of Health, which has sought to improve the equal opportunities policies of health trusts throughout the country:

A working group was set up by the Secretary of State for Health in September 1992, comprised of individuals from both within and outside the NHS, to advise on what action should be taken to address the barriers facing Ethnic minority staff. The group proposed the creation of an action programme to be promulgated, co-ordinated and reviewed by Ministers and NHS Management Executive Directors, and for which chief executives would be accountable. (Programme of Action on Ethnic Minority Staff in the NHS, Equal Opportunities Review, No. 54, March/April 1994, p. 25)

The proposed programme sets out eight goals, of which the most significant is the first:

NHS trusts and health authorities are to include in their business plans a local objective to increase the proportion of Ethnic minority staff in areas and grades where they are under-represented within a specified timescale, until a fair representation is achieved. (Programme of Action on Ethnic Minority Staff in the NHS, Equal Opportunities Review, No. 54, March/April 1994, p. 25)

One other important factor which has led the Trust to review their equal opportunities policy is the publication of a report based on my research findings (the circulation of which was restricted), which showed wide disparities in promotion rates for ethnic minority and White staff.

Personnel versus ward managers: the battle for control of the recruitment process

As in many other organizations there has been a decentralization of responsibility for recruitment and promotion away from the personnel department and towards ward managers. All the ward managers are given two days' training on equal opportunities in recruitment and, after this, the personnel department adopt a very 'hands off' approach, preferring to leave recruitment to ward managers. The equal opportunities training programme was the subject of various comments from ward managers, for example:

Personnel introduced the two-day equal opportunities in selection course in the mid-1980s. Personally, I could not see the point of it. I have been recruiting for years now and I know what to do. It is supposed to be compulsory, but I was quite successful at avoiding it. I kept bumping into the senior personnel manager and she would always nag me about going on the course. Finally, they got me after about five years and I did it. It was a complete waste of time. (Ward manager, hospital A)

Another ward manager argued that the course was largely irrelevant to her needs:

The equal opportunities course is all very well. But we rarely get Black applicants and when we do get a vacancy it is much easier to fill it from within, so it hardly seems that useful. (Ward manager, hospital A)

In an interview with a ward manager at hospital B, the impact of the high numbers of disciplinary cases involving Black staff was described in the following way:

Whether I like it or not there *is* a problem with Black workers and absenteeism in this Trust. There have also been a lot of disciplinary cases involving Black workers, and I have to say that it is always at the back of my mind when I am interviewing ethnic minority candidates. (Ward manager, hospital B)

The managerial structure within the Trust has profound implications for the implementation and development of the policy, as Jewson and Mason note:

The power struggles between different levels of management will have a direct effect on the capacity to implement policy. The relationship between line management and the personnel department is of particular importance. The issue of the involvement of the personnel department in equal opportunities policies is not simply one of the degree to which personnel is willing to extend its responsibilities...rather it is a question of the extent to which the structure of the organisation, and the pattern of power struggles within the establishment, allows, or indeed impels, the personnel department to become involved. (Jewson and Mason 1987, p. 134)

In interviews with personnel managers and line managers within the Trust it became clear that, despite the formal recruitment policy, there were wide variations in practice. In particular, ward managers believed the personnel function to be distant from the day-to-day concerns of ward managers. Ward managers often stated that, as far as they were concerned, the role of personnel in selecting candidates should be limited since the ward managers, knew what and, perhaps more importantly, who they wanted for a particular post. The way in which ward managers sought to control the recruitment process reflects a deeply embedded notion on their part that because of their detailed knowledge of the work task, they are in a unique position to make judgements about candidates. The implementation of an equal opportunities policy overseen by a central personnel function was regarded as both peripheral and irrelevant to the process of selection by many.

Ward managers, in particular, have had radically to rethink the way they perform their jobs because of financial constraints. The Trust has already undergone restructuring to remove layers of middle management and devolve responsibility to ward managers, which has reinforced the autonomy that they already had. The continuing emphasis on performance indicators and financial targets has increased pressure on managers to be more 'efficient'. For many a key part of increasing efficiency is ensuring that they have a team working on their ward that they know they can trust. In an organization with high levels of internal recruitment, this has often meant that ward managers have decided on a candidate for a post long before the interview takes place.

Evidence from the two hospitals suggests that there is a clear difference between the way in which line managers see the recruitment process and the way in which the personnel officers see it. The senior personnel manager provided the following account:

> Line managers draw up the job specification and are sometimes helped by personnel managers to write it, often so that there is some element of self-selection in terms of experience and qualifications. Skills may appear in the ad and the job description is also drawn up in conjunction with personnel. Some managers prefer to use a person spec., others will stick to a job description. A person spec. has three elements to it, namely qualifications, experience, and skills and attributes. A shortlist is drawn up from these three criteria. There is a two week closing date. We set up a job file which contains information on the number of application forms sent out, the number received and the ethnic returns if they are completed. All the information is sent to the manager concerned who will draw up a shortlist using the Trust-wide stated criteria and any others which they feel are relevant. There are six standard criteria which get a yes, no or inferred next to them. We will then call the shortlisted candidates to interview. We make it a practice never to have it conducted by one

person. There are always two people at least who will interview. The interview should take place within two weeks of the ad going in and the unsuccessful applicants will get standard regret letters.

The recruitment process was described very differently by a ward manager at hospital A:

> Of course, people know how to get round it [the equal opportunities policy]...what usually happens is that if there is a vacancy they often have someone in mind for that post; they know people who would be good in that particular job. It makes the recruiting process more difficult because you have to go through the process formally, to show that you have been fair. But you end up taking on the person who you thought would be good in the first place, but you have to be seen to be doing it correctly. (Ward manager, hospital A)

Access to, and knowledge of, the labour market are crucial factors which help determine who gets what jobs. Such knowledge and access, if restricted, help to create areas of the labour market which are socially closed to those without the necessary knowledge and information. The importance of informal networks within the hospital was emphasized by one of the few African-Caribbean managers, at hospital B:

> If you take the way they run the bank it shows you a lot about how this place works. If a ward manager is short they basically ring their friends and ask them if they want some work. My husband who is a nurse did some bank work here and his name is on the list, and there were times when I have been telephoned at home by a ward manager saying that they can't get a bank nurse and that they have tried every-one, and my husband would be sitting beside me and I would say, have you gone right through the list? And they would say yes, and then I would say well have you got as far as L because he is sitting next to me and he can come in if you want him. Then there would be an embarrassed silence and they would say, yes send him in. It all goes on in the social club here, that's where they all go boozing and the make their contacts there. (Caribbean manager, hospital B)

Many of the staff at hospital B believed the interview process to be little more than a rubber stamp on preferred candidates and that the equal opportunities policy was a symbolic commitment to equality. This anonymous questionnaire response from hospital B is indicative of a wider feeling among other members of staff, particularly those of minority origin:

> Jobs go to people who please managers. They are not all advertised and there are ways of getting people out or demoralizing them.

Other questionnaire responses revealed similar views:

> My observations and experiences are that while one or two Black staff have made senior management jobs, racial discrimination where possible in favour of White applicants does take place. Senior managers still feel safe with Black staff confined to specialist areas through the process of marginalization and are not as comfortable with senior Black staff in mainstream areas.

> The equal opportunities policy cannot tackle individual managers' prejudices and preferences. If a manager wants a particular individual for a post, interviewing makes no difference. Personnel should be more stringent in applying equal opportunities for interviews.

The above quotes illustrate the way in which staff who were prepared to respond perceive the policy. There was widespread cynicism among nurses at the lower end of the hierarchy in relation to the equality policy. Numerous ethnic minority workers at hospital B expressed the belief that the Trust's equal opportunities policy had little bearing on the way in which recruitment and promotion processes operated. One African-Caribbean, staff nurse B, said:

> There are occasions when a job is advertised and the interview is a bit of a farce. You know a job has to be advertised, but they are just going through the motions because the ward manager already has someone in mind for the post. (African-Caribbean nurse, hospital B)

A Ugandan Asian nurse who works at hospital B had a more phlegmatic view of the way in which line managers sought to manipulate the recruitment process:

> It happens in all areas of work, wherever you are. They have to go through the motions to make it look fair. (Asian nurse, hospital B)

A Chinese community psychiatric nurse who works at hospital A made some interesting observations about the discretion ward managers have over the outcome of the selection process:

> I have worked for six different health authorities as I have followed my husband around the country so I know what conditions are like...I can see what the selection process is like from the other side because I have been a ward manager myself. There are two ways you can look at appointments, first you can think I will appoint someone who I know will get on with everyone and be part of the team, which is like closing ranks. Or you can go for the outsider. Most of the panels which I have been a part of have had a nursing officer, a consultant and myself. On all the occasions I have sat on those panels I try to favour the outsider because they are just the same as I was and if you don't appoint new people nothing ever changes. Most people here are not very open minded, the ward managers just want control over their staff. (Chinese community psychiatric nurse, hospital A)

Many of the staff at both hospitals believe that ward managers exercise considerable discretion over the recruitment process and that the Trust's equal opportunities policy is for cosmetic purposes only:

> The ward managers are so powerful. In the old days we had a nursing officer who was attached to the ward who did all the interviewing, which was much better because it was impartial. But now ward managers seem to be able to do what they want. It is obvious because they have their own favourites and they are always the ones that get the jobs. And there is so much of it going on, I have seen it happen, they just do what they want. There are a lot of people grumbling about it, but they won't say anything because they are so afraid. There is one particular ward here where it is very bad. (African Caribbean nurse, hospital B)

Since ward managers in the Trust have considerable power to determine the outcome of interviews and to select candidates who will 'fit' with their view of what is both suitable and acceptable the question arises, how are their decisions justified? Or, how are they able to resist pressures from personnel to adopt procedures that are more likely to produce egalitarian outcomes? Many of the ward managers at hospital

A believed the role of personnel to be, at most, advisory. Many felt themselves to be the best possible judge of a candidate's suitability for a post and that the role of personnel should be marginal. The following remarks from interviews with ward managers at hospital A outline how they see their role in the recruitment process:

> I have to work with whoever is appointed so I believe that it's right that I have the most important say over who we recruit.
>
> It should be central, they should be able to recruit their own staff and they know the ward and they know the sort of people they want.
>
> Ward managers should do everything in the recruitment process, I do. I write the advertisement, I do the shortlisting and I do the interviewing.
>
> It should be a fundamental one, the ward manager must have the final say, because they are going to be working with the person they appoint.
>
> They should have a paramount role...the Sister should have a big say in who gets recruited because they know who will be right for the job, they know the sort of skills they will be looking for, they also know the team that they are working with and be aware of the fact that any new staff have to fit with that team, so you must make some assessment of an applicants personality which I know is very subjective. But you have to use your judgement as to who will fit in with the team.

Many of the ward managers were critical of the role of personnel in the recruitment process, for example:

> Personnel should be there to support ward managers. They need to be much more active. We have trouble getting hold of people from personnel, which makes me think there are not enough of them.
>
> The role of personnel should be minimal, emphatically minimal. Trying to get hold of them is impossible, they are never there. There are times when it is useful to have someone from personnel sitting in on an interview, but I have had great difficulty in getting hold of anyone. I am not sure I know what their role really is. In fact, I am not sure if *they* know what their role really is.

They should be there to give us advice. Unfortunately, we don't get a very good response from personnel as they seem to be very stretched. It seems like the guts of the personnel department has been taken out.

Personnel's role should be not much more than an advisory role, co-ordinating dates, times, checking contracts, and so on.

It is important to emphasize that the recruitment process is one in which there may be several different outcomes. The outcome of the process is contingent upon a range of different factors which include the way a post is advertised, the criteria used to select and shortlist candidates, the way in which the interview panel is constituted, and on occasion the predetermined decision of an employer to discriminate in favour of one or other of the candidates.

Although formally the personnel function has control over the recruitment process it is clear that within Unicorn Trust line managers have a high degree of autonomy in the recruitment and promotion process. The role of personnel within the Trust is to ensure that the procedure as specified in the equality policy is adhered to and that recruiters are able to justify their selections in ways that fit with the aims of the policy. However, it was clear from interviews with ward managers that they regarded any attempts by personnel officers to enforce the equality policy as 'unnecessary interference'. As other writers have noted, line managers are often able to circumvent formal procedures and are able to manipulate the outcomes of interviews in a way that discriminates against non-White workers and women workers. Thus, having an equal opportunities policy is no guarantee of equality of outcome. Underlying the decisions of line managers are common-sense assumptions about ethnic minority workers, based on their experience of working in a specific organizational context. In the case of hospital B there are two significant factors which may affect the way in which they are perceived by line managers responsible for promotion and recruitment. First, there have been a number of well-publicized disciplinary cases which have been 'race'-related. Figures from the questionnaire show that ethnic minority workers have been disciplined more than their White counterparts. It is possible that line managers at hospital B have come to regard ethnic minority workers as potential or actual troublemakers, something that is likely to affect their decisions about the suitability of ethnic minority candidates for promotion. Given the emphasis that line managers place on 'not rocking the boat', the issue of discipline may have profound effects for ethnic minority workers in the Trust.

Unicorn Trust and Industrial Tribunal cases

There have been two very high-profile Industrial Tribunal cases which have had considerable effects within the Trust. In the UK the Industrial Tribunal is one of the main methods available to ethnic minority groups to gain legal redress in cases of racial discrimination. The Tribunal consists of a panel of three judges, one of whom is legally qualified while the other two have experience as employers or as union representatives. These Tribunals assess cases of racial discrimination in employment. They have powers to compel employers to compensate individuals who have experienced racial discrimination. Apart from this, Tribunals have no other powers to sanction employers or organisations are found guilty of discrimination. For many employers the threat of negative publicity attached to such cases is a serious enough penalty in itself. Banton (1994) argues that when an employer is found guilty of racial discrimination it sends a clear message to other employers that they must review their own employment policies. It should also be mentioned that standard of proof required to establish guilt at an Industrial Tribunal is different from that in the criminal courts. In criminal cases guilt must be established 'beyond reasonable doubt'; for an Industrial Tribunal the standard of proof to establish guilt is 'on the balance of probabilities'.

There are, however, a number of factors that may deter ethnic minorities from going to an Industrial Tribunal. Among the most obvious is awareness that discrimination has actually taken place. Even if individuals are aware of behaviour that is discriminatory, they may be unaware of the legal processes for redress.

At Unicorn Trust the most controversial case that went to an Industrial Tribunal involved a community psychiatric nurse of Asian origin. He was a member of the Inner City Mental Health Team who took the then health authority to the Tribunal alleging discrimination. He describes the case thus:

> I applied four times for a job following my Registered General Nurse training in 1984 as a charge nurse [equivalent to ward manager] and I was rejected four times. I was quite distressed and angry – it was a definite example of discrimination in my mind. There was no justification for it. It was not that the four people who got the job should not have, they all had the right qualifications and experience, but so did I and I did not get it. I went through the grievance procedure, in fact I was the first person to take the health authority to Tribunal. The Tribunal felt that there had not been discrimination and that the decisions that

the interview panel had made were correct. It was a perverse decision. The Tribunal were very critical of the health authority but they concluded that no racial discrimination had taken place. It chewed me up.

The aftermath of the Tribunal did, however, cause some changes within the then health authority:

The health authority got criticized and the criticism brought about some changes. It was also a big issue in the media, and the health authority had to push through an equal opportunities policy. Although I personally lost, the Commission for Racial Equality and the local Race Equality Council all began to focus on the health authority. Their pressure brought some changes and did a lot of good.

The Tribunal clearly had a dramatic personal effect. In an informal discussion with a personnel officer at the Trust she described the way this nurse changed after the Tribunal decision:

It really radicalized him. I don't know this for sure, but my feeling is that he was incensed by the Tribunal decision and after that he became quite aggressively anti-racist. I think it was then that the Black Workers Forum started. The Black Workers Forum have been such a nuisance to this Trust. They are always trying to gain the maximum political capital out of the smallest event, simply to put pressure on the Trust. He found an ally in a newly appointed West Indian community psychiatric nurse. They get away with blue murder and they have *never* been disciplined, all because the Director of Personnel wants to avoid an embarrassing 'situation' arising with them alleging that they have been disciplined on the basis of their race.

The existence of an articulate, radical, anti-racist, group who were openly critical of the Trust and who appeared, at least, to be exempt from the usual forms of discipline served only to heighten the perception among White workers that ethnic minority workers were treated favourably by management.

Equal opportunities and bad faith

The history of events at Unicorn Trust undoubtedly led to bad faith on the part of ethnic minority workers. There was a widespread belief among them that there was tacit acceptance of discrimination within the Trust and that tackling discrimination was a low priority for middle and senior managers. At the same time, White nurses and workers within the Trust frequently expressed the view that ethnic minority nurses were 'fireproof' and could do no wrong. The gap between the perceptions of each group by the other could hardly have been wider.

The existence of bad faith can be understood as a social conflict in which expectations of different social groups are not met. The expectations of different groups are, of course, subjectively defined by the participants in a conflict who often have a predetermined agenda. In the case of the equal opportunities policy at Unicorn Trust there are two clearly recognizable groups: ethnic minority workers and White workers. The ethnic or 'racial' dimension to the conflict could not have been more apparent or sensitive. What unites almost all the ethnic minority workers in the Trust is that they have first-hand experience of racism, whether they are managers, professional psychiatrists or nursing auxiliaries. This is a clear example of the way in which race or ethnicity cuts across class boundaries.

Ethnic minority nurses and workers frequently referred to the equal opportunities policy as little more than lip service, or a paper commitment, for the social reality of the situation for them is that discrimination persists, albeit in a covert form. White workers who were interviewed tended to perceive the equal opportunities policy as a form of political correctness gone mad. Some of the White nurses and other workers who were interviewed regarded the policy with open contempt. A number of White workers who took part in the research felt that the equal opportunities policy conferred preferential status on ethnic minority workers. For example, some White workers seemed to think that ethnic minority workers were exempt from disciplinary procedure because managers at the Trust were anxious about being accused of racism.

The mood of suspicion and mistrust has not been improved by highly publicized Industrial Tribunal cases, which have reinforced the view prevalent among many ethnic minority workers in the Trust that equal opportunities is paid lip service only. With few ethnic minority workers at senior levels and little evidence that the Trust is actively trying to promote equality of opportunity, the scepticism of ethnic minority workers in the Trust is understandable. The mood of many is summed up by a Chinese nurse at the hospital A:

> If you ask managers about a particular issue they always have an answer for it. They always say that 'something is in progress'. Of course, you never get to see the end-result. If you ask about the

equal opportunities policy they show you some glossy brochure but nothing ever gets done. (Chinese community psychiatric nurse, hospital A)

The power of ward managers

While ward managers clearly have considerable influence over the recruitment process, they also have the ability to make the everyday life of subordinates pleasant or unpleasant. The extent to which a ward manager can make a person's life difficult is illustrated in an interview with Chinese-born community psychiatric nurse. When asked if she had any personal experience of discrimination she replied:

I have worked in other health authorities and I had never felt that there had been discrimination. Sometimes you would get people trying to take advantage of you, but if you stand up to it then there is no problem with it, once people know that you won't take it, you get their respect. I would like to stress that Unicorn Trust as a whole have been fine, it was just that one manager, my last one, treated me much less favourably than others because of my race. I think he was frightened of me, I was the only foreigner in the unit. But I am sure that it was because I was not White that treated me less favourably. I thought to myself, if you are going to make a claim about this man then you are going to have to have evidence of the sorts of things he has doing. So I collected my evidence and took it to my union. They said they thought I had a strong case, but that they would prefer to deal with it informally rather than make it official. I agreed and took the case to the manager above the person who was the cause of the problem and he kept him in check and the problems stopped. (Chinese community psychiatric nurse, hospital A)

What makes this case so interesting is the pressure exerted on the complainant to keep the matter informal. When asked about the role of the union in the case, she replied:

I did approach them, but I got the impression that they really were not that interested.

Unicorn Trust, clearly sensitive to matters of racial discrimination, has, according to other ethnic minority workers, a preference for dealing with such matters informally. Problems then inevitably arise if harassment or unfair treatment continues, precisely because there is no formal record of it, as happened in this case:

> The problems started up again as soon as that senior manager left. The replacement was a woman who knew my ward manager from another health authority, and her line was basically, 'If you shut up I will make sure that your ward manager does his job properly and does not bother you.' That was OK, but then she left and was replaced by someone who did not want to get involved. (Chinese community psychiatric nurse, hospital A)

This case illustrates the extent to which informal networks can be used to put pressure on people. It also suggests that attempts to deal with harassment informally are largely unsuccessful. A similar example of hostility from white colleagues is explained by an Asian community psychiatric nurse, now working with the inner city mental health team:

> All my experiences of racism have been at hospital B...I have met people who would not even speak to me because they felt so uncomfortable around me. On the ward where I was working there was a charge nurse who was constantly trying to catch me out. She felt threatened by me. When I challenged her about it she said that it had nothing to with the fact that I was Asian. She changed after I had confronted her, but she had tried to create trouble for me. The ward manager above her was sympathetic to me and asked me if I wanted to take it any further, but it was all very formal and by the book and I knew that if I made a complaint, she would simply deny that her behaviour was racially motivated. No one ever says 'yes I am a racist'...if you take a case of racial discrimination forward, it is never treated seriously; you are always told that it is your imagination. (Asian community psychiatric nurse, Inner City Mental Health Team)

The constitution of the interview panel

The way in which an interview panel is constituted can have a real effect on the outcome of the recruitment process. The question of who has the casting vote on a panel is, of course, of some significance. The senior personnel manager at hospital A explained the constitution of the interview panel thus:

The panel will always include the manager who the person will be working with. We are trying to devolve responsibility to line managers as much as possible and helping them to deal with personnel issues. Notes of the interview will always be kept for reference. The candidates will be graded on their performance and then the panel will have a group discussion to select the candidate. The line manager will always have absolute authority in choosing the person for the job, although the candidate that is selected is almost always a consensus selection, it very rarely comes to the line manager stating their preference for a candidate. We emphasize that selection is a panel decision, so that if there is an Industrial Tribunal then it is the panel that go before the tribunal. One of the panel will look at the references for the candidates before the interviews so that questions can be asked, then the rest of the panel will read the references after they have made their decision hopefully to confirm their choice. We do not place too much emphasis on references, but we never appoint without references even if it is only a verbal reference...at the end of the process we look at the ethnic returns. Only personnel managers see the ethnic returns not the line managers. The figures then get collated. (Senior Personnel Manager, Unicorn Trust)

Ethnic minority staff at hospital B frequently expressed concern that the interview panels rarely contained any ethnic minority representatives. In an interview with a community psychiatric nurse, the problems of having more ethnic minority staff on the panel were alluded to:

Sure it will help, but it won't sort the problem and doing that imposes pressure on staff who are ethnic minority, you know, we still have a job to do, and it is very time-consuming to get involved with interviews. Of course, not all the ethnic minority people share the same dialect or meanings in their speech – people have a different understanding. There is also the problem that some African Caribbean and Asian people have rejected their own culture because they see it as the culture of failure. It is like that old thing: a Black slavemaster will always whip harder than a White one. But it is still a check on the interview process. The panels I have been on have been pretty good, but then I react if someone says something and I don't mince words. The interviews I have been involved with have all followed the process very well and I have seen some successes for Black people. But White people will always tone down what they think, but then later after work, down at the pub, you can hear them talk about Pakis and niggers, they just don't say it at work. (Asian community psychiatric nurse, Inner City Mental Health Team)

Other non-White workers at hospital B have made similar points. One in particular, stated:

In my own opinion, I think we need to look at the interview panel. Usually it is not well constituted, so, for example, if there is an interview panel of three people at least one of them should be of minority origin. It will help things along, no question about it. (African ward manager, hospital B)

Some of the non-White workers at hospital B remain less optimistic about the possibility of change:

I don't think the system will change. I just don't know what will change it, because whoever is at the top wants to hang on to that position and it is difficult to promote fresh interests. But it is more difficult for Black managers because they have to prove themselves not just once but again and again. (African-Caribbean nurse, hospital B)

In light of the absence of ethnic minority workers within the Trust and the reluctance of line managers to cede power to personnel function, it seems unlikely that the constitution of the interview panel will change significantly.

Aspects of acceptability

The question of the criteria that are used for selection is discussed in some detail by Jenkins (1986). His division between suitability and acceptability provides sociologists with a useful conceptual tool to describe the mechanisms that allow discrimination to flourish.

The most common method of selection for a job is the interview. It is in the institutional interview that both the suitability and acceptability of candidates is determined. The interview is a social situation which has a number of characteristics of note. First, there are usually two or more people involved and the roles of interviewer and interviewee are unmistakable and clearly delineated. Second, the participants in the interview do not possess equal status, because the interviewer has the power to determine the distribution of scarce resources (in this case, a job). Third, the interviewer has the power to define what the necessary social and cultural skills are for a particular job. The question of cultural competence is often crucial in determining the success or failure of a candidate. It has been argued that such judgements are prone to ethnocentric bias:

> It is not simply the case that Black workers are disadvantaged by their own cultural repertoires or lack of native competence. Given the power relationship which exists between the two sides of the interview, it is more a question of the refusal of the interviewer to accord legitimacy to, or validate, the culture and practices of the interviewee than anything else. This is another dimension of the routine ethnocentricity of the selection process. It is the power of the interviewer to define the situation and to make that definition count, which transforms ethnocentricity into racism in this context. (Jenkins 1986, pp. 128–9)

The question of what criteria are used to sift applicants is crucial, and even more so in a depressed labour market where employers can expect large numbers of applicants, often with broadly similar qualifications. Both Jenkins (1986) and Collinson et al. (1990) refer to two types of criteria employers use: acceptability criteria and suitability criteria. Suitability criteria refer to the skills, experience and qualifications that are relevant to a particular job. Acceptability criteria refer to qualities that are less easily quantified. Jenkins suggests that they include attitude to work, personality, self-presentation and, most significantly, the ability to fit in with other workers.

> Although the specific content of notions of acceptability will obviously alter with the nature of the job, its position within the class hierarchy of organisations and occupations and the nature of the organisation concerned, the principle of a threshold of suitability, beyond which criteria of acceptability come into play, is common to all job recruitment. The emphasis throughout, in all notions of acceptability, is upon the predictable and reliable person who will not cause management any problems. (Jenkins 1986, p. 49)

It is possible to argue that acceptability criteria are more significant than suitability criteria. Indeed, in an organization like the Unicorn Trust being able to fit into a team is considered to be one of the most important criteria for a successful candidate. Given the importance of 'fitting in' customs that do not conform to what is acceptable are at best regarded as curious and at worst as justification for denying a person a job:

Some of them [ethnic minority nurses] have got a funny outlook on life, not exactly taboos, but that sort of thing. I used to work with a nurse who was Black and he used to roll up the sleeves of people who had died to let their spirit free because he thought that their spirit got trapped up their sleeve. It is a bit strange. (White nurse, hospital B)

As Beishon et al. note:

Non-formalisation of selection criteria is rare, but informal criteria can be hidden beneath formal procedures...where this occurred it is possible that informal selection criteria may play a role in reproducing the relative disadvantage of Ethnic minority nursing staff...We did not find that employers prioritised equal opportunities or race related training as it affected recruitment and selection. We found little evidence of employers' commitment to recommendations as outlined in the CRE's code of practice for the elimination of racial discrimination and the promotion of equality of opportunity in employment (1994), or to the NHS management executive's publication, 'Ethnic Minority Staff in the NHS a Programme of Action'. (1993, p. 52)

It is easy to imagine occasions where people may not be quite so accepting of different cultures. In situations where there are large numbers of candidates with similar qualifications it is likely that acceptability criteria will prove to be much more important. Ward managers at hospital A have tended to reinforce Jenkins' hypothesis that employers will always prefer the predictable and reliable candidate. In an interview with one ward manager at hospital A this was made abundantly clear:

All the ward sisters have had their two days of training with a senior personnel manager so we know all about equal opportunities. We make sure we ask all the candidates the same questions which makes the system fairer and there is a points system and the person with the highest number of points usually gets the job. If two people have the same number of points then I look for the person who is going to fit in with the team best, someone who won't rock the boat, my senior staff nurse and I usually know who to appoint. (Ward manager, hospital A)

The importance of 'fitting in with the team' was emphasized repeatedly by ward managers at the Trust. For example, one ward manager stated:

The ward manager has to make a judgement about how well the person will fit in with the team. There is no room for candidates who you don't think will get on with the other people in the team. (Ward manager, hospital A)

The significance of acceptability criteria was underlined by a ward manager who argued that candidates could be employed without the necessary qualifications, provided they undertook on-the-job training. Therefore, the sole criterion on which they had been appointed were whether or not they were 'acceptable':

We recently had two senior posts which we couldn't fill so we recruited two people at a lower grade and gave them in-house training and within a year we had trained them to the required standard. (Ward manager, hospital A)

A similar situation arose with one of the workers at the Inner City Mental Health Team:

I would not have got the job if the selection process had been run by Unicorn Trust. They constantly stress the necessity of formal qualifications, so even if you have the relevant experience and skills you will not get the job unless you have got the qualification. When I got this job I did not have all the formal qualifications that were needed, but I got them through on-the-job training. So there are ways and means of employing people. (Asian community psychiatric nurse, Inner City Mental Health Team)

The above case is of particular interest since one of the key aspects of acceptability criteria for working in the inner city mental health team appears to be membership of a ethnic minority group and a clear commitment to anti-racism. Indeed, one personnel manager argued that such appointments were controversial:

I was not very happy about that appointment. She did not have the right qualifications, but it was not my decision. It was decision of the people at the ICMHT and I am sure that they wanted an Asian candidate for that post regardless of their qualifications. (Senior Personnel Manager, Unicorn Trust)

A charge nurse at hospital B made the following observation:

> The criteria for a job are often weighted towards having formal qualifications at the expense of experience, and at interview experience is not taken into account. Experience is incredibly important. Although a candidate may have all the formal qualifications and may appear more knowledgeable you can never beat experience. Let me give you an example. When I first started nursing I was on a ward where there was an elderly lady who was very ill. At the beginning of the shift the charge nurse told me to take a look at her and see if she was OK, which I did but she seemed fine. I couldn't find anything wrong with her, but the charge nurse told me to keep an eye on her. So later on that day we did a lot of tests, you know, pulse, blood test, respiration, everything and she seemed normal. Just as I was going off the ward at about 5.15 that evening she had a massive stroke and died. So what I am saying is that all the formal qualifications in the world do not give you that sort of experience and you cannot compare one with the other. (Charge nurse, hospital B)

The question of what criteria should be applied to candidates is a matter that has caused considerable division within the Trust. Members of the Inner City Mental Health Team have argued for relaxing formal criteria and appointment on the basis that a group or groups are under-represented. There is a very clear division between the radical policy advocated by members of the team and the stress on formal qualifications by personnel managers. Attempts to introduce a more radical policy are described by a member of the team:

> There were people who argued strongly for removing all the Community Psychiatric Nurse requirements because they ruled out a lot of Black people and that most Black people were not worried about credentials anyway. Others disagreed violently and argued that their Asian clients were worried about the credentials of the nurses who visited them and that they were right to demand that nurses should be fully trained.

One of the key aspects of acceptability that emerged during the research was the question of English language. It was referred to frequently by other ethnic minority workers at hospital B, for example:

There is a big cultural barrier. What I mean is that when you have a Black applicant and a White applicant you often find that the White candidate is more fluent and more open than the Black candidate. You get short answers from the Black candidate which means that you don't learn a lot about them. If you ask a Black candidate 'where were you born?' and they say Ghana, it is very different from asking a White candidate 'where were you born?' and them saying 'London, but my parents are from Manchester and my wife is from Southampton'. People should be aware of cultural differences and probe Black candidates more; they should be able to ask rigorous questions. (Asian community psychiatric nurse, hospital B)

Other ethnic minority workers at hospital B made reference to the question of language:

The main problem is language. It does not matter how many degrees you have got behind you, you need to be able to convey what you are trying to say clearly, there seems to be a problem with the way Black applicants come across at interview and the way they are interpreted. (Asian staff nurse, hospital B)

There is also the problem that a lot of ethnic minority staff do not do themselves justice at interview. I think it's to do with culture. Ethnic minority people just tend to give short answers to questions and they don't come over very well at interview. A lot of it is to do with schools. If you are not encouraged to push yourself at school, then you just end up doing any old thing. People don't perform at the level they are capable of. Like I say, they don't come over in interviews very well because they don't elaborate on their answers, therefore people are kept back. (African-Caribbean nurse, hospital B)

Let's just say that it [employment] is not as equal as I would like it to be. You get treated well enough on the surface, but behind the public face it is a different matter. You get the feeling that you are not the same as White people, you are not one of their own. Take recruitment and interviewing, for example, ethnic minorities don't come across very well at interview. Maybe it is because in some cases their English is not very good. It is a cultural thing and English people seem to have an advantage. (Vietnamese nurse, hospital B)

A community psychiatric nurse expressed similar concerns about culture and language in interviews:

> There is a big cultural gap between the panel and ethnic minority people. Ethnic minority people may apply, but they do not get the job or they are not shortlisted. If the criteria are strict enough and a person is saying the right things then there could be progress, but the will needs to be there. It is an issue of language. I could know all the right words, but I do not know some of the nuances of grammar, or the right way of synthesizing sentences because I come from a different culture. Whereas with two White people at interview all that is unspoken, they have grown together culturally, they are in tune if you like. Sometimes it comes down to understanding the question. For example, compare the way Americans speak English to the way the English speak English. Americans will tell you straight, exactly what they think. Britain is somewhat different. There is a roundabout way of saying things so that you do not offend someone and there is a lot of non-verbal communication which is taken for granted and is tied up with the culture. This country is very Americanized, through the media and so on, and with all the influence of America there are still fundamental misunderstandings between the British and Americans. So imagine a situation where you come from a culture that has no impact on Britain. It is a hundred times harder to communicate. For example, Asian people, well at least those born, say, in India or Pakistan, will tell you their history before they actually answer your question. If you ask them, how do you like living in Oxford? They will say, 'Oh, we don't have relations here so we are not very happy' or 'We have lived in Cardiff and Cardiff was better because so and so'. They won't just say they don't like it here, they have to give you some history. It is just a particular way of speaking and explaining things that is different, and that sometimes lets them down when it comes to the interview panel. The panel think, I don't want to know all this, all I want to know is can they give an injection? So there needs to be a way of coping with that. (Asian community psychiatric nurse, hospital B)

The question of verbal competence was frequently mentioned by staff at both hospitals. Ward managers referred to the importance of speaking the Queen's English. Reasons for the stress on language competence include being able to understand instructions and communicating with other workers, patients and the public, all of which are closely tied up with managerial control. Thus speaking The Queen's English could be seen as another aspect of fitting in, that is, of being an ideal worker who does what they are told. Few ward managers were actually able to give any objective indication of how they measured a candidate's ability to speak English, indeed, what is good English seems a highly problematic concept. What a particular ward manager defines as good English seems likely to be bound up with their own cultural expectations that may or may not be ethnocentric. As Jenkins points out:

> The whole notion of linguistic competence, is largely a matter of the judgements of significant others...by their very nature they tend to be ethnocentric and, on occasions highly personal. (Jenkins 1986, p. 72)

In many cases the interviewer is likely to be White and has the power to define what is good English. Such a definition seems likely be closely linked to ethnocentric and idiosyncratic conceptions of 'good English'. Thus any deviation from their own definition of good English may be defined as not up to the required standard.

The question of what constitutes acceptability is one that may have considerable bearing on ethnic minority candidates. In an occupational area that is predominantly White, as hospital A is, it is possible that one of the key elements of acceptability is being White. Given the reputation which ethnic minority workers seem to have acquired within the Trust, it is probable that they are perceived by line managers as potentially disruptive. When the reputation of ethnic minority workers is combined with the emphasis on candidates who will 'not rock the boat' it seems that ethnic minority candidates face a substantial disadvantage in the recruitment process. Jenkins makes a similar point about the recruitment of ethnic minority workers in mainly White occupational areas:

> The selection criteria used in the recruitment of manual and routine non-manual workers will tend to be informally specified, allowing for idiosyncratic, inconsistent and implicit decision making which may be difficult to account for after the event...to take a concrete example, as in the following quotation from the personnel officer of a public sector organisation, it is clear what the implications of such informality may be for the Black job seeker.
>
> I can recall sitting in an interview situation where there has been a Black who has been the best candidate and you get this sort of attitude, 'the blokes won't like it'. Sometimes there is an accepted sort of silent

acceptance that you'll share the same attitudes, 'you know we don't want him'. Sometimes, for example, that candidate will be ignored and they will discuss someone else instead. (Jenkins 1986, p. 131)

Notions of acceptability do not develop in a vacuum. At Unicorn Trust management notions of what constituted a 'steady and reliable' worker were very clearly related to the way in which acceptability criteria affected the decisions made by managers responsible for recruitment. The production and reproduction of acceptability criteria takes place through the decisions that managers make and through the processes that reinforce their power to make discriminatory decisions. In the case of Unicorn Trust the sorts of assumptions outlined by Jenkins clearly inform selection outcomes as well as other ethnocentric assumptions which influence the selection process in spite of the formal equal opportunities policy.

Ethnic monitoring

Ethnic monitoring is regarded by many as an integral part of an equal opportunities policy. In the UK the Commission for Racial Equality make the point that while ethnic monitoring is not a legal requirement of the Race Relations Act it is impossible to make judgements about progress in terms of recruitment and attracting ethnic minority applicants without some form of measurement. The CRE suggest that ethnic monitoring should have three distinct strands:

1. Obtain information on the ethnic origin of their employees and applicants, and add the data to their personnel records.
2. Examine, by ethnic origin, the distribution of employees across the organization, and the success rates of candidates for jobs, training, transfer and promotion, according to the type of job, grade, department, section, shift, category, etc.
3. Assess, regularly, whether the distribution of staff and the success rates of applicants reflect equal opportunities or reveal possible racial discrimination.

At Unicorn Trust managers' attitudes towards ethnic monitoring appeared to be ambivalent. Figures on the ethnic origin of applicants were collected regularly but the information was not used to inform any changes in policy. Moreover, while the ethnic monitoring that took place could be described as basic, there was no systematic use of the data to examine the effect of the equality policy or to examine movement and promotion within the organization. Indeed, the Trust has been very sensitive about who has access to the information on ethnic monitoring. One of the reasons for this is that personnel managers believe that the statistics may exacerbate feelings of disenchantment among ethnic minority workers within the Trust. As the Black Workers Forum have consistently alleged that discrimination is widespread within the Trust, it seems possible that the figures may support such accusations. More radical members of the Black Workers Forum believe that the refusal of the Trust to circulate the figures on ethnic monitoring is in itself prima facie evidence of discrimination.

Ethnic monitoring at Unicorn Trust is well developed for the process of applications in recruitment. Every quarter statistics are compiled from each directorate showing the ethnic origin of applicants, the ethnic origin of those shortlisted for posts and the ethnic origin of successful applicants. The figures are discussed and analysed every quarter at the Equal Opportunities Action Group of the Trust, usually chaired by the head of personnel. In an interview with an African-Caribbean woman manager who is part of the EOAG, the way the statistics were dealt with proved interesting:

> Every meeting it's just the same. We look at the statistics and they always tell us the same thing, that we fail to attract ethnic minorities to apply for jobs with us. The figures are consistently low. And every meeting they draw a veil over those figures. I was at one meeting of the Equal Opportunities Action Group and it started, as usual, with a discussion of the figures and then the chairman said, 'Well, nothing unusual there, let's move on to the next item'. I couldn't believe it. I said, 'Hold on, is that all we have to say on the statistics? I mean they are always the same, don't we need to look at why that might be the case?' The chairman replied by saying that we didn't have time to discuss it. (African-Caribbean manager, hospital B)

During my research at the Trust it was not possible to gain access to the data that had been collected on ethnic monitoring as senior managers denied access.

Efficiency and equality

Throughout the research at Unicorn Trust it became apparent that there was a tension between the management style or culture and the aims of achieving equity in recruitment and selection. The dominant managerial paradigm within the Trust is that of New Public Management (NPM). As a management style this has been discussed in detail elsewhere (for a particularly useful discussion see Pollit et al. 1991 and Hood 1991). None the less, it may be helpful to outline some of the key aspects of NPM as it is widespread in many public sector employers in both the UK and the US. As a style of management NPM typically employs performance indicators, parsimony in resource use, producing more for less, the use of internal markets and competitive tendering. Overall, it is a results-driven management style, in which the underlying goal is always to improve efficiency. It often involves the devolving of power away from administrative centres and towards budget centres or line managers.

The NPM model involves thinking very much in terms of rational choice about the costs and benefits of a particular course of action or, indeed, inaction. The tension between efficiency and equality becomes tangible when managers regard the pursuit of equality of recruitment and promotion as a cost rather than a benefit. The notion of equality as a cost became clear in interviews with ward managers who regarded equal opportunities training as 'a waste of time'. Similarly, the rigid adherence to the letter of the employment policy meant for many ward managers advertising a post, interviewing different candidates and then appointing the candidate they thought was suitable for the post in the first instance.

I have written in more detail about the tension between efficiency and equality elsewhere (see Carter 2000), but it is important to note that one of the consequences of devolving power away from a central personnel function and towards line managers is that it allows space for ethnocentric assumptions to influence selection outcomes. When allied to a climate in which there is an emphasis on the reliable and predictable worker, there is a tendency for line managers to use informal networks to assess the suitability of candidates. The use of informal networks allows managers to select candidates who do not threaten the stable running of the organization. In light of the poor history of race relations within Unicorn Trust it is not hard to see why many White ward managers regard Black candidates as a risk. The tendency has been for managers to push ethnic minority candidates towards those areas where ethnic minority nurses are already concentrated precisely because they are more likely to 'fit in' with the existing workforce.

Of course, there need not be a tension between efficiency and equality. The question that needs to be asked is, what do different social actors within an organisational framework define as efficient? The answer tends to be that what is efficient is easily quantifiable and measurable, most obviously in the shape of (say) profit or in the case of a hospital, the number of patients who have been treated. Measurable aspects of equality in terms of recruitment and promotion tend to be accorded much less weight than what managers are fond of calling the 'bottom-line' indicators.

Overall, the impact of NPM has been to marginalize equality issues, to increase the scope and space for managers to make ethnocentric selection decisions, and to intensify rather than reduce the patterns of segregation that exist within the NHS.

Conclusions

The dominant theme in the research was the extent to which ward managers were able to resist the Trust's equal opportunities policy. Ward managers made explicit and implicit references to the importance of control over staff. Given that ethnic minority nurses in the Trust have gained a reputation as troublemakers as result of the comparatively high numbers of them who have been formally disciplined and a reputation for absenteeism, it is not surprising that ward managers are reluctant to recruit or promote ethnic minority nurses. Whether ethnic minority nurses genuinely are more troublesome is not important. What is important is the acquisition of the label. Becker (1963) makes the point that once a label is attached to a person or group it is very difficult for them to shed the label. The research at Unicorn Trust makes clear the ability of line managers to bypass the formal recruitment policy in favour of one based largely on ethnocentric and stereotypical notions about the acceptability of ethnic minority candidates. An additional complicating factor at Unicorn Trust is the tense relationship between the inner city mental health team and senior managers, which has served to harden attitudes within the Trust about how difficult ethnic minority workers are to manage. The underlying significance of the controllability of workers makes it unlikely that there will be much progress within the Trust until ethnic minority workers are able to cast off the image of troublemakers with a poor record on absenteeism. While the equal opportunities policy at Unicorn Trust could have potentially made a difference to the promotion and recruitment process there is abundant evidence to suggest that the impact of the policy has been, at best, limited. Nursing as an occupational sphere is one in which the employment experiences of men and women are very different, with male nurses tending to reach higher grades, which is reflected in their higher levels of pay. More generally, the pay and conditions of the nursing profession are poor in comparison to other public sector workers such as police officers and teachers. But within the nursing profession the experience and conditions of ethnic minority nurses are so fundamentally different and inferior to that of their White peers that it is possible to talk of nursing as both a gendered and racialized professional sphere.

There is clear evidence of gender discrimination within the NHS (Finlayson and Nazroo 1998). However, it is only relatively recently that questions of ethnic origin have started to figure in discussions about equality. If the experience of Unicorn Trust is typical, there is enough evidence to suggest that questions of ethnic inequality should be considered alongside the questions of gender inequality.

7
Racism, Institutional and Otherwise

Introduction

The development of the notion of institutional racism is an important step forward in understanding the impact and nature of racism and discrimination. It forces us to consider racism and discrimination as a part of the structure of organizations. It is a clear shift away from the notion that racism is the result of one or two prejudiced individuals, or 'bad apples', within an organization. Institutional racism, then, is an integral part of organizations.

If we take the example of the criminal justice system in the UK, figures for 2001 show that some 20 per cent of the prison population of the UK are from the ethnic minorities. This compares to 5.5 per cent of ethnic minorities in the population as a whole. It would seem unlikely that this disparity is the result of a small number of prejudiced individuals within the criminal justice system. Instead, it suggests a system that both consciously and unconsciously discriminates against ethnic minorities at every step in the process, from stop and search to trial, conviction and sentencing. Similarly, it is worth stopping to consider why it is that a survey of 1,210 health visitors and community nurses by the health union MSF found that 5 per cent of ethnic minority staff got performance-related pay rises compared to 14 per cent of their White peers (*Guardian* 21 June 2000). The MSF report suggests that the differences cannot be explained by age, grade or regional variations. Instead, the most likely explanation appears to be discrimination. The award of discretionary pay awards is just the sort of area where both conscious and unconscious assumptions about ethnicity and racism might be reflected. What this sort of report highlights is not necessarily that there are managers who actively discriminate against ethnic minority staff. Instead, it tells us more about how unconscious assumptions about ethnic origin are both rarely challenged and also how they influence the work experience of ethnic minority employees. Differences in pay are not confined to the health service. Research by the Association of University Teachers (2000) suggests that White academics are three times more likely than ethnic minority academics to be high earners (on a salary of over £35,000 per year). One of the major conclusions of the Macpherson Report is that institutional racism is not confined to one specific location within society. Instead it is widespread and is embedded in all the major public service institutions in the UK. Given the evidence of research that has been published since the Macpherson Report, it is hard to disagree.

But before taking the analysis of institutional racism any further, we should ask what is new and different about institutional racism as defined by Macpherson. The current debate about institutional racism is one that has been informed by the work of Stokely Carmichael and Charles Hamilton (1970), who were part of the Black Power Movement. The starting point for their analysis of US institutions was that White supremacy was both a conscious and unconscious element of their constitution. Moreover, they argued that African-Americans had been oppressed, subdued and brutalized by White society. Many of the themes identified by Carmichael and Hamilton emerge in the Macpherson Report. Not least of these is that racist assumptions are so closely interwoven into the fabric of society that, for many white people, they remain an implicit and unrecognized part of social life.

What is new and different about the Macpherson Report is the acknowledgement of a canteen culture that emphasizes fitting in with what are predominantly White, male-dominated cultures. This culturally loaded backdrop, which exists in many organizations, is manifested in jokes, conversation, attitudes and actions of individuals throughout organizations. It is thought to be a major deterrent to ethnic minorities who wish to work in areas that are traditionally dominated by a white workforce. It also reinforces the ethnic boundaries that exist within specific labour markets, so that specific sectors of a labour market, or indeed specific shifts, come to be seen as populated exclusively by ethnic minority workers as they may self-select these types of work in order to avoid precisely the sort of low-level racism that Macpherson calls 'canteen culture'.

Since the Macpherson Report was published the question of institutional racism has hit the headlines in a variety of different contexts. Those organizations that have been accused of institutional racism include the Prison Service, the Crown Prosecution Service, the theatre, the news media, the Fire Service and the education system. In fact, it might be easier to identify those organizations that have not been accused of institutional racism. Despite the frequent use of the term, there seems to be little agreement on what it actually means. The former Chief Executive of the Commission for Racial Equality in the UK, Gurbux Singh, expressed his dissatisfaction with the term, preferring instead to talk of under-representation, though to talk only of under-representation ignores some of the subtle and not so subtle forms of racism that influence behaviour and decision-making in the workplace. For those organizations that have a commitment to challenging institutional racism, the task of operationalizing it and confronting it in a way that is understandable to ordinary people is even greater.

One of the major disadvantages of the use of the term institutional racism is that because of the focus on structural and unconscious aspects of discrimination and racism it under-emphasizes the fact that institutional racism is nothing more than the aggregation of many individual acts of discrimination that individual social actors are responsible for. Or to put it another way, it draws attention away from those individuals within institutions who deliberately and consciously perpetuate racism. Whether or not they do so in a social structure or framework in which racism is an integral part may add to our understanding of how discrimination is perpetuated, but ultimately we should not lose sight of the fact that, for many, the discussions about institutional racism often under-emphasize the extent of overt forms of racism and discrimination.

Analytically, the term institutional racism conflates discrimination and racism, the implication being that racism cannot exist without discrimination (and vice versa). The interrelationship between racism as a set of beliefs or an ideology and discrimination as way of articulating those beliefs is a close one. However, there remains a real difference between racism as an ideology and racism as a practice, a difference that is not obvious in the official definition of institutional racism. Indeed, the use of the term disadvantage rather than discrimination suggests unconscious rather than conscious differential treatment.

One of the major conclusions of the empirical research that forms the basis of this book is that professions are highly racialized. Throughout the 1970s, 1980s and 1990s feminist sociologists have written extensively about the impact of patriarchal ideology and the way in which it shapes the experience of women, both in specific occupational spheres and in society more broadly. Until the publication of the Macpherson Report the impact of race has to a greater or lesser extent been underplayed, within the literature on social identity and the impact of different dimensions of identity on the experience of work. Feminist thinking about occupational segregation and social closure has enjoyed a hegemonic dominance over debates about professions, while the position of ethnic minorities in professions has until recently remained in the background of such debates.

In earlier chapters I presented empirical data on discrimination and racism within the NHS. In order to illustrate the extent to which forms of racism and discrimination cut across occupational cultures I will refer to a second piece of research that I conducted with Steve Fenton and Tariq Modood in 1999. This examined the position of ethnic minority academics in the UK university system. I have written elsewhere about the how the university system constitutes a very different type of employer from the NHS (Fenton et al. 2000). Indeed the genteel traditions associated with universities could not be further from the harsh realities of a working life in the nursing profession. The manifestation of racism and discrimination in each of these areas is very different, so, for example, while ethnic minority nurses may frequently report violence, intimidation and abuse from patients and staff, it is much less likely that ethnic minority academics experience the same sorts of discrimination and harassment. Although there are major differences in the experience of ethnic minority employees in these two occupational areas, there are also some significant similarities, not least of which are notions of promotion and recruitment based on merit that dominate these occupations. Where the concept of institutional racism does help us to gain some practical grip of the problems encountered by ethnic minority staff in different occupations is in gaining some understanding of how notions of merit are far from objective and neutral, but are in fact laden with a wide range of socially determined assumptions about the extent to which different social groups are appropriate for different types of work.

Ethnicity and employment in higher education

In 1999 the results of the research I conducted with Steve Fenton and Tariq Modood were published as *Ethnicity and Employment in Higher Education*. The research sought to examine the distribution of ethnic minority staff throughout the academic system in the UK as well as to examine the experience of individual members of staff, with particular reference to the impact of equal opportunities policies on recruitment and promotion practices. It also sought to provide some benchmark figures to show how many universities and colleges had equality policies specifically aimed at ethnic inequality. Overall, the aims of the report was to provide some global statistical references to the under- and over-representation of ethnic minority staff in different parts of the university system, again, for benchmark purposes.

The research was jointly sponsored by the Commission for Racial Equality, the Committee of Vice Chancellors and Principals, the Standing Committee of Principals, the Higher Education Funding Council for England and the Scottish Higher Education Funding Council and the Department of Education in Northern Ireland.

The data for the study were generated using different methodologies. First, an analysis of the Higher Education Statistics Dataset for 1996–97 which are the most complete and reliable data available. This dataset contains individual records for every individual member of academic staff in the UK. It was used to determine whether ethnic minority staff are over- or under-represented in specific subject areas, types of employment or grade, or types of university.

Second, all academic institutions in the UK were sent a questionnaire to assess how developed their institutional equal opportunities policy was and whether there was a specific focus on 'race' or ethnic origin.

Third, questionnaires were sent to a representative sample of ethnic minority staff in universities throughout the UK which generated more data about the experience of individual ethnic minority staff members.

Fourth, a number of focus groups also took place with academic staff in selected universities throughout the UK as well as with ethnic minority postgraduate students to assess the extent to which they regarded the academic sphere as a desirable career path and what the experiences of ethnic minority staff were, particuarly in relation to promotion and recruitment.

The dataset from HESA for 1996–97 contains a total of 126,142 cases. Of these, 23,000 are recorded as information refused when asked to categorize their ethnic origin. Similarly 5,609 cases contained no information about nationality. Thus the base figure for all tables that follow is 97,533. A decision was taken to maintain a distinction between those ethnic minorities who were born in the UK and those ethnic minorities who were born overseas. The rationale for this decision was that universities in the UK have an increasingly heterogeneous body of academic staff. This reflects the growing globalization of the academic labour market. The distinction between British-born and non-British-born minorities also serves to illustrate the similarities and differences of the different ethno-national groups.

The ethnicity and nationality of those cases included in the 1996–97 dataset were distributed in the following way.

Table 7.1:   Academic staff by ethnic national group

	(n)	%
White British	82,911	85
White non-British	9,287	9
Minority British	2,418	2
Minority non-British	2,917	3
Total	97,533	100

Significantly, the numbers of non-British minorities (2,917) are greater than those of British minorities (2,418). Definitions of nationality are problematic. For example, there some people who have settled in the UK without acquiring British nationality. None the less, the majority of those recorded as non-British will be academic staff who are not permanent residents of the UK and who are likely to be postdoctoral staff on short-term research contracts. The bulk of this group are part of an increasingly international labour force who migrate globally in search of employment.

The distinction between British and non-British staff is an important one to sustain as significant differences between and within the groups emerge later in the analysis.

Tables 7.2 and 7.3 show the ethnic origin of staff without reference to nationality. Table 7.2 shows that the largest group is the White group (94 per cent), followed by the Chinese group (2 per cent) and the Indian group (1 per cent).

Table 7.2:   Total academic staff by ethnic group

	(n)	%
White	92,198	94
Chinese	1,673	2
Indian	1,390	1
Other Asian	873	1
Black African	556	1
Black Caribbean	310	0
Pakistani	291	0
Other Black	167	0
Bangladeshi	75	0
Total	97,533	100

Table 7.3:   Ethnic groups as a percentage of all minorities

	(n)	%
Chinese	1,673	31
Indian	1,390	26
Other Asian	873	16
Black African	556	10
Black Caribbean	310	6
Pakistani	291	5
Other Black	167	3
Bangladeshi	75	1
Total	5,335	100

(Figures may not add up to 100 per cent due to rounding.)

By excluding White staff (see Table 7.3) it is possible to see the distribution of ethnic minority staff more clearly, with the Chinese, Indian,
other Asian and Black African categories emerging as the largest groups.

The distribution of ethnic groups within UK universities becomes
clearer when the White ethnic group is removed from the analysis, as
shown in Table 7.3.

One factor likely to affect career progression through the academic
system is the age of the respective groups and thus their length of service. The British ethnic minority population has an age profile that is
different from that of the total academic population, being much more
concentrated in the younger age groups. This is reflected in academic
staff distributions. The older age groups in academic posts have higher
proportions of whites: 92 per cent of older staff are White and British;
80 per cent of younger staff are White and British.

Since the nature of the academic labour market has changed considerably over the last twenty years it is likely that one consequence of the
younger age of ethnic minority staff is that they are more likely to be

Table 7.4:   Age by ethnic national origin

	Age 45 and under	Age 46 and over
White British	80%	92%
Minority British	3%	2%
White non-British	13%	5%
Minority non-British	4%	1%
Total	100	100

competing for jobs that are offered on short-term contracts rather than permanent, tenured jobs. This is a reflection of the way in which the nature of the academic job market has changed, with a pronounced shift away from full-time tenured posts towards short-term contracts, which may or may not be renewed. As a result, the academic job market has become increasingly characterized by instability of employment. One of the major indicators of the extent to which institutional racism has affected the progress of ethnic minorities within the UK university system is whether or not they are more likely than their White peers to secure full-time tenured employment in teaching and research. As I will show later, the preponderance of ethnic minority academic staff who are employed on short-term contracts reflects not only the increasingly contractualized nature of employment in UK universities, but also some of the unspoken assumptions about ethnic and national origin.

Ethnicity, nationality and sector of higher education

The division between different sectors of the higher education system used in the research is between 'new' universities (i.e. former polytechnics, which were granted university status in 1992) and 'old' universities, medical schools that are free-standing and all other higher education institutions.

Generally speaking, posts at old universities are regarded as more prestigious and have greater status. They also tend to attract more research grants, thus the fixed term contracts that are associated with research are concentrated in the pre-1992 or old universities. Old universities often have long-established traditions of science and engineering, disciplines in which there are often a large number of research projects and where, typically, young non-British and British Whites are to be found. These posts may represent an important stepping-stone onto employment and advancement, either within the global academic system or outside of academia in industry. Such posts can be seen as a stepping-stone to further careers and this should be borne in mind when discussing fixed-term posts as a form of disadvantage.

When examining ethnic minority representation by sector it is notable that the greatest proportion of ethnic minority staff are in medical schools, while in the 'other HE institutions' category representation is particularly low. Differences that are exacerbated when taking into account ethnicity and nationality. See Tables 7.5–7.6.

When both ethnicity and nationality are taken into account, the under-representation of British-born ethnic minorities in the university

Table 7.5:   Minority academic staff by higher education sector

	Total % non-white academic staff	% non-white academic staff aged under 45
Medical schools	11	12
Old universities	6	8
New universities	5	7
Other HE institutions	2	3

Table 7.6:   Academic staff by ethnicity/nationality group and higher education sector

	Medical schools	Old Universities	New Universities	Other HE institutions
White British	78	82	89	94
Minority British	6	2	3	1
White non-British	12	12	5	4
Minority non-British	4	4	2	1
Total	100	100	100	100

sector becomes apparent, with 2 per cent of academic staff within old universities being British-born ethnic minorities and 3 per cent in new universities.

The UK academic sphere is of particular interest as it shows how gender, ethnicity and nationality combine in specific ways to produce and reproduce disadvantage. The disadvantage experienced by different social groups within the academic system may, of course, be a result of factors such as length of time within the system and the possession of qualifications. Comparisons of the mean age of different ethnic groups does indeed suggest some differences, although, as Table 7.7 shows, the difference in mean age would not necessarily explain the different occupational position of men and women, and ethnic minorities within the university system.

Table 7.7:   Mean ages of gender and ethnic groups

Male White	43.06
Female White	39.31
Male minority	38.45
Female minority	36.70

Table 7.8: Staff holding PhD qualification by ethnicity/nationality group

Minority Non-British	49%
White non-British	39%
Minority British	40%
White British	41%

While the average age of minorities is lower than that of White staff, any variation in occupational position is unlikely to be explained by the difference in age. Similarly, the possession of professional qualifications may also explain differences in the occupational position of different groups. For most current academic posts the possession of a PhD is regarded as essential. Table 7.8 shows that British-born ethnic minority staff have a similar proportion of staff who have a PhD, while overseas ethnic minority staff are more likely to have a PhD.

The HESA data show that ethnic minority staff tend to be concentrated in particular grades (principally in research posts). Many of these are short-term contracts with little long-term job security. In grades such as senior lecturer and professor, the representation of ethnic minority staff declines considerably (see Table 7.9).

The concentration of ethnic minority staff in the lower grades of the academic system is made more apparent when the grade structure is divided simply into high and low grade posts (see Table 7.10). Professorial posts and senior lecturer posts are classified as high grade posts. There are almost a quarter of all academic staff in high grade posts compared to 28 per cent White British, 16 per cent minority British, 15 per cent White non-British and 8 per cent minority non-British.

The preponderance on the lower rungs of the employment ladder is a key aspect of the ethnic minority experience in the academic sphere. However, another key indicator of disadvantage is the number of ethnic minority staff who are employed on fixed-term contracts. The use of fixed-term contracts is becoming increasingly common as free market-

Table 7.9: Grade by ethnic national group

	Research	Lecturer	Senior lecturer	Professor	Other grades
Minority non-British	52	32	7	1	7
White non-British	40	35	10	5	11
Minority British	30	42	13	3	12
White British	20	42	19	9	10

Table 7.10:   High/low grade posts by ethnic national group

	High grade posts	Low grade posts
Minority non-British	8%	92%
White non-British	15%	85%
Minority British	16%	84%
White British	28%	72%
Total	24%	76%

style employment practices are introduced into the academic sphere. These practices allow employers greater flexibility in the hiring and firing of employees (see Table 7.11).

The data suggest that a major division between White and non-White staff is their employment status, with 48 per cent of British-born ethnic minority staff being employed on short-term contracts compared to 34 per cent of White British academic staff. For non-British academics the figures of staff employed on short-term contracts is notably higher, though this probably reflects the increasingly international flavour of the labour market and the fact that most non-British academics may be likely to return to their country of origin once they have acquired sufficient experience in foreign universities. Even so, it is interesting that a higher proportion of non-British minorities (68 per cent) are employed on short-term contracts compared with White non-British academics (61 per cent).

Critics of the UK university system argue that these data illustrate exactly what the Macpherson Report referred to as institutional discrimination. That is, there are structural aspects of the academic system that systematically place ethnic minority employees at a disadvantage. Discrimination is a key feature of the very fabric of UK universities. This is reflected in the concentration of ethnic minority staff in short-term

Table 7.11:   Contract status by ethnic national group

	Permanent contract	Fixed-term contract
Minority non-British	32%	68%
White non-British	38%	61%
Minority British	51%	48%
White British	64%	34%
Total	57%	41%

contracts in the less prestigious research-only posts, as well as in the lack of senior ethnic minority academics. Even taking into account the fact that the average age of ethnic minority staff is lower than that of their White counterparts, and that therefore they have spent less time in the system, the fact remains that ethnic minority staff tend to be lodged in inferior academic positions. The extent to which the assumptions about ethnic minority groups within the academic system reflect either conscious or unconscious discrimination is hard to gauge. It is note-worthy that in the questionnaire that was sent to a sample of staff throughout the UK academic system some 20 per cent of British-born ethnic minority and 16 per cent of non-British born ethnic minority staff reported experiencing racial harassment.

Without more systematic research on the attitudes of those respon-sible for employment within the academic system it is unlikely that any hard conclusions can be drawn. None the less, the anecdotal evidence gathered in the course of this research suggests that ethnic minority academics feel that they are often 'pigeon-holed' as being suitable only for some, usually the less prestigious, posts rather than others.

While there are major differences in the experiences of ethnic minor-ity staff within the National Health Service and the UK university sector, one of the features of their experience that is similar is that cer-tain parts of each profession have come to be identified as being spaces in which Black and ethnic minority staff are concentrated. The colon-ization of certain occupational niches by Black and ethnic minority groups is as much to do with the fact that ethnic groups are trying to get a foot in the door of certain professions as it is with the ability of other dominant social and occupational groups to restrict the access of ethnic minority groups to the more desirable parts of such professions. Thus specific jobs and spaces within occupations take on a racialized character. So fully to understand the process that leads to the encir-clement of ethnic minority employees requires analysis of how the structures of the labour market affect the decisions that ethnic minority job-seekers make and the way in which recruiters target recruitment, as well as some understanding of the way in which assumptions about eth-nic identity shape the assumptions made by recruiters during the selec-tion process. This interplay between structure and agency is not fixed and is in a constant state of flux. However, what we can be certain of is the extent to which ideas and assumptions about ethnic origin shape the way in which decisions are made about successful job-seekers. So it is the nature of the job that determines the final occupational destin-ation of ethnic minorities as much as the skills that they bring with them

to that job. Particular jobs come to be seen by ethnic minorities themselves and by employers as being 'Black' jobs, while others are seen as
'White' jobs. An additional contextual factor is the impact of the use of
short-term contracts in higher education. Until the early 1980s the
majority of academics enjoyed tenure. That is, they were full-time, permanent empoyees. However, throughout the 1980s and 1990s more and
more posts within UK universities have become fixed-term, with little
or no guarantee of job security at the end of the contract. At the same
time, there has been a rapid expansion in the numbers of students
entering higher education in the UK and a corresponding intensifica-
tion of labour. Thus job insecurity and a marked deterioration in pay
and conditions have affected the nature and experience of work within
UK universities. The extent to which these factors have deterred able
applicants from entering the academic sphere is difficult to assess.
While pay and conditions have declined there has been a corresponding
increase in pay in parts of the private sector, and there is anecdotal evidence to suggest that many of the brightest graduates are going into the
private sector instead of taking up jobs in universities. This affects both
ethnic minority and White graduates. But for ethnic minority graduates
thinking of working in UK universities the fact that they are more likely
to be located in unstable forms employment compared to their White
peers and that they are less likely to reach senior levels within the
system are extra deterrents.

The impact of ethnic identity on the progress of academics is clearly
demonstrated in this research, but it is also important to emphasize what
Steve Fenton refers to as the two-step difference, namely that ethnic
minorities tend to fare less well than their White peers but that ethnic
minority women tend to do less well than ethnic minority men. In other
words, UK universities are not only racialized but also gendered. The
impact of gender is illustrated in Table 7.12, which shows the distribution of men and women across academic grades within universities.

Table 7.12:   Males and females by high/low grades and ethnic national groups,
HESA dataset

	High grade	Low grade
Minority non-British (males)	9%	90%
Minority British (males)	21%	79%
Minority non-British (females)	5%	95%
Minority British (females)	8%	92%

Table 7.13:   Primary employment function by gender, HESA dataset

	Teaching only	Research only	Teaching and research
Males	9%	27%	64%
Females	13%	34%	53%
Total	10%	30%	60%

Table 7.12 shows a clear pattern, with minority British males most likely to be high-grade posts than minority non-British males, followed by minority British females and lastly minority non-British females. Taking into account all the usual qualifiers about length of service, qualifications and career breaks, what these data show is that gender and ethnic origin combine in a specific way within the UK university system to constrain the career paths of ethnic minority women particularly compared to ethnic minority men.

Further investigation of the HESA dataset shows that women tend to be concentrated in teaching only or research only posts while the men are concentrated in the more prestigious and secure teaching and research posts (see Table 7.13).

In addition to the data supplied by the Higher Education Statistics Agency, the data from the questionnaires that were distributed as part of the research show that some 28 per cent of ethnic minority women in our sample reported experience of discrimination in job applications, while 16 per cent of ethnic minority women reported experience of discrimination in job promotions. Clearly these findings have to be treated with some caution because of the difficulties in establishing the motivation of employers who are alleged to have discriminated. Of equal interest is the fact that some 28 per cent of ethnic minority women reported some experience of racial harassment compared to 16 per cent of ethnic minority men. Again, while it is problematic to define harassment without knowing the circumstances of each case, the fact that over a quarter of ethnic minority women in our sample felt able to report some experience of harassment is something of an indictment of UK universities.

The next 5–10 years will prove to be a watershed in the employment of ethnic minority staff within UK universities. Those Black and Asian academics who have persevered should be reaching a point in their careers where they will be eligible for senior posts, such as heads of department and professors. Whether universities, as institutions, have learnt the lessons of research such as this will be measurable in the numbers of ethnic minority academics who have reached the top of the academic tree. Another key indicator will be whether or not members of those ethnic groups (particularly Bangladeshis and Pakistanis) who have been under-represented in academic posts have increased in number.

The research established the existence of three central divisions within academic employment. First, that the position of non-British non-Whites is more disadvantaged than those of British ethnic minorities, especially in relation to permanent contracts. Second, that certain groups are greatly under-represented (particularly the Black Caribbean, Pakistani and Bangladeshi groups) while others are over-represented (Black Africans and Chinese). Third, that within each group of staff, as defined by nationality and colour, the position of women was worse.

Conclusions

If we compare the experience of ethnic minority employees in the areas of higher education, nursing, the police force and the fire service a series of similarities and differences are apparent. In all these occupational spheres there is evidence that ethnic minority employees are confined to particular parts of the profession; they may also be confined to certain grades and/or specific forms of tenure. Similarly, in all of these professions there is an absence of ethnic minorities at the senior levels of each respective hierarchy. What is different is the way in which racism and discrimination are articulated. Thus in both the fire service and the National Health Service racism is often experienced through overt forms of discrimination, for example, physical or verbal abuse. Indeed, the recent confidential report conducted for the Department of Health suggest that such discriminatory behaviour is endemic. A survey conducted for the report showed that 46 per cent of respondents had experienced racial harassment over the last twelve months. Such discriminatory behaviour may be part of a wider occupational culture in which there are deeply embedded assumptions about gender and race or ethnicity as indicated in the Home Office report on the fire service. However, when compared with UK universities the sort of discrimination experienced by ethnic minority groups is quantitatively and qualitatively different. While overt forms of discrimination do occur, discrimination takes a more subtle and pernicious form in the shape of unspoken assumptions about the suitability of particular ethnic groups for different types of work. This partly explains why ethnic minority academics are more likely than their White counterparts to be located in insecure forms of employment on short-term contracts with little prestige. Within the university sector the notion of a monoculture is very real and imposes constraints on ethnic minority academics trying to break into privileged academic spheres. It is a monoculture that is imbued with assumptions about 'race', ethnicity and nationality. As Fenton et al. (2000) point out, it is also a culture inextricably linked to class subcultures. What is particularly interesting about the culture of UK universities is the coexistence of notions of meritocracy in relation to seniority within the system and evidence of highly ethnocentric assumptions about ethnic minority groups within the system.

What the evidence suggests is that there are qualitatively different experiences of racism and discrimination in different occupational spheres, but also that there are broadly similar quantitative outcomes in terms of the position of ethnic minority groups within professional spheres. Thus, in the course of the research on UK universities it was extremely unusual for respondents to talk about physical or verbal abuse in the same way that nurses working in the NHS describe their experiences. However, there are many overlapping themes: being passed over for promotion; being channelled into types of employment that lack prestige, security and good pay; feelings among ethnic minority respondents that to be as successful as White candidates they have to be twice as well qualified; and, most importantly, structures within organizations that militate against ethnic minority candidates because there are unspoken assumptions about the inferiority of ethnic minority employees that are part of the fabric of organisations, in exactly the way that Sir William Macpherson describes.

8
Conclusions

Introduction

Professional spheres, so often presented as occupational areas where position is based on achievement and there are strong meritocratic traditions, are as riddled with stereotypical assumptions about 'race' and gender as any other form of employment. No one should doubt the impact of 'race' within professional spheres and that it continues to exert a powerful influence over occupational mobility or that, as well as individual acts of discrimination within professional spheres, there are structures that reflect highly ethnocentric assumptions about ethnic minorities and are inextricably part of organizations. As significant as the existence and explanation of institutional and individual racism within an organizational context is the ability of White groups to resist change that seeks to overcome different forms of discrimination and racism. If the example of the National Health Service and other major public services in the UK is in any way indicative of the ability of the White establishment to resist change, then real change is likely to take a considerable amount of time.

To appreciate how and why ethnic minority groups are confined to specific parts within professional organizations requires an understanding not only of the concepts of 'race', racism, discrimination and segregation but, crucially, a socio-historical understanding of the way any given profession constructs and reconstructs itself. Or to put it another way, it is essential to understand the way that notions of 'race' and racism are built into the structure and fabric of professional spheres. In the case of the UK nursing profession the debate that took place within and between government departments during the mid-1950s illustrates precisely the sorts of assumptions that both directly and indirectly led to the encircling of migrants from the New Commonwealth and Pakistan into areas of nursing that lacked prestige, status, security and prospects of promotion. The consequences of these historical decisions have are far-reaching, in that they create a self-fulfilling prophecy that justifies the exclusion of ethnic minority groups from positions of power and status. When combined with different forms of social closure these interlock in ways that make upward mobility from what are essentially occupational ghettos extremely difficult.

Notions of social closure have rarely been employed as a conceptual tool in order to understand the position of ethnic minority groups in the labour market, or society more broadly. However, what the empirical data that I have referred to demonstrate beyond any doubt is that different forms of social closure operate within occupational spheres in ways that constrain the choices and career mobility of ethnic minority groups. The important conceptual link is between common-sense notions of race and the way they are operationalized and understood by those in positions of power who are able to determine selection outcomes. It is precisely this understanding of what 'race' means in terms of those who make decisions about who to employ and who not to employ that has been closely explored by Jenkins in *Racism and Recruitment*. The analytical framework that he employs to understand the way in which selection decisions are made suggests that the dual concepts of acceptability (does the candidate fit in?) and suitability (does the candidate have the right qualifications and experience?) are riddled with ethnocentric assumptions that remain implicit and unspoken and reproduce the sorts of ethnic divisions within profession that already exist. As I have stated earlier, Jenkins' analysis is extremely powerful in understanding how ethnic divisions within workforces are set up and sustained, but lacks an appreciation of how the structure of labour markets themselves influences what constitutes both acceptability and suitability.

That is, jobs become Black jobs not just because the Black job-seekers do not fit in with White workforces. It is also because specific niches of the labour market that, historically, have been filled by Black workers and are characterized by low pay and conditions, have themselves taken on a racialized significance. Or to put it another way, it is not only the social characteristics of the person who is applying for a job that determine what part of the labour market they end up in, but also the nature of the job itself. If an occupational area is populated by other Black workers then there is tendency to push other Black job-seekers into those parts of occupations, not just because they are more likely to 'fit in' with other Black workers, but because the nature of the work is quantitatively and qualitatively worse than other parts of the occupation and the nature of the work task itself has become imbued with a racialized significance.

Thus in the case of the UK nursing profession there is increasing evidence to suggest that Black nurses are more likely to work in the least desirable parts of the profession. Thus when recruiters make decisions about who to recruit and to what parts of the profession they should be recruited it is precisely these notions about what are areas of Black work that help to determine where Black job-seekers end up. For those women who migrated from New Commonwealth countries to the UK in the 1950s and 1960s to work in nursing it is quite clear that their experience is best described as being part of a racialized class fraction in the way that Miles and Phizacklea (1980) describe. Their experience was and is determined by a specific combination of gender, class and ethnic origin. It should be remembered here that many women from the Caribbean migrated independently of men and, as the material in the earlier chapters shows, were recruited to work in feminized professions. The class background of many of those women can be understood only in relation to their ethnic origin, which meant that they were often confined to poorly paid employment with little prospect of promotion.

Whether or not the young men and women of ethnic minority origin in the UK and the US are likely to experience employment in the same way as their parents and grandparents is as yet unclear, though we can hope that the increasing numbers of young ethnic minorities who are entering education in the US and the UK are less likely than their parents and grandparents to experience the same sorts of racism and discrimination.

Throughout a wide variety of occupations and professional spheres ethnocentric assumptions and racism (both individual and institutional) continue to exert a powerful force over Black and Asian employees and job-seekers. What the study of different occupational spheres shows us is that professions are not only gendered, but also racialized. Strategies of social closure have been developed and employed to maintain professional boundaries in ways that seem to be objective and non-discriminatory. However, these strategies are aimed at ensuring that some social groups remain inside the boundary while others remain on the outside. What the material I have referred to suggests is that there are gendered and racialized boundaries both between and within professions. The impact of these boundaries forces us to rethink notions of double discrimination for ethnic minority women and also reconsider causal relationships that might be said to exist between race and gender.

Gender, 'race', work and exclusion

The question of which aspect of social identity assumes primacy over another within a given social interaction is complex and has been the subject of wide debate within sociology, feminism and the study of 'race' relations. In terms of understanding the position of ethnic minority women within the labour market generally and specific occupational spheres, the shape and direction of the debate are significant. Feminist writers such as Walby (1990) have sought to emphasize the primacy of gender and an organizing concept that explains the subordinate position of women within the workplace. However, the experience of paid employment is both quantitatively and qualitatively different for women of ethnic minorities – a fact emphasized by Phizacklea (1990). Thus gender divisions can be said to be cross-cut with divisions based on notions of 'race'. The analysis of the data about UK universities and the UK nursing profession shows that Black women do indeed occupy positions that are both distinct and inferior to that of White women. Indeed the primacy of ethnicity as a dimension of social identity for Black women is emphasized by a number of writers (e.g Floya Anthias, Nura Yuval-Davies and Annie Phizacklea). If we add to this that differences between migrants who came to the UK and the US in the 1940s and 1950s and their sons and daughters are starting to emerge it becomes essential to add age as a dimension of social identity which is likely to have a determining effect on the labour market position of ethnic minority women. The impact of socio-economic class should not be ignored either, with different ethnic groups in both the UK and the USA possessing very different amounts of cultural and financial capital, which contribute to their class position. Indeed in the US it is possible to talk of a Black middle class, while in the UK there are a growing number of Asian entrepreneurs who have 'made it', although this should not conceal the fact that Asian people are disproportionately represented in the poorest income quintile in society.

Where then does this leave us? Writers such as Bradley (1999) argue that it is impossible to disentangle the effects of gender, class and ethnic origin.

While this may be true in a general sense, in that it is impossible to talk of any overarching theory that satisfactorily explains why different social groups occupy different and unequal positions in the labour market, it is possible to explain how and why ethnic minority women are predominantly located in occupational ghettos if the social, historical and economic context of a given occupational sphere is examined in detail.

Feminist sociologists have advanced arguments about the ways professions and other occupational areas are gendered and how different forms of social closure act to exclude women from the most prestigious parts of professions. What has been underemphasised is the extent to which forms of closure and exclusion based on gender are cross-cut by forms of closure and exclusion based on 'race' and ethnicity. If it is true to say, as Davies and Rosser (1986) do, that the NHS is staffed by women but run by men, then it is equally true to say that if the NHS is staffed by women, then Black women within the NHS tend to occupy the least desirable parts of the profession. Not only that, but that White nurses have been successful in socially closing the most desirable parts of the profession. Indeed as the numbers of migrants born in the Caribbean and other parts of the New Commonwealth decline there is anecdotal evidence that they are being replaced by migrants from all over the globe, including China, South Africa and Australia, so the real acid test will be the extent to which the experiences of 'new' migrants are the same as 'old' migrants.

What is currently taking place within the nursing profession within the UK is a very good case in point. The factors that shaped and continue to shape the experience of migrants from the New Commonwealth and Pakistan and ethnic minorities more generally include a) a desire to migrate to the UK in order to seek employment and higher standards of living, b) the efforts of employers to attract labour from former colonies, c) the relative ease of access as the majority of migrants possess UK passports, d) the fact that there were severe labour shortages in parts of the profession that had been abandoned by White labour because of a lack of prestige, opportunity and pay. In addition, there were two crucial underlying assumptions that shaped the experience of these women: first, that nursing was principally a woman's job; and second, a desire on the part of the nursing establishment and the government to ensure that migrants were restricted to the lowest grades and the least desirable types of nursing, i.e. this occupational sphere is one that is both gendered and racialized. The effects of this have been that until the 1990s migrant women have remained stuck in the lower rungs of the profession with little opportunity to acquire the necessary qualifications to escape and, as they have reached retirement age, gaps in the nursing profession have started to appear, with the result that the NHS have begun to recruit women from around the world, but particularly from the Philippines. All the anecdotal evidence that is available to date suggests that the experience of migrant women from the New Commonwealth is being reproduced in a contemporary context with the majority of those who are being confined to the least desirable parts of the profession being migrants.

'Race', ethnicity and gender: the notion of double discrimination

The debate about the intersection of 'race' and/or ethnicity with gender is one that has been taking place within the context of postmodern notions about identity that emphasize the notion of multiple and fractured identities. Or, put more crudely, different aspects of our social identities become socially significant at different times and in different social spheres. There has been, quite correctly, a rejection of the notion that women are a homogeneous category whose experience is similar. The understanding of the interrelationship between class, 'race' and gender has been discussed in some detail by authors such as Bradley, Anthias and Yuval Davis. The common theme in the literature is the rejection of essentialist forms of categorization and thinking that accord one aspect of social identity, for example, gender, over other aspects of social identity. We should not forget that there are very real differences starting to emerge between the experience of first-generation migrants and their second-, third- and fourth-generation sons and daughters. There is also an emphasis not only on the interrelationship between different forms of social identity but also the social and physical context in which it takes place. Thus the aspects of social identity that assume importance in the domestic sphere may not be the same as those that assume prominence in the sphere of paid employment. As writers such as Anthias and others have emphasized there is no clear-cut relationship between class, 'race' and gender and their interrelationship is not always the same. The corollary of this is that the notion of double disadvantage for Black women should be reassessed, Thus gender disadvantage and racial disadvantage are not always cumulative. Instead we should examine the particular intersections of each aspect of identity in specific social circumstances. Thus in the case of Black women working in the NHS it is possible to say that their experience is both gendered and racialized. Women have entered a profession that is defined as feminine, but within that profession there is evidence to show that Black women have been confined to the parts that White women define as undesirable. There are also important differences beginning to emerge between those first-generation migrants who came to the UK to work as nurses who are now approaching retirement and the new waves of migrants from Europe, Australasia and the Far East.

Some of the contemporary debates about intersectionality seem to be debates about semantic issues. It is well established within sociology as a whole and within the sociology of work that different aspects of social identity interact in different ways in different contexts. Rather than discussing just how problematic it is to explain these different intersectionalities perhaps the discipline should start to consider what the effects of being male or female, White or ethnic minority actually *are* in any given context.

What the analysis of the position and experience of ethnic minorities within professions suggests is that closure of desirable, secure and prestigious parts of occupational areas is not only a gendered experience, as Witz (1992) suggests, but that it is also racialized and that these forms of subordination cut across each other in ways that are not always easy to unravel, particularly in terms of causality. However, there is one way in which the gendered and racialized nature of the experience of Black women within a specific occupational sphere can be quantified. That is, through the analysis of levels of pay. A quantitative analysis of levels of pay within the NHS came to the following conclusion:

> The nursing profession is a...public sector, female dominated 'caring' profession, with a high proportion of staff from the ethnic minorities. One might expect that a profession with these characteristics would be less likely to engage in racial and gender discrimination. Our conclusion is not entirely consistent with this view. Particularly when the endogeneity of training and participation history is taken into account, White nurses are found to have significant advantage in terms of speed of promotion – amounting in cash terms to some £40,000 more in additional earnings over a whole career. (Pudney and Shields 2000, p. 39)

In light of the evidence about the occupational position of Black and other ethnic minority women not only in nursing but in other professional spheres too it is difficult to be optimistic about the impact of equality policies. Until recruiters regard the recruitment of a diverse workforce as a benefit rather than a cost such policies will continue to have a modest effect. In the short term one way to try to maximize the impact of such policies would be to increase the penalties for those found to be engaging in discriminatory behaviour. This type of clearly measurable outcome would fit closely within the framework of new public management if the achievement of equality goals was regarded as management priority. In the long term, as others (such as Cockburn and Webb and Liff) have noted there has to a transformation in workplace attitudes towards race if there is to be any real change in the position and experience of ethnic minority employees. In that respect the Macpherson Report represents a watershed in that it has alerted organizations to the ways that racism and discrimination are part of not only 'shop floor' cultures but also of management cultures, and form part of the very framework of many organizations. The real test will be over the next 10–15 years, which should see major changes in public service organizations with regard to race. In light of the experience of ethnic groups who have been successful in entering professional spheres, there is much to learn. What much of the evidence suggests is that as ethnic minority groups become better qualified, they are able to overcome forms of credentialism that restrict entry into specific occupational spheres. Once within an occupation or profession they are often sidelined or pushed into part of the profession that lack security or prestige and the opportunities for upward or outward mobility are limited. Breaking the stranglehold that established professional groups have within their spheres requires a systematic analysis of how and why they have been able to retain positions of privilege, often through a complex combination of forms of social closure, and an increase in the transparency of the way in which appointments are made. Certainly the trends that have been identified in this book are entrenched and will be hard to break down, but change in attitudes and practices is not impossible, particularly when it is regarded as a social and political priority at both the micro and macro level.

References

Abrams, P. (1982), *Historical Sociology*, Open Books, Shepton Mallet.

Adamson, K. (1994), 'Racial Equality Issues in Theory and Practice: A Critical Look at the Assumptions Underpinning Equal Opportunities', in Erikson, M. and Williams, S. (1994), *Social Change in Tyne and Wear*, University of Sunderland.

Agobolegbe, G. (1984), 'Fighting the Racist Disease', *Nursing Times*, April.

Akinsanya, D. (1988), 'Ethnic Minority Nurses, Midwives and Health Visitors: What Role for Them in the National Health Service?', *New Community*, Vol. 14, No. 3.

Allen, I. (1988), *Doctors' Careers*, Policy Studies Institute, London.

Allsop, J. and May, A. (1993), 'Between the Devil and the Deep Blue Sea: Managing the NHS in the Wake of the 1990 Act', *Critical Social Policy*, 38, Autumn.

Anthias, F. (1992), *Ethnicity, Class, Gender and Migration*, Avebury Press, Aldershot.

Anthias, F. and Yuval-Davis, N. (1992), *Racialized Boundaries, Race, Nation, Gender, Colour and Class and the Anti-Racist Struggle*, Routledge, London.

Anwar, M. and Ali, A. (1987), *Overseas Doctors*, CRE, London.

Armstrong, P. (1985), 'Changing Management Control Strategies: The Role of Competition between Accountancy and Other Organisational Professions', *Accounting, Organisations and Society*, Vol. 10, No. 2, pp. 129–48.

Ashton, D.N. and Brown, P. (1987), *Education, Unemployment and Labour Markets*, Falmer Press, Brighton.

Bacchi, C. (1996), *The Politics of Affirmative Action*, Sage Press, London.

Balibar, E. and Wallerstein, I. (1991), *Race, Nation and Class: Ambiguous Identities*, London, Verso.

Banton, M. (1977), *The Idea of Race*, Tavistock, London.

Banton, M. (1983), 'Categorical and Statistical Discrimination', *Ethnic and Racial Studies*, Vol. 6, No. 3, July.

Banton, M. (1987), *Racial Theories*, Cambridge University Press, Cambridge.

Banton, M. (1988), *Racial Consciousness*, Longman, London.

Banton, M. (1989), 'Racial Discrimination at Work: Bristol Cases, 1980–89', *New Community*, Vol. 17, No. 1.

Banton, M. (1994), *Discrimination*, Open University Press, Milton Keynes.

Barrett, S. and McMahon, L. (1990), 'Public Management in Uncertainty; a micro-political perspective of the health service in the United Kingdom', *Policy & Politics*, Vol. 18, No. 4, pp. 257–68.

Baxter, C. (1988), *The Black Nurse: An Endangered Species*, National Extension College for Training in Health and Race, Cambridge.

Becker, G. (1957), *The Economics of Discrimination*, University of Chicago Press, Chicago.

Becker, H.S. (1963), *Outsiders*, Free Press, New York.

Beishon, S., Virdee, S. and Hagell, A. (1995), *Nursing in Multi-Ethnic NHS*, Policy Studies Institute, London.

Bindman, G. (1992), 'Proof and Evidence of Discrimination', in Hepple, B. and Szyszack, E., *Discrimination The Limits of the Law*, Mansell, London.

Blackaby, D., Leslie, D., Murphy, P.D., O'Leary, N. (2000), 'White/Ethnic Minority Earnings and Employment Differentials in Britain: Evidence from the LFS', Swansea University discussion paper.

Blakemore, K. and Boneham, M. (1994), *Age, Race And Ethnicity*, Open University Press, Buckingham.

Boddy, M. (1995), *TECS & Racial Equality, Training, Work Experience and Ethnic Minorities*, SAUS Publications.

Borgas, G. (1992), 'Ethnic Capital and Intergenerational Mobility', *Quarterly Journal of Economics*, Vol. 123.

Bourn, C. and Whitmore, J. (1993), *Race and Sex Discrimination*, Sweet & Maxwell, London.

Bradley, H. (1989), *Men's Work, Women's Work*, Polity Press, Cambridge.

Bradley, H. (1996), *Fractured Identities, Changing Patterns of Inequality*, Polity Press, Cambridge.

Bradley, H. (1999), *Gender and Power in the Workplace, Analysing the Impact of Economic Change*, Macmillan, Basingstoke.

Braham, P., Rhodes, E. and Pearn, M. (eds) (1981), *Discrimination and Disadvantage in the Labour Market*, Harper and Row, New York.

Brennan, J. and McGeevor, P. (1990), *Ethnic Minorities and the Graduate Labour Market*, CRE, London.

Brooks, D. (1975), *Race and Labour in London Transport*, Oxford University Press, Oxford.

Brooks, D. and Singh, K. (1979), 'Pivots and Presents: Asian Workers in British Foundries', in S. Wallman (ed.), *Ethnicity at Work*, Macmillan, Basingstoke.

Brown, C. (1984), *Black and White Britain*, Policy Studies Institute, London.

Brown, C., McCrudden, C. and Smith, D. (1991), *Racial Justice at Work*, Policy Studies Institute, London.

Brown, C. and Gay, P. (1985), *Racial Discrimination 17 Years after The Act*, Policy Studies Institute, London.

Buchanan, D. and Boddy, D. (1988), 'Getting In, Getting On, Getting Out and Getting Back', in Bryman, A. (ed.), *Doing Research In Organisations*, Routledge, London.

Cameron, I. (1993), 'Formulating an Equal Opportunities Policy', *Equal Opportunities Review* 47 Jan/Feb.

Carline, D. (1985), *Labour Economics*, Longman, Harlow.

Carmichael, S. and Hamilton, C. (1970), *Black Power: The Politics of Liberation in America*, Random House, London.

Carpenter, M. (1980), 'Asylum Nursing before 1914, a Chapter in the History of Labour', in Davies, C., *Rewriting Nursing History*, Croom Helm, London.

Carter, J. (2000), 'New Public Management and Equal Opportunities in the NHS', *Critical Social Policy*, Vol. 20, No. 1, pp. 61–83.

Carter, J., Fenton, S. and Modood, T. (1999), *Ethnicity and Employment in Higher Education*, Policy Studies Institute, London.

Carter, T. (1986), *Shattering Illusions*, Lawrence & Wishart, London.

Casey, B. (1995), *Redundancy in Britain: Findings from the Labour Force Survey*, Department of Education and Employment Research Paper No. 62.

Cashmore, E. and Troyna, B. (1983), *An Introduction to Race Relations*, Routledge & Kegan Paul, London.

Castles, S. and Kosack, G. (1992), *Immigrant Workers and Class Structure in Western Europe*, Oxford University Press, Oxford.

Clarke, L. (1980), *Occupational Choice: A Review of Research in the United Kingdom*, HMSO, London.

Cockburn, C. (1989), 'Equal Opportunities: The Short and Long Agenda', *Industrial Relations Journal*, Vol. 20, No. 3, Autumn.

Cockburn, C. (1991), *In the Way of Women: Male Resistance to Equality in Organisations*, Macmillan, London.

Cockburn, C. (1991), *Brothers: Male Dominance and Technological Change*, Pluto, London.

Coker, N. (2001), *Racism in Medicine*, King's Fund, London.

Collinson, D. (1988), *Barriers to Fair Selection*, Equal Opportunities Commission, London.

Collinson, D., Knights, D. and Collinson, M. (1990), *Managing to Discriminate*, Routledge & Kegan Paul, London.

Coombes, M. and Hubbuck, J. (1992), 'Monitoring Equal Opportunity at the Workplace', *Ethnic and Racial Studies*, Vol. 15, No. 2.

Coote, A. and Campbell, B. (1982), *Sweet Freedom*, Picador, London.

Corrigan, P. (1981), *Schooling The Smash Street Kids*, Macmillan, London.

Coussey, M. and Jackson, H. (1991), *Making Equal Opportunities Work*, Institute of Personnel Management, London.

Coussins, J. (1976), *The Equality Report, One Year of The Equal Pay Act, The Sex Discrimination Act & The Equal Opportunities Commission*, NCCL, London.

Cox, O.C. (1970), *Caste Class & Race*, Monthly Review Press, New York.

Cross, M. (ed.) (1992), *Ethnic Minorities and Industrial Change in Europe and North America*, Cambridge University Press, Cambridge.

Cross, M. (1992), 'Black Workers, Recession, and Economic Restructuring in the West Midlands', in Cross, M. (ed.), *Ethnic Minorities and Industrial Change in Europe and North America*, Cambridge University Press, Cambridge.

Cross, M., Wrench, J. and Barnett, S. (1990), *Ethnic Minorities and the Careers Service, An Investigation into Processes of Assessment and Placement*, Research Paper No. 73, Department of Employment, London.

Cunningham, S. (1992), 'The Development of Equal Opportunities Theory and Practice in the European Community', *Policy and Politics*, Vol. 20, No. 3.

Curran, M.M. (1988), 'Gender and Recruitment: People and Places in the Labour Market', *Work, Employment & Society*, Vol. 2, No. 3.

Dale, K. and Liff, S. (1994), 'Formal Opportunity, Informal Barriers: Black Women Managers Within a Local Authority', *Work Employment & Society*, Vol. 8, No. 2, pp. 177–98.

Daniel, W.W. (1968), *Racial Discrimination in England*, Penguin, Harmondsworth.

Darity, W. and Mason, P. (1998), 'Evidence on Discrimination in Employment: Codes of Color, Codes of Gender', *Journal of Economic Perspectives*, Vol. 12, pp. 63–90.

Davies, C. (1992), 'Gender, History and Management Style in Nursing: Towards a Theoretical Synthesis', in Savage, M. and Witz, A. (1992), *Gender and Bureaucracy*, Blackwell, Oxford, pp. 229–52.

Davies, C. and Rosser, J. (1986), *Processes of Discrimination: A Study of Women Working in the NHS*, Department of Health and Social Security, London.

Davis, K. and Moore, W.E. (1967), 'Some Principles of Stratification', in Bendix, R. and Lipset, S., *Class, Status and Power*, Routledge & Kegan Paul, London.

Dex, S. (1986), 'The Costs of Discriminating: A Review of the Literature', Research Paper No. 39, Home Office, London.

Doeringer, P. and Piore, M. (1971), *Internal Labour Markets And Manpower Analysis*, Lexington Books, Lexington, Mass.

DoH (1998), http://www.msfcphra.org./hr/hvstats.html.

Donaldson, L. (1993), 'The Recession: A Barrier to Equal Opportunities?', *Equal Opportunities Review*, No. 50, July/August.

Dresser, M. (1986), *Black and White on the Buses*, Bristol Broadsides, Bristol.

Dworkin, R. (2000), *Sovereign Virtue*, Harvard University Press, Cambridge, Mass.

Edwards, R.C., Reich, M. and Gordon, D. (eds) (1975), *Labour Market Segmentation*.

EOC (1991), *Equality Management*, Equal Opportunities Commission, Manchester.

Esmail, A. and Everington, S. (1995), 'Racial Discrimination against Doctors from Ethnic Minorities', *British Medical Journal*, No. 306.

Fenton, S. (1984), *Race Health & Welfare*, CRE, London.

Fenton, S. (1988), 'Health, Work and Growing Old: The Afro-Caribbean Experience', *New Community*, Vol. 14, No. 3, Spring.

Fenton, S. (1996), 'Counting Ethnicity', in Leviats, R. and Guy, W., *Interpreting Official Statistics*, Routledge, London.

Fenton, S. (1999), *Ethnicity*, Palgrave, Basingstoke.

Fenton, S., Modood, T. and Carter, J. (2000), 'Ethnicity and Academia, Closure Models, Racism Models and Market Models', *Sociological Research Online*, Vol. 5, No. 2.

Feuchtwang, S. (1979), 'Collective Action and English Law against Racial Discrimination in Employment', *Power and Politics*, No. 4.

Feuchtwang, S. (1982), 'Occupational Ghettos', *Economy and Society*, Vol. 11, No. 3.

Fevre, R. (1984), *Cheap Labour and Racial Discrimination*, Gower Press, Aldershot.

Fevre, R. (1989), 'Informal Practices, Flexible Firms and Private Labour Markets', *Sociology*, Vol. 23, No. 1.

Fevre, R. (1992), *The Sociology of Labour Markets*, Harvester-Wheatsheaf, Hemel Hempstead.

Finlayson, L. and Nazroo, J. (1998), *Gender Inequalities in Nursing Careers*, Policy Studies Institute, London.

Fishkin, J. (1987), Liberty versus Equal Opportunity, in Paul, E. et al. (eds) *Equal Opportunity*, Blackwell, Oxford.

Forbes, I. (1991), 'Equal Opportunity: Radical, Liberal and Conservative Critiques', in Meehan, E. and Sevenhuijsen, S. (eds), *Equality Politics and Gender*, Sage, London.

Frank, A.G. (1986), *On Capitalist Underdevelopment*, Oxford University Press, Oxford.

Fryer, P. (1984), *Staying Power*, Pluto Press, London.

Gallie, D. (1988), *Employment in Britain*, Blackwell, Oxford.

Gillborn, S. and Gipps, C. (1996), *Recent Research on the Achievement of Ethnic Minority Pupils*, HMSO, London.

Gray, P., Elgar, J. and Bally, S. (1993), *Access to Training and Employment for Asian Women in Coventry*, Coventry City Council, Economic Development Unit, Research Paper.

Gregory, J. (1987), *Sex Race and the Law*, Sage, London.

The Guardian (2000), 'NHS Pay Awards Riddled with Racism', 21 June.

The Guardian (2001), 'Report Reveals Racism Reveals Racism in Medical Profession', 19 June.

Gupta, Y. (1977), 'The Educational and Vocational Aspirations of Asian Immigrant and English School Leavers', *British Journal of Sociology*, Vol. 28.

Halford, S. (1992), 'Feminist Change in a Patriarchal Organisation', in Savage, M. and Witz, A. (eds), *Gender and Bureaucracy*, Blackwell, Oxford.

Ham, C. and Hill, M. (1984), *The Policy Process in The Modern Capitalist State*, Harvester Press, New York.

Hamnett, C. and Randolph, W. (1988), 'Ethnic Minorities in the London Labour Market. A Longitudinal Analysis 1971–1981', *New Community*, Vol. 14, No. 3.

Harding, N. (1989), 'Equal Opportunities for Women in the NHS: The Prospects of Success?', *Public Administration*, Vol. 67, No. 1.

Hartmann, H. (1982), 'Capitalism, Patriarchy, and Job Segregation by Sex', in Giddens, A. and Held, D. (eds), *Classes, Power and Conflict, Classical and Contemporary Debates*, Macmillan, London.

Heath, A. and McMahon, D. (1995) *Education and Occupational Attainments: The Impact of Ethnic Origins*, Paper 34. Centre for Research Into Elections and Social Trends, February.

Hepple, B.A. (1983), 'Judging Equal Rights', *Current Legal Problems*, Vol. 36.

Hepple, B.A. (1992), 'Have Twenty Five Years of the Race Relations Acts in Britain Been a Failure?', in Hepple, B.A and Szyszack, E. (eds), *Discrimination: The Limits of the Law*, Mansell, London.

Hiro, D. (1971), *Black British, White British*, Eyre & Spottiswode, London.

Home Office (1999), *Equality and Fairness in the Fire Service*, available on the world wide web at *http://www.safety.odpm.gov.uk/fire/fepd/pdf/equal.pdf* accessed on 28 June 2002.

Hood, C. (1991), 'A Public Management for All Seasons?', *Public Administration*, Vol. 69, Spring.

Howard, A. (ed.) (1979), *The Crossman Diaries*, Methuen, London.

Hubbock, J. and Carter, S. (1980), 'Half a Chance: A Report on Job Discrimination against Young Blacks In Nottingham', CRE, London.

Iganski, P. and Mason, D. (2002), *Ethnicity, Equality of Opportunity and the British National Heatlh Service*, Ashgate, Aldershot.

Iganski, P. and Payne, G. (1996), 'Declining Disadvantage in the British Labour Market', *Ethnic and Racial Studies*, Vol. 19, No. 1.

Jary, D and Jary, J. (1995), *Dictionary of Sociology*, Collins, London.

Jenkins, R. (1986), *Racism and Recruitment: Managers, Organisations and Equal Opportunities in the Labour Market*, Cambridge University Press, Cambridge.

Jenkins, R. (1996), *Rethinking Ethnicity*, Sage, London.

Jenkins, R. and Solomos, J. (1987), *Racism and Equal Opportunities Policies in the 1980s*, Cambridge University Press, Cambridge.

Jenkins, R., Bryman, A., Ford, J., Keil, T. and Beardsworth, A. (1983), 'Information in the Labour Market: The Impact of Recession', *Sociology*, Vol. 17, No. 2.

Jewson, N. and Mason, D. (1986a), 'Modes of Discrimination in the Recruitment Process: Formalisation, Fairness and Efficiency', *Sociology*, Vol. 20, No. 1.

Jewson, N. and Mason, D. (1986b), 'The Theory and Practice of Equal Opportunities Policies: Liberal and Radical Approaches', *Sociological Review*, Vol. 34, No. 2.

Jewson, N. and Mason, D. (1987), 'Monitoring Equal Opportunities Policies, Principles and Practice', in Jenkins, R. and Solomos, J. (eds), *Racism and Equal Opportunity Policies in the 1980s*, Cambridge University Press, Cambridge.

Jewson, N. and Mason, D. (1992), 'Race, Equal Opportunities Policies and Employment Practice: Reflections on the 1980s and Prospects for the 1990s', *New Community*, Vol. 19, No. 1.

Jewson, N. and Mason, D. (1993), 'Equal Opportunities Policies in the 1990s: A Policy Principle Comes of Age', University of Leicester Discussion Paper.

Jewson, N., Mason, D. Lambkin, C. and Taylor, F. (1992), 'Ethnic Monitoring Policy and Practice', Department of Employment, London.

Johnson, R.A. (1990), 'Affirmative Action Policy in the United States: The Impact on Women', *Policy and Politics*, Vol. 18, No. 2, pp. 77–90.

Jones, T. (1993), *Britain's Ethnic Minorities: An Analysis of the Labour Force Survey*, Policy Studies Institute, London.

Kalton, G. and Moser, C.A. (1958), *Survey Methods in Social Investigation*, Basic Books, New York.

King's Fund (1990), *The Work of the Equal Opportunities Task Force – A Final Report*, King Edward's Hospital Fund for London.

Lawrence, D. (1974), *Black Migrants, White Natives*, Cambridge University Press, Cambridge.

Lee, G. and Loveridge, R. (1987), *The Manufacture of Disadvantage*, Open University Press, Buckingham.

Leonard, A. (1987), *Pyrrhic Victories: Winning Sex Discrimination and Equal Pay Cases in the Industrial Tribunals 1980–84*, HMSO, London.

Levitas, R. and Guy, W. (1996), *Interpreting Official Statistics*, Routledge, London.

Liff, S. and Webb, J. (1988), 'Play the White Man: The Social Construction of Fairness and Competition in Equal Opportunity Policies', *Sociological Review*, Vol. 36, No. 3, pp. 543–51.

Lloyd, C. and Seifert, R. (1995), 'Restructuring in the NHS: The Impact of the 1990 Reforms on the Management of Labour', *Work Employment & Society*, Vol. 9, No. 2, pp. 359–78.

Lovenduski, J. (1989), 'Implementing Equal Opportunities in the 1980s an Overview', *Public Administration*, Vol. 67, No. 1.

Lowery, S. and Macpherson, G. (1988), 'A Blot on the Profession', *British Medical Journal*, Vol. 296, pp. 657–8.

Lustgarten, L. (1980), *Legal Control of Racial Discrimination*, Macmillan, London.

Macdonald, I. (1977), *Race Relations, The New Law*, Butterworths, London.

Marable, M. (1995), *Beyond Black and White: Rethinking Race in American Politics and Society*, Verso, London.

Mason, D. (1994), 'Employment and the Labour Market', *New Community*, Vol. 20, No. 2.

McCrudden, C. and Baldwin, R. (1987), *Regulation and Public Law*, Weidenfeld & Nicolson, London.

Miles, R. (1989), *Racism*, Routledge, London.

Miles, R. and Phizacklea, A. (1980), *Labour and Racism*, Routledge & Kegan Paul, London.

Mirza, H. (1992), *Young Female and Black*, Routledge, London.

Modood, T. (1998), 'The Indian Economic Success (a challenge to some race relations assumptions)', *Policy and Politics*, Vol. 19, No. 13.

Modood, T. et al. (1997) *Ethnic Minorities in Britain* (4th National Survey), PSI, London.

Moore, R. and Wallace, T. (1975), *Slamming the Door: The Administration of Immigration Control*, Martin Robertson, London.

Morris, A.E. and Nott, S.M. (1991), *Working Women and The Law, Equality and Discrimination in Theory and Practice*, Routledge, London.

Murphy, R. (1984), 'The Structure of Closure: A critique and development of the theories of Weber, Collins, and Parkin', *British Journal of Sociology*, Vol. 35, pp. 547–67.

Neale, J. (1983), *Memoirs of a Callous Picket: Working for the NHS*, Pluto Press, London.

Nemerowizc, G. (1979), *Children's Perceptions of Gender and Work Roles*, Praeger, New York.

Nichols, T. (ed.) (1980), *Capital and Labour*, Athlone Press, New York.

Oakley, R. (1988), 'Employment In Police Forces: A Survey of Equal Opportunities', CRE, London.

Owen, D. (1991), 'Ethnic Minorities in Britain' (1991 Census statistical paper 1), ESRC, London.

Parkin, F. (1974), 'Strategies of Social Closure in Class Formation', in Parkin, F. (ed.), *The Social Analysis of Class Structure*, Tavistock, London.

Parkin, F. (1982), *Max Wober*, Routledge, London.

Patterson, S. (1963), *Dark Strangers*, Tavistock, London.

Paul, E.F., Miller, F.D., Paul, J. and Ahrens, J. (eds) (1987), *Equal Opportunity*, Blackwell, Oxford.

Peach, C. (1968), *West Indian Migration to Britain*, Oxford University Press, Oxford.

Peach, C. (1991), 'The Caribbean in Europe: Contrasting Patterns of Migration and Settlement in Britain, France and the Netherlands', Research Paper No. 15, Centre for Ethnic Relations, Warwick University.

Phizacklea, A. (1988), 'Gender, Racism and Occupational Segregation', in Walby, S. (ed.), *Gender Segregation at Work*, Open University Press, Buckingham.

Phizacklea, A. (ed.) (1983), *One Way Ticket*, Routledge, London.

Phizacklea, A. (1990), 'Unpacking the Fashion Industry', Taylor & Francis, London.

Pilkington, A. (1984), *Race Relations in Britain*, University Tutorial Press, London.

Pollert, A. and Rees, T. (1992), 'Equal Opportunity and Positive Action in Britain: Three Case Studies', Warwick Papers in Industrial Relations, No. 42.

Pollit, C., Harrison, S., Hunter, D. and Marnoch, G. (1991), 'General Management In the NHS: The Initial Impact 1983–1988', in *Public Administration*, Vol. 69. pp. 61–83.

Pollit, C. (1990), *Managerialism and the Public Services*, Oxford, Blackwell.

Premru, F. (1995), *Sun-a-Shine, Rain-a-Fall*, London Transport Museum, London.

Pryce, K. (1979), *Endless Pressure*, Penguin, Harmondsworth.

Pudney, S. with Shields, M. (2000), 'Gender, Race, Pay and Promotion in the British Nursing Profession. Estimation of a Generalised Ordered Probit Model', *Journal of Applied Econometrics*, 15, pp. 367–99.

Ram, M. (1992), 'Coping with Racism: Asian Employers in the Inner City', in *Work, Employment & Society*, Vol. 6, No. 4, December, pp. 601–18.

Rennie, S. (1993), 'Equal Opportunities as an Ethical Issue', *Equal Opportunities Review*, No. 51.

Rex, J. and Moore, R. (1967), *Race, Community and Conflict*, Oxford University Press, Oxford.

Rex, J. and Tomlinson, M. (1979), *Colonial Immigrants in an English City*, Routledge, London.

Roberts, K., Dench, S. and Richardson, D. (1986), *The Changing Structure of Youth Labour Markets*, Research Paper No. 59, Department of Employment, London.

Rubenstein, M. (1987), 'Modern Myths and Misconceptions: Equal Opportunities Make Good Business Sense', *Equal Opportunities Review*, No. 16, Nov/Dec.

Ruck, S. (ed.) (1960), *The West Indian Comes to Britain*, Routledge, London.

Sapsford, D. (1981), *Labour Market Economics*, Allen and Unwin, London.

Schmid, G. and Wietzel, R. (eds) (1984), *Sex Discrimination and Equal Opportunity*, Gower, Aldershot.

Silverman, D. and Jones, J. (1976), *Organisational Work*, Collier Macmillan, London.

Sloane, P. (1985), 'Discrimination in the Labour Market', in Carline, D., *Labour Economics*, Longman, Harlow.

Smith, A. (1994), *New Right Discourses on Race and Sexuality*, Cambridge University Press, Cambridge.

Smith, D.J. (1977), *Racial Disadvantage in Britain*, Penguin, Harmondsworth.

Smith, D.J. (1980), *Overseas Doctors in the National Health Service*, Policy Studies Institute, London.

Smith, D. and Troyna, B. (eds) (1983), *Racism School and The Labour Market*, National Youth Bureau, Leicester.

Smith, R. (1993), 'Deception in Research, and Racial Discrimination in Medicine', *British Medical Journal*, Vol. 306, pp. 668–9.

Solomos, J. (1988), *Black Youth, Racism and the State*, Cambridge University Press, Cambridge.

Solomos, J. (1989), 'Equal Opportunities Policies and Racial Inequality: The Role of Public Policy', *Public Administration*, Vol. 67, No. 1.

Sooben, P. (1990), *The Origins of the Race Relations Act*, ESRC research paper in ethnic relations No. 12, Centre for Research in Ethnic Relations, University of Warwick.

Thomas, M.E. and Hughes, M. (1986), 'The Continuing Significance of Race: A Study of Race Class and Quality of Life in America, 1972–1985', *American Sociological Review*, Vol. 51, December, pp. 830–41.

Turner, R. (1971), 'Sponsored and Contest Mobility and the School System', in Hopper, E. (ed.), *Readings in the Theory of Educational Systems*, Hutchinson, London.

Wainwright, D. (1979), *Discrimination in Employment*, Associated Business Press, London.

Wainwright, D. (1983), 'Through the Bureaucratic Maze: Managing an Equal Opportunities Programme', Runnymede Trust, London.

Walby, S. (1986), 'Segregation in Employment in Social and Economic Theory', in Walby, S. (ed.), *Gender Segregation at Work*, Open University Press, Milton Keynes.

Walby, S. (1987), *Patriarchy at Work*, University of Minnesota Press, Minnesota.

Walby, S. (1990), *Patriarchy*, Blackwell, Oxford.

Walby, S. (1992), 'Gender Work and Post Fordism', paper presented to the First European Conference of Sociology, Vienna, August.

Walsh, M.J. (1977), *Doctors Wanted: No Women Need Apply, Sexual Barriers in the Medical Profession, 1835–1975*, Yale University Press, New Haven, Conn.

Walvin, J. (1984), *Passage to Britain*, Pelican, London.

Webb, J. and Liff, S. (1988), 'Play the White Man: The Social Construction of Fairness in Equal Opportunities Programmes', *Sociological Review*, Vol. 36, No. 3.

Whitting, G., Moore, J. and Warren, P. (1993), 'Partnerships for Equality: A Review of Employers Equal Opportunities Groups', Employment Department Research Paper No. 19.

Wilkinson, B. (1992), 'Implementing Equal Opportunities', *Equal Opportunities Review*, No. 46.

Williams, P. (1997), *The Rooster's Egg*, Harvard University Press, Cambridge, Mass.

Williams, W.M. (1974), *Occupational Choice*, Allen & Unwin, London.

Wilson, M. (1994), 'A Career in the Health Service: Making the Most of Equal Opportunity', cited in *Healthy and Wise, The Essential Health Handbook for Black Women*, London, Virago.

Wilson, W.J. (1980), *The Declining Significance of Race*, University of Chicago Press, Chicago.

Wilson, W.J. (1987), *The Truly Disadvantaged: The Inner City, the Underclass and Public Policy*, University of Chicago Press, Chicago.

Witz, A. (1992), *Professions and Patriarchy*, Routledge, London.

Wrench, J. (1993), 'Employment and the Labour Market', *New Community*, Vol. 19, No. 2.

Index

acceptability criteria   13, 66–7, 128
  English language   151–4
  and possession of social
    characteristics   73
  Unicorn Trust   147–55
advertisements
  equal opportunities statement   45–6
  media for   121, 122
  restricted   122–4, 127
affirmative action policies   3–4,
    31–2, 40–1
  for equal opportunities   49–50
  and equality of outcome   81
  hard (radical)   43, 52, 83
  reaction against   33–4, 82–3
  in US   32–4, 50–1
African-Asian groups
  employment rates   **18**, 19
  in professions   25
  relative success   27
African-Caribbean groups   13
  labour market position of post-war
    migrants   25, 89
  sponsorship for immigrants
    111–13, 114
  unemployment   18, **18**
African-Caribbean women
  the 'dirty jobs' in NHS   80–1,
    99–102, 115, 178
  experiences of immigration
    84, 94–7
  experiences (research interviews)
    93–4
  in labour market   25
  nursing qualifications and training
    70, 75–6, 79, 80, 102–5, 111
  post-war recruitment to NHS   91,
    96–7, 109–14, 116–17
  retiring from nursing   68,
    76–7, 79
Anthias, F. and Yuval-Davis, N.   26,
    179, 181
Anwar, M. and Ali, A.   89

Asian groups   7, 13
Association of University Teachers
    161

Bacchi, C.   31–2, 50
Bangladeshi groups   13, 27
  unemployment   18, **18**, 28
  women in labour market   25, 26
Banton, M.   6, 15, 20, 141
Barbados, recruiting offices   96,
    110, 115
Becker, H.S.   158
Beishon, S. et al.   70, 93, 122, 149
  Working in a Multi-ethnic NHS report
    76, 106
beliefs, and choice   15
Black Power Movement   161
Black and White Britain
    (PSI report 1984)   16–17
Black Workers Forum   142, 156
Blackaby, D. et al.   30
Bourn, C. and Whitmore, J.   38
Bradley, H.   49, 54, 64, 69,
    91, 179, 181
Brennan, J. and McGeevor, P.   19
Bristol, 'race' riots   7
British National Party   36
British Rail   87
Brooks, Dennis, *Race and Labour
    in London Transport*   13
Brown, C.   9, 15, 18

California, University of   50
'canteen culture'   43, 161
Caribbean, economic
    underdevelopment   86
Carmichael, Stokely   161
Carpenter, M.   91
Carter, J., Fenton, S. and
    Modood, T.
  *Ethnicity and Employment in Higher
    Education*   4, 27, 70, 72, 78
  research   163–75

Carter, T.   94
'chill factor'   20, 21, 67
Chinese groups
   employment rates   19
   relative success   25, 27, 64, 165
choice
   and discrimination   15
   of occupation   20–1, 120, 171–2
civil rights
   legislation (US)   53
   US movement   11, 33
class (socio-economic)
   and education levels   71
   and labour markets   11, 21,
      29, 179
   in US   11–12
Cockburn, C.   54–5, 68, 182–3
Coker, N.   69
Collinson, D.   35, 57, 148
colonial ideology   87, 88, 116
Colonial Office, and recruitment
      of nurses   85, 110, 111–13,
      114, 115, 116
Commission for Racial Equality
      26, 162
   and discrimination in labour
      market   28–9
   and ethnic monitoring   155–6
   higher education study   164
   and positive action   40
   powers under Race Relations
      Amendment Act   39
   on recruitment methods   122
Commonwealth Immigration Act
   (1962)   90
contracts, fixed or short-term   81,
   169–70, **170**, 172
credentialism   66–9, 77, 183
   and acceptability criteria   151
   in nursing   79, 80, 92, 127
credentials, variations between
      qualifications   69–71
criminal justice system (UK)   160
Crown appointments   39
Crown Prosecution Service   162
culture, and acceptability criteria
   153
culture change   54, 55–6, 183
Curran, M.M.   92

Dale, K. and Liff, S.   57
Daniel, W.W.   9, 15, 19
Davies, C. and Rosser, J.   91, 180
decision-making, objectivity in   83
difference, notion of   64, 65
Din v *Carrington Viyella*   38
direct discrimination   16, 36
   defined by Race Relations Act   37
   in NHS   103, 174
disadvantage
   accumulated   19
   assumptions about   25
   compared with individual
      discrimination   59, 162
   and power structures   54
   radical view of   52–3
discrimination   2, 15
   changed attitudes to   29, 183
   double (race and gender)   178,
      181–2
   gatekeeper   104–5
   individual   59, 162
   in labour market   28–9
   in NHS   101–2, 103, 174
   in pay awards   160
   in promotion   124–9
   in recruitment   101, 121–4, 182
   reverse (positive)   32, 40–1
   see also direct discrimination;
      indirect discrimination;
      racism; victimisation
diversity policies   51
Dworkin, R.   50, 51, 70

Eastern Europe, post-war migration
      from   88
economic restructuring, effect on
      ethnic minority workers   23–4
education levels   15, 19, 25
   and class   71
   and employment rates   18–19,
      18, 22
   and promotion   **126**
   see also qualifications
education system   162
efficiency, and equality   156–8
employers
   and equal opportunities
      policies   45–6

factors in discriminatory decisions
15–16
see also recruitment
employment
discrimination in 2, 30
patterns of 10
Employment Appeals Tribunal 38
engineering industry 68
English language 14–15
as acceptability criterion 151–4
equal opportunities 2
aims of 3–4
and bad faith 142–4
in employment practice 30
Equal Opportunities Review (journal)
57–8
equal opportunity policies
compared with affirmative action
31–2, 49–51, 53
and cost 46, 182
liberal 41, 42, 52, 131
and outcomes 62, 81, 140
personnel managers' adoption of
56–8
radical 41, 42–3, 52–3, 83
typologies of 53, 54
see also recruitment
Equal Oppportunities Commission,
nursing training courses 75–6
equality
concept of 30, 32, 34, 41–5
and efficiency 156–8
'hard and soft' 51–6
and opportunity 45
equity, concept of 34
Esmail, A. and Everington, S. 14
ethnic difference 1
ethnic minority groups
differences within 13–14
dual closure (women) 27, 78,
80, 178
education levels 22
effect of economic restructuring 22
and equal opportunity policies
55–6
extra effort required 27
historical migration (UK) 85–6
labour market position of 9,
12–13, 22, 28, 64–5, 84, 89

marginalized within occupations
5–6, 78, 137, 183
as negatively privileged
(Weber) 12
and NHS advertisements 121–4
and qualifications in higher
education 169
and shift work 119–21
university academic staff 165–6,
165
view of affirmative action 53–4
women in higher education 173
ethnic monitoring 155–6
ethnic penalty, concept of 26
ethnicity
of academic staff **165**
and labour markets 13–23, 24–5
and shift work 119–21
*Ethnicity and Employment in Higher
Education* study 4, 27, 70, 72, 78
European Volunteer Workers
Scheme 88
examinations, use of 70

feminism, impact of 29–30
feminist ideology 3, 179–80
Fenton, S. 6, 163, 172
see also Carter, J.
Feuchtwang, S. 118
Fevre, R. 20, 123, 127
Finlayson, L. and Nazroo, J. 159
fire service 65, 162, 174
Ford Motor Company 22
Frank, A.G. 86
Fryer, Peter 85

gender differences
in higher education 168, **169**,
172, **172**, 173
in labour market 25, 179
within ethnic groups 13–14
within professions 77–8, 162–3
generational differences 18, 26,
30, 178
perception of discrimination
75, 181
geriatric nursing 67, 90, 92
Gray, P. et al. 14
Grunwick dispute 36

Ham, C. and Hill, M.   47
Hamilton, Charles   161
harassment, 'racial'
   physical attacks   106
   verbal abuse   105–9
Heath, A. and McMahon, D.   26
hierarchies   5, 63, 107
   and policy   47
   and power struggles   134
higher education
   ethnicity and employment
      research   4, 27, 70,
      72, 78, 163–7
   see also universities
Higher Education Statistics Dataset
   (1996–97)   164
Hiro, D.   86, 89

ideologies, used by personnel
   managers   57
Iganski, P. and Payne, G.   26, 41
immigrants
   class origins of   26
   and colonial identity   115–16
   experiences of (research interviews)
      94–6
   and 'myth of return'   98–9
   as 'strangers'   97–9
   in US   11
immigration (from New
   Commonwealth)   9, 28, 85–90
   culture shock   97–8
   pattern of   85–6
   pull factors   86, 95–6, 180
   push factors   86–7, 95, 180
   as temporary   89, 98–9, 116
   see also African-Caribbean women
Immigration and Nationality
   Directorate (Home Office)   39
India, post-war migration to UK   86
Indian groups   13
   relative success   25, 27, 28, 64
indirect discrimination   16, 36, 75
   defined by Race Relations Act   37
   proof of   36–7
   in recruitment   122
industrial tribunals
   interpretation of legislation   37
   Unicorn Trust   131, 141–2

institutional racism   35, 36,
   57, 160–2
interviews, recruitment   60, 136–7,
   145–6, 147–8
Ireland, migration from   88

Jenkins, R.   4, 6, 35, 57
   informal recruitment   60
   on interviews   148
   Racism and Recruitment   13, 177
   suitability and acceptability criteria
      66–7, 73, 77–8, 154–5
Jewson, N. and Mason, D.   52, 53,
   54, 60, 131, 134
jobs, stereotyped   55, 64
Jones, T.   15

King, Rodney (King Affair)   6–7

labour, division of
   international   23
   racial (NHS)   99–102
Labour Force Survey (2000)   25
labour markets
   academic   164
   changing   2, 4, 22, 26–7
   ethnicity and   13–23, 89
   exclusion and segregation
      in   24–7, 28
   and informal networks   136–7
   internal   121, 122, 127
   restructuring   14, 23
   see also occupations
labour shortage (post-war UK)   9–10,
   86, 87–8
   government response to   109–14
Lawrence, D.   86, 89
Lawrence, Stephen, murder of   3, 7
   see also Macpherson Report (1999)
legislation
   civil rights (US)   53
   UK   35–7, 53
   see also Race Relations Act
Liff, S. and Webb, J.   55, 183
line managers
   autonomy of   60, 82
   recruitment responsibilities   58–9
   see also ward managers
Liverpool, 'race' riots   7

local government 39
  radical equality policies 52
London, 'race' riots 7
London Transport 13
  direct Commonwealth recruitment
    87, 90, 96

Macpherson Report (1999) 3, 35,
    36, 57, 162–3
  'canteen culture' 43, 161
  effect of 183
Major, John 88–9
management structures 129, 134,
    156–7, 183
managers
  and enforcement of equal
    opportunities policy 129
  harassment by (NHS) 107–8
  and promotion 128
  self-interest of 59
  see also line managers; personnel
    managers; ward managers
manufacturing industry
  decline of 14, 23, 25
  ethnic concentrations in 14, 28
Marable, Manning 9, 12, 33–4
markets, primacy of 43–4
medical profession
  doctors' qualifications 69
  dual closure 77
  recruitment from New
    Commonwealth 89–90
  sponsorship in 71
  see also nursing
merit, as objective 83
meritocracy 42, 52, 175, 176
metalworking industries, West
    Midlands 89
Metropolitan Police 57
  see also Macpherson Report
migration
  patterns of 27–8, 85–6
  see also immigrants; immigration
Miles, R. 6, 15, 87–8
Ministry of Health, and NHS
    labour shortage 85, 110,
    111–13
Ministry of Labour, and NHS labour
    shortage 85, 110, 113, 115

Modood, T. 9, 14–15, 17, 18, 163
  on ethnic disadvantage 25–6
  labour market 19
  see also Carter, J.
Murphy, R. 65

National Front 36
National Health Service (NHS) 84,
    90, 174
  direct Commonwealth recruitment
    87, 91
  discrimination in 101–2, 103,
    107–9, 174, 182
  equal opportunities policies 4, 129
  informal networks in 74
  positive action policies 41
  post-war labour shortages 9, 85,
    89, 90–1, 109–14
  segregations within 91–2, 99–102,
    109, 128, 180
  see also medical profession; nursing;
    ward managers
national identity 44
nationality, definitions of 165
Nemerowicz, G. 91
networks
  and access to sponsorship 72
  informal 74–5
  informal recruitment 59–60, 63,
    82, 136–7, 157
  used to pressurize 145
New Public Management (NPM)
    style 157–8
New Right
  and national identity 44
  political resurgence 7, 36
  and primacy of market 43–4
news media 162
newspaper industry 67–8
nursing
  credentialism in 79, 80, 92, 127
  disciplinary policies 106, 130,
    134, 140
  gendered occupation 80, 90–2,
    159, 180
  harassment by staff 106–9, 116
  qualifications 70, 75–6, 80
  'racial' division of labour 99–102,
    158–9, 177, 180

nursing – *Continued*
recruitment (current)   76, 180
retirement of New Commonwealth
    nurses   68, 76–7, 79
SEN and SRN training system
    102–5
social closure in   67, 80, 99–100,
    104, 116
training courses   75–6, 93, 111–12
verbal abuse from patients   105–6,
    116
see also Unicorn Trust

occupations
factors in choice of   20–1,
    120, 171–2
racialized niches   21, 118,
    171–2, 177–8
see also labour market
opportunity, concept of   45–6
opposition, culture of   82
organizations
policy-makers and   46–7
power structures within   54,
    82, 134

Pakistan, post-war migration
    to UK   86
Pakistani groups
relative disadvantage   27
in textile industry   20, 67, 89
unemployment   18, **18**, 28
women in labour market
    25, 26
Parkin, F.   65, 70
patronage   73–4
Patterson, S., *Dark Strangers*   10, 86,
    89, 90–1
Peach, Ceri   87
personnel managers
and equal opportunity policies
    56–8
function marginalized   58,
    129, 157
role in recruitment process   60,
    133–4, 139–40
Philippines, NHS recruitment
    from   76, 180
Phizacklea, A. and Miles, R.   178, 179

policy
defining   47
outcomes   41
policy implementation
bottom-up   48, 49
equal opportunities   58–62
process of   34–5, 41–2, 47
top-down   47, 48–9
policy-making   46–7
political correctness, and opposition
    to equality policies   82, 143
Political and Economic Planning
    Reports
    (1968)   14
    (1977)   14
positive action   40–1
power, within organizations   54, 57,
    82, 134
Price v *Civil Service Commission*   37
prison service   40, 162
probation service   40
professions   1–2, 3, 5
entry into   5
ethnic minority groups in   3, 25,
    174, 182
job vacancies   122
marginalization within   5–6, 78,
    174, 176, 183
patronage and sponsorship in
    74, 82
post-war migrants in   89
racialized   3, 162
use of credentialism   66–7
see also medical profession;
    universities
promotion
and acceptability criteria   128
applications   **124**
discrimination in   101, 104–5,
    124–9
influence of personnel
    managers on   57
numbers (by ethnic groups)   **125**
nursing profession   76
and qualifications   126, **126**
temporary   126–7, **126**
and training   125, 127, **127**
in UK universities   173–4
psychiatric nursing   67, 90, 92

public authorities, duties under Race
    Relations Amendment Act   38–9
Pudney, S. and Shields, M.   182

qualifications   5, 75, 151
    as artificial barriers   52–3, 66
    and promotion   **126**
    variations between   69–71

'race', use of term   6
race relations   10, 32
    UK National surveys   19, 20, 25
Race Relations Act (1976)   16–17,
    22, 35
    impact of   29, 35–6
    provisions of   37–8
Race Relations Amendment Act
    (2000)   22, 29, 35
    provisions of   38–9
    scope of   39–40
race riots   32
    1980s (UK)   7
race-awareness training   61–2
racism
    'canteen culture'   43, 161
    'common-sense' assumptions   15,
        103, 129, 175, 176
    debate in US   6–7
    institutional   35, 36, 57, 160–2
    new (New Right)   44
    and social closure   177
    see also discrimination
Racism in Medicine (King's Fund
    report)   69
Reagan, Ronald   44
recruitment
    and acceptability criteria   147–55
    constitution of interview panels
        145–7
    discrimination in   101, 121–4, 182
    fairness in   62–3
    formality in   60–1, 62–3
    informal   59–60, 63, 82, 130, 158
    role of personnel managers in   6,
        57, 133–4, 138–40
    role of ward (line) managers   58–9,
        133–40
    see also advertisements
redundancy, factors in   24

Rennie, S.   58
research analysis
    (Unicorn Trust)   118
Rex, J. and Tomlinson, M., *Colonial
    Immigrants in an English City*   10

self-employment   19, 25
service industries, immigrant
    labour in   89
Sex Discrimination Act (1975)
    35, 36–7
shift work
    ethnicity and   119–21
    and promotion   125
    textile industry   20, 67, 89
Simpson, O.J., trial   6
Singh, Gurbux   162
skills, stereotyped definitions of   92
Smith, A.   44
Smith, D.J.   9, 15, 16, 20, 69, 72, 74
social closure
    and access to jobs   21, 73
    concept of   8, 11, 64, 177
    definitions of   65
    dual   77–8, 80
    and professions   79–81
    resistance strategies   75–7
    strategies of   66, 104, 183
    see also credentialism;
        sponsorship
social identity, gender and race   179
social mobility, increased   26–7
sponsorship   71–3
    for Caribbean immigrants
        111–13, 114
state intervention, conservative
    view of   43–4, 45
stereotypes   15, 176
    and redundancy   24
suitability criteria   13, 66–7, 147, 148

textile industry, concentration of
    Pakistani men in   20, 67, 89
Thatcher, Margaret   44
theatre   162
Thomas, M.E. and Hughes, M.
    11–12
trade unions   68
    role of   144–5

training
  nursing   75–6, 93
  and promotion   125, 127, **127**
  SEN and SRN system   102–5
Trinidad, economic weakness   95
trust, failure of   143
Turner, R.   72

unemployment
  by ethnic group   14, **17**
  by qualification   **18**
  female   **18**
  and recession   23–4, 28
unemployment rates   14, 17, 18
Unicorn Trust
  acceptability criteria   147–55
  Equal Opportunities Action Group
      156
  equal opportunities policy
      129–30, 131, 132–3, 140
  industrial tribunals   131, 141–2
  interview panels   145–7
  managerial structure   129, 134,
      156–7
  public image   132, 141
  research analysis   118
  see also promotion; recruitment
United Kingdom
  direct recruitment from New
      Commonwealth   87–8
  government response to labour
      shortage   109–14, 116
  perception as mother country   88,
      94–5
  see also equal opportunities policies;
      legislation
United States
  affirmative action policies   32–4,
      50–1
  Black middle class   11,
      28, 179
  economic recession   23
  institutional racism in   161
  and Islamic and Arabic
      identities   1
  'Philadelphia Plan'   33
  race relations   11–12
  racism debate   6–7
  Walter McCarran Act (1952)   86

universities
  academic staff by ethnic group
      165
  access to sponsorship in   72
  affirmative action policies (US)
      50–1
  age structure of staff   166, **166**
  elite (UK)   50, 167
  employment function   **173**
  fixed-term contracts   169–70,
      170, 172
  hierarchies of   69, **169**
  minority staff by ethnic group
      168
  research   163–7
  social closure in   81
  staff grades   **169**, **170**, **172**
  structural discrimination in
      170–1, 174–5
usurpation, strategies of   75–7

victimization, defined by Race
    Relations Act   16, 38

Wainwright, D.   62
Walby, S.   3, 6, 68, 69, 179
Walter McCarran Act (1952) (US)   86
Walvin, J.   86–7
ward managers   129
  and control of recruitment process
      128, 133–40, 158
  power of   144–5
  see also line managers
Weber, Max *see* social closure
West Indies, post-war recruiting
    offices   90
Wilkinson, B.   59–60
Wilson, W. Julius, *The Declining
    Significance of Race*   11, 12
Witz, A.   6, 8, 65, 77–8, 79, 182
women
  and changes in employment
      cultures   56
  and dual closure   28, 77–8, 80, 178
  and feminized jobs   68–9
  in higher education   168, 172,
      172, 173
  in professions   6
  see also Sex Discrimination Act (1975)

ISBN 978-0-9565029-0-2

Published by Louise Mclean's Publishing,

London, UK.

Legal Disclaimer: This book is written as an educational resource for the public. It is not intended to replace appropriate diagnosis and/or treatment by a qualified physician.

Introduction

Homeopathy is a highly effective form of natural medicine which treats a multitude of ailments. Recently it has been experiencing a resurgence in popularity, though it has been in use around the world for over 200 years.

I first discovered homeopathy in 1986, after initially buying a self help book to treat myself and my family and in 1993 I decided to sign up for the 4 year course. However once I started reading the homeopathic text books, I realised that it was a lifetime's study!

So often, it is a positive personal healing experience which make practitioners decide to study and practise it themselves. Since I started using it, I have witnessed people being healed of a wide range of conditions by myself and other homeopathic practitioners. I have personally treated hayfever, flu, bronchitis, fevers, tonsillitis, middle ear infections, tinnitus, cystitis, rheumatism, fractures, broken ankles, cold sores – and countless other maladies.

Then in 1996, something happened to me which really put homeopathy to the test! After an emotional shock, I developed a lump in my right breast, which appeared a few days later. My confidence in homeopathy made me determined to find out whether I could find a remedy to heal it, as I had seen these listed in the homeopathic repertory. When I found the indicated remedy, causing the lump to disappear overnight, I never looked back!

I now only use homeopathic remedies and 1991 was the last time I took antibiotics or any other pharmaceutical medicine. After 24 years of using it exclusively, I wanted to write a book to tell people about its exceptional and long lasting benefits.

Millions worldwide can testify to the excellent results produced when conventional drugs have failed them. This is because people are tired of suffering the side effects of chemical drugs and are looking for something safe that works.

This book is for you and people everywhere who want to discover the exceptional benefits of using this inexpensive and very effective healing medicine. I sincerely hope it answers some of the questions you want to ask, as it is has been written to explain homeopathy in a simple and straight forward way.

The possibilities for homeopathy are endless and once you experience it yourself, you will never doubt its fast acting results! It could be healing you and your family right now!

You can try it out by buying a first aid kit from a homeopathic pharmacy but for chronic conditions, visit a qualified and registered homeopathic practitioner (see Chapter 15). For further information, have a look at the Homeopathy Heals website, which has masses of good articles and scientific studies, as well as a useful selection of Links pages at **www.homeopathyheals.me.uk**

Louise McLean, LCCH MHMA.

Contents

1. What is Homeopathy and How does it Work?

2. Who Uses Homeopathy?

3. How Can Homeopathy Help Me?

4. What Does Homeopathy Treat?

5. Every Patient is Unique – Individualisation

6. Homeopathic Remedy Types

7. The Homeopathic Practitioner

8. How Quickly Will I Get Better?

9. How Safe are Homeopathic Medicines?

10. How are Homeopathic Medicines Made?

11. Homeopathic Medicine compared to Modern drugs

12. Homeopathic Hospitals and Scientific Trials

13. Brief Homeopathic History

14. First Aid Remedies

15. Useful Contacts

16. References

17. Self Help Books and Further Reading

1. What is Homeopathy and How does it Work?

Homeopathy is a complete system of medicine, systematically developed over 200 years ago by Dr. Samuel Hahnemann, a German doctor and chemist (see Chapter 13). It is an evidence-based, empirical form of medicine. Comprehensive and wide-ranging, it treats all conditions and illnesses whether of the mind, emotions or body.

Hippocrates the 'Father of Medicine' stated that there were two laws of healing – the Law of Opposites and the Law of Similars. The Law of Opposites is the way conventional doctors treat illness by giving medicines which are 'anti' such as antibiotics, antihistamines, antipsychotics, anti-inflammatories, anti-convulsants, etc. The Law of Similars or 'Similia Similibus Curentur' is a Latin phrase meaning 'Likes cures Like' and is the chief way in which homeopathy works.

Homeopathic theories are based on the Law of Similars which also corresponds to the Law of Attraction. Like Attracts Like, Like Cures Like. We can see the law of attraction in every day life where you find people with similar life situations helping and sympathising with each other.

Through like for like, a substance (plant, mineral, etc.), which would cause symptoms in a healthy person, can be used to cure the same symptoms in a sick person, when given in a dilute and dynamically potentised dose. An example would be the remedy Apis Mellifica made from honey bees which can be given to cure a bee sting or diluted snake venom to antidote a snake bite.

Every human body has its own natural curative powers, also known as chi or prana, which homeopaths call the Vital Force. Homeopathic medicine works by stimulating and awakening the patient's curative powers, to create a healing reaction.

The human race has survived because we have this self-healing mechanism. All that is needed is the right stimulus (remedy) to start the process of restoring health. The potentised remedy acts as a catalyst, setting healing into motion. It powerfully stimulates the immune system or Vital Force to heal the body, through 'like for like'.

Internally our bodies electrically transmit messages to all parts and systems. Illness is caused when these messages are not getting through or where there is a blockage. All systems of the body should be communicating with each other at all times. Our bodies are made up of a large percentage of water which is a great conductor of electricity. Homeopathic medicines communicate a current, pattern or frequency of potentised energy throughout the whole system which kick starts the body's many healing mechanisms.

The remedies work on the basis of resonance and respond to a matching symptom pattern, through like heals like. They stimulate the body to heal through this vibration. If there is no matching energy pattern there is no effect. Just as when you pluck a string on a violin, the same string will vibrate on another violin in the room.

Homeopathy is highly effective at combating the symptoms of ill health in a safe and thorough manner, re-balancing the body and strengthening the defences and this it does very effectively, giving long term benefits. For example, after proper treatment, many people discover that their overall level of health improves for longer periods so that they can enjoy a better quality of life.

2. Who Uses Homeopathy?

According to the World Health Organisation, homeopathy is the 2nd most popular and most widely used medicine in the world today with 400,000 homeopathic doctors in India alone!

Homeopathy has always had the support of the elite in society in Europe and America. Britain's present Queen Elizabeth II and Prince Charles endorse it and English royalty have traditionally always had their own homeopathic doctor. Today this is Dr. Peter Fisher of the Royal London Homeopathic Hospital. According to rumour, Queen Elizabeth never travels anywhere without taking her homeopathic vials and occasionally dispenses pills to her royal staff.

Homeopathy was popular among many of the most respected writers in Britain such as Charles Dickens, William Makepeace Thackeray, George Bernard Shaw, W.B. Yeats, Sir Arthur Conan Doyle and Alfred, Lord Tennyson. Famous American authors include Henry James, Henry Wadsworth Longfellow, Louisa M. Alcott, Mark Twain and J.D. Salinger.

Many American Presidents such as Abraham Lincoln, James Garfield and William McKinley, had treatment and in Britain Prime Minister Benjamin Disraeli. Artists and musicians who used it include Renoir, Van Gogh, Monet Gaugin, Yehudi Menuhin, Beethoven, Chopin and Schumann. Other famous supporters were the Russian writers Dostoevsky, Chekhov and philosopher Johann Wolfgang von Goethe.

Nowadays, there are many celebrities who enjoy the benefits of homeopathy. Americans stars include Tina Turner, Whoopi Goldberg, Pamela Anderson, Jane Fonda, Cher, Martin Sheen, Lesley Anne Warren, Mariel Hemingway, Lindsay Wagner, Cindy Crawford, Linda Gray, Susan Blakely, Cybil Sheppard, Dizzy Gillespie, Angelica Houston, Priscilla and Lisa Marie Presley,

Jennifer Aniston, Jerry Hall, Diane von Furstenberg, Ashley Judd, Naomi Judd, Australian stars Olivia Newton-John and Natalie Imbruglia and Swedish celebrity Britt Ekland.

British celebrities include Catherine Zeta-Jones, Jane Seymour, Susan Hampshire, Susan George, Marie Helvin, Paul McCartney, Michael Caine, Michael York, Vidal Sassoon, David Beckham, Roger Daltrey, Annie Lennox, Kim Cattrall, Orlando Bloom with tennis stars Boris Becker and Martina Navratilova using it for sports injuries. A comprehensive list can be found on the website of Sue Young and in Dana Ullman's book 'The Homeopathic Revolution'. (1) (2)

Homeopathy is practised nowadays in countries all over the world and is especially popular in France, Germany, South America and India. It is also popular in Russia, South Africa, Saudi Arabia and the USA. In India there are 100 homeopathic medical schools and the number of patients taking homeopathic medicines has increased from around 800,000 patients in 1997 to 13 million patients in 2006. (3) Mahatma Ghandi was largely responsible for its huge popularity in India today.

In a 2008 Global TGI survey people were asked whether they trust homeopathy. The following percentages of people living in urban areas said YES: India 62%, Brazil 58%, Saudi Arabia 53%, Chile 49%, United Arab Emirates 49%, France 40%, South Africa 35%, Russia 28%, Germany 27%, Argentina 25%, Hungary 25%, USA 18%, UK 15%. (4)

The popularity of homeopathy has increased in the past 30 years and estimated to be growing the world over.

3. How Can Homeopathy Help Me?

It is important to understand that homeopathy is a completely different system of medicine to the current conventional medical model and that it can be used to treat every type of illness. Unlike pharmaceutical drugs, it not only helps heal your existing complaint(s) but also improves your whole state of being - mentally, emotionally and physically.

Conventional medical doctors give out the same drug to a wide range of people for a given condition, whereas homeopathy individualises a medicine which best fits the patient, carefully noting their personal symptoms.

Homeopathic practitioners believe in preventative medicine. It is important to go for treatment at the first symptoms and signs of ill health before they worsen and you end up on medication for the rest of your life or succumbing to the surgeon's knife! You can save yourself a huge amount of trouble in the future and this cannot be emphasised enough.

Many of us know of friends and family who started out with minor symptoms and ended up on prescription drugs. These caused side effects needing additional medication or operations that caused more problems, needing further interventions or surgery, etc. etc.

Homeopaths believe that disease manifests for four main reasons. Firstly, it is inherited through parents, grandparents, ancestors. Secondly, it can be caused by an event such as a shock, death of a loved one, divorce, job loss - any event that has a serious impact upon a person's life. Thirdly, it can be caused by the side effects of drugs, vaccines and environmental toxicity and these can be passed down through the genes to your children. Fourthly, it can be caused by accidents and injury.

In acute illness which comes on suddenly such as pain, fever, headache, diarrhoea, vomiting, a well chosen homeopathic remedy can work very fast. In deeper chronic conditions of longer duration, improvement can be more gradual. The general rule is a month for a year, so if you have had a complaint for 5 years, it will take at least 5 months to clear completely. All the time you will be getting better, instead of worsening, which is the usual trend for long term illness. The rate of healing depends upon your overall state of health which will determine how fast you get better. There are many levels of health and these are taken into consideration during treatment.

There is also a strong body/mind connection, where over time a negative state of mind will eventually affect the physical body causing disease. Many people become 'stuck' in an emotional state, cannot move on in their lives and this is where homeopathy can help tremendously.

All diseases follow a pattern and no organ becomes diseased without first giving signs and symptoms. Just as diseases follow a pattern, healing also follows a pattern—in the reverse order the disease followed.

People sometimes buy self help books and treat themselves with over the counter homeopathic remedies (see Chapter 9) and this can be fine for acute ailments. However, although prescribing for yourself might work well initially, it is always better to visit a qualified homeopath to resolve deeper problems, as they have undergone the full training and are able to assess the totality of your symptoms. This is because it is hard to be completely objective about yourself, which is absolutely necessary in order to find the correct remedy, as the homeopathic practitioner must take into consideration your whole state of being.

In the UK healthcare is delivered free through the National Health Service, so people readily take advantage of this but paying a little money to save yourself years of chronic health problems, is money very well spent. After all, without good health, your life becomes greatly restricted. As many people say, 'Health is Wealth'!

You can find a homeopathic practitioner on the websites listed at the end of this book under Useful Contacts.

4. What does Homeopathy Treat?

All conditions of whatever nature and type are treatable with homeopathic medicine. Not all are completely curable but in difficult cases, symptoms can be greatly alleviated. It depends upon the skill and experience of the practitioner.

Typical examples include headaches, conjunctivitis, toothache, sinusitis, middle ear infections, tinnitus, tonsillitis, hayfever, asthma, flu, fever, bronchitis, colic, constipation, diarrhoea, haemorrhoids, cystitis, shingles, herpes, measles, chickenpox, ulcers, abscess, warts, black eye, burns, bruises, rheumatism, arthritis, which can be healed with homeopathic medicine. There are homeopaths who have had great success treating much more serious illness such as heart and liver disease, etc., and in India there are experienced homeopathic doctors who have cured many cases of cancer.

For women, problems with their monthly cycle or menopause are usually treatable. Sexual dysfunctions and infertility can be helped and male issues of confidence and impotence successfully remedied.

In our modern world, the greatest problems are depression, stress, anxiety, panic attacks, fear and phobias. There are many homeopathic medicines for these states. Similarly grief and unhappiness when they become a long term problem, can be greatly alleviated after taking one of the many homeopathic remedies available.

It is also common to find that the onset of a physical illness can stem back to an important event in the life of the patient such as a shock, fright, loss or grief. The homeopath will select a remedy that corresponds to the way the patient reacted to that event, mentally, emotionally and physically, in order to clear the state which caused the illness. In other words you treat the cause, to remove the effect.

In the homeopathic model of health, illness and disease often develop through negative states of mind. Nowadays it is better understood that the state of mind will affect the physical body. Therefore the homeopath gives the remedy which addresses and treats those traits and this in turn will usually heal the physical malady, if it was caused by an unhappy mental state and negative emotions.

In order to find the best homeopathic medicine for you, the practitioner will search through the many volumes of Materia Medica of homeopathic medicines as well as the Homeopathic Repertory of symptoms. These advanced homeopathic books can only be obtained through specialist bookshops (see Chapter 15). Nowadays many homeopaths use computer software programmes which contain all of this information.

The Homeopathic Repertory, typically 2000 pages, contains all of the information derived from Homeopathic Provings (e.g. testing remedies out on healthy people - see Chapter 10), as well as the many years of clinical practice of expert practitioners. Remedies are listed in abbreviated form, such as Sulph for Sulphur or Phos for Phosphorus, alongside the symptoms (rubrics). It is divided into sections in this order: Mind, Vertigo, Head, Eye, Vision, Ear, Hearing, Nose, Face, Mouth, Teeth, Throat, External Throat, Stomach, Abdomen, Rectum, Stool, Bladder, Kidney, Prostate Gland, Urethra, Urine, Male, Female, Larynx, Respiration, Cough, Expectoration, Chest, Back, Extremities, Sleep, Dreams, Chill, Fever, Perspiration, Skin, Generals. Some sections are bigger than others.

In the volumes of Materia Medica, thousands of homeopathic medicines are listed alphabetically with symptoms for each listed in the same physical order as the Repertory. Again these are taken from the Homeopathic Provings, as well as verified by famous homeopathic practitioners through many years of clinical practice.

Every symptom of mind, emotions and body is listed in these books. Symptoms that would mean little to a medical doctor can almost always be looked up and the curative remedy found.

Homeopathy is like a vast study of human nature, showing how states of mind and emotions correlate with the physical body and can culminate in illness. The homeopath must be able to retain an encyclopedia of symptoms in his/her head to be a successful prescriber who can quickly find the correct remedy.

From broken bones to ingrowing toenails, homeopathy can help all! See Chapter 14 for a list of some of the First Aid Remedies.

5. Every Patient is Unique - Individualisation

Homeopathy individualises every person treating people with unique personalities as well as different physical looks and emotional temperaments. It treats their diverse patterns of symptoms and looks at the patient as a whole. Why does the patient need their perfect remedy to be individualised? This is because on close examination during case-taking, people are so very different.

Is it not true that no two people are alike? That every person is unique? This is why it is possible to see 20 people with asthma and they might all need a different homeopathic medicine! There are in fact about 250 homeopathic medicines for asthma but the correct one for each person must be selected after taking into consideration what makes the condition better or worse, what time of day the attacks tend to come on, whether the person is hot or cold, worse for damp, needs fresh air or prefers the windows closed and so on. You would be amazed how each person's symptoms can be so different and yet they have all been diagnosed with the same condition - asthma.

Your GP may not distinguish much between individual asthma cases, other than their severity and may prescribe a ventilator for all but a homeopath will carefully note the different symptoms of each case. Common traits are present but these are not necessarily of value to the homeopathic prescriber. Only the symptoms that are specific to the patient are of use. Anything unusual is especially important and can usually be found in the Repertory.

For example, diarrhoea is something millions of people suffer but if it is experienced very early in the morning driving the patient out of bed, we think of the remedy Sulphur. Fever is a common symptom but in the Belladonna fever we see dilated pupils of the eyes, red face and the patient (very often a child), becomes delirious. Migraine is a common symptom but in a Bryonia case the patient must lie still in a dark room and is worse from any movement whatsoever. Lots of people suffer from sore throats but those who need the remedy Causticum can completely lose their voice with a raw burning sensation.

In order to individualise a remedy, questions must be asked about the mental and emotional state, the intensity of a physical problem and anything that helps or worsens these. Also important are sensitivity to the environment, noise, crowds, weather, heat or cold, drafts, need for fresh air. Desires or aversions, as well as allergies to certain foods, are important. Food and drink cravings are recorded. Pattern and quality of sleep, as well as recurring dreams, are noted.

Another very useful indicator is the patient's phobias, such as fear of exams, dentists, doctors, heights, open spaces, darkness, being alone, burglars, thunderstorms, water, flying in aircraft, animals, spiders, etc. Anything that is at all unusual in a case can be extremely useful, differentiating it from other remedies.

Some patients may be worse at night, others in the day, still others first thing in the morning. Certain remedy types are well known for being worse at a particular time, for example, Aconite at midnight, Arsenicum at 1 a.m; Natrum Mur at 10 a.m; Sulphur at 11 a.m, Belladonna at 3 p.m. and Lycopodium at 4 p.m.

Every person is a fully functioning and integrated organism, affected by their inner and outer environment, by other people, by their job, their family, their spouse, their friends, the weather and atmospheric conditions, the food they eat, all the influences around them and these all need to be taken into account. Something that affects one person might have no affect upon another.

6. Homeopathic Remedy Types

Homeopaths very often see patients as falling into specific remedy types. They choose the remedy for a condition which most closely fits their mental, emotional AND physical symptoms. They do not attempt to treat different parts of the patient separately as they find giving the remedy that fits the totality of symptoms is most likely to cure the complaint. It is completely different from conventional medicine which utilises a one-size-fits-all approach.

There are about 100 well known remedy types which cover the majority of patients but thousands more to choose from if these do not fit the overall symptom picture. Some of the most well known constitutional remedies are listed below with an abbreviated description of the type of patient who needs them. You will probably recognise people you know here!

Argentum Nitricum - hot, very anxious and impulsive, lots of phobias, craves sweets.

Arsenicum Album – very chilly, anxious and fearful, critical, very tidy, need to depend upon someone, vomiting, burning pains, worse midnight to 2 am.

Aurum Metallicum – dutiful, workaholic, guilty, anger and violence, severe depression, oversensitive, heart complaints and worse night.

Bryonia – warm-blooded people, hardworking and industrious, suffer from severe migraines, constipated, thirsty, pains worse any movement.

Calcarea Carbonica – fat, fair, chilly but perspiring types who are shy and fearful.

Causticum – dark-haired, nervous, sympathetic people, idealistic and intolerant of injustice. Suffer from arthritis and can develop paralytic conditions.

Colocynthis – for pent up emotions causing cramping, abdominal colic where bending double relieves.

Graphites – chilly, constipated, itching eczema with cracks and fissures behind knees, elbows.

Ignatia – grief, fright, disappointment, unhappy love and shame. Very emotional types.

Lachesis – talkative, ambitious, jealous. Menopausal remedy for hot flushes. Worse after sleep and tend to work late at night.

Medorrhinum – warm-blooded people who like to stay up and party through the night. Hurried types who go to extremes and shun responsibilities. Sexually promiscuous with chronic discharges from vagina and penis, as well as bladder infections, conjunctivitis, arthritis.

Natrum Mur - bottle up their problems, dutiful, hide their grief and are worse when consoled, love of music. Fluid imbalances, hayfever.

Phosphorus – fair, dark or red hair, excitable, nervous, dreamy, chilly and very sociable.

Phosphoric Acid – exhaustion, apathy, indifference, disappointed love, chilly, craves fruit, painless diarrhoea.

Pulsatilla – mild, gentle, clingy, weepy blondes and small children, tend to be hot, crave fresh air, thirstless, with moods changing quickly.

Sepia – dark-haired women, like to be alone, uncommunicative, enjoy violent exercise, chilly. Menopausal remedy, never well since taking the Pill and suffer lower back pain.

Silicea – very chilly, obstinate (children) but sensitive, lack self confidence, hard swollen glands. Slim blondes. Abscess remedy and helps push splinters out of body.

Staphysagria – people who feel victimised, suppress their emotions, get very indignant and easily offended though do not show it. Some form of addiction, especially smoking.

Sulphur – hot, lazy, hungry, thirsty, tired types who suffer from very itchy red skin eruptions which are worse from bathing and heat of the bed.

Thuja – closed people with fixed ideas, feel unlovable but hide this. Outer appearance important to them. Can be tricksters and deceitful. Prefer to be alone. Warts and yellow/green discharges.

Veratrum Album – Chilly, haughty, ambitious types who can lie and cheat to get to the top, suffer from vomiting and cramps.

These are only very short descriptions of different constitutional remedy types. In the Materia Medica books all aspects of a remedy are listed which can go into several pages for each one.

To illustrate how remedies need to be differentiated and individualised, we can look at the type of reactions a person might have after a shock. If a person becomes very tired, indifferent to everything and everyone, the remedy Phosphoric Acid would be indicated. If they become terribly restless, anxious and frightened, it would be Aconite. Arnica is for shock when people say they are absolutely fine afterwards but are obviously not. These are all different ways people react to a shock and homeopathy must treat the individual. So it is important to observe closely how people are behaving in order to ascertain which remedy they need.

If you decide to self-prescribe and suffer for example, with hayfever, you might decide to try Natrum Muriaticum (see above), which is an excellent remedy for this. It may work well initially but the hayfever might come back and not be cured for good, if it was not the remedy that was the best fit. Again, itching eczema with cracks and fissures behind the knees or in the elbows can be cured with the remedy Graphites but it will work best if a person's other general symptoms also fit this remedy. So it must be emphasised that it is best to visit a qualified practitioner for long lasting results.

Remedies are easier to prescribe in First Aid situations though even these have to be individualised but fortunately there are less to choose from. (See Chapter 14)

The Miasms

Homeopaths take into consideration inherited genetic traits, tracing their origins to 5 main causes or Miasms, which are: Tuberculosis, Syphilis, Gonorrhoea, Psora, Cancer. For example the person who has continual chest colds, bronchitis or pneumonia may have ancestors who had tuberculosis. Patients suffering from violent mental derangement, alcoholism, a succession of abscesses or ulcers show a syphilitic ancestry. A parent or grandparent who contracted gonorrhoea, will pass on a susceptibility to thick yellow discharges to successive generations. The psoric miasm relates to skin conditions and Hahnemann believed it to be the underlying basis of all disease patterns.

We all have a mixture of these miasms in our physical makeup and especially tuberculosis, dates back thousands of years. However one or more of the miasms tends to be uppermost and it is an important aspect of treatment to take into account these inherited traits when finding the best homeopathic medicine. This is because each homeopathic medicine can usually be categorised under one or more of these miasms.

7. The Homeopathic Practitioner

All qualified lay homeopathic practitioners undergo a four year part time or a three year full time course at an accredited College. Medical doctors and nurses generally complete courses of shorter duration. The syllabus includes a thorough study of the Homeopathic Repertory and Materia Medica, as well as an understanding of the principles, theories and philosophy of homeopathy. A firm foundation in anatomy, physiology, pathology, disease and clinical medicine is also included in the course. The study of homeopathy is a lifetime's work, as there is so much to learn.

A qualified homeopathic practitioner should have the following:-

1. A recognised qualification, full insurance, as well as membership of a registering association.

2. Knowledge of diseases with application of curative procedures.

3. Thorough knowledge of homeopathic medicines, quality of medicines, quantity of medicines, correct procedure of dispensing doses, repetition of doses, etc..

4. Understanding of homeopathic philosophy, of health and sickness, removal of symptoms of disease.

5. Obstacles and hindrances to the restoration of health.

6. The practitioner should be open to current medical and health research and comply with government regulations.

In homeopathic education there are different schools of thought and methods of prescribing may differ. There is the classical homeopath who tends to prescribe on the whole picture, gives fewer remedies and leaves the body to respond to them for longer periods of time. Then there is the practical prescriber who might treat symptoms therapeutically and give more remedies to take. Some practitioners specialise in a particular area, for example, infertility, menopause, autism or children's conditions. There are many other ways of prescribing, depending upon the condition being treated.

The first homeopathic consultation will last for one to two hours in order for a detailed case history to be taken to find the homeopathic medicine which most closely matches the patient's unique pattern of symptoms. Follow up visits are shorter once the full history is recorded.

When a patient visits a homeopathic doctor or practitioner, he or she will be asked a series of questions in a thorough manner. The practitioner will also ask for a full medical history with as much information as possible regarding the existing complaint(s). Physical symptoms from head to toe are recorded including any accidents and injuries, as well as childhood illnesses. In addition, the health of your parents and grandparents are important, as this shows inherited conditions.

The homeopathic practitioner must take into consideration and account a great many factors in order to choose the correct remedy. Complaints and sensations that would be of no interest to your doctor, are of great importance to the practitioner. Sometimes it is only the most unusual and seemingly irrelevant things that can act as confirmation of a particular homeopathic remedy!

In addition to what you want healed, the homeopathic practitioner will also want to know something about your job, your hobbies and a little about your relationships. As mentioned, the homeopathic practitioner endeavours to search for and treat the CAUSE of the disease in order to heal and REMOVE the EFFECT, as illness can often be the result of a traumatic experience.

Homeopathic practitioners try to restore the healthy functioning of what they call the 'Vital Force', the invisible life force in each of us that is constantly creating new cells, breaking down old ones and repairing the body.

There are so many homeopathic medicines to choose from that the consultation must be conducted with great attention to detail. Very often, the homeopathic practitioner will know immediately which remedy is needed but can sometimes research for up to two hours after a consultation to find the one that will work best.

Worldwide, homeopaths have millions of written case notes that demonstrate the positive benefits of treatment. Some have before and after photographs as well as video proof of successful cases. It is important to visit a trained homeopathic consultant for long lasting results because homeopathic remedies are chosen only after complex case-taking.

Most homeopaths treat patients who have been referred to them by word of mouth, by friends and family who have had regular successful treatment. Patients seek out homeopathy because conventional treatment has not benefited them or because it poses too great a risk of side-effects.

If you are taking prescribed pharmaceutical drugs for your condition, you will find that as your condition improves, you may be able to safely reduce your medication with advice from your doctor.

As the founder of homeopathy, Samuel Hahnemann, said: 'The physician's highest and only mission is to restore the sick to health, to cure, as it is termed.'

Potency and Dosage

Generally speaking, the homeopath may start off by giving only one or two doses of a chosen remedy. Each dose acts to stimulate your own healing powers and it is not always necessary to repeatedly stimulate them.

There are different levels of health and the choice of the potency of a remedy should reflect this. Some homeopaths give lower potencies for more serious illness and higher potencies for the young or stronger patients whose problems are emotional or of the mind. Repeating a higher potency remedy too often, such as the 200c and 1000c (1M) can sometimes spoil a cure because the remedy should be left alone to work more deeply over time.

So in some cases only one high potency – 200c, 1000c (1M) or 10,000 (10M) is given, which can work for weeks or months at a time, with no repeat dose being necessary because when 'like finds like', it is as though the remedy substance resonates/vibrates at the same frequency as your own unique energy field and so can stay in your system a long time. Remember this system of medicine is completely different from orthodox medical treatment! Outcomes of homeopathic treatment are measured by the LONG TERM curative effects and complete eradication of the disease state.

Unlike orthodox pharmaceutical medicine, you may not be given a bottle of pills. The general exception to this, is patients with a serious chronic disease, who can take regular doses of very low potencies. The decimal X potency is an even lower potency scale and ideal in the initial treatment of long term chronic disease. Seriously ill people will be seen more often and given these lower potencies, such as the 30x or 6x. If there is organ damage, they may be given X potencies of specific remedies which target these organs, known as drainage remedies, which help to clear toxicity.

It is important to note that homeopathic medicines obtained from health shops tend to be restricted to either a 6c or 30c potency and higher potencies can only be obtained from homeopathic pharmacies. There are thousands of remedies available at the homeopathic pharmacies but only about 25 of the well known ones are available in high street health shops. It is anyway better not to take the higher potencies, unless given to you by a qualified homeopath.

How to Take Your Homeopathic Medicines

Remedies must be sucked and taken on an empty stomach. They should be taken at least 15 minutes after food or drink and no further food and drink must be ingested for another 15 minutes. It is best therefore to take them at a time when you are not eating or drinking.

You should avoid substances that will antidote your remedies, such as coffee, mint sweets or strong smelling substances like eucalyptus, camphor and clove oil, which your homeopath will explain to you. There are toothpastes available in health shops that will not antidote your remedies, which contain fennel instead of mint. Remedies should be stored away from heat, sunlight and strong smelling products, which will reduce their effectiveness.

It is also essential that you take no other homeopathic remedies during treatment, other than the ones that have been prescribed to you, as these may stop the curative action.

8. How Quickly will I Get Better?

How quickly you get better depends upon how long you have had the condition. As mentioned, homeopaths estimate a month for a year. So if you have had arthritis for 10 years, it would take around 10 months for you to get completely better but the healing may be quicker depending upon how strong you are.

With some conditions you will need to see your homeopath every month but in other cases only every two or even three months, which can be quite economical. As explained, this is if you are given the higher potency medicines which can keep working for a long time. This also depends upon the skill of the homeopathic practitioner.

Very often a homeopathic medicine will clear your illness quickly and efficiently. However, in chronic conditions, you may experience a slightly increased intensity or worsening of your symptoms for a short time and this is considered to be a good sign. If you experience this 'healing crisis' or 'aggravation' of your symptoms, known as the primary reaction, then the secondary healing reaction will surely follow. If you have been ill for any length of time, it can be necessary for you to go through this detoxification process before the true healing can take place and you will feel a lot better after it.

When visiting a practitioner for follow up appointments, a careful analysis is taken of the Direction of Cure of a patient's symptoms. The 'Law of Cure' (see Chapter 11) states that symptoms are cured from above down, from the inside out and in the reverse order of their appearance. Through many years of homeopathic clinical experience this observation has stood the test of time, though conventional doctors are rarely aware of it.

An example would be that after a curative remedy is given to someone suffering with eczema covering their body, we would observe the eczema moving downwards (from above down) and when it reaches the ankles, we know it is nearly cured. Although sometimes it might go quickly and completely after the remedy.

The wonderful thing about the way a higher potency homeopathic medicine can keep working for months, is that all the time your illness is clearing, as the remedy works more deeply in your physical body. As stated, the remedies work from above, downwards. Firstly on your state of mind, then your emotions and then on your physical body.

This is when the chosen remedy was the best possible choice and when it progressively improves your health. Your symptoms will be alleviated and the disease will be gone, subject to there being no disturbance of the remedy action through taking anything that will antidote it, as mentioned above.

Most people go to the homeopath with a problem they need fixing and find that other minor problems are also healed. At the same time they notice an improvement in their state of mind, feel emotionally better and enjoy an increase of energy. This is because the remedy chosen was the closest match to their whole state - mental, emotional and physical.

As Dr. Samuel Hahnemann stated: 'The highest ideal of cure is the rapid, gentle and permanent restoration of the health, or removal and annihilation of the disease in its whole extent, in the shortest, most reliable, and most harmless way, on easily comprehensible principles.'

9. How Safe Are Homeopathic Medicines?

- Homeopathic medicines are safe for young and old alike, as well as during pregnancy.

- Homeopathic medicines are especially good to give to children who enjoy them because they are pleasant tasting and easy to take. Children really thrive on homeopathic treatment, as they are young and vital and it helps their growth.

- Homeopathic medicines are not tested on animals but can be excellent to give to your pets!

- Homeopathic medicines are non-addictive.

- Homeopathic medicines are non-toxic.

- Homeopathic medicines are generally without side effects, as long as you do not continually take repeated doses of the higher potencies, when they are not indicated.

- Homeopathic medicines can be taken alongside prescribed drugs, as they will not interfere with their action.

Caution for Self-Diagnosis

Taking an incorrect remedy that is not indicated can mean little will happen but repeatedly taking it might bring on the symptoms of that remedy and make you worse (see Homeopathic Provings in Chapter 10). If self-prescribing, when you get real improvement, you need to stop taking the remedies, as they can continue working in your body for days, weeks and even months after you stop taking them.

Though it's tempting to self-diagnose remedies, you will not know the correct potency, dosage and time of repetition and could end up taking the wrong one. In addition, you will not be able to judge when a change of remedy is needed. Although this may not necessarily be harmful, it may not result in the long term relief of your symptoms.

However, it is a very good idea to invest in a homeopathic first aid kit for emergencies, which usually comes with an instruction book (see Chapter 14).

10. How are Homeopathic Medicines Made?

Every homeopathic medicine is generally made using one substance – whether plant, mineral, metal, etc. However, nowadays some homeopathic pharmacies make 'combination remedies' for example for jetlag. The exact substance(s) are always known, unlike most modern drugs where we are not always aware of the ingredients.

In order to make a homeopathic remedy, the substance is made up into a tincture by firstly steeping it in pure alcohol which absorbs the essence of the substance and simultaneously acts as a preservative. If it is a plant, the whole plant is put into a bottle and immersed in alcohol for 24 hours. After that time, the fluid is decanted off for medicinal use.

When a substance is not soluble in alcohol, a specific method of trituration is employed, which involves grinding the material in a mortar and pestle for a total of 3 hrs. The trituration method brings the substance into a form which is then soluble in alcohol or water. This first level method of preparation enables the energetic potential of the material substance to be liberated and changes its physical and chemical properties.

Substances are then diluted and shaken (succussed) to a point where they become potentised, i.e. more powerful and energised, which removes the potential for causing side effects.

For the centesimal or 'c' potency, one drop of the tincture is put into a bottle and 99 drops of a 60% distilled water + 40% pure alcohol mix is added. The bottle is then forcefully struck against a firm surface between 40 to 100 times (Succussion). This is now a 1c potency of the remedy being made. Then one drop of the 1c is put into a new bottle, 99 drops of the alcohol and water medium is added and the bottle is shaken a further 40 to 100 times, to make up a 2c potency. The process is repeated over and over to make up the higher potencies, such as the 6c or 30c and above.

The succussion brings out and imprints the formative intelligence of the substance being made, upon the 60% distilled water + 40% alcohol medium. The potentised signature of the substance is carried up the through the successive potencies, with the alcohol acting as a preservative. Succussion is nowadays done by machines but originally by hand.

There have been lots of articles in the press stating that homeopathic medicines are made using ONLY dilution. This is a fallacy, as dilution alone would do nothing in itself. All homeopathic medicines are made by a process of dilution and SUCCUSSION at a every step of the procedure. Potentisation is achieved through the vigorous shaking between each potency - i.e. between a 1c and a 2c, between a 2c and a 3c potency, between a 3c and a 4c, and so on.

When the liquid tinctures of the different potencies of the homeopathic medicines have been made up, a couple of drops are dropped onto lactose or sucrose based tablets or pillules which quickly soaks in to medicate them. All homeopathic medicines of every potency are made first into tinctures and then dropped onto (usually) lactose tablets.

As stated earlier, most homeopathic medicines can be bought in either 6c or 30c from high street health shops. Higher potencies of 200c, 1m (1000c), 10m (10,000c) and above, can be obtained only from homeopathic pharmacies.

There are TWO homeopathic potency scales – the centesimal or 'C' potency which is on a scale of 1 + 99 drops and the decimal or 'X' potency which is on a scale of 1 + 9 drops. Any remedy up to a 12c or a 24x potency still contains the original molecules of the substance and this is known as Avogadro's number.

Dr. Samuel Hahnemann's Experiments

Since homeopathy was first discovered over 200 years ago by Dr. Samuel Hahnemann, a large number of the thousands of homeopathic medicines have undergone scientific PROVINGS to ascertain their indications for prescribing. Dr. Hahnemann was in fact the first doctor to conduct clinical trials on medicines!

When Hahnemann first experimented, though perfectly healthy at the time, he found that by giving himself repeated doses of Peruvian Bark (quinine), he brought on all the symptoms of a malaria attack - fever with heat and chills! He then wondered if a substance that could cause a disease, might in tiny doses, also cure it (Like Cures Like - The Law of Similars), which he found to be the case.

He then set about discovering the healing properties of plants, metals, minerals, etc., by testing them on himself and on healthy volunteers or 'Provers'. He even created a 'Provers Union'!

After some years of practising like this, Hahnemann was still not satisfied. The substances he was using, while more effective than current medical practice, were still causing side effects. Or, if he reduced dosage too far, there was no effect. This is when he developed the concept of succussion or potentisation, that opponents of homeopathy criticise.

He noticed that by diluting then succussing a substance, it became safer to use on the sick than by giving the material dose. He found unwanted side effects were reduced and medicines were made more effective.

Hahnemann went on to test hundreds of substances on himself and healthy volunteers or Provers, matching the tested substances to heal symptoms in his patients and all the while keeping accounts of detailed observations. Far from being ideas-based, this is completely evidence-based, empirical medicine - an almost unique concept at that time.

Anybody who has an understanding of the principles of homeopathy can be left in no doubt that this is a scientific therapeutic method based on observation, facts and phenomena which follow the rules of inductive logic that can be tested in daily practice. It is a comprehensive mode of therapy, which in many countries is the first line of treatment for a whole range of acute and chronic conditions.

Homeopathic Provings

Nowadays when conducting a Proving, around 50 to 100 people repeatedly take the 30c potency of a remedy and all must record in detail the symptoms they experience, many of which they never had before. All this information is then put into a database in order to discover the predominant indications for prescribing the remedy and then added to the volumes of Materia Medica. The Provers must be healthy and symptom-free, so that the symptoms they experience are new ones that are caused by the remedy.

They must keep a careful daily note of all the symptoms they experience, mental, emotional and physical, and must not discuss these with any of the other Provers. Then whatever symptoms the Provers all experienced in common become the bold type symptoms of the remedy, which are then added to the Materia Medica and the Homeopathic Repertory (encyclopedia of symptoms). So the symptoms the majority of Provers experience are added in bold type, the symptoms that many but not all Provers experience are added in italic type and other less common ones that only some of the Provers experience, are added in plain type. Thus the curative indications of a remedy are obtained for clinical use and the remedy undergoing the Proving can be used to treat a person who is ill with those same set of symptoms - Like cures Like.

In addition to homeopathic Provings, remedy indications have also been obtained through historical records of accidental poisonings of, for example, arsenic and belladonna. Poisoning by arsenic causes vomiting, diarrhoea, restlessness, anxiety and extreme chill. So if you get a patient in this state (possibly after food poisoning), the remedy Arsenicum in a homeopathic tablet will quickly alleviate them. Belladonna causes high fever and delirium with dilated pupils of eyes, so in a potentised dose it is very useful for treating fever, especially in children.

Plants, trees, minerals such as calcium, magnesium, zinc as well as metals such as gold, silver, iron, are made into homeopathic medicines, as well as nearly everything on the Periodic Table.

11. Homeopathic Medicine compared to Modern Drugs

Homeopathic theories are based on principles corresponding to the unchanging Laws of Nature - unlike medical theories which are constantly changing.

Dr. Samuel Hahnemann first coined the word 'homoeopathy' ('homoios' in Greek meaning similar, 'pathos' meaning suffering), to refer to the Law of Similars. He understood the energetic basis of health, well before the paradigm of 'matter as energy' was put forward in modern physics.

Modern medicine utilises the Law of Opposites, in the form of antibiotics, anti-inflammatories, anti-convulsants, anti-hypertensives, antidepressants, antispasmodics, antifungals, anti-psychotics, antihistamines, etc. etc. It seeks to 'fight' the symptoms of illness and in doing so, attacks the whole body as well as the disease. This causes symptoms to be suppressed and driven deeper, eventually creating a more serious condition, bringing the patient to a lower level of health. If symptoms are continually suppressed, then the disease takes hold and progresses to the point where the person develops a chronic condition.

Homeopathy does the opposite, stimulating the body to heal itself, bringing the symptoms to the surface in order to clear them out of the body, while continually brings the patient to higher levels of health.

So it is important to note that the disappearance of symptoms does not equal cure! Examples of this would be a patient whose skin symptoms have been suppressed, going on to develop asthma or the arthritic patient whose joint pains are suppressed, eventually going on to develop heart disease.

Constantine Hering, who first espoused the Law and Direction of Cure, was a converted skeptic. Hering stated that according to the Law of Cure, symptoms move from above down, from inside out and in the reverse order of their appearance.

As a young man he had been assigned the task of reviewing homeopathy. His medical mentor had been asked to write a book exposing homeopathy as false. Hering conducted a detailed study but after seeing the results, he concluded the opposite and became a homeopath himself! Actually a huge number of medical doctors converted to homeopathy in the 19th century, especially in Britain.

The modern medical doctor is not usually aware of and makes little connection with the Direction of Cure. Medical science has divided the body into specialised parts, such as neurology, ear, nose and throat, cardiology, gastroenterology, gynaecology, and does not study how the body works as a whole. Very often treatment of one part will result in a 'new' condition appearing in another and the doctor does not necessarily notice that powerful prescribed drugs have caused deeper illness but goes on giving the patient more and more, making them sicker still. Then when the patient dies, the doctor says, 'We did everything we could!'.

Interestingly, at the end of the 19th century, the Arndt-Schulz rule or Schulz' law was cited as a guideline of importance in pharmacology texts. It concerned the effects of medicine or poisons in various concentrations and it stated: 'For every substance, small doses stimulate, moderate doses inhibit, large doses kill, meaning that highly diluted medicines or poisons enhanced life processes, while strong concentrations may inhibit these processes and even terminate them'. There were exceptions to the rule, as many paralysing substances have no exciting effects in weak doses, and what constitutes a weak, medium or strong stimulus is highly individual, as pointed out by Arndt himself. However this Rule certainly appeared to support homeopathic theory.

Nowadays, it is certainly true that many pharmaceutical drugs are poisonous to the body and the bill for dangerous side-effects can run into millions in negligence claims. Yet one UK leading insurance company reported only 'a couple' of claims against homeopaths in a ten year period! Hence insurance cover for homeopathic practitioners is very low compared to that of medical doctors, reflecting safety and negligible risk.

In addition, pharmaceutical drugs can be prohibitively expensive compared to homeopathic medicines, which cost very little. In 200 years there has never been a single homeopathic medicine being recalled!

There is only one true science and that is the science of Nature. Doctors should look to Nature in order to study disease. Doctors and scientists could learn much and find answers. They should also study health before they study sickness, as medical schools are often financed by drugs companies and they are taught only drugs and disease, rather than health and prevention of disease. In addition, doctors do not take into account the many and varied causes of illness nor inherited conditions or miasms.

12. Homeopathic Hospitals and Scientific Trials

In the UK, there are four homeopathic hospitals - in London, Bristol, Liverpool and Glasgow, but there were once fourteen! (5) These four cost the National Health Service around £4 million a year compared to the over £110 billion for the total annual NHS budget for 2009! Right now these homeopathic hospitals are threatened with closure despite huge public demand.

The Tunbridge Wells Homeopathic Hospital has already been forced to close because the NHS Primary Care Trust refused to pay for patients being referred. The total drugs bill for homeopathic medicines in 2009 was £152,000 compared to £11 billion for pharmaceutical drugs. These savings were shown in 2005 when Prince Charles commissioned the Christopher Smallwood Report which revealed that the NHS would save a lot of money if it utilised homeopathy and complementary medicine. (6) (6a)

At one of the earliest debates on the National Health Service Act of 1948, the Government pledged that homeopathy would continue to be available on the NHS, as long as there were 'patients wishing to receive it and doctors willing to provide it'. Yet in 2006 a group of professors hostile to homeopathy sent a letter to all the Primary Care Trusts (PCTs) putting pressure on them not to refer patients to the homeopathic hospitals. They wrote the letter on NHS headed paper to give it more authority! (7)

Many people in the UK who depend upon it, are alarmed at the possibility that homeopathy may no longer be available on the NHS. Provision has always been made for people to be treated at homeopathic hospitals in the UK and until PCTs began to stop referring and paying for patients, there had been long waiting lists, some 6 months or more.

Those who criticise and pass judgment on homeopathy have rarely taken the time to study it. Yet in the past 200 years, there have been numerous medical doctors who converted to practising homeopathy. (8) It can take years to master but the rewards for patients, practitioners and the health of the nation are great. Before those who preach science come down on homeopathy too heavily, they should ask themselves how many of the accepted treatments within the National Health Service have a true scientific evidence base?

Scientific Trials

In 2005, the World Health Organisation created a favourable draft report on homeopathy, showing it to be the second most popular medicine in the world but the report was quashed when antagonistic forces discovered its existence and very soon afterwards the Lancet published its selective meta-analyses of trials and its editorial of 26th August 2005.

Dr. Peter Fisher is the Queen's homeopathic physician at the Royal London Homeopathic Hospital. In his article in PubMed, he discusses this 'End of Homeopathy' editorial and the analysis of the Lancet clinical trials, where nearly 100 successful studies showing homeopathy worked were thrown out and only a few that were inconclusive were analysed. Dr. Fisher wrote:

'The Lancet meta-analysis in 2005 of homeopathic trials was said to be based upon 110 placebo-controlled clinical trials of homeopathy and 110 clinical trials of allopathy, which were said to be matched but were in fact reduced to 21 trials of homeopathy and 9 of conventional medicine and further reduced to 8 and 6 trials.'

'The final analysis which concluded that 'the clinical effects of homeopathy are placebo effects' was based on just eight clinical trials of homeopathy. The Lancet's press release did not mention this, instead giving the impression that the conclusions were based on all 110 trials. One of the most serious criticisms is the complete lack of transparency: We have no idea which eight trials were included in the final, damning, analysis. The literature references are not given, nor any information on the diagnoses, numbers of patients, etc., nor can these be deduced from the article. Prof. Egger has refused several requests to disclose the identity of the eight trials. This is not even a matter of scientific method but of natural justice: the accused has the right to know the evidence against him.' (9)

With regard to the famous BBC2 Horizon programme on homeopathy, Prof. Madeleine Ennis who was cited, was not involved in the actual Horizon test. The test was carried out by Wayne Turnbull of Guys Hospital, London. It has been conceded that the Horizon test was not an exact replica of Ennis' successful trials. Many of Turnbull's protocols were different. He added an ammonium chloride lysis step which would have ended up killing the very basophils that were such an integral part of the test. Ennis' original test had been successfully replicated in 4 different labs in 4 different countries. (10)

There have been hundreds of studies and clinical trials which prove homeopathy works. In most cases, the researchers concluded that the benefits of homeopathy went far beyond that which could be explained purely by the placebo effect.

Though homeopathy can never be properly tested through double blind randomised trials because of its individualised approach, as the giving the same medicine for a single condition would be unlikely to be indicated for all subjects. This is because 10 people suffering from a condition may all need a different homeopathic medicine.

41

Yet conventional medicine, with its one-size-fits-all approach to prescribing, tests out the same drug on large numbers of people. In homeopathy, all may need different medicines!

One of the most comprehensive patient outcome surveys was an analysis of over 23,000 outpatient consultations at the Bristol Homeopathic Hospital from November 1997 to October 2003. This represented over 6,500 individual patients whose outcomes were recorded at follow-up. More than 70% of these follow-up patients recorded clinical improvement after homeopathic treatment. (11)

In addition, a major CAM Pilot Project in 2008, implemented by Get Well UK, was commissioned by the Department of Health, Social Services and Public Safety in two primary care trusts in Northern Ireland. The result was a 79% improvement in the level of health for those who had homeopathic treatment. (12)

One of the best studies on homeopathic medicines was the 'Groundbreaking Research regarding Homeopathy using Spectroscopy' (13) and some of the important studies on the properties of water were performed by Dr. Rustum Roy and his paper provides an interdisciplinary base of information on the structure of liquid water. (14)

In 2009, Nobel Prize winner, Luc Montagnier and his team reported the results of a series of rigorous experiments investigating the electromagnetic (EM) properties of highly diluted biological samples. They found that pathogenic bacteria and viruses show a distinct EM signature at dilutions ranging from 10-5 to 10-12 (corresponding to 3CH - 6CH homeopathic dilutions) and that small DNA fragments (responsible for pathogenicity) were solely accountable for the EM signal. It was noted that the samples needed be 'vortexed' (a process akin to succussion) for the EM effects to be present. They propose that specific aqueous nanostructures form in the samples during the dilution process and are responsible for the EM effects measured. (15)

The argument that homeopathy is only placebo falls short when it successfully treats animals and babies. Animals are especially responsive to homeopathic medicines. (16) When Prince Charles treats his farm animals at Highgrove, how would they know that a remedy has been put in the water they drink?! For years, farmers have successfully used homeopathic medicines for their cows suffering from mastitis. Can it be the placebo effect when a baby quickly gets better after being given a homeopathic medicine?! As anyone who has treated animals and babies will tell you, homeopathy works even more quickly than it does for adults! If proof were needed, this is it and definitely not placebo. Registered vets treating animals homeopathically can be found here: http://www.bahvs.com

The 21st century scientists simplify things into mechanisms and formulas, often mathematically expressed, bringing everything down to the reductionist model, yet it doesn't occur to them that perhaps there are some things which the human mind cannot grasp. Those who claim to be scientists, should at least try to understand different paradigms. If not, they look more like people who have settled into a comfortable world view, which might soon become very outmoded indeed! As the great musician and conductor Sir Yehudi Menhuin once said: 'Homeopathy is one of the few specialised areas in medicine, which carries no disadvantages but only advantages.' (For lots more scientific studies and research, please go to www.homeopathyheals.me.uk)

13. Brief Homeopathic History

Dr. Samuel Hahnemann

The founder of homeopathy, Dr. Samuel Hahnemann, was born on 11th April 1755 in Meissen, Saxony, Germany. He envisioned an entire system of medicine based on the Law of Similars and then fully developed it within the span of a single lifetime.

The Law of Similars was known to both Hippocrates and Paracelsus and utilised by the Mayans, Chinese, Greeks, Native American Indians and Asian Indians, but it was Hahnemann who developed it into a systematic medical science. A Greek physician, Galen, had laid these rules down in about 150 AD.

Hahnemann was a genius, who was skilled in many fields. After training as a doctor he became a master pharmacist. He was also a linguist, translator and fluent in seven languages. In 1790 he translated Cullen's Materia Medica and discovered the fever-producing properties of cinchona bark, which was to him like the falling apple to Newton. From this single experiment he became convinced of the pathogenetic effects of medicines which would give the key to their therapeutic power (see Dr. Samuel Hahnemann's Experiments, Chapter 10).

In his work, he also promoted the humane treatment of the mentally ill, as well as curing them with his remedies. In 1792, Hahnemann was invited by the Duke of Saxe Gotha to take charge of an asylum for the insane in Georgenthal, in the Thuringian forest where he treated the inmates with his homeopathic medicines until 1794.

In 1796, Hahnemann wrote his *Essay on a New Principle*, which ascertained the remedial power of medicinal substances and where he firmly expresses his belief that medicines should be employed which have the power to produce similar affections in the healthy body.

Hahnemann, when living in Konigslutter, had abandoned giving the complex mixtures of medicines of the time. He encountered jealousy towards his rising fame as an innovator and the local physicians incited the apothecaries to bring a legal action against him. Though Hahnemann had shown himself a master of the apothecaries' art by the writing of his learned and laborious Pharmaceutical Lexicon, he was prohibited from dispensing his own simple medicines.

However, in 1799, a scarlet fever epidemic gave Hahnemann the opportunity to demonstrate his concept of highly diluted and potentised homeopathic medicines. He created a sensation when he successfully used Belladonna as a cure and a preventive for this epidemic.

The antagonistic attitude of what he called the 'old school doctors' meant that he was forced to continually move and after living in Hamburg, Altona and Mollen, he settled in Leipzig where he lived happily from 1810 to 1821.

In 1810 he published the first edition of his immortal *Organon of Medicine*, which was an extension of his published *Medicine of Experience*, put into a more methodical form, in the model of some of the Hippocratic writings.

Long before Koch and Pasteur, Hahnemann understood the principles of contagious illnesses and successfully treated the deadly epidemics which ravaged Europe in the first half of the nineteenth century.

Success was achieved for him again in 1814, when Hahnemann used homeopathy to treat an epidemic of typhus which affected Napoleon's soldiers after their invasion of Russia. Soon the epidemic spread to Germany, where Hahnemann cured the first stage of illness with the remedies Bryonia and Rhus Tox.

In 1831 homeopathy triumphed again. This time over the cholera epidemic which spread westward from Russia, while allopathic medicine was helpless against the virulent disease. The remedies Hahnemann used - Camphor, Cuprum and Veratrum - would still be among the top remedies used for cholera today.

Hahnemann developed his understanding of chronic diseases, which was the concept of inherited conditions or miasms. He published his discovery in 1828 in the first edition of *The Chronic Diseases*. As his success grew, his supporters and detractors increased!

Homeopathy began to become popular in the other countries of Europe and also in America. This increased the bitterness and ferocity of the attacks on him by the medical doctors. Hahnemann had ignored these attacks but in 1830 he published a pamphlet against his foes entitled *Allopathy: a Warning to all Sick Persons*, which was an excellent caricature of the medicine of the day.

In that same year, Hahnemann lost his wife, the mother of his numerous children.

However, in 1834, something happened that surprised everyone who knew him. A beautiful and vivacious Parisienne, Marie Mélanie d'Herville-Gohier, took the lengthy journey to consult Hahnemann in Germany for the treatment of her neuralgic pains. She swept the 80-year-old widower off his feet and they were married only three months after they first met! Mélanie convinced Hahnemann to come back to Paris with her, to enjoy the adulation of French society, many of whom had already adopted homeopathy.

After years of adversity, Hahnemann was able to enjoy the end of his life with a young, beautiful and well-connected wife, who brought many members of the French nobility and high society to see him. Hahnemann had great fame and success in France and completed his 'most complete and best method', described in the sixth edition of the *Organon of Medicine*. The manuscript was in the hands of his publisher when Hahnemann died in 1843, at the ripe old age of 88.

Homeopathy in Europe

Homeopathy was extremely popular in Europe and America during the 1800s and early 20th century, especially with Royalty. Its aristocratic patronage in the UK extended well into the 1940s and beyond, as can easily be seen in the lists of patrons of the dispensaries and homeopathic hospitals shown in the Homeopathic Medical Directories. (17)

Homeopathy was introduced into Britain in the 1830s by Dr. F. H. F. Quin (1799-1878). Dr. Quin became the Duchess of Devonshire's family physician and travelled with her entourage. He met Hahnemann and travelled extensively in Europe, residing for a time both in Rome and Naples. He successfully used the homeopathic medicine Camphor against cholera in Moravia (now Czechoslovakia) and cured himself of the condition on Hahnemann's advice.

Quin introduced homeopathy into the highest levels of English society - to Dukes, Counts, Lords, minor Royals and Baronets. British homeopathy never really shook off its aristocratic gloss, so it never established itself at a popular level amongst the working people. It was regarded as the 'rich man's therapy' and exclusive to the wealthy, privileged and titled. While this allegiance with the upper classes undoubtedly worked to the benefit of British homeopathy in its early days, later on it became a great burden, especially when it sank into decline after the 1880s.

However, there was a resurgence in the 1960s and 1970s. Its leaders include Phyllis Speight (born1920), John Da Monte (1916-75) and Thomas Maughan (1901-76). Suddenly in 1978 and after twenty years of inactivity, a group of lay practitioners established their own Society of Homeopaths, a Register, The London College of Homeopathy, a Journal (The Homeopath) and a Code of Ethics. (18)

Opposition from Orthodox Medicine in America

Nowadays, few in the United States know that in the early 1900s there were 22 homeopathic medical schools, over 100 homeopathic hospitals, 60 homeopathic orphanages and old people's homes, as well as over 1,000 homeopathic pharmacies!

Homeopathy was very popular among women in America, not only as patients but as its practitioners. The first women's medical college in the world was the homeopathic Boston Female Medical College, founded in 1848. Homeopaths also admitted women physicians into their national organization considerably before orthodox physicians allowed them.

Then as now, orthodox medicine was fiercely opposed to homeopathy. After its formation in 1847, Members of the American Medical Association had great animosity towards it and they decided to purge all local medical societies of physicians who were homeopaths. This purge was successful in every state except Massachusetts because homeopathy was so strong among the elite of Boston.

The AMA wanted to keep homeopaths out of their societies and discourage any type of association with them. In 1855 the AMA established a code of ethics which stated that orthodox physicians would lose their membership if they even consulted with a homeopath! If a physician lost his membership, it meant that in some US States he no longer had a licence to practise medicine.

At an AMA meeting, Dr. J.N. McCormack from Kentucky, who was the driving force behind the reorganisation of the American Medical Association in 1903, said: 'We must admit that we never fought the homeopath on matters of principles. We fought him because he came into the community and got the business.'(!)

Drug companies were antagonistic towards homeopathy, collectively trying to suppress it. The medical journals they published were used as mouthpieces against it and in support of orthodox medicine.

It is quite remarkable in itself that homeopathy survived the incessant and harsh attempts to destroy it. After the turn of the century, however, the AMA became increasingly effective in suppressing it. In a strategic move the AMA chose to 'allow' graduates of homeopathic medical schools to join the AMA., as long as they denounced homeopathy or at least didn't practise it.

In 1910 the Carnegie Foundation issued the famous Flexner Report. The Report was an evaluation of American medical schools chaired by Abraham Flexner, in cooperation with leading members of the AMA. As one might easily predict, the homeopathic colleges on the whole were given poor ratings. There had been 22 homeopathic colleges in America in 1900, but by 1923 only two remained.

Things might have been different if, in the early 1900s, John D. Rockefeller had bequeathed major grants of between $300-$400 million intended for homeopathic institutions but which were instead given to orthodox medicine. This was due to pressure from his son and his financial advisor, Frederick Gates. Rockefeller referred to homeopathy as 'a progressive and aggressive step in medicine' and was under homeopathic care throughout the latter part of his life, living to 99 years of age. (19)

Homeopathy in Epidemics

In the 19th century, homeopathic medicine was proven to be extremely effective in epidemics such as scarlet fever, cholera, typhoid, diptheria, yellow fever, polio and influenza and was used extensively for these in Europe, Britain and America.

In 1854 there was a cholera epidemic in London which was found to be caused by a contaminated public water pump. As soon as it was closed, the epidemic ceased. The House of Commons asked to see a report about the methods of treating the epidemic but when they received it, patients who had received homeopathic treatment were not included. The House of Lords demanded an explanation and it was later shown that under conventional medical care the death rate was 59.2% but for patients under homeopathic care, only 9%.

Diptheria was another epidemic disease treatable with homeopathy. From 1862 to 1864, in the records of diphtheria in Broome County, New York, there was a report of an 83.6% mortality rate among the medical doctors and a 16.4% mortality rate among homeopaths.

Deaths rates in the yellow fever epidemic of 1878 in America for those under homeopathic care were approximately one-third of those using orthodox medicine. Statistics indicate that the death rates in homeopathic hospitals from these epidemics were often one-half to as little as one-eighth of those in orthodox medical hospitals.

Homeopathy was also very effectively utilised in the major Influenza Pandemic of 1918. The Journal of the American Institute for Homeopathy, May, 1921, published a long article about this. Dr. T. A. McCann, from Dayton, Ohio reported that 24,000 cases of flu treated medically had a mortality rate of 28.2% while 26,000 cases of flu treated homeopathically had a mortality rate of 1.05%! This last figure was supported by Dean W.A. Pearson of the Hahnemann College, Philadelphia, who collected 26,795 cases of flu treated with homeopathy with this result. The most common remedy reportedly used was Gelsemium, with some cases needing Bryonia and Eupatorium.

In Buenos Aires, Argentina, there was a polio epidemic in 1957, where the symptoms of the epidemic resembled those of the remedy Lathyrus Sativa. Dr. Francisco Eizayaga, a homeopathic doctor, told how the homeopathic doctors and pharmacies prescribed Lathyrus 30c as a prophylactic and "thousands of doses" were distributed. "Nobody registered a case of contagion." (20) (21)

More recently in Cuba during 2007 and 2008, medical researchers successfully prevented the annual outbreak of Leptospirosis using homeopathy among a population of 5 million people across two regions. Cuba goes through a yearly cycle of Leptospirosis epidemic, especially in August when the hurricanes flood the countryside and water pollution reaches its height. Annually, many are left homeless, flooded out and under the stress of a disaster situation. Leptospirosis is an infectious disease caused by the spirochaete Leptospira transmitted to humans from rats, giving jaundice and kidney damage which can cause death.

Until August 2007, conventional treatment of the population was with a vaccine, which had resulted in thousands of infections and a number of fatalities, at a cost of US $2 million but the homeopathic solution cost just 10% of that, at US $200,000.

Using Homeoprophylaxis, (the equivalent of vaccinations in homeopathy), a nosode of Leptospirosis was prepared. 5 million doses were administered to a population of 2.5 million people. Two doses were given, the second dose being 7-9 days after the first. In 2007, the incidence of infection was brought down to 10 people with no fatalities and in 2008, there were no deaths, with infections at less than 10 a month. Homeopathy was first introduced to Cuba in 1842. (22)

14. First Aid and Remedies

One of the most indispensable additions to your medicine cupboard is the Homeopathic First Aid Kit which usually comes with an instruction book. It can be extremely useful for sudden illness in the middle of the night, Sundays or Bank Holidays! If you had any doubts about the veracity of homeopathy, these will quickly be dispelled when you use it in emergencies! This is especially true if you have children or babies, who so often get ill unexpectedly. These Kits can be purchased from the homeopathic pharmacies listed below under Useful Contacts.

Probably the most well known first aid remedy is **Arnica Montana**. It is excellent for bruising of the soft tissue, sprained ankles, muscle strain, injuries to the head to prevent concussion, as well as shock after an accident.

Hypericum, being a nerve remedy, works well if you crush your fingertips, fall downstairs bruising your coccyx or tailbone, stub your toe or bang your elbow. It is also very effective for pain after dental extractions.

Ledum is the remedy to take after injections from needles, as it is suitable for all types of puncture wounds.

Splinters or any foreign object in the body will be quickly drawn out when you take **Silicea** and therefore should not be used by anyone with metal plates, pins or breast implants. Silicea is also very effective for treating abscesses.

Another excellent first aid remedy is **Symphytum** for fast healing of fractures and broken bones. Breakages of tendons and cartilage will also heal with this remedy.

The list overleaf contains a number of first aid remedies and includes other common conditions.

Condition	Remedy
Abscess	Silicea/Hepar Sulph
Abdominal surgery/Caesarian	Staphysagria/Bellis Perennis
Back strains from over-lifting	Rhus Tox
Black Eye/blow to eyeball	Arnica/Symphytum
Blows to breast/testicles	Conium Mac.
Blows to a bone	Ruta Grav.
Bowels (no movement)	Opium/Hydrastis
Broken Bones	Symphytum
Broken Ankle	Symphytum/Rhus Tox
Bruises to soft tissue	Arnica
Burns	Cantharis/Causticum
Cuts & bleeding wounds	Calendula (remedy or cream)
Fever (high with delirium)	Belladonna
Fever (after cold winds)	Aconite
Food poisoning	Arsenicum
Fractures	Symphytum/Calc Phos.
Frozen shoulder	Ruta Grav.
Genital warts	Thuja

Hangovers	Nux Vomica
Head injury (concussion)	Arnica
Incised wounds (surgery)	Staphysagria
Influenza with bone pains	Eup Perfoliatum
Muscle sprains	Arnica
Nerve injuries	Hypericum
Puncture wounds	Ledum
Scar tissue healing	Silica/Thiosin
Shock with panic	Aconite
Splinters/foreign objects	Silica
Sprained Ankle	Arnica
Sunstroke	Belladonna
Tennis Elbow	Ruta Grav.
Thrush in mouth	Borax
Ulcers (burning)	Arsenicum Alb.
Varicose Veins (collapsed)	Hamamelis
Warts (main remedy)	Thuja
Warts on Cervix	Calendula

Chronic conditions need to be individualised through in depth case-taking because there are a number of remedies for each condition. Contact a qualified homeopathic practitioner.

15. Useful UK Contacts

Find a Homeopathic Practitioner in your Area:-

Alliance of Registered Homeopaths

http://www.a-r-h.org/

Homeopathic Medical Association

http://www.the-hma.org/

Homeopathic Pharmacy & Supply Company:-

Helios Homeopathic Pharmacy

(International Orders)

http://www.helios.co.uk/

Homeopathic Supply Company

http://www.homeopathicsupply.com/

Homeopathic Booksellers:-

Emryss Publishers

http://www.emrysspublishers.com/

Serpentina Books

http://www.serpentinabooks.com/

Narayana Publishers

http://www.narayana-publishers.eu/

Homeopathic Educational Services

http://www.homeopathic.com

Homeopathy Colleges:-

School of Homeopathy

Gloucestershire, UK.
www.homeopathyschool.com

The College of Practical Homeopathy (UK) Ltd.

London, UK.

www.college-of-practical-homeopathy.com

Homeopathic Colleges in the UK
http://www.hcpf.org.uk/members

Useful USA Contacts

Homeopathic Educational Services

http://www.homeopathic.com

North American Society of Homeopaths

http://www.homeopathy.org/directory.html

American Institute of Homeopathy

http://homeopathyusa.org/member-directory.html

USA - Professional Orgs

http://bit.ly/6FI2KB

Worldwide Directory

http://www.holisticmed.com/www/homeopathy.html

http://abchomeopathy.com/l.php/8

http://www.extendedyears.com/lib/40101.php

16. References

1. The Homeopathic Revolution by Dana Ullman, MPH.
   www.homeopathicrevolution.com
2. A-Z of Famous People who used Homeopathy – Sue
   Young, RSHom.
   http://www.homeopathy.wildfalcon.com/archives/2009/05/18
   /homeopathy-a-z-2/

3. Savvy marketing sees surge in alternative therapies Press
   Trust of India June 30, 2009.   http://www.business-
   standard.com/india/news/savvy-marketing-sees-surge-in-
   alternative-therapies/66042/on

4. Global TGI survey 2008
   http://www.tgisurveys.com/documents/TGIbarometerhomeop
   athy_Jan08.pdf
5. Fourteen Homeopathic Hospitals in Britain
   http://www.homeoint.org/morrell/londonhh/outbreak.htm
   http://www.homeoint.org/morrell/londonhh/munoffer.htm

6. Homeopathic hospitals SAVE money for the NHS, as the
   Smallwood report commissioned by Prince Charles
   has demonstrated.
   http://news.bbc.co.uk/1/hi/health/4312780.stm   Alternative
   therapies could save the NHS money - Christopher
   Smallwood report commissioned by Prince Charles -
   original report
   http://research.freshminds.co.uk/files/u1/freshminds_report_c
   omplimentarymedicine.pdf
7. Letter to NHS Primary Care Trusts from professors
   opposed to homeopathy
   http://www.senseaboutscience.org.uk/pdf/Baum%20letter.pdf
8. Doctors who Converted to Homeopathy
   http://homeopathy.wildfalcon.com/?s=converted&submit=Sea
   rch
9. Lancet - End of Homeopathy by Dr. Peter Fisher
   http://www.pubmedcentral.nih.gov/articlerender.fcgi?artid=13
   75230

10. **Professor Madeleine Ennis' experiments**
    http://www.homeopathic.com/articles/view,55
11. **A study of 6500 patients at the Bristol Homeopathic hospital was conducted showing that over 70% of patients reported complete cure or significant improvement of their symptoms.**
    http://news.bbc.co.uk/1/hi/england/bristol/4454856.stm
    http://www.trusthomeopathy.org/research/homeopathic_hospitals/Bristol_study.html
12. **Northern Ireland: Complementary and Alternative Medicines Pilot Project (see page 31)**
    http://www.dhsspsni.gov.uk/final_report_from_smr_on_the_cam_pilot_project_-_may_2008.pdf
13. **Groundbreaking Research regarding Homeopathy using spectroscopy**
    www.bodyandsoulclinic.blogspot.com/2007/09/groundbreaking-research-regarding.html
14. **The Structure Of Liquid Water; Novel Insights From Materials Research; Potential Relevance To Homeopathy Rustum Roy1, W.A. Tiller2, Iris Bell3, M. R. Hoover4**
    http://www.rustumroy.com/Roy_Structure%20of%20Water.pdf
15. **Nobel Prizewinner Luc Montagnier Proves Homeopathy Works** http://avilian.co.uk/2009/09/luc-montagnier-foundation-proves-homeopathy-works/
16. **The Relevance of the Placebo Effect in Homeopathy**
    http://avilian.co.uk/2009/11/the-relevance-of-the-placebo-effect/
17. **A History of Homeopathy in Britain by Peter Morrell, Honorary Research Associate in the History of Medicine, Staffordshire University, UK.**
    www.homeopathyhome.com/reference/articles/ukhomhistory.shtml http://www.homeoint.org/morrell/articles/pm_arist.htm
18. **Hahnemann Revisited by Dr. Luc De Schepper**
    http://www.wholehealthnow.com/homeopathy_pro/hahnemann_rev1.html
19. **A Condensed History of Homeopathy by Dana Ullman, MPH.** http://www.homeopathic.com/articles/view,19

20. **More on Epidemics: Homeopathy in Epidemics**
http://www.whale.to/v/winston.html
21. **On the Genus Epidemicus**
http://www.wholehealthnow.com/homeopathy_pro/wt10.html
22. **Successful Use of Homeopathy in Over 2.5 Million People Reported from Cuba**
http://homeopathyresource.wordpress.com/2009/01/01/successful-use-of-homeopathy-in-over-5-million-people-reported-from-cuba/ **Cuba prevents annual epidemic among 2.5m people using homeopathy**
http://www.irishhomeopaths.com/homeopathy-cuba

17. Self Help Books and Further Reading

Everybody's Guide to Homeopathic Medicines

Stephen Cummings, MD & Dana Ullman, MPH.

http://www.homeopathic.com/store/product=1817

The Homeopathic Treatment of Children: Pediatric Constitutional Types

by Paul Herscu, ND

http://www.minimum.com/b.asp?a=treatment-children-herscu

A Homeopathic Guide to Partnership and Compatibility

by Liz Lalor

http://www.homeopathicbooks.co.uk/products?id=1737

Emotional Healing with Homeopathy

Peter Chappell, RSHom.

http://www.homeopathic.com/store/product=1022

Impossible Cure

by Amy Lansky, PhD. (Homeopathy for Autism)

http://www.impossiblecure.com/order.html

The Spirit of Homeopathic Medicines: Essential Insights to 300 Remedies

Didier Grandgeorge, MD.

http://www.randomhouse.ca/catalog/display.pperl?isbn=978 1556432613

Prozac-Free: Homeopathic Medicine for Depression, Anxiety, and Other Emotional and Mental Problems

Judyth Reichenberg-Ullman ND, MSW and Robert Ullman, ND.

http://www.homeopathic.com/code=ULL-PRO

Whole Woman Homeopathy

Judyth Reichenberg-Ullman ND, MSW.

http://www.healthyhomeopathy.com/store/product2.html

Homeopathy for Pregnancy, Birth & Your Babies First Years

by Miranda Castro

http://www.mirandacastro.com/zencart/

Homeopathic Care for Cats and Dogs

by Donald Hamilton, DVM.

http://www.wholehealthnow.com/books/cats-dogs.html

The Science of Homeopathy

by Prof George Vithoulkas http://www.vithoulkas.com/

The Homeopathic Revolution

by Dana Ullman MPH. www.homeopathicrevolution.com

Printed in Great Britain
by Amazon

Radiant
Princess

STEVE BRENNAN

Radiant Princess

Radiant Princess

FOR NIAMH

Our very own Radiant Princess

INTRODUCTION

When Kate first suggested Niamh as a name should our unborn child be a
girl, I'd never heard the name before. Niamh Brennan. Had a nice ring to
it. When she went to Primary School there were another two Niamhs in
her class. Suddenly popular, that name.
It was only when I decided to have her name tattooed that I looked into it.
Radiant Princess it meant. The original Niamh had been a minor figure in
Irish mythology, wife to Oisin (pronounced Oh-shun) who was the son of
the legend Finn McCool. Oisin's tale was recorded by the Irish poet James
Joyce in The Wanderings of Oisin.
But Niamh's story had never been told. So here it is. It's a bit of Celtic
mythology and a lot of invention.
You can decide for yourself which is which.

Radiant Princess

Radiant Princess

HE WAS ALONE. Well, he was alone apart from his horse and the two giants with swords striding towards him.

There was nothing friendly about them. They were clearly about to give him a hard time.

Kill him, maybe.

Probably, actually.

Smart thing to do would be run.

But he didn't do running away. He wasn't climbing on his horse and heading for the hills. He was standing his ground. It was his ground. He got there first. And they weren't having it, however big and ugly they were.

No words were spoken.

He drew his sword.

There was no need for this, he thought.

But he was having none of it.

He was never going to win.

This was going to hurt.

NIAMH woke in the night again.

Three nights running the same dream had broken her sleep.

Not a nightmare. Not even scary, really. But it disturbed her, nevertheless. And she didn't know why.

Niamh was the hero in her own dream. For three nights she had been asked to come to the rescue of a stranger. She knew him. And yet she didn't.

He was strong and brave and handsome and yet Niamh had to save him. He was a giant of a man in trouble and he puzzled her.

She pulled on her dressing gown and wandered along the corridors, down the great staircase and through the reception hall to the gateway that never needed to be locked. Tir-na-nOg was a fine place to live and Niamh had no worries about leaving the palace to take a walk in the gardens, even in the depths of the night.

There was no point in trying to sleep. She had tossed and turned every other night the strange dream had come to her so tonight, she knew, would be no different. A nice walk would be better, until she cleared her head. Then, maybe, she could sleep some more.

The castle gardens were a magical place. The whole island was. The moon shone on the lawns and flowers as she strolled the paths. Niamh could wander the grounds in the wee small hours, knowing she was safe. Everyone was.

So the stranger in her dream was a true disturbance.

Who was he?

Why was he in trouble?

Where was he, for goodness' sake, because he surely wasn't on Tir na nOg? She would know him otherwise.

What was she meant to do about it?

And how?

She turned all this over in her head, again and again with no answer.

She was going to have to ask someone. Someone who wouldn't tell her she was mad and forget about it. Someone who cared that she dreamed.

She was going to have to tell The Queen.

First thing in the morning, she decided.

At breakfast.

It was just as well The Queen was her mother, thought The Princess.

WHEN the light broke into Fand's bedroom she woke gently and knew her daughter would want to see her that morning. Niamh was strong-willed, defiant even, and refused guidance daily. But that day Fand knew Niamh wanted to talk.

It was a nice feeling. In Tir-na-nOg no-one ever got old or sick. People only got hurt in accidents. But even when there was so much to be happy for, the young still needed to rebel. Fand knew that and she'd done it herself but it still hurt when Niamh didn't want her help.

That morning, though, she did and Fand went to the breakfast room with a smile wider than her usual.

Breakfast was a grand affair. Manannan, Niamh's father, was the island's king, not because he fought, although he could and was good at it. Manannan was king because he was smart and was respected for it. When a decision was needed, he was your man. Which is why the people were happy for him to live in the country's biggest building with his family. But they didn't live alone. Dozens of people tended the gardens and ran the kitchens and kept the farms. And every morning they gathered for breakfast.

Sometimes even Manannan would be found in the kitchen, scrambling eggs or grilling scallops but more often than not he was bustled away. Tir-na-nOg needed him thinking, not cooking.

It was an open table for breakfast. One big room for 40 or so chairs around two giant tables and you sat where there was an empty seat, whether you were a king or a cook.

Fand helped herself to the buffet table and picked a seat at a corner of the table. That way, she figured, she and Niamh would almost be facing each other, not side by side.

"Morning Fand," said Dimpna, making for the seat The Queen had hoped her daughter would use. "Did you sleep well?"

Fand's brow furrowed.

"Dimpna, can I ask you a favour?"

"Of course you can Fand. What's the problem?"

"It's Niamh. I've got a feeling that she'll need to talk to me this morning and I'm hoping she'll sit right here. It seems really rude but, do you mind leaving that chair for her?"

Dimpna looked across the room.

"D'ye think she's had a dream maybe?"

"Could be. I don't know but I think she needs me today."

"I'm going nowhere Fand. I'm for standing here until Niamh arrives so you don't have to ask anyone else for her chair.

"And, since she's just stepped through the door, that's only a matter of moments, anyway. Here she comes Fand. Good luck."

Dimpna smiled at Fand and Niamh before moving round the table.

"Morning Mum," said Niamh.

"Sleep well?" asked her mother.

Niamh hesitated a moment then said: "Mum, I keep getting this dream."

And so Niamh told her mother about the stranger who needed her help.

"Does it mean something, Mum?"

"Of course it does child," said Fand. "You've been due a dream for a while now but I didn't know when it would come. And now it has."

"But what does it mean?"

"How in Tir-na-nOg do you expect me to know that Niamh? I'm no dream reader. For that you need the Well of Dreams and that's a two-day ride on a good horse. I'll ask some of the girls to get a travel pack together for you.

"And you'll need to ask Dad who's to go with you. That's his job. I'll start the preparations and you go see Dad. You'll need to be on the horse at dawn tomorrow."

"What?" said Niamh. "I'm not spending two days on a horse because of a dream, Mum. I'm not that bothered who this stranger is. And if he's that desperate for my help, then I suggest he comes to me."

Fand smiled at her daughter and reached for her hand, readily given for a change.

"Niamh, it's not a dream you're having. It's destiny. It's about the rest of your life and how you live it. Only the Well of Dreams can give you the answer.

"I don't know who your stranger is.

"Your father certainly won't know and will probably want to horsewhip him before you meet him.

"He might be just around the corner or far, far away. He might be here tomorrow or you might need to ride to him next year. But whatever and whoever, Niamh you must meet your stranger and give him a name."

Niamh looked in her mother's eyes. There was always love and tenderness there but today there was something else. An authority that told Niamh that she had, for once, to do what she was told.

She saw something else, too, something she hadn't seen before. Was it concern? Sorrow, even?

"Mum, I'll go. But there's something else, isn't there. What's wrong? What am I getting into here?"

"I'm sorry darling," said Fand. "Every mother fears for her child when a dream comes calling. You've got to find yourself and maybe I'll lose a bit of you.

"You've got to go to a place where I can't protect you and none of us know what you'll find when you get there.

"But go you must and that's the end of it. Go see your father and I'll get your camping gear."

Fand managed to leave the table and turn her back on her daughter before her first tear slipped from her eye. She wiped it away before the hall could see.

"Dimpna?" she called. "We've got work to do."

MOST MORNINGS Manannan saddled his horse and jumped the fences around the palace.

This morning he decided to wait in his private meeting room.

It wasn't a room he used very often. In fact, it had been months since he'd been in it. But it was an important room. It was a room where the people of Tir-na-nOg could ask their king for help. Anyone was welcome to visit Manannan and ask for his help. It was a very public place for that. But it was very private too. When the Tireans – which is what the people of the country called themselves – asked to meet Manannan in the Purple Room they knew only those present would know of what they spoke.

Manannan didn't know why he chose not to ride Embarr over the fences that morning but he was smart enough to know there was a reason he had to be available.

He was, however, astonished when Niamh burst through the door. His daughter had been a stranger for some time. They only met during tantrums and when Manannan had decided she needed guidance. But Niamh didn't take guidance. Manannan gave it anyway. So they fought as only a father and daughter can, throwing words instead of punches and hurting the more for it.

"Right Dad, I've to go to the Well of Dreams, that I've never heard of by the way, in a place I've never heard of, with a sidekick you've to pick. Does that sound right to you, eh?"

Manannan sighed.

"I'm getting too old for this stuff," he thought, but didn't say.

"I take it you've already spoken to Mum, then?" he asked.

"Not more than 10 minutes ago. It's her that's sending me to this Well of Dreams place. I've said I'll go but I don't have to like it, do I?"

"So you've had a dream then?"

"How do you know that, then?

"You don't spend two days on a horse going to the Well of Dreams unless you've had a dream, do you?"

Niamh had to accept that her dad made sense but she still wasn't giving in.

"Dad, I had never heard of the Well of Dreams until half-an-hour ago and now I'm supposed to go halfway across the kingdom because of a stupid dream? You're supposed to be the smartest guy around this place so maybe, before I saddle up, you'll tell me what this is all about. Eh?"

Manannan had been putting this off for years and despite being the smartest guy in the Purple Room that minute he was stumped. Because Niamh wanted an answer he didn't have.

"We're lucky, Niamh," he said. "Very lucky.

"We don't get sick. We live long and well. Other people have so many sicknesses they have to give them all names just so they know what sickness they've got.

"And they do strange things. They fight for daft reasons. And they lose friends for daft reasons.

"You're a lucky girl, Niamh but you don't know it yet.

"Now, you're going to the Well of Dreams for three reasons: first, your Mum told you to go; second, I'm telling you to go and I'm not just your dad, I'm King around this place; and third – and I don't understand what you don't understand about this – your dream told you to go.

"The others get ill and they fight. We get to dream.

"There's a whole new thing out there waiting for you Niamh.

"Go get it, Niamh"

And suddenly Niamh understood why her dad was a king.

"So who's going with me?" she asked quietly.

"It's Sean. If ever I was in trouble, he'd be the man I'd want at my side. And I think your mum's probably already putting a saddle on Merlin and loading him with gear for you. So you've got my best friend and the man I know will defend you to the death, and a fine horse loaded with supplies.

"Anything else you think you might need?"

Niamh found a lump in her throat. Her dad might be King but the best things he had weren't things and he'd just given her several of them.

"Any chance of a hug, Dad?"

It didn't take long for Manannan to say: "Aye Lass."

FAND WAS getting ever more tetchy. Her daughter was leaving home for the first time and she just wouldn't do it the way she was told.

"So now you know where you're going and how long it's going to take, do you?" she demanded. "And clearly you've allowed for all the unforeseen events that might crop up. Doubtless you'll know exactly what to do if your horse breaks a fetlock?"

"I thought that was what Sean was for," Niamh shot back.

Sean surveyed the situation calmly but with interest. He had neither a wife nor daughter and was fascinated at the bickering.

Not much taller than the Princess himself, his wiry frame leant against the castle wall while the talks over luggage carried on.

"Ah, now, Princess, even I don't know what might be waiting on us out there. Lions? Tigers? Bears?" he teased. "We might be lucky with a broken fetlock."

"Don't be ridiculous man. There's no bears in Tir na nOg," said Niamh.

"There might be no bears today young lady but how do you know about tomorrow?" Fand almost shouted, her anxiety getting the better of her.

"In that case why are you sending me to the edge of the country with a one-man escort?"

"Enough!" shouted Manannan. "Niamh, you're going with Sean and you'll take as many supplies as you can reasonable carry. And Fand, there's no bears in Tir na nOg."

The King was clearly in no mood for an argument so his wife and daughter buckled down to the last of the packing.

It didn't take long and Fand, Niamh, Manannan and Sean wandered back to the castle for breakfast while the stable lads checked the load and the horses' tack.

Once they were settled, Manannan turned to his daughter.

"Now, Niamh, you're the Princess of Tir na nOg and Sean will make sure anyone you meet knows that and accords you every courtesy. But there's a duty that comes with being a princess. It's only because our people respect us that we have our position. And that means you have to respect them back. Especially the strangers. I know you respect everyone around our castle here but there are people on the island who don't know you yet. It's important that they're happy for you to be their princess too. You understand?"

"Yes Dad," she said. She'd been feisty for long enough but now the mission daunted her. She missed her mum and dad already.

"Here Niamh," said Fand, hands held out. In them lay an elegant, slim sword, shining bright silver, decorated at the hilt with delicate emeralds of the deepest green.

"And what am I supposed to do with that?" asked Niamh. "You wouldn't let me peel a potato 'til last summer."

"I don't expect you to do anything with it. In fact, I'm hoping you'll bring it back without it ever coming out of the sheath. But if you ever need to draw a sword, I'll feel a lot happier knowing you've got one."

"Just in case you meet a bear, eh?" said Sean. "You'll not be needing a sword Princess, but it's a lovely thing to look at. And I bet it's a belter for a young lady to wave about a bit. Bring it with you. Make your mum happy. Well, happier, anyway."

"This is my sword Niamh," said Fand. "I never had to draw it but my mum had wanted me to have it. It was hers before mine and her mum's too. We Tirean women haven't had to draw a sword for generations and long may that continue.

"I'm past the thought of ever using it. So I want you to have it and never to need it either."

Niamh took the sword and wrapped its belt around her waist, letting it drop lightly at her right hip, left handed as she was.

"Love you, Mum," she said.

"And I love you Niamh." Fand drew a deep breath and said: "Right. Be off with the pair of you. Come back soon, but don't come back without some answers Niamh, alright?"

They walked to the waiting horses and mounted up, Sean on his horse of many years, Shelbourne, a grey stallion as wiry and lithe as its rider and Niamh on Merlin, magnificently white and majestic, clearly a king's horse.

Manannan slapped Merlin's hind quarters and the horse stepped into a gentle trot, seemingly aware of his precious cargo.

Sean and Shelbourne followed. They had a long day ahead of them.

SEAN LED them away from the castle and Niamh pulled alongside him as they reached the open fields.

"So, Sean, I've got a notion of where we're going but I'm hoping you've got a plan in your head. We can't ride through the night, can we?"

"Indeed you're right Princess. So I've got a wee notion as to how to get you to the Well of Dreams and back safely and relatively comfortably in four days. But it's only a rough guide. I've no idea why people go or how long you end up staying there. Might take a day or two before you get the answer you're looking for. Don't know."

"What do you mean you don't know why people go?" asked Niamh. "Don't you have dreams?"

"Never had one. Never want one either. Seem to cause nothing but bother. I'm told it's like being awake and all sorts of stuff that's not likely to happen actually does and you've no control at all. Sounds pretty grim Princess."

"But dreams can be magical and lovely and funny," she said. "It's a real shame you can't enjoy them Sean."

"Princess, we're 10 minutes into a trip that's going to take at least four days because you've had a dream you don't get and we've no idea what happens when you do get it. Think maybe I've got the better deal eh?"

Niamh smiled and stayed quiet for a bit: Sean did have a point, after all.

When next she spoke it was her turn to surprise Sean.

"Sean, do you mind calling me 'Niamh', instead of 'Princess'?"

"And why would that be Princess?" asked Sean. "I'm proud to call your father by his first name but we've been through a lot of stuff together and maybe I've earned that right as a friend. But you're the King's daughter and you're a princess and I've hardly earned the right to call you by your name."

"You get called 'Princess' because of who your parents are. I'd rather be called for who I am," said Niamh.

"And who, exactly, might that be," said Sean after a moment's thought.

"I think we'll have to wait until we find out what the Well of Dreams has to say before we know Sean. But I don't think it's a bad person."

Sean laughed loud and long.

Eventually he said: "D'ye think I'd be out here on a horse trip like this if I thought you were a bad person, Princess? Sorry, Niamh. And I thank you for the privilege. There's not many men asked to call a princess by her name."

"Sean, if my Dad thinks you're the man to look after me on this journey, you've certainly got the right to call me 'Niamh'. Now where on Tir na nOg are you planning we should sleep tonight?"

Sean laughed again. Any tension between them had gone. They were a pair on a mission and they might as well make the best of the trip.

"I figured we'd have a picnic lunch whenever you feel hungry and that we'd get to the O'Bamas' house in time for dinner. It's short notice but they're grand company and they'll not pass up the chance of entertaining Manannan's daughter. I've a feeling there might be a bit of a party on offer this evening Princess. Sorry, Niamh."

"Sounds good to me Sean."

Niamh gave Merlin a gentle kick and they were off. The road might be long but there was fun to be had on the way.

NIAMH was surely sore when she spotted the smoke.

"What's that?" she asked Sean.

"The O'Bamas," he replied. "You can't see the house yet but that smoke tells you Michaela's got a fire going. Dinner can't be far away."

"But they don't know we're coming, Sean. How can we just turn up and ask for food?"

"Princess – sorry, Niamh – Michaela could rustle up a meal for a dozen if she had to. They don't get many visitors to the farm and they like to make the most of it when they do."

"Just seems really rude to turn up unannounced," said Niamh.

"Well, the only way to announce an arrival would be to send someone ahead unannounced and that seems less than useful. And anyway, you're a princess of this island My Lady. You can turn up unannounced in any quarter and be welcome."

"Still seems rude," she said, unconvinced.

"Not if your mum's packed a present from the Queen as a thank-you to the hostess," said Sean.

"What present?"

Sean pulled a slip of paper from his top pocket and read from it.

"Packet in the rear left saddle bag with Michaela's name on the wrapper," he said.

Suddenly Niamh realised why their horses were so loaded.

"Have we got other presents tucked away I don't know of?" she asked.

"Some. Not many. Your mum just wants people we might run into to know she's grateful for their hospitality. The O'Bamas are the only family we were definitely going to meet so there's something specially for Michaela for looking after you."

"You mean us, don't you?"

"No Princess. Sorry, Niamh. Fand expects me to be able to look after myself. That's so I can look after you."

"So what's the present for Michaela?"

"No idea. It's wrapped up isn't it? I suggest you give it to Michaela and tell her it's from your mum. She'll be delighted whatever it is."

They topped the ridge and a new valley opened out before them. Cattle and sheep roamed the grass, a river winding past the farmhouse belching the smoke Niamh had spotted earlier. A man on a horse was herding the livestock. A couple of young children were splashing in the river. Chickens flapped.

"That's Doreck on the horse," said Sean. "Dereck's the dad. They've got this family tradition that male children have to take their father's name but that got confusing with so many men in the house with the same name. So they take the name but change is slightly every time. Daft if you ask me. One of these days they're going to have a right famous O'Bama with a right daft name."

It had been a long day in the saddle and the valley below almost said "come in" to Niamh.

It's going to be grand to get off this horse, she thought.

THERE was a welcome party. Doreck had spotted them enter the valley and rode to the house to alert his mother who immediately flew into a panic over her clothes, hair and dinner arrangements for visitors. She didn't get visitors often and wanted to give her best impression.

Hair freshly brushed, frock freshly changed, dinner still under consideration, Michaela stood at her garden gate with her husband and four children awaiting arrivals.

"Good evening you O'Bamas," hailed Sean pulling Shelbourne to a halt and dismounting in a single fluid action.

"Sean, it's grand to see you. Been way too long," said Dereck, throwing his arms around his guest.

"Indeed, indeed Dereck. And you Michaela. Looking well, all of you."

"You're not so bad yourself Sean," said Michaela, planting a kiss on Sean's cheek.

"Might I introduce you to my travelling companion?" asked Sean, indicating towards Niamh.

"This is Princess Niamh of Tir na nOg."

Michaela's knees nearly buckled. She didn't know whether to bow, curtsy or what. She stared at Sean.

"Could you not have given us a bit of notice that you were bringing the Princess to visit Sean?" she said in a tone that suggested Sean was to be severely dealt with later.

"Actually," said Niamh, "It's my fault. We didn't know we were coming until yesterday and then it was too late to send notice."

Dereck bowed and Michaela decided to curtsy. The children took their cue from their parents and bowed or curtsied as seemed proper.

"Thank you for coming Princess," said Dereck. "We've nothing but a farm and a home here but we'd be proud and happy to share it with you."

"That's true Princess, whatever we've got is yours," said Michaela, beginning to regain her composure.

"Right now," said Niamh, "all I want is to get my backside off this horse," at which the O'Bama youngsters broke into laughter. Even royalty got sore in the saddle, it seemed.

Michaela spotted the chance to buy some time before she had to serve up a dinner fit for a princess.

"I don't suppose a nice warm bath would help?" she said.

"It's Michaela isn't it?" said Niamh. "Sean only got half way through the introductions, you know."

"It is indeed, Princess," laughed Michaela.

"Well, Michaela, that's the best idea I've heard for days. And I'd like you to call me Niamh."

"Yes Princess. Sorry, Niamh," said Michaela, turning to her husband.

"Get the water piping. I'll show the Princess – Niamh – to her room."

Dereck was no fool. When he saw that look in his wife's eye, he knew exactly what to do: whatever he was told.

THE BATH did the trick and Niamh felt much better when she joined Sean and the assembled O'Bamas for dinner. Dorreck was the eldest son at the same age as Niamh. Domineck was next in line with Siobhan and Sinead making up the clan.

They all soon relaxed in the company of a princess who was determined to be as normal as a princess could be among strangers.

"I've got something for you from my mum," said Niamh, handing the parcel to Michaela.

"There's no need for presents, Princess," said Michaela.

"She wants you to have it," said Niamh, keen to find out what the wrapper was hiding.

Michaela unwrapped the most beautiful tablecloth she could have imagined.

The O'Bamas lived well and wanted for little but their life was basic. Happy but basic. There were few luxuries in the O'Bama household.

Michaela gasped as she unfolded the fabric to show the brightly woven pattern.

"It's gorgeous," she whispered. Instantly she threw it over the dining table.

"Will you look at that?" she said. "If only I'd a meal worthy of a table looking like that."

Sean said: "I've come from a palace and ate with a king, a queen and a princess and I can tell you now Michaela that whatever you've managed to pull together in the hour since we sprung our surprise on you will be the finest in the land and fit for any royalty. What do you say Princess? Sorry, Niamh."

"You know," said Niamh, "Princesses like the same food as everyone else."

They all laughed and sat at Michaela's table where she truly did serve a meal fit for a princess. Not fussy. Not fancy. Just exactly what a young woman who had spent a day in the saddle needed.

Niamh and the O'Bamas became firm friends over dinner. They laughed, joked and forgot any notion of royalty. By dessert they were just a bunch of friends having dinner.

And they were all fascinated by the nature of Niamh's mission.

"The Well of Dreams, eh?" said Michaela. "What do you think it's going to tell you?"

"If I knew that I wouldn't have to spend four days on a horse," said Niamh.

They agreed it was a puzzle and Michaela begged Niamh to tell them the answer on the return trip. But Niamh had to decline.

"I can't promise Michaela. It all depends if it makes any sense or not."

"Quite right, Princess," said Dereck. "It's nobody's business but yours."

He paused, then added: "But you'll tell us what you can eh? We've got to know who this big handsome fella is, don't we?"

Niamh nodded but inside her stomach was fluttering. She had never been afraid of anything before – never had a reason to be. And now she had butterflies and could feel her heart pounding. It was the fear of the unknown.

She couldn't even promise to tell the O'Bamas her story later because she didn't know if it had a happy ending or not.

Sean filled the gap in the conversation.

"Sounds to me this handsome man needs a hand," he said. "And as soon as Niamh finds out who he is, we'll go and give him one."

"Do you know something I don't?" asked Niamh.

"Princess we're not going to the Well of Dreams for an answer that finishes a story. We're looking for an answer that's a start. I figure when you get your answer we've then got to go and find your man and get him out of whatever trouble he's in. And that could take a while."

"I'm going to be home in three days Sean," said Niamh. I didn't sign up for any odyssey."

"Aye Niamh, we'll be back with your mum in three days. But I've a feeling this journey's just starting."

THE SUN rose and with it the Princess.

It was, she thought, an important day and she had no idea what to expect.

She was curious rather than apprehensive, excited more than wary. Maybe today the stranger in the night would become clear.

She dressed for a day in the saddle but wore her brightest blouse, knowing she might spend some time in new company before nightfall.

It was no surprise to her that Sean had seen to the horses and the saddles before she arrived in the O'Bamas' front room for the monster breakfast Michaela was already building, slice by slice, rasher by rasher.

"Your mum would expect you well fed and watered anywhere in Tir na nOg Princess. You'll not be leaving this house with a belly wanting more of a breakfast, Your Highness."

Niamh sighed. Clearly no amount of telling would persuade people to call her by her name. She resolved that in future she'd tell people they could call her Niamh and let them decide what to call her. As long as it wasn't rude, of course.

"I'm not sure I'm that hungry, to be honest Michaela," said Niamh.

"Ah, that's nothing but the nerves Princess, and no wonder. I'd be hiding butterflies myself if I was you. But you'll take a breakfast Princess because I'm not having your mum worry that you're in the parish of the Well of Dreams and your tummy rumbles just as the secret unfolds. Fried or scrambled?"

Michaela waved a handful of eggs plucked from the henhouse minutes earlier.

"Scrambled please," said Niamh. She'd eat her fill to ease the fluttering of those butterflies, she decided.

Niamh said her farewells but asked Michaela's indulgence for another night. She and Sean would need to stop on the return trip.

"If you try and pass this house or go another way I'll send Dereck out with the dogs to fetch you Princess. It's an honour to have you and a pleasure to know you."

"You're good people, Michaela," said Niamh. "I'll never pass your door without knocking and I'll expect the same from you. See you tomorrow, whatever it brings."

Sean strapped the last of Niamh's kit to Merlin and she climbed aboard. Her mother's sword brushed her leg as she mounted and, oddly, she felt comforted by it.

And then they were off. Who knew what the day would bring? But the Princess knew it was not to be like any other she'd had before.

They settled into an easy pace. No need to tire horses on such a trip.

"How do you know where we're going Sean?" asked Niamh.

"I've been there before Princess," said Sean.

"And when was that?" she asked.

"Many years ago. With your dad, since you were about to ask.

"What for?"

"He'd had a dream. Kept coming to him and he couldn't work it out. He's a clever man your dad and we figured if he couldn't work it he'd have to ask the Well of Dreams. Worst day of my life it was."

"How?"

"We went to war, Princess. Your dad's dream was that the giants across the sea were jealous and wanted Tir na nOg as their own. We know we're lucky, that we live long and well and, generally, happy. They knew it too and they wanted it for themselves.

"None of us knew this but it came to your dad in a dream and the Well

16

of Dreams helped him understand what had to be done.

"It was why we took arms and crossed the water to meet them. Your dad's scared of nothing Niamh, but he feared a battle with his wife and child at risk. So we took the fight to them rather than wait for them to come."

Sometimes the loudest sound is no sound at all. Niamh waited for Sean to carry on but he stayed quiet.

"What happened Sean?" she asked, eventually.

Sean sighed.

"We won," he said and kicked his horse into a gallop.

Niamh resolved to ask her dad what happened when she got home.

THE SUN was high as they crested a bluebell-covered hill. At the top Sean pulled his horse to a stop.

"We're here," he said.

Niamh pulled Merlin up beside him.

"Where?" she said.

"There," said Sean. "That wee copse of trees. That's it."

A group of maybe 20 trees stood in the middle of an empty plain. It looked as ordinary a place as she could think of.

"What now?" she asked.

"First, we eat. I've no idea how long you'll take doing your business but you don't want to be hungry Princess. I'll build us a fire and we'll take a drop of lunch, then you head on down."

Niamh was still full from breakfast but only said: "You're not coming with me?"

"It's your dream Princess. I'd only get in your way."

So they took tea and bread and cold meats. Niamh watched Sean unpack the horses.

"What's your plan?" she said.

"I'll get us some shelter up. I'm all for sleeping under the stars but I'm not sleeping in the rain. Might not rain but if it does, we're not sleeping in it. So I'll have things ready for when you get back."

Niamh finished her lunch and gazed at the copse.

"Right," she said suddenly. "Let's get on with it."

"I'll see you when I see you Princess," said Sean.

With that, Niamh mounted Merlin and headed gently down the slope to the unremarkable little grove.

Even up close there was no sign of life or activity. Just a few trees. Certainly no Well of Dreams, she thought.

She dismounted and tethered Merlin to a branch of the first tree. Not that she needed to. He wasn't going anywhere.

A little nervously, she walked into the copse.

"Good day Niamh," said The Voice.

She knew instantly The Voice was important which was why she gave it capital letters. She also knew The Voice was like no other. Because Niamh heard The Voice in her head. Not through her ears like she heard ordinary voices. This was actually inside her head. It was talking to her and her alone.

All of Niamh's compusure evaporated in a heartbeat. In that instant she was, once again, the little girl that Manannan and Fand had brought into the world.

"Who are you?" she whispered, trembling.

"You came all this way to talk and you don't know me? Very odd Niamh," said The Voice. It sounded female.

"Are you the Well of Dreams?" she asked.

"That's what some call me," said The Voice. "But then, that's probably because in Tir na nOg people generally only come to talk when they've got a dream to talk about. Like you Niamh."

The Voice was oddly calming. Reassuring.

Niamh relaxed.

"You know my dreams then?" she asked.

"Indeed I do Niamh."

"And can you tell me what they mean?"

"Well…yes…and no," said The Voice.

"And what's that supposed to mean?" asked Niamh, emboldened. She might be awed but she wasn't overawed.

"Dreams are strange. They're like bits of stories, often with the start, middle or end missing. I think you've got the middle of a story so I can't tell you how it starts or ends. Or what to do about it. If anything should be done about it all, for that matter."

"I spent a long time on a horse for this," said Niamh, "You've told me less than I already know."

"Not at all Niamh, I'm just explaining how I can't help. If you understand that, maybe I'll be able to tell you how I can help."

Niamh thought for a moment.

Then: "Alright. I've got a wee bit of the picture now and you can help me with the other bits. Like a jigsaw puzzle?"

"Correct. And you might need to go elsewhere to find the missing bits for the full picture. In fact, I'm sure of that Niamh," said The Voice.

By now Niamh was getting used to talking to something she couldn't see and heard only in her head. She was glad Sean hadn't come, though. She probably looked a complete eejit, jabbering away in a wood.

"OK. So we don't know where we're going, just the direction?"

"Very good, Niamh. I wish everyone who had questions understood the answers as well as you."

"But you can't get many people chasing dreams out here. Do you?"

"Oh no," said The Voice. "The last person who came here to talk was your dad. But I'm not just here Niamh. I'm everywhere. It's just that people like to have a proper meeting place. And this is as good as any for the people of Tir na nOg."

This last statement called many more questions to mind for Niamh but she had a feeling they'd take all day. And she'd rather have answers to her dream questions first.

"Alright," she said. "Who's the stranger who comes and wakes me up every night? And why?"

"His name's Oisin. Written down it looks funny but it sounds like 'Oh-shun'. He's a ranger and poet, which can be a bit awkward, making up rhymes when riding to hounds.

"Anyway, he lives across the water and he's part of a ranger clan called the Fianna, led by his father Finn McCool, whose real name also looks funny written down. They hunt and roam the land and Oisin writes down their adventures.

"Now, Oisin's in danger. He's a big lad and a fair fighter, but he hasn't got the killer instinct his father has and he's a little too trusting."

"So what's that to do with my dream?"

"There's a strong connection between you Niamh. It's fair to say you'd make a perfect couple, which is odd since you've never met. But sometimes there's a bond between people that can't be explained. Twins have it often. They know when the other is in trouble without being told. Somehow they just know.

"You've got a bond like that with Oisin and that's why you believe he's in danger. Your dream is your heart telling your head you have to help him."

"And how exactly am I supposed to help a ranger poet in another land?" demanded Niamh, a little exasperated.

"No idea Niamh," said The Voice. "You're not much use to him riding into battle with your Mum's pretty wee sword are you? But you might be able to persuade him to leave."

"To quit the fighting and turn to the writing."

"What, turn his back on his family?" said Niamh. " I doubt that. The little I know of rangers is that they'd suffer almost anything for pride. They'd die rather than look bad, the eejits."

"Maybe that's why Oisin's different then?"

"This is daft," said Niamh. "You're telling me to head off across the water to save some fella I've never met from an unknown threat and take him to safety to become a full-time writer?"

"I'm telling you nothing of the sort Niamh. All I'm doing is explaining your dream."

"So is this supposed to be my destiny then? My fate? To team up with this writer man?"

"Destiny? Fate? What nonsense have they been teaching up in that castle Niamh? These are foolish words made up by people too daft or too lazy to think up better reasons for things they can't explain or who just won't accept things for what they are. Like there's some big giant hiding somewhere that's got their lives all planned out for them. Those that peddle that nonsense do it just so they've got someone – or something – else to blame for their own poor decisions.

"No Niamh, it's not fate, or destiny. It's just a young man with whom you've a bond in need of help. It's your call whether you answer him or not."

Niamh had to think long and hard about that one.

"Is he waiting for me? Does he know he's in trouble?"

"No Niamh. He's troubled by a regular dream with you in it but he doesn't know who you are or why he dreams of you. And Finn McCool isn't the type of father to listen to him and send him to a Well of Dreams."

"There's more than one?" asked Niamh.

"Sort of. Different folk have different names and ways of coming to me."

"Oh, this is hopeless," sighed Niamh. "I came here with one question and now I've got dozens. But worse than that, I'm confused now and don't know what I'm meant to do."

"You're meant to do what you want to do," said The Voice. "Sometimes people have to do things that they don't want to do but those are very rare occasions. Mainly you should do what you want to do. Reasonable people generally get along fine that way."

"Should I go?" whispered Niamh.

"You should certainly go back to Sean now Niamh. The light's beginning to fade. And I've no more answers to help you. It's over to you now."

"And if I need to talk to you again?"

"I'm all over the place, Niamh. You just need to find the right way to reach me. I'll be around."

"Thanks. I think. If I need you again, what should I call you?"

"Whatever you want Niamh. I've many different names depending on who's calling"

"If I give you a name another day, will you know it?"

"I will Niamh. Now farewell. And good luck. Whatever you decide."

Niamh turned and walked back to Merlin.

"Come on boy," she said. "Time to head for home, I think."

SHE WAS too tired and too confused to give Sean the full story. All she could manage was a brief account of Oisin and his vague situation and the decision that lay ahead.

Sean shrugged.

"It's as well I keep my sword sharp," he said, more to himself than to Niamh.

They ate and drank and the Princess thought and thought until she thought her head would explode.

When they turned in to their separate shelters, the Princess fell asleep in a heartbeat and was only mildly disturbed when Oisin appeared looking quite unruffled astride a horse alone in a field.

He really was quite handsome, she thought.

WHEN morning arrived, Niamh had made at least one decision: "Sean, I want to press on for home, not stay overnight at the O'Bamas'."

"It's a day and a half's ride Princess. Can't be done in a day."

"We can stop for a break at the O'Bamas' than press on til evening and use our shelters. That way I'll be home early tomorrow. I'd like that rather than spending the afternoon away from home just thinking."

Sean took a moment to look kindly at Niamh.

"That we can do Princess. So the sooner we're on our way the better."

Sean insisted they took some breakfast before breaking camp and heading for home. Next stop was some hours off and he wasn't having the girl in his charge feeling hungry on the way.

They kept a steady pace and made the O'Bamas' by mid-day where Michaela was disappointed not to have overnight guests. But she understood.

"You'll be wanting to talk to your mum and dad about all this. But you'll take a hot lunch with us before you head."

She sent the children out to bring Dereck and Doreck in from their work, against Niamh's pleading.

"There's not often we get a princess for lunch and he'd give me a right shirricking if you came and went with him in the field," she said.

Niamh gave them the same basic story she'd given Sean as they took lunch.

"So what do you do now?" asked Michaela.

"No idea," said Niamh. "That's why I'm in such a hurry to see my mum and dad. They might not know everything but they know me well enough."

With the horses fed and watered, they pressed on. As the sun began to dip behind the hills they were still half a day from home and Sean called a halt. There was a small copse beside a stream that Sean reckoned was ideal for an overnight stop.

"It'll be dark soon and we don't want to be running the horses about when we can't see."

The shelters were up in jig time and they sat down for a light dinner under the stars again. This time she found herself looking forward to seeing Oisin in the night. She was no longer scared by his visits. He was no longer a threat.

And as she slept, without her even knowing, she made up here mind.

SHE SLEPT soundly and woke with the light, a strange, new determination in her heart.

Over breakfast, Sean noticed the change.

"Everything alright, Princess?"

"No Sean," she said. "Not yet."

RIDERS approaching Tir na nOg's castle were few and far between so the pair were spotted long before they arrived and Fand was waiting at the gates for her daughter.

"Come here, my gorgeous girl," she bubbled. "How did it go? You must be exhausted. I've got the girls running you a bath. You'll be all sore after the travelling. Are you hungry? I've got a grand bit of lunch all arranged….."

Truth was, Fand knew that whatever Niamh had learned from the Well of Dreams was unlikely to make her settle down and stick to a nice, peaceful life in Tir na nOg.

So she prattled on, hoping Niamh wouldn't give her any news she wasn't going to want to hear.

"Mum, I'm grand. A wee bit sore but I'm grand. I'll have a bath later. Right now I need to talk to you and Dad. Where is he?"

"He's out hunting with some of the lads. We thought you'd be later, so…."

"Dangit," said Niamh. "He could be out for hours then."

She paused. Then breathed deeply. She knew suddenly that the meeting with her parents was important. But in that moment she realised it wasn't urgent. Trying to find her father in the fields was a hopeless exercise and she'd rather he was in a good mood on his return than hot and sweaty having been called from the chase.

"It's fine Mum," she said. "But you'll have to wait 'til I tell you my news because Dad needs to know it too and I'll need you both to be with me. I can't tell it twice, separately. So, please, I will take that bath and that lunch. And if it's alright with you I'll take your arm on the way to them both."

Fand regarded her daughter and knew. She knew that Niamh wasn't a wee lassie any more. And she knew that the woman before her, however slight, had a mind of her own. And that she had a mission. And that she'd just have to wait to find out what that mission was.

MANANNAN was never any good at quiet entrances. When he came home with the dogs and the spoils of the day's hunt, everyone knew about it. Much barking, shouting and general malarkey but when he spotted Merlin padding about the paddock, the noise grew.

"Is there a princess in the house?" he bellowed. "Where's our Princess Niamh then?"

The dogs, all fine wolfhounds who had never seen a wolf but looked like they could handle one anyway, loped off to the kennels and their dinners.

For years Niamh had run down the stairs to meet the sounds of her dad's return. But today, she walked.

Manannan looked up at the young woman he'd last seen as a girl. Long brown hair flowing over her shoulders, sparkling gray/blue eyes, a hint of freckles on her pale cheeks and a grin on her lips that told him two things: she was delighted, as always, to see him and; she had a secret she was bursting to tell.

They gave each other a big, warm hug.

"So, my gorgeous girl, how was your trip?" asked Manannan.

"Let's find Mum and I'll tell you all about it," she said.

Fand was fussing over the evening meal preparation, mainly to fill the time until she sat down with Niamh and her husband. When the pair appeared, the cooks sighed in relief, content they could now get on with the task at hand of feeding the palace without a queen's interference.

The three of them retired to Manannan's study where Niamh told them, from start to finish about her trip: from the party at the O'Bamas' to the decision she had come to in the shelter the previous night.

"I'm going to go and find him and bring him here," she said.

Fand and Manannan exchanged glances. They'd suspected the trip to the Well of Dreams might lead to something like this. They'd never discussed it, just felt it and understood the other felt it too. They weren't minded to try to stop her. That way only arguments lay and she'd go her own way in any case.

"The Well of Dreams," said Manannan. "Did he tell you to do that?"

Niamh was surprised. The Well of Dreams she had spoken to – The Voice – had been a woman. But then, she reasoned, the Well of Dreams could probably pick any voice it wanted. It made sense it sounded like a man to her dad.

"No Dad. Actually she didn't tell me to do anything. She just told me what my dream was about and left me to the decision.

"Isn't that how she was with you Dad? She surely didn't tell you to go to war did she?"

Manannan's shoulders slouched a little, as though he'd just remembered a heavy weight lay over them.

"No, Niamh. And it was a man I spoke to. But that's probably of no consequence. The Well of Dreams is what it is to each of us, I suppose.

"All he did was lay out a situation for me and there was a decision to be made. Well, there was another option, but there was no chance of the right outcome that way."

"What happened, Dad," asked Niamh.

Manannan looked at Fand who nodded her approval.

"It's not a secret Manannan. She's grown enough to know now, too."

Manannan drew a long breath and threw his shoulders back in his high-backed armchair.

"I'd had this dream that a band of giants was gathered on the shore across the sea and preparing to attack. I couldn't understand why anyone would want to harm us so I went to the Well of Dreams to find out.

"I'd always felt we were lucky on Tir na nOg but it took the Well of Dreams to spell it out for me. We take it all for granted but we live well here Niamh and the giants – a clan by the name of Hooligan – were jealous. They wanted the same health and good living even if it meant they had to steal it.

"My decision was simple. Either build barricades and try to defend our shores or meet them on their own ground. Win or lose, it was an easy decision. Even if we lost on their land, they'd still have to cross the sea to take the island and, hopefully, we could do enough damage to weaken their fighting capability.

"If nothing else, they'd think twice about boarding the boats.

"There were about a hundred of us. Took to the boats and set out for the mainland late in the day so we'd arrive in the deepest dark of the night.

Embarr's a fantastical horse – he doesn't need a boat to cross seas – but my place was in the boats with the men.

"There was good cloud cover and we had a few problems finding our positions in the drear but we had the advantage of surprise and were pretty much where we wanted to be just as light began to break.

"By the time the sun was up the main party was in position. And that left about 20 of us to go and stir it up a bit.

"The Hooligans aren't really giants. They're big, right enough, all of them, unnaturally big: seven, maybe eight feet tall some of them. So the likes of me and Sean were on a hiding to nothing if we went toe-to-toe with them

"They'd set themselves a camp by a wee bay, with their boats lined up ready for the invasion. But the Hooligans were no sailors so they'd spent days looking at the sea, waiting for it to calm so they could come our way. They're not the smartest people, Hooligans. A calm sea between the mainland and Tir na nOg is almost unheard of. Their fear of the water gave us the edge because they stayed put while we travelled.

"The first they knew we were there was when we rode straight through their camp and threw our torches into their boats. They scrambled out of their tents to see their fleet already ablaze. When they reached for their swords we were upon them. Not big and strong but fast and furious.

"This, unfortunately, made them very, very angry. Their big and strong started to batter our fast and furious and we lost 10 men in the next few minutes, half our forward force. And then we ran.

"We turned and ran as fast as our horses could run, straight for the hills that surrounded the bay. It was a bit of a gully and when we made it half way up the foothills we turned to face them; dozens upon dozens of them baying for blood. Our blood. And the blood of our wives and our children.

"When they were in the neck of the valley, we unleashed our archers. From the hills around the Hooligans we rained arrows of fire on them. Relentlessly. Volley after volley of death rained down on them.

"And while they whirled and danced in the fire we raised our swords and rejoined battle before they could retreat.

"I made straight for their leader, Mingin Hooligan, but he was a monster of a man and threw me from Embarr to the ground. He was just about to run me through when Sean caught him square in the eye with one of those little throwing daggers of his. When he reeled back I managed to ram my sword right into his chest and pushed it as hard as I could.

"When he finally fell, you could feel the ground tremble. With their leader down, the rest of the Hooligans knew they were beaten. They dropped their swords and we let them carry their dead back to their camp.

"We gathered our dead and wounded and came home to Tir na nOg.

"And we've had no trouble from Hooligans ever since."

The telling had taken its toll on Manannan. He seemed suddenly older and sadder.

"Who did we lose Dad?" Niamh whispered.

"Our best," said Manannan. "They had to ride into the heart of the enemy. I lost two brothers – your uncles. So did Sean. And good friends too. No one was unaffected.

"It was a once-in-a-generation battle. We lost many of our best and it's taken a generation for sons to replace their fathers. We don't need another threat like that, another reason for so many young men to die."

There was silence in the room as Niamh took her father's words in.

"Sounds like you did the right thing, though, Dad."

"It was better than the alternative, anyway," said the King.

It was Fand who finally broke the mood.

"Right, enough of the past. We've a whole new dream to chase now Niamh, eh?"

"Yes Mum. And it feels like I'm supposed to get someone out of a fight rather than pick one, if you know what I mean."

"I do, lass, I do," said Manannan. "But you don't have to pick a fight to end up in one. You'll need a squad with you. Small enough not to cause alarm but big enough not to be messed with.

"I'll go and check on the lads. Fand, can you tend to your daughter for us?"

And with a tender kiss to both their cheeks Manannan strode from the room with a purpose in mind.

EACH EVENING after the chores were complete – the cattle settled, the pigs fed, horses tended – the men of Tir na nOg met in the castle fields for exercise. Not lifting and running for fitness; daily life on the island kept men fit. This was sword play and unarmed combat exercise. It was training. Practice.

When Manannan had returned with the dead and wounded and his depleted force from the mainland, he decreed that all the men of Tir na nOg should be able to defend their home and family to the best of their abilities. So, from a young age, they met and trained daily, the skilled passing on what they knew to those new to the notion of the fight.

Manannan maintained that the island did not have an army. They would never invade anyone. But, if push came to shove, they were ready.

Every now and again Manannan called them together for some full battle exercises, just to remind them that there was more to it than pretend kicking and punching and swinging swords about. There were few complaints; no-one needed reminding of the losses against the Hooligans.

These gatherings gave the King the chance to run his eye over the men from outlying settlements who had to show they could still run and fight and hadn't put the flab on around the waist since they'd last met.

He'd have no need to send for men from elsewhere now though. Manannan knew he'd have the makings of an escort group from among the men of the castle and its surroundings.

"I'm looking for an honour guard, lads, a bunch ready to ride to the mainland with the Princess Niamh for a few days, maybe a bit longer. Will you go if asked?"

And to a man, they shouted they were ready.

"Good lads," said Manannan. "Good lads."

Sean had already canvassed the field, eyeing up the candidates.

"Alright Sean," said Manannan. "Anyone take your eye for this trip?"

"I'd travel with any of them, you know that," said Sean. "But I figure this is a diplomatic mission, not a raiding party. So I'm thinking we want men for their manner as much as their skills. How many you thinking of?"

"I thought six. Enough but not too much of a presence. You?"

"Sure, I'll be there," said Sean.

"That wasn't what I meant Sean. I was asking what you thought."

"Sure. Six, and me at the front. Your daughter's not going anywhere with a bunch of lads that's never been further than the castle fountain."

"I was thinking maybe…" Manannan began but Sean cut him off.

"Your place is here Manannan. We can't have a king and his princess roaming the mainland together. Anything goes wrong and we've lost too much. And because you'd be a bigger target, you'd need a bigger party and then you'd look like more of a threat and then…well, you know what I mean.

"I'll take Niamh and a few of the lads and we'll be back in a few days."

"What's your thoughts on the mission Sean?"

He thought for a moment then said: "It's risky, rather than dangerous. If we stay smart we'll be fine.

"And we've got no option, anyway We've got to go. Or the Princess does and that means us, doesn't it?"

"It does, Sean, it does. When will you leave?"

"We'll prepare tomorrow and leave the day after. No point in hanging around, is there? Best get to it."

"I'll leave you to pick your team, Sean," said Manannan. And then he was off to check on the transport. Niamh's next trip involved more than a horse ride.

THE BUZZ in the dining hall was louder than normal and more intense. The talk was of nothing but the Princess's expedition.

Manannan kept a seat for Sean who joined him with his plate and told the King, Queen and Princess who was to travel.

Mindful of the pain when a family loses more than one, he'd refused to pick brothers together. And he'd avoided only sons, lest their parents lose everything.

"Got them," said Sean, taking his seat.

"And are they ready?" asked Niamh.

Sean looked at her sideways along the table.

"They said we could catch this evening's tide if we hurried Princess. I'd say they're ready."

"So," said Manannan, "who've we got?"

"Six strapping lads that know how to handle themselves: Tom Dooley, Michael Flannigan, John Dempsey, Sean Devlin, Pat McCourt and Andy Hanlon. All good, well-behaved lads that won't go looking for trouble. Pat's the youngest at 20 and Tom's the oldest at 26. Apart from myself, of course, at 93 or so."

Manannan laughed.

"And a match for any of them, I'm sure Sean. I wouldn't have anyone else lead a guard for my daughter."

"Have they family?" asked Niamh.

"There's none of them married Princess, but they've all got girlfriends. Some of them more than one actually. The youngsters don't want to settle down too quick these days. It's a long, long life if you pick the wrong wife, they say.

"I think you'll find the girls have a similar view Sean," snapped Fand. "You don't want to spend decades washing the wrong socks, believe me."

"Of course, My Lady," said Sean. "I'm sure their feelings are mutual."

"Settled then," said Manannan. "I've been down to the harbour and Finnegan's getting the Silver Spur ready. Not that she needs much doing. He keeps that boat sparkling so he does. But he's getting all the fishing gear out the way so our Niamh doesn't have to climb over nets and tackle on her way."

"I'll see him in the morning," said Sean. "Make sure he's got a quiet corner I can hide in. Hope she's as fast as I remember her."

"It's not fast we want, Sean," said Fand. "It's steady we want."

"Sean's not much of a sailor, remember," said Manannan. "He wants this voyage over as quickly as possible."

"Never liked boats," said Sean. "Even good ones make me ill so the faster the better. Needs must, though Manannan. Needs must."

"To be sure Sean. But now I reckon a good night's rest is needed. It's going to be a busy day tomorrow."

NONE of the lads needed any introduction, either to each other or to Niamh. In Tir na nOg everyone knew everyone and was most likely related somehow or other, by blood or marriage.

They met as a group, though, for the first time after breakfast and Sean spelled out the nature of the mission. It didn't take long.

"We're heading for the mainland where the Princess hopes to track down a stranger. We know his name and family and that's about all, apart from the fact that he's in some kind of danger. The Princess is going to try to persuade him to leave the mainland and come back with us.

"Our job is to keep her – and him, if it comes to it – safe. We're not looking for a fight with anyone and we'll talk our way out of anything we can. Only if we can't will we draw swords.

"Any questions?"

Well, of course, there were plenty, starting with who the Tir this stranger was and why was the Princess out to get him? But none of the lads said a word out of respect for Sean and Niamh. They'd find out soon enough, they figured.

"Right then. We need the boat readied, supplies loaded, shelters stored, clothes packed, horses tended, weapons sharpened and a whole load of other stuff that'll become apparent as the day wears on so I suggest we get to it, eh?"

And so began a full day of preparation. Every time one of the lads thought he'd finished, something else cropped up. They couldn't guarantee finding spare shoes for the horses if needed, so decided to take spares. And so it continued.

Come the evening Fand spent time fussing over her daughter, checking and rechecking she had enough good, clean clothes for the trip. She wanted her to make an impression on anyone she ran into.

"Here, take this too. For luck."

Fand handed her a little pouch full of stemmed leaves.

"Shamrock Mum? What's that for?"

"It's an old island thing Niamh. It doesn't grow anywhere else and it's meant to bring you good luck. It's probably just superstitious nonsense but it won't do any harm to have it about you."

The Princess laughed.

"If you want Mum, but I can't see a few leaves saving the day if it needs saving."

Eventually they hugged and retired to bed.

Nobody expected much sleep.

"SEA'S a bit choppy," said Sean unhappily. He wasn't worried about the mainland. It was getting there that bothered him.

"It's nothing at all," said Fran Finnegan, skipper of the Silver Spur and veteran of 25 years on the boats of Tir na nOg, bringing home vast catches of fresh seafood for the grateful islanders every week.

The "choppy" sea he was looking at was good sailing weather.

"There's a good wind blowing our way Sean. Get us across in jig time, so it will. It's nothing at all to worry you."

Sean remained unconvinced but led Shelbourne up the gangway anyway, a little unsteadily as the Silver Spur rose and fell at the quayside.

Niamh had a last hug from her parents. Anything to be said had already been said.

"Come home safe. And soon," said Fand.

Niamh was nervous too but, unlike her parents, she was looking forward to her adventure.

"I'll see you in a few days," she said and turned to board.

Quite a crowd had gathered at the quay. It had been a long time since Tir na nOg had sent an expedition off. When the cables were cast off and the boat parted from the quay a cheer went up wishing the party safe passage.

Finnegan's three-strong crew of fit, young men hoisted the sails and pulled on various ropes as the Silver Spur headed out to deep water.

And they were off, picking up speed across the swell, Finnegan's wake trailing behind.

THE SKIPPER was proven right. The wind was right behind them and the sun looked like it was trying to break through the light cloud.

Once the boat was pointing in the right direction there was little to be done apart from keeping it straight. That was Finnegan's job so the others settled down to enjoy the trip as best they could.

All bar Sean, that is. He sloped off to the back of the boat – the stern, Finnegan called it –where he curled into a small ball and wished for land to be close. His stomach churned and occasionally he had to be sick and he'd rather be left to his misery than endure everyone's company.

But the journey passed swiftly enough and eventually the mainland came into view. Gradually it filled the horizon until they were close enough to see its buildings and then, closer still, signs of life.

Close to shore now, the sea settled and Sean recovered enough to find his feet.

"We'll need a landing spot," he said.

"Right enough," said Fran. "We'll follow the coast a bit until we find one."

And soon enough they did, just around a headland lay a bay with a sizeable village and a quay perfect for mooring the Spur.

"Looks like we've got a welcome waiting," said Tom Dooley, eyeing the shore from the Spur's prow, where he'd perched himself since boarding.

They'd been seen from some distance so the village inhabitants had had the time to collect themselves and form a reception committee. They were clearly wary of a strange vessel approaching their land. A dozen or so citizens had gathered on the quay while a larger group hung back at the village edge.

With only a tiny foresail remaining up for power, the Silver Spur edged gently towards the pier as Sean stepped up to the prow with Tom.

"May we be granted permission to land?" he called to the committee.

"And who's asking?" came the reply from the big man in the middle of the reception group.

"Princess Niamh of Tir na nOg and her royal escort on a diplomatic mission," called Sean.

A quick huddle of the gathering followed. The Silver Spur didn't look like a threat and was flying the royal ensign of Tir na nOg, although it was certain none of the locals would recognise it. And it would be rude to turn away visitors politely asking to dock.

"Bring her alongside, Sir," shouted the group's spokesman.

The last sail dropped and as the boat drew gently up to the quay, Finnegan's three lads jumped ashore trailing cables to tie the Spur up to the pier. They slid out the gangway and Sean stepped ashore.

"Thank you for your permission, Sir," he said. "There are seven of us in the escort, plus our Princess and a crew of four who plan to remain with our ship while we continue our mission ashore. Can we disembark?"

"Not sure whose place it is to grant permission," said the big man, "but, then, since that means I don't know whose place it is to refuse, you'd better come ashore."

"Thanks again," said Sean, offering his hand in friendship. "The name's Sean and, for want of a better description, I'm the head of the escort party."

"Connel Ferry," said the big man, shaking Sean's hand. "Village spokesman by virtue of being the biggest man in the village. How can I help?"

"We'd like to see to our horses, get unloaded, find some shelter and take some advice if that's alright Connel. May I introduce our Princess?"

Niamh, looking every bit a royal, glided slowly down the gangway and stepped ashore.

"Princess Niamh of Tir na nOg, this is Connel Ferry, who graciously allowed us to dock at his quay," said Sean.

"Thank you very much Mister Ferry," said Niamh. "I hope somehow we can repay your kindness."

Ferry had never met a princess before and was instantly in awe.

"A pleasure to meet you Your Highness," he blurted nervously. "I'll see if we can find somewhere for you to find your land legs again."

He turned to one of his companions.

"Get up to Bernie's and tell him to get the place tidied up. We've got visitors, tell him."

The man bolted for the village with the news. A princess had landed in Coltoun.

"If you'll come this way Your Highness, we'll do what we can to make you welcome but I'm afraid it's all a bit basic. This is a working fishing village, you see."

"It's very good of you to have us, unannounced as we are," said Niamh. "But aren't we taking up a berth for your own boats if they're out fishing just now?"

"This time of year they're further up the coast, where the fish are," said Ferry. "They dock at other villages to put their catch ashore and come home only every now and again. And they only come back one at a time until the fish come back down the coast in the autumn. Then the quayside can get pretty busy. But you'll be fine where you are just now."

The party walked the horses into the village and up to an inn where they could tend to the horses and take some rest. It was late in the afternoon by now and Sean decided they would make camp for the night.

But Bernie, the landlord of The Anchor Inn was having none of it. He had enough room for his visitors and the Princess would be made most comfortable. Sean figured they could set sentries outside her bedroom as easy as outside a tent so he agreed.

They settled in and joined the locals in the tavern for an evening of getting-to-know-you. The travellers and the residents were still wary of each other but a few pleasant hours of story-telling and beer put them all at ease.

Sean had decided that the exact nature of their mission didn't need to be broadcast. Enough that they had business with the clan of Finn McCool. The villagers were happy to offer advice and directions as to how they should proceed to find him.

They set sentries at the Princess's door and agreed a rota so that they could all get a good night's sleep before heading out into the wilds of the mainland in the morning.

FERRY had shown them the way and in the morning they took it. Pat McCourt took the lead, carrying the flag of Tir na nOg high on a pole wedged in his saddle. Niamh rode between the rest, Sean at her side as they headed for the hills in the distance.

They rode at an easy pace. There was no point in tiring the horses. There was no telling when they'd need to burst into a gallop. Neither, though, did they want the trip to take any longer than necessary. The longer they were away from the island the more the risk of danger.

Finn McCool's territory was two full days ride from the coast and even then he might prove hard to find.

"He moves around a fair bit," Connel Ferry had warned. "Hard man to pin down. Always up to something so he's got places he calls home scattered all over the place. I think he prefers a saddle to a chair, to be honest."

So they rode in a general direction, not necessarily with a destination in mind.

The chat was free and easy and either about what they might find or home. Home was all any of them knew, apart from Sean.

And, of course, the lads wanted to know all they could discover about the man they were after, Oisin. Why, they wondered, was he so special?

And, of course, Niamh couldn't tell them.

She didn't know.

THEY CAMPED at the base of the hills they'd seen from the village, preparing for the ascent in the morning. The hills didn't look a major obstacle but they wouldn't crest them by nightfall and they didn't feel like sleeping on the slopes.

The weather continued to favour them and they woke to a fine morning, the sun hidden by the crest of the hills they set out to climb.

By the time they reached the crest the sun was high and they badly needed to break for some lunch and to rest themselves and their horses. And to take in the view.

From the hilltop they could see beyond the bay where the Silver Spur lay berthed. On the other side the greenery rolled out as far as they could see, hills and fields and the odd village dotted around.

What looked like the largest village they could see was some distance beyond the foot of the hill, settled on the bank of a silver river. They decided that would be their resting place for the night and began their descent.

IT WASN'T so much a welcome party as an inspection this time. The good people of Myleen didn't let just anyone ride into their town, royal banner or not.

Once again, Sean explained the nature of their visit and they were allowed to spend the night at the larger of the town's two inns. This was more comfortable than camping and allowed Niamh the chance of a warm bath, which she much appreciated, especially as she might well meet the man in her dream the following day.

In the bar that night they were assured that Finn McCool was roaming in the east, not far from Myleen.

The town's suspicion subsided as the evening wore on. Niamh was chatty and bright, charming the locals while her escort stayed pleasant but alert. Sean had drilled them well. Only moderate drinking, eyes and ears open and your sword within reach - with a smile on your face.

"How will we find Finn McCool in the country?" Niamh asked a local. She felt revived after her bath and excitement was rising at the thought of what the morning might bring.

"He'll find you, Your Highness," was the reply. "This is his territory and he probably already knows there are strangers around. He'll want to know who you are if you wander into his hunting ground."

"Sounds like a plan, then," said the Princess.

Sean agreed. They'd just saddle up and head east in the morning.

WHEN DAWN arrived, they tended the horses, took breakfast and headed out into the fields, the sun low in the sky ahead of them. Few of them spoke, aware of a tension in the Princess. She was aware that, whatever the day brought, life was unlikely to be the same ever again.

They rode without urgency, prepared to be found rather than expecting to discover. Generally, they were wandering vaguely further inland.

They had been on the move for around and hour when Patrick's horse, in the lead with the standard, took fright and reared, clearly alarmed. In his path, curled and upright at the head, lay a snake, hissing and angry.

Patrick, as startled as his horse, was thrown to the ground, still clutching the standard. His sword remained sheathed though. He'd been ready for an attacker on horseback or running from the trees but he'd never seen a snake before. None of them had, apart from Sean maybe, back in the day.

Sean instinctively reached for Merlin's rein to stop him taking fright. He shouldn't have worried. Not much spooked Merlin. He should have paid more attention to the horse's rider.

Niamh, shocked to see Patrick fall, leapt from her saddle to help.

Patrick, shaken but unhurt, lay staring at the snake, which was seemingly getting ready to strike. Bright yellow, with black stripes, the snake weaved on the spot as its tongue lashed and whipped furiously.

Niamh drew alongside Patrick and, strangely, the snake began to retreat. It hissed and curled but it appeared, rather than angry, scared. It practically cowered and skulked its way back into the long grass.

And then it was gone.

"Did you see that," said Patrick, astonished not to have been bitten.

"I saw it," said Sean, clearly livid. "And it had better not happen again."

"Sorry Sean, but that snake caught me and Marcus completely by surprise," said Patrick. "Last thing I expected."

"That's not the point," snarled Sean.

"Princess," he said, turning to Niamh. "The whole point of you having us to guard you on this mission is to keep you safe. You do not run to the aid of your guards. You just put yourself and this whole mission in danger by leaving your mount. I'll thank you to take more care in future and leave any danger to those of us entrusted in dealing with it."

Niamh felt chastised by Sean's tone. She'd never seen him angry before, only quietly in control.

"I'm sorry, Sean," she said. "You're right. I wasn't thinking. Or actually, I was thinking about Patrick instead of why we're all here. I'll be more careful from now on, I promise."

Sean nodded, satisfied his message had got through.

Patrick rose to his feet and brushed himself down.

"There's something else though," he said. "Did you not see the way that snake ran off when the Princess got near to it. It was just about to attack me when Her Highness arrived and then it legged it. So to speak. Like it was scared of something."

Sean thought for a moment.

"True enough," he said. "'It's not like a snake to back down for a young woman. But who knows? Not me. Maybe we just got lucky. Let's not rely on luck next time, eh?"

Drama over, they remounted and continued their foray to the east in search of Finn McCool and his son.

WHEN McCool appeared, there was no dramatic entrance. The royal party neared a copse of trees and there he was, a giant of a man astride a giant of a horse.

He was heavily clothed but not armoured, out for the hunt rather than the fight. His bow and quiver were strapped to one flank, his sword, an evil, shiny thing, slung by the other. A dead deer straddled the rump of his mount.

With Tom now in the lead with the standard, they approached the chieftain at a gentle pace and pulled up some 20 yards from him so as to not appear aggressive.

McCool was first to speak.

"Well, well, what have we here then?" he mused loudly. "A royal party from Tir na nOg? Most unusual, I'll say."

Sean stepped up to respond.

"You're correct, Your Lordship. Allow me to present the Princess Niamh of Tir na nOg. I am Sean, leader of her protection party. Am I to assume that we have encountered Finn McCool, master of this territory?

"I'm McCool, right enough. Not sure about the master bit though. I just get to do what I want around these parts. And that includes greeting royal delegations, it would appear.

"Your standard announces you Princess. It's not been seen around here for generations but it's still a sign to be recognised.

"What brings you here Your Highness? I doubt it's the hunting."

Sean spoke again. He'd been practising this bit, hoping he wouldn't make a fool of himself and his Princess.

"It's complicated Your Lordship but I'll try to explain. The Princess has been having a recurring dream of a young man in danger. The Well of Dreams in Tir na nOg has named him as Oisin, son of Finn McCool. The Princess is compelled to meet Oisin, so we are escorting her in a bid to ensure a safe introduction."

McCool laughed and slapped his thigh, a deep, throaty, honest laugh.

"A mission of love, you say? A date with destiny? I've heard of such events but it's the first time I've actually come across one. And of course I believe it. Why would anyone make up such nonsense?"

Niamh spoke up in reply.

"I remain unconvinced about destiny, my lord. And fate. And you can't love those you haven't met. But my dreams are real enough. And the threat to your son feels real enough. That's why I'm here."

McCool raised himself upright in the saddle.

"Well," he said. "I'd better take you to the lad then. He'd have been here with me had his horse not thrown a shoe. I figure the lads will have him fixed up back at base by now. They should have the fire going and the venison ready for dinner. Would you care to join us Princess? And your men, of course."

"That's very gracious of you Mister McCool. We'd be very grateful."

"Settled then. And call me Finn. I always find 'McCool' a bit formal, Princess."

"I know what you mean Finn," said Niamh. "Please call me Niamh. I've been trying to persuade Sean here to do so for ever and it hasn't worked."

"That's called respect Princess. Don't knock it. But I'll be glad to call you by your name. Now, if you'll follow my lead?"

McCool turned his horse due north-west and urged him forward. The royal party fell into line behind.

MCCOOL'S camp was fairly close. Why camp far from your hunting ground?

Several large tents were arranged in a circle around a central living area large enough to act as a corral for a dozen or so horses and allow their riders to congregate and eat and drink. It wasn't a village, but neither was it an overnight stopover.

McCool rode straight into the middle, the royal party following.

"Oisin!" he shouted. "Oisin, you've got a visitor."

A tall, muscled young man tending to a horse turned and walked towards the new arrivals, first spotting Tom bearing the standard, then Sean, before freezing, as though struck by a thunderbolt.

For the first time Oisin set eyes on the girl he had spent months dreaming of. And Niamh first saw her stranger in the night.

There was silence as their eyes met and they registered that, somehow, they knew each other. They stood and stared, neither knowing what came next.

Finally McCool broke the silence.

"Well, I don't know what just happened there but it's not something you see every day.

"Oisin, this is Princess Niamh of Tir na nOg and she's come looking for you because she's had a dream you're in danger.

"Niamh, this is my son Oisin and he's clearly had you on his mind too, though he's kept himself pretty much to himself about it."

Niamh's heart was pounding. The man of her dreams, literally, was standing before her, looking as strong and handsome as she could have hoped for.

Oisin, in turn, was in awe. Unlike Niamh, the encounter had come to him as a complete surprise. Even had he had time to prepare he'd have been struck dumb, not just by his immediate recognition but by the striking beauty of the young woman on the horse before him.

It was Niamh who spoke first.

"I've come a long way over sea and land to find you Oisin. I think we need to talk."

Finally finding his voice Oisin stepped forward.

"Can I help you from your horse, Princess?" he asked.

Niamh held out her hand and considered that here was one man she may allow to call her Princess rather than Niamh.

"We'll be having some venison stew in a bit," said Oisin. "It's a bit rough and ready Princess, but we weren't expecting royalty for dinner."

The pair stood awkwardly as the royal party and McCool's men looked on curiously.

Then Sean had a notion

"You know McCool, I think we should let these youngsters tell each other their dreams in private. Meanwhile me and the lads are parched. What you got to drink around here?"

McCool laughed long and hard once more.

"I'm beginning to like you Sean of Tir na nOg," he said, then shouted: "Francis! Break open another barrel, of beer. I think we're going to need it."

NIAMH and Oisin sat apart from the rest and explained their dreams. Niamh told Oisin about Tir na nOg, the Well of Dreams, her family, her life. Oisin told Niamh of his adventures, his rugged lifestyle, his love of the hunt and his writing.

History had been passed from generation to generation by stories told over campfires and at bedtime. Oisin had started to collect those stories and write them down. And he loved poetry, despite his father thinking it unmanly.

The night wore on and the pair gradually became a couple, holding hands as they talked, laughed and fell in love as the royal party, McCool and his men each did their best to drink more beer than the next man.

The hours passed like minutes.

MORNING came, a dull and misty affair, just like most of the camp. Unlike Niamh and Oisin, though. At first light the pair were at pains to make sure they looked their best and were in no hurry to seek out the other in case they appeared too eager.

The men rose gradually, all moving rather more slowly than they had just a few hours earlier. But their mood was excellent. Who could not be moved by watching a young couple find their life's love?

Breakfast took a while. And why not? The deer would still be there to be hunted in the afternoon. And curiosity filled the air.

"Right Sean," said McCool, pushing away an empty plate that had previously held an impossible portion of food. "What's your plan?"

Sean, who had taken the same time to eat a third of the food McCool had packed away, looked thoughtful.

"Haven't got one McCool. All I'd ever planned was getting the Princess here and home safe. Part one's complete. Just got to get her home now. But I've got a feeling both Niamh and your boy might have an opinion on the matter."

McCool laughed again. His laugh spread around the camp. Everyone was in fine spirits.

"It occurs to me that you'll be trying to persuade the lad to go with you, Sean," said McCool. "Unless I'm mistaken, that was the entire purpose of the enterprise."

"Not at all," said Sean. "The only purpose was to find him and find out whatever trouble he was supposed to be in. Never thought for a second the pair would be hit by a thunderbolt. But now we'll have a bit of a job telling either one the other's not hanging about.

"And if you think I'm going back and telling Manannan I've left his daughter in a field with a bunch of strangers, you're mistaken."

"Aye, Sean, I hear you," said McCool. "But then, I've got to ask why I'd let my boy ride off to a far-off island with a bunch of strangers who turned up in my camp with a big old destiny story. He might be his own man, Sean, bit I'm still his old man, you know."

"Fact, McCool," said Sean. "I've no clue what to do now."

"There's another puzzle, Sean," said McCool. "Niamh says her dream was all about rescuing Oisin from danger. Take a look around. The boy's in no danger. He's running free in his own huge back garden."

"I'd thought of that too, McCool," Sean said back. "That lad's a happy, free spirit in no danger at all that I can see. Well, no more than any of the rest of us at any rate. All I do know is that he's probably a happier man this morning than he was yesterday."

McCool, it seemed laughed as much as he spoke. And so he did so again.

"Yer a fine fellow Sean," he said when he'd stopped his laugh. "What do you say we go out and find ourselves a few deer for dinner and leave our love-struck children to see if they feel the same this morning as they did last night? You leave a couple of your lads and I'll leave a couple of mine. We can have a right good run around and only be minutes from the camp. Can't rush these affairs of the heart, you know."

"I'll join you in that McCool. Think the lads can handle any problems that come up in a field. The horse hasn't had a good run for a week. And a good gallop might clear my head."

"That's a remarkable brew you've got in those barrels McCool. What d'you call it?"

"Glad you like it Sean. We called it after the idiot who first made it. Accidentally burnt the barley he was toasting to make normal beer then used it to make this dark beer thinking nobody would notice. Turned out to be a fabulous mistake and naturally he claimed it was deliberate, which was how we gave him the nickname "Genius". The beer's been called that ever since. Good stuff, eh?"

Sean looked at McCool from half-closed eyes.

"It was better last night," he said.

YOU SHOULD eat," said Oisin, watching Niamh push food around her plate.

"I've a strange feeling Oisin. My tummy keeps turning over and it's making me not hungry. And it's worse every time I look at you."

"Charming," said Oisin with a grin. "But I've the same feeling Princess. It feels like part of my inside is trying to get out. Something remarkable is happening to us – to you and me – and I'm pretty sure I'll need to be fit and fed to meet whatever's coming next. Eat."

Niamh ate.

"What do we do now?" she asked when her plate was fairly clear.

"Hah," shouted Oisin. "Who knows? I know what we don't do and that's be apart. I've no notion of heading off with the lads if you're left behind. I think we're stuck with each other for now Princess. Is that alright with you?"

"Perfect," said Niamh. "But I can't live in a field."

"Point taken Princess. But today we're not heading anywhere. Too complicated. A ride out in the country perhaps? Just the two of us?"

"She's going nowhere without an escort Oisin," said Sean, arriving in perfect time.

Oisin looked at the grizzled wee man in front of him with the determined face.

"Respect, Sean. The Princess is coming to no harm on your watch or mine. We'll take a ride out with a healthy guard. We'll not need them out here but it's a strange day and I'll be glad of some back-up."

Sean nodded.

"Good lad," he said.

They split into three groups: one went hunting, one tended camp and the other went for a gentle wander to let Niamh and Oisin learn more about each other.

THE TROUBLE with hunting deer is that, while deer aren't exactly the smartest animals in the countryside, they don't fancy getting killed and eaten, so when there are humans about they tend to make themselves scarce for fear of ending up in a pot. So McCool took his party a fair stretch of the horses' legs to get away from the camp. No deer would come near that, he reasoned.

They took some time to find their prey – a lone deer grazing idly in a copse – and even longer to approach it. They had to remain upwind of it so the deer wouldn't catch their scent and bolt.

As always, Sean felt a little sad at stalking the deer. He'd have been happy to let it roam free if he didn't have to eat.

It was McCool who brought the deer down. His first arrow brought it to its knees and the second, just an instant later, finished its short life.

"Nice work, McCool," said Sean, glad it was over. "A fair size too. Should keep the camp fed for a day or two."

It took three men to lift the deer onto the rear of McCool's horse and tie it down. As they were doing so, a shout went up.

"Rider approaching!" shouted the man McCool had tasked with keeping an eye open for uninvited guests as the rest hunted.

As the lone rider drew closer it became clear it was one of McCool's own men, returning from a mission into town to fetch supplies. But his pace was urgent. This rider was in a hurry.

He arrived with important news.

"There's a bunch of Hooligans planning an attack on the camp, Finn. They heard we had a princess from Tir na nOg with us and they're looking for revenge for a battle they lost some time back."

"Some time back?" snorted Sean. "It's been hundreds of your years. There have been many, many generations come and gone since then."

"These are Hooligans, Sean," said McCool. "The passage of time doesn't dull their bitterness. Or their stupidity, I'm afraid. Double the time and they'll still be angry. Different generation, same anger. You should see how they celebrate battles they won over 300 years ago. Shameful it is."

He turned to his rider.

"What do we know?" he asked.

"There's about eight of them over at Marne. They think they'll be heroes if they go it alone so they're planning an expedition tomorrow then a dawn raid on us the following morning. Element of surprise, they're thinking."

"Only a Hooligan would let the enemy know they were going to surprise them," said Finn, shaking his head. He turned to the group.

"Right lads, back to camp in a hurry and get the rest of the boys together."

UP ON the hill, Niamh and Oisin wandered gently and discussed their future. They had, by now, agreed that it would be spent together. How, was the question.

Oisin had decided that their dreams were a sign of destiny, even if Niamh was minded of the Well of Dreams' warnings of such notions.

Their options were limited. Oisin had little to offer in the way of a home. He lived with his band, roving the land and living from it. They more they talked the more it became clear that Oisin would have to follow his heart – and his Princess.

Sudden movement in the fields below caught his eye. The hunting party was heading for the camp at top speed.

"Something's wrong," said Oisin. "Back to base at a gallop, lads."

Oisin had expected to bring up the rear with his Princess but Niamh was astride Merlin and no-one was about to leave them trailing. They were back at camp in no time.

"What's going on?" asked Oisin as he rode in.

"Seems our old friends the Hooligans have learned we have visitors from Tir na nOg and they want to make a name for themselves by bringing them harm, my boy," said McCool. "Looks like we're in for a bit of a shindig. They're out for revenge for a fight they lost three centuries ago."

Sean explained how he and Niamh's father had laid the trap that killed off the Hooligan plan to invade the island so long ago.

"But how can that be?" asked Oisin. "That was 300 years ago. No-one lives that long."

"Time works differently in Tir na nOg, Son," said McCool. "As I've a feeling you're going to discover before long."

Oisin shook his head, as if to clear it. Things were moving very quickly in a land where things had always taken their time.

"What's the plan Dad?" he asked.

"Well, we're not sitting here waiting for those numbskulls to turn up waving swords, that's for sure. We've got today and tomorrow to decide how we handle them.

"But right now we've got another decision to make."

Niamh let out small cry, as if suddenly in pain. A dreadful thought had just come to her.

"Wait," she said. "My dream was to find Oisin and rescue him from danger. But when I found him there was no danger.

"What if, by finding him, it's me who has put him in danger?"

Sean and McCool exchanged glances.

Eventually McCool answered for them.

"That would appear to be the case, Princess."

OISIN was having none of this. He strode to his horse and drew his sword from its scabbard.

"I don't need rescuing from anyone, least of all those idiot Hooligans. I say we go and teach them a lesson right now."

But McCool shook his head, an air of sadness suddenly on his shoulders.

"You'd have been right two days ago Oisin," he said. "But two days ago we weren't in this position. Everything, don't you see, has changed. Call it destiny if you want. Call it fate if you want. Call it good luck that the Princess Niamh has entered your life. Call it bad luck that we've got Hooligans to deal with.

"But we are where we are. And you're not drawing a sword against Hooligans today. You, my son, are leaving with Niamh and Sean."

"I'm not running away from anyone," shouted Oisin.

"I know that," said McCool. "But two days ago you were my son, expected to ride fast with a sword in your hand, headlong into any threat.

"Today your job has changed. Today you are the guardian of a princess. It's your job to protect your princess. It's your job to get her safely back to Tir na nOg. She's your number one priority. And you can't put her first and still set out on a Hooligan raid."

McCool's voice cracked. His eyes welled up.

"Oisin, you have to go," he said.

Oisin's shoulders slumped and his sword hand fell to his side. He knew his father was right. The joy he had known just minutes ago had turned to despair at the thought of leaving his father and friends just as they faced a battle.

"I might never see you again Dad," he said.

"That's probably the case Oisin. Time works differently in Tir na nOg. I expect you to live long, well and happily there."

They threw their arms around each other, father and son in tears at saying farewell forever.

"You best get your things," said McCool.

"What about the Hooligans?" said Oisin.

"You leave them to us, Oisin."

McCool turned to his men: "What do you say lads? Can we handle these Hooligans and let these good people go about their business?"

The camp let up a cheer. They'd have taken on any number of Hooligans just for the craic if McCool gave them the nod.

"Hold a minute there," said Sean. "Think long and hard before you enter battle McCool. How do you think the rest of the Hooligans will react if you slaughter eight or so kinsmen on behalf of Tir na nOg? They still remember what we did three centuries ago.

"It'll be war.

"You'll drag your whole clan into a war you have no part in and it could last generations.

"Just let us take Niamh and Oisin to safety and let you get back to your riding and hunting. Tell them we sneaked away in the night."

The lads looked kind of disappointed as they realised Sean was right. McCool knew it too.

"I'll think of something else," he sighed. "Now be off with you before you cause any more trouble."

IT ONLY took Oisin minutes to gather his belongings. Some clothes, some bedding. He had his sword. He was ready.

"Is that it?" asked Niamh.

"What do you mean?" he asked.

"Well, it's not an awful lot, that's all," said Niamh.

Oisin looked puzzled.

"Clothes, bedding, horse, sword." He counted them off. "What else do I need?"

Niamh laughed.

"Nothing we can't get for you," she said.

McCool's men formed a guard or honour, swords raised for the royal party as they left camp. McCool himself stood silent and still and watched his son's back grow small as he rode off with his new love.

Eventually he spoke.

"Those Hooligans are going to wish I had killed them," he growled.

OISIN might have now been Niamh's guardian but Sean was still in charge of the mission.

"It's a straight run for the Silver Spur Niamh," he said. "Sorry Oisin, but there's no point in alerting anyone else that we're on the move. We're bypassing the towns, resting only when the horses flag and setting sail as fast as the tide will let us."

Oisin nodded. His new life might be just beginning but this was a mission that had to be finished quickly.

So they skirted Myleen unseen, the royal standard rolled and tucked into a saddlebag, and pressed on for the hills. They camped and fed themselves as dusk fell and set a rota of double sentries, aware that danger was in the air.

The night passed uneventfully and breakfast was a simple affair, avoiding the need for setting a fire.

It was still early when they mounted and scaled the hills, descending with the sea in sight in the distance.

They rested the horses at the bottom and ate some lunch. Sean hoped to make the boat by nightfall.

They were in open country when the spotted a lone rider approaching at speed. He cut off their route and stood smack in their way, clearly determined to block their progress.

"It's a Hooligan," said Oisin.

"How the Tir did he figure this out?" wondered Sean. "They're supposed to be stupid aren't they?"

"Aye, but they've got a nose for trouble," replied Oisin. "Let's see if he knows what's going on."

The Hooligan stood his ground, challenging them to pass.

The party pulled up in front of him.

"Will you give way Sir?" shouted Oisin.

The Hooligan grinned a stupid grin.

"I will not. That there's Niamh of Tir na nOg and I want to show her to my cousins."

"Where are your cousins?" asked Sean, scanning the area.

"They're over the hills. I'm here to get my horse some shoes before a big day tomorrow. But it looks like it's today that's my lucky day," grinned the Hooligan. "Hand her over."

The Hooligan was indeed a giant. Sean figured the party could take him easily enough but they'd have to get him first off his horse and then his feet.

But it was Oisin who took charge.

"I'm not handing over anything or anyone without a fair fight. You're challenged ya big ugly eejit. Get off yer big ugly horse and show me what you're made of, man to eejit."

"Oisin, don't," begged Niamh.

Oisin leapt to the ground, rolling up his sleeves. Quietly he said to Sean: "I'll expect your arrow through his ribs if this doesn't work."

Sean fingered his bow.

"My pleasure, I'm sure," he said.

The Hooligan grinned. He figured he'd pummel Oisin. Big as he was, the Hooligan was bigger by far.

He dismounted and stepped towards Oisin, fists raised.

"Right," said Oisin. "So this is a fair fight, let's get the rules straight."

The Hooligan was nonplussed.

Dropping his fists and looking confused he said: "Rules? There aren't any rules."

"Good," said Oisin as he kicked the Hooligan smack between the legs with every ounce of energy he had.

"I was hoping you'd say that," he added as the Hooligan doubled over in agony.

Oisin drove his huge fist straight into the Hooligan's face. His nose exploded, spurting blood in all directions.

The Hooligan reeled and Oisin punched him solidly in the ribs, then spun him and broke several ribs on the other side. With the Hooligan now defenceless, Oisin planted one final massive blow to the head and the giant rocked backwards and slumped to the ground. He'd fight no more today.

"Very nice," said Sean.

"Thanks," said Oisin.

Niamh leapt from Merlin and ran to him.

"That was incredible Oisin," she shrieked, hugging him tightly. "And so brave to square up to that giant on your own."

"Oh, I wasn't really alone, was I Sean?" asked Oisin.

"Never moved a muscle," said Sean. "You did the job, lad."

Patrick went to check the Hooligan's condition.

"We don't really want him dead, do we?" he said. "Might start trouble we won't be here to deal with."

Patrick checked the giant was still breathing and stood up just as a yellow-and-black-striped snake slithered from the grass, seemingly intent on biting the Tirean.

Almost without thinking, Niamh threw her bag at the snake. She'd had it round her shoulders throughout the trip and was the closest thing to hand.

She missed. But you'd have thought she had hit it from the snake's reaction. It recoiled, as if in terror, and slithered rapidly away.

Patrick stood still, astonished. Again.

"Princess, that's twice you've scared the daylights out of a snake about to bite me. How do you do it?"

Niamh looked puzzled herself.

"I've no idea," she said.

"Do you mind if I take a look at that bag of yours, Princess?" asked Sean.

"Carry on," she said. "But I missed, didn't I?"

"I know," said Sean. "I'm just wondering what's in it."

Niamh's bag had only the essentials you'd expect in any young lady's bag.

Apart from the purse of shamrock leaves Fand had given her for luck in Tir na nOg.

"Beats me," said Sean, handing back the bag. "Maybe snakes don't like shamrocks."

"Think we can still make the quay by nightfall?" asked Niamh.

"As long as we don't get any more surprises," said Sean. "Shall we get to it?"

They remounted and pointed themselves at the village, urging the horses into a gallop.

BOTH SUN and moon were in the sky as the approached the village, the sun just preparing to dip behind the hills to the west. As they neared, they saw the Silver Spur's mast rising high above the houses.

Rather than a cavalry charge into the town, they dismounted and walked the horses in, hoping to create less of a fuss. A handful of villagers stepped up to greet them, Connel Ferry included.

"Successful mission then, it seems," he said to Sean, indicating Oisin with a tilt of the head.

"So far Connel, so far," said Sean. "I'll not be happy til we've got them back home, though."

"It's nearly nightfall, Sean. Will you be looking for rooms at the inn?"

"I need to speak with the crew first, Connel. Let me let you know in a minute."

Sean marched down the quay where Joe McGlone was standing guard before the Spur's gangway. The rest of the crew were busy with the sort of stuff sailors did and Sean didn't understand.

"Any trouble?" asked Sean.

"Not a thing, Sean," said Joe. "The locals have been good with food and drink and we've kept ourselves to ourselves. All quiet."

Finnegan made an appearance from below a hatch.

"Sean," he shouted. "Thought I heard voices. Everything alright?"

"How quick can we set sail Fran?" asked Sean.

Finnegan leapt to the deck and surveyed the water level.

"Immediately Sean, if you don't mind a night crossing."

"Can you do that?" asked Sean warily.

"Water's high enough to carry us out, seems calm enough out there, the moon's bright and the sky's clear so we can navigate by the stars. No problem. We can."

"Get ready for passengers, then Fran."

Sean strode back up the quay.

"Right lads, escort the Princess and Oisin to the boat," he said. "Connel, we'll decline your offer of hospitality this time, much as I'd appreciate a bit of a rest and a beer. But we'll have to be on our way.

"Thanks for your help my friend. There's no secret here. Nothing to hide. You can tell anyone you want that the second the Princess and Oisin clapped eyes on each other it was love.

"And now he's escorting his new Princess to safety. There's a bunch of Hooligans out to cause her harm and he's taking her home. As am I."

"Safe home," said Connel. "Maybe see you again sometime."

Sean hesitated. He knew it was highly unlikely he'd ever see Connel and his pals again but he didn't want to say so.

"Maybe we will, Connel," he said. "Maybe we will."

Then he spun and headed back to the Spur where Oisin was eyeing the boat warily.

"Is this thing safe?" he asked.

"Where's the big, brave warrior now," giggled Niamh. "Of course it's safe. It's how we got here. And that was my first time on a boat, by the way. It's actually quite pleasant."

Oisin allowed Andy to lead his horse onto the boat and he and Niamh followed. The walkway rose and fell gently as the waves washed the far side of the vessel.

Oisin hoped he wouldn't be on the Silver Spur for long.

FINNEGAN'S crew had been taking it in turns to rest while the shore party had been searching out Oisin so there were enough fresh hands to hoist the sails and point the Silver Spur out towards the open sea.

The shore party, on the other hand, were exhausted and all found a corner to sleep despite a fair swell causing the Spur to pitch and roll through the waves.

Even Sean slept. Even Oisin, wholly unused to having the floor beneath him rise and fall on its way, slept. The horses, exhausted, slept too.

Away from the coast the sea settled into a steady rhythm, allowing the Spur to travel gently, rocking those beneath the deck like babies in cots. They slept well as the ship closed the gap to Tir na nOg.

The night slipped away and dawn came gradually, rousing the passengers slowly from their slumber.

Niamh gave herself a shake and washed as best she could on a ship designed for business rather than pleasure. Oisin did the same, conscious that he would shortly be introduced to the King and Queen of Tir na nOg. Or more importantly, Niamh's parents. He also knew he'd be getting a fair amount of attention from the islanders, wondering just who the Princess had brought to live among them.

The pair stood at the bow, watching the island grow bigger before them. Oisin remained quiet, his head full of a thousand thoughts.

"Thinking of your dad?" asked Niamh.

"Aye," he replied. "The Hooligans are planning a dawn raid on the camp and I'm not there to help them."

"Relax son," said Sean. "You're in Tir na nOg waters now and time works differently. Whatever was going to happen has already happened. But there's not many on this planet equipped to put one over on your dad, let alone a bunch of Hooligans. And he's had two days warning. They'll have done fine, trust me."

Sean paused for a moment then said: "I do wonder what he did, though. Something special I'm sure."

THE RETURN of the Silver Spur caused much excitement in Tir na nOg and most of the castle's residents made their way to the quay for her arrival. It wasn't every day a ship came in from the mainland. Not even every generation, actually.

Manannan and Fand were at the quayhead, anxious to greet their daughter and greatly relieved to see her wave happily from the Spur's prow as she approached.

Niamh was the first down the gangway, into the arms of her parents, full of excitement.

Then she turned and held out her hand to Oisin who stepped forward and took it in his.

"Mum, Dad," she said, "This is Oisin."

"The man of your dreams, eh?" asked Manannan, eyeing the young man up and down. He held out his hand.

"Welcome to Tir na nOg, Oisin," he said.

"Thank you, Sir," said Oisin. "And I should tell you that I recognised Niamh the moment I saw her, from my own dreams."

"Ah," said Fand. "Destiny, then."

She smiled and gave the young man a hug, struggling to reach his broad shoulders.

Niamh sighed.

"Destiny, eh? A name for stuff that people can't explain, that's all. What I can explain is the rumbling in my stomach. There's not much of a kitchen on that boat."

Fand laughed.

"I figured that. They're working up a morning feast at the castle."

She looked over Niamh's shoulder.

"Sean, looks like you and the lads did a grand job. There's a mountain of food getting ready for you as soon as you're ready for it."

"Think you'll find everyone's ready right now, Fand, thanks," said Sean.

With that, Fand took her daughter's arm and with Oisin at Niamh's side, they set off for the castle and breakfast.

Manannan fell into step a few yards behind, signalling Sean to join him.

"Well Sean, what do we make of this man Oisin?" he asked.

"He's going to be just fine Manannan," said Sean. "Just fine.

"He's a big strong, smart lad with his heart in the right place. He's as brave as any man I've met. Just watched him go toe-to-toe with a Hooligan on his own and leave him flattened. And he's clearly daft about the Princess. Left everything he had and knew behind him to come here with her.

"He's going to be just fine I reckon."

"I was afraid of that," sighed Manannan.

"What," said Sean, taken aback. "There's not much more you can ask for in a man for your daughter.

"No, that's not it, Sean. It means she's not my wee girl any more. "She's someone else's woman now and that's going to be hard to take."

"With all due respect, Your Highness, yer an eejit. The Princess will always be your wee girl and you, of all people, should know that she's stronger now that she's got two men to care for and them to care for her."

Manannan stretched his arm round Sean's shoulders.

"You're probably right Sean. Doesn't make it easy though,"

"Be happy for her," said Sean. "You both deserve it."

THE KITCHENS excelled themselves. Manannan was almost moved to complain that their breakfast should be standard rather than exceptional. But he knew there was a new kid in town and everyone wanted to impress. They also clearly wanted Niamh to know her new friend deserved the best. And since his daughter was clearly besotted with the new kid – and he with her – he decided to let it go. He made a note to order those breaded truffles again, though. Far too long off the menu, he figured.

Manannan sat with Fand: Niamh and Oisin across the table from them.

"So," said Manannan after a superb breakfast, "Where do we go from here Oisin? Your thoughts please?"

"But Dad…" started Niamh.

"I'll talk to you in a minute Niamh. Right now, I'm talking to Oisin. And I think you'll find I'm not just your dad, I'm still King around these parts."

Oisin rose to the occasion.

"Manannan – Your Highness – two days ago I first met your daughter.

But I dreamed of her months ago. And she came to find me. There's something magical and mystical about that and I don't understand it.

"All I do understand is that I'm here, alone, with people I hope will be new friends and family. I've never asked anyone for anything and I'm not asking you for anything other than a bit of time and tolerance. I've no idea what happened to the Princess and me but I'd appreciate it if you'd let us find out."

Manannan considered Oisin for a moment then looked across at his daughter.

"That seems a perfectly fair request," he said. "I suggest we find you somewhere to live and something to do until you figure it out. Fand, can you get Dimpna to sort out Oisin's quarters. Doesn't look like he's got much luggage but he'll need somewhere comfortable to settle what he does have. Looks like he's here indefinitely."

"It's all organised," said Fand. "We thought Niamh was likely to bring back her stranger so we've got that little cottage just outside the main gate set aside for him. Bed's made up and everything."

"Seems I'm a bit behind the times here Oisin," said Manannan. "I'll leave you to settle in. And I'm sure Niamh will want to show you around. There's not much to Tir na nOg but what we have we like."

"I hope you'll like it too."

OISIN declared himself well pleased with his new accommodation: a pleasant cottage with just one bedroom, a living room and a kitchen – well, it was more a food preparation area with a table and chairs.

"That's in case you ever want to invite me to dinner," said Niamh.

"But who would cook it?" asked Oisin. He'd never cooked a thing in his life. McCool's camp had always travelled with a cook so there had never been a need.

Niamh thought and realised she'd seldom been allowed in the castle's kitchen so had little idea of how to cook for herself.

"Maybe we'll have to take lessons," she said. "I don't fancy our every meal being in the company of Mum, Dad and hundreds of onlookers."

It was just one of dozens of new issues the young couple were going to have to deal with. But the cooking would wait. Oisin had to find his way around first.

They spent the day wandering the castle and its grounds, exploring. Niamh showed Oisin the dining hall, the various meeting rooms and all the castle's workings. She showed him the playing fields and the drill ground, the horse ring, the flour mill, the river that drove the flour mill and all along the way she introduced him to the locals who would become his neighbours and, she hoped, his friends.

As the day drew to a close she showed him the tavern. Niamh had never been in it. It was where the men went in the evening after dinner to drink and talk and her parents had not so much banned her from going as suggested she wouldn't like it. She'd probably not be welcome either. Oisin made a mental note to visit as soon as he could.

In there, he thought, he'd make friends.

AND SO BEGAN Oisin's task of making a home and life for himself with Niamh. He rose every morning and joined the castle complement for breakfast. He helped with the animals in the fields and the tending of the crops. He hunted deer most days, successfully, much to the delight of the kitchen staff.

On the training ground he was made very welcome. The Tireans had practiced their fighting in the same way as their fathers and their fathers before them every day for decades. When Oisin arrived he brought new techniques, not all dependent on size and strength. He showed them how to use an opponent's weight against him, allowing the smaller of the fighters to throw him to the ground.

He showed them how to twist a sword or a knife from an enemy's hand and how to stop a man with a single punch – if you put it in the right place.

Sean, who had led training for years, watched on with approval: the Tireans were getting better and better at defence. He'd been taking more and more of a supervisory role of late and he was happy that a natural successor was emerging

Oisin spent as much time as he could with Niamh and found himself growing ever more in love with her – and she with him.

She took to the fields for combat practice with him and proved more than capable. Her friends joined too and soon Tir na nOg had a whole new fighting force of women.

Later of an evening he'd wander to the little tavern and drink some beer and talk with the locals. Everywhere he went people called him by his name and made him welcome. As the new kid in town, he wasn't hard to spot.

For Oisin, though, settling in didn't prove straightforward. He figured it could take him years before he would know the Tireans by name well enough to call each of them by their names. And how could he remember that the local in the tavern was the father of the milkmaid? That she was married to the farrier? That the father of the farrier was the mason? And that the mason was the local at the other end of the bar who had just bid him welcome?

As his love for Niamh grew Oisin realised he'd struggle ever to be considered a local. He knew he could never go back to his previous life and that he'd better just get used to being the newcomer the Princess had brought over from the mainland. He had hundreds of acquaintances and men he could laugh and drink beer with.

But he had no friends.

"How come you call everyone 'Pal,' Oisin?" asked one local one night.

"It's safer than trying to call everyone by their name and getting it wrong," he answered truthfully.

Niamh noticed he was troubled and redoubled her efforts to make him happy. But Niamh wasn't the problem.

"Look, Princess," he told her, "I'm happier than I've ever been when I'm with you. I love you completely and always will. It's when I'm not with you that the problems start. Just in my head. Missing my friends and a life I know is gone forever. And I know there's nothing to be done about that. So I have to get on with it and be as content as I can be when I'm so far from what used to be home."

Niamh frowned but nodded.

"If you're happiest when we're together, maybe we should try to spend more time together," she said.

"I've been thinking about that," said Oisin. "There truly is nothing I want more and there's only one way I can think of making it happen."

Oisin stopped and took a breath.

"Niamh," he said, "will you marry me?"

The Princess looked him in the eyes and blushed.

"Do you think I went all the way to the mainland to bring you back here for someone else?" she asked. "You and I are meant to be married Oisin. The answer's yes."

And they kissed. Softly and lovingly, knowing they had just sealed the rest of their lives together.

IT WAS only right that Oisin should ask Niamh's father for her hand in marriage, so he asked for an appointment. Now, Manannan wasn't a hard man to find around Tir na nOg so when Oisin asked for a private word, the King had a suspicion as to what was afoot.

They met in the evening in Manannan's meeting room.

"Well Oisin," he said, "what can I do for you?"

Oisin had thought long and hard about this. Should he make a speech about longing to stay and live long with his Princess? Should he thank Manannan for the welcome and the hospitality before asking for his daughter's hand? Or should he get straight to the point, the way Manannan himself probably would?

"I'd like your permission to marry your daughter Manannan," he said.

Manannan smiled. He'd been expecting it and, while he didn't like seeing his little girl stop being a little girl, he couldn't help but enjoy watching her blossom and he knew much of that was down to Oisin.

"Have you asked Niamh for her permission?" he asked, not entirely seriously. "I can't give my permission without her's"

"I have Manannan. She said 'yes'."

"And have you plans for the future? Where will you live? And how?"

"We thought we could live in the cottage I'm in now. And I can keep us by tending the land and the cattle and hunting. I think I'm contributing to Tir na nOg now and I'll carry that on."

"Aye lad," said Manannan. "You've fitted in well for a stranger in these parts. And I've never seen Niamh so happy so you must be doing something right. Long may it continue. Of course you can marry my daughter."

Manannan stepped forward, grabbed Oisin and hugged him like a brother. Then he strode to the giant cabinet in the corner and pulled out a flagon made of fine bone china and two glasses.

"I've had this for years, waiting for a special occasion," said Manannan. "If this isn't a special occasion, I don't know what is, eh? Time it was opened I reckon."

He poured two large measures of the golden liquid, handing one to Oisin. He raised his glass to the young man.

"To life, love and happiness Oisin. May the pair of you have them all in abundance."

They chinked glasses and sipped the fiery Water of Life. It slipped down a treat, warming them inside as it went.

"So," said Manannan, "we must make an announcement. You tell Niamh, I'll tell Fand and we'll tell the people after dinner eh?"

"So soon?" asked Oisin, taken aback.

"We don't get to marry off a princess that often in Tir na nOg, Oisin. The people sense there's a party coming, so we might as well tell them."

"Fine by me Manannan," said Oisin. "And what about the wedding?"

"Same, I reckon. Can't think of a single good reason for keeping the pair of you apart any longer than necessary.

"But I think you'll find that you and I will have very little say in events. Niamh and Fand will banish us from the arrangements and call us out to do as we're told when they're good and ready."

They both laughed at that, not least because they knew it to be true.

A DELIGHTED Fand gave her daughter a huge hug.

"Congratulations Niamh. I couldn't be happier for you. He's a lovely lad and I'm sure you'll be very happy together."

"Thanks Mum," said Niamh. "I'm really nervous, though."

"And who isn't when they agree to take a life partner? It's the biggest decision of your life and you'd be mad if you weren't nervous. But you'll know yourself if you've made the right decision."

Fand paused a moment, then said: "You do know, don't you?"

"It's the right decision Mum, no doubt about that," said Niamh.

"Then we'd better start planning a wedding," said Fand.

THAT EVENING, after dinner, Manannan rose and rapped his tankard on the table before him several times to attract the room's attention. When the assembled company was silent, waiting on the King's word, he announced: "People of Tir na nOg, the Princess Niamh and Oison, son of Finn McCool, are to be married."

A great cheer went up and immediately the couple were surrounded by well-wishers. Oisin's hand was shaken and his back slapped by all. Niamh found herself in a whirlpool of women who seemed mainly interested in her choice of wedding dress.

"And so the madness begins," murmoured Manannan. Pleased as he was he knew the wedding would dominate all proceedings on the island until the pair were wed. Fand would see to that.

Secure in that knowledge, Manannan did what any father would do in the circumstances and reached for another tankard of ale.

THE WEDDING was scheduled just three weeks after their engagement. It made sense to take advantage of the weather. They'd have the harvest gathered and could hold the celebrations in the arena, rather than indoors. That meant the whole island could witness the event.

It also made the invitations easy. Everyone was invited.

The news went out across the land and the nation geared up for the biggest party for years. Smart suits and fancy frocks were looked out and skilled hands worked flat out on new outfits.

Fand fussed and fretted more than Niamh who was happy with a simple white shift and a tiara of fresh flowers to match her bouquet. In the end they reached a compromise and the seamstress went to work.

Both Oisin and Manannan were fitted with new suits. Manannan's favourite ceremonial outfit appeared to have shrunk since he'd last had occasion to wear it. Or so he claimed anyway. Oisin had never had one.

The menfolk were given some relief from their chores. With so many expected for the wedding there was a pressing need for more venison so all available hands were sent hunting, Oisin and Manannan included. Hunting was no hardship for the men of Tir na nOg.

Teams of craftsmen worked flat out to prepare the couple's new quarters. Oisin's notion of staying in his cottage with his new wife was ruled out in an instant by Fand who insisted they were to live inside the castle's grounds. Manannan and Fand had earmarked a cottage when Niamh had been just a child but it needed work before it could welcome a royal couple.

As the day approached time itself appeared to gather pace. It only appeared to, right enough. Time worked differently in Tir na nOg.

Hikers, horses, ox-drawn carts and all manner of transport began arriving in droves, pitching their shelters in the fields surrounding the castle. Whole families, four generations often, arrived, all of them up for a party.

And what a party it was shaping up to be. Fand had counted the population of the island and added some as a guide as to how many meals they'd serve on the day. Every barrel of beer available had been shipped in. Vats of blackcurrant and lemonade were stationed around the arena. The chefs lost count of the deer used for stews and barbecues were erected throughout the ground for those who would prefer to grill their steaks. No-one was going to go hungry or thirsty at this party.

It was tradition that the wedding couple held separate parties before the big day. Niamh and Oisin decided on the Thursday before the Wedding Saturday, aware that it could be a late night and they wanted the Friday to recover before the ceremony.

Niamh invited the friends she'd grown up with and gone to school with – they were all to be bridesmaids anyway. And so she had Kaitlin, Khloe, Molly, Daisy Lauren and Laura as Maids of Honour. Ava, Lucy, Carla, Leyla, Molly (another one), Olivia, Abigail, Sinead, Robyn, Eisha, Natalie, Orla, another Lauren, Ella, Ife, another Laura Shania, Grace, Kitty and two Karaghs were bridesmaids. Kyle, Peter, Owen and Wee Kamie were to form an Honour Guard.

It was quite a list. But there were no rules as to how many bridesmaids a Tirean bride could have.

Niamh and her pals had a private all-girl ceilidh in the castle's smaller function room. Five bands offered their services but only one, The Partons, had a girl singer, so Niamh chose them.

They ate good food, drank nice wine and sang and danced til the band was played out and they all went home tired and happy.

Oisin went to the tavern. He had no friends close enough to single out from his pals who drank there, so everyone was invited.

Sean was there, though, tight to Oisin's shoulder. He'd seen enough bachelor parties to know the groom needed looking after. He recalled one young man arriving at his wedding without eyebrows. His "friends" had shaved them off. And there was the young man who woke up tied to the back of a horse not knowing where he was on the morning of his wedding. And there were more such stories.

So Sean acted as Oisin's minder. Manannan, as King, couldn't be seen in the tavern with his soon-to-be-son-in-law so close to the wedding. And the crowd would have behaved differently had their King been in attendance. So Manannan decided to allow Oisin to enjoy himself without him.

The beer and the laughter flowed and the groom was the toast of the town til the wee small hours when Sean escorted him home and made sure he got to his bed safe and sound and ready for marriage.

EXCEPT he wasn't. Oisin woke with a thick head late in the morning with a vague sadness around him. It hung over him like a cloud.

He shook himself and ventured outdoors, stretching before plunging himself into the chill of the pool that formed in a tiny gully off the river. The shock of the cold brought him to life in an instant. Job done, he climbed back out, pulling his towel around him for heat. And comfort. For the cloud still hung over him.

The girls in the castle had been keeping an eye on the cottage and had rustled up a handsome breakfast as soon as Oisin had made an appearance. The lads almost started a fight over who should take it to him.

Oisin was back in his cottage, dried and dressed when Michael Flannigan and Sean Devlin burst in with steaming food and tea.

"How's the head Oisin?" shouted Michael, rather louder than Oisin considered necessary.

"Lovely day outside," shouted Sean. "Breakfast?"

Ever grateful for the hospitality, Oisin thanked them and sat at the table. He ate. Not well, though. His appetite didn't do the fine fare on offer justice.

"Cheers lads," he said. "And tell your excellent cooks it's all my fault, not theirs, that the plate isn't cleared."

He stepped outside the door again, drawing a deep breath and looking for his horse.

"Where's Django?" he asked.

"Ah," said Michael. "The Queen's had some of the horses put into stables so none of the wedding party can spoil the big day by getting themselves injured going over a fence or two."

Sometimes a small black cloud can quickly develop into an entire weather system capable of great strength and damage.

Oisin turned slowly to Michael and said quietly: "Where is my horse?"

Michael knew instantly he'd lost the argument and pointed to the stables just beneath the castle's west gate.

Oisin burst through the stable door.

"Where is my horse?" he practically hissed at the stable lad.

"Queen Fand says all the royal horses are to be kept quiet for a couple of days," said the lad, clearly wishing it was someone else's job to tell Oisin what was happening.

Oisin whistled. It was low, sharp and musical and Django knew the sound instantly, raging and kicking the stable door to let Oisin know where he was. Grabbing his saddle, Oisin turned to the stable lad.

"This horse hasn't been in a stable in its life and it doesn't start today," he said.

With Django unchained, Oisin saddled him and led him to the door where several other stable lads seemed anxious to keep him from riding.

"Don't think of trying to stop me," he growled. "Not everyone does what the Queen says."

He dug Django in the ribs and headed for the hills.

Oisin rode and rode and rode. Finally, at the top of a fine hill, he dismounted and looked down on the island that was now his home.

Alone, apart from his horse, Oisin let out a roar from the bottom of his lungs that echoed round the valleys around him. Out of breath, Oisin took a minute or two to take in his surroundings and let out another roar, every bit as intense.

Oddly, he felt better. He hadn't changed anything but just shouting made things better. He breathed easier.

But the cloud still followed him, despite the sunny day. It should have been one of the happiest days of his life but Oisin felt his happiness tinged with misery.

Then there was movement below him. A rider, running fast, as if on an urgent mission. One man on a horse. Oisin stood and waited, expecting a full instruction from Fand to get back to the castle slowly and immediately, without injury.

The rider was still some way off when Oisin realised it was Sean, riding Shelbourne at full tilt. It didn't take Sean long to top the hill at a clip and pull up a few yards away from the runaway groom.

"Morning," said Sean. "You alright?"

"Been better," said Oisin.

"Bad beer?" asked Sean.

"Good beer," replied Oisin. "Too much good beer."

"Problem, then?" insisted Sean.

"Clearly," said Oisin.

Sean dismounted and stood beside Oisin to look over the land. The sun was high and the island looked at its best.

"Why are you here, Sean?" asked Oisin.

"I thought you might need a friend," said Sean.

"That's good of you Sean," said Oisin.

They stood and looked at the scenery for a moment, saying nothing.

Then Sean spoke up.

"You don't have the look of a man about to marry a beautiful princess, Oisin," he said.

Oisin had to agree he was troubled.

"Look Sean, it's just that all this stuff is happening to me. I'm not actually doing anything, or, more to the point, deciding. It's just happening. Where I live, how I live. I'm just being swept along on a great big wave with no voice or vote. And while I've clearly been made very welcome, you can't just replace your family and lifelong friends with someone else's."

Sean took a moment to reply.

"It's funny how you can feel lonely when you're surrounded by people, eh?" he said.

Oisin sighed. Sean was exactly right.

"There's times I think it's just Niamh and me but now it seems it's just me, what with all these preparations and the fuss. And while Niamh will be attended hand and foot tomorrow, I'll still feel a stranger at my own wedding."

"Have you not made one friend who would stand with you in the morning?" asked Sean.

"Ah, they're all nice enough lads and I get on well enough with them but I've only known them a wee while. And I don't know any of them well enough to ask them to watch my back."

Oisin paused and thought for a moment.

"Unless…unless…" he paused.

"Sean, we're making new rules all the time here. It doesn't have to be a lad I grew up with who stands with me.

"It's better it's someone I trust and whose company I enjoy.

"Sean, I know you'll cover my back because you've done it before, the only Tirean who has.

"Sean, would you, maybe, think of standing with me tomorrow?"

Sean let out a little whoop of delight.

"I was wondering if you were ever going to ask ya eejit. Thought maybe you didn't want an old man at your shoulder on the big day, and who could blame you? I'd be delighted and proud to stand with you at your wedding Oisin. Delighted and proud."

Oisin drew a long, deep breath and looked out over the fabulous vista that was his new home. He smiled.

"Looks like I have got a friend after all," he said.

COME the morning, Tir na nOg was buzzing with excitement. The hum of thousands of well-wishers began quietly at dawn and began to grow as the islanders went about the business of preparing for a giant party.

Oisin and Niamh were served their breakfasts in their rooms, their last before they moved into their new home as man and wife.

Both had opted for simple suits for the day. The tailor had run Oisin up some smart black trousers with a billowing white shirt and a black waistcoat to match the trousers.

Niamh's choice, naturally, had been rather more complicated. With dozens of advisors, she had been drawn in many directions before she settled on simplicity: a plain, white shift with lace borders and a few embroidered flowers to add some colour. She had also chosen a simple tiara of flowers and a bouquet to match. Just a hint of make-up added a final touch to her glowing face.

Fand sat in Niamh's room and surveyed her daughter.

"Will I do, Mum?" asked Niamh.

Fand was too choked to speak. Where had the years gone, she wondered? She had never wanted her little girl to grow up and stop being a little girl and here she was, ready to be wed.

Fand found enough voice to say: "You'll more than do my darling. You're beautiful. More beautiful than ever before. And that's hard to believe."

SEAN came to Oisin after breakfast, already dressed in the only outfit he'd never worn on a horse. Very smart he looked too, also decked out in black and white with a bright yellow flower pinned to his lapel. He'd brought one for Oisin too.

"Can't have anyone saying we didn't make an effort, can we Oisin?" he said.

He pinned the flower to the groom's lapel and stood back to check his charge. With his hair and beard neatly trimmed and his new suit and shoes,

Oisin had scrubbed up pretty well.

Sean sniffed the air, the stepped closer to Oisin, sniffing again.

"Are you wearing perfume?" he asked.

Oisin blushed ever so slightly.

"The girls put some kind of oil in a bath for me this morning," he said. "I thought it smelled quite nice actually."

"Quite right," said Sean. "Can't have you turning up at your wedding stinking of horses and dogs can we? Splendid. Now you're looking like a man who's just about to marry a princess."

With Sean's approval, Oisin relaxed.

"Right," said Sean. "One last thing."

He pulled a small flask from inside his jacket.

"Manannan sent this. A drop of his special reserve. Said it would help calm any nerves on the big day."

"Very good of him too," said Oisin, taking a draft of the fiery spirit, feeling it warm the inside of his chest.

They took a few minutes to savour their drinks.

Then Sean said: "Ready?"

Oisin looked him square in the eye.

"Aye," he said.

IT WAS A glorious day for a wedding. The sun beat gently on the island's arena, decked with traditional green and gold bunting hanging from and between every available fixing point.

The crowds had begun pouring in early. The stadium had been built generations before and was big enough to hold the island's whole population but everyone wanted a good vantage point.

They had built the stadium in the shape of a horseshoe, with a huge field in the middle for sporting events and a stage between the two ends allowing a clear view of formal events from all parts of the ground.

Oisin and Sean entered the arena and began their walk to the end of the horseshoe where a large table decked in the royal colours stood with two chairs facing the crowd that had already started to gather.

Those already assembled rose to greet the groom and his friend. The applause began slowly and gently but grew to a loud happy cheer as the pair reached the table, Oisin waving his thanks for the welcome and approval.

Anyone who had not taken a seat rushed to find one now, knowing that the bride's arrival was imminent.

When she came she caused a momentary ripple of excitement and an almost immediate silence as the eyes of thousands fell on the beautiful young woman standing alone at the entrance. Tiny and fragile, she truly was a radiant princess.

Manannan stepped forward to his daughter's side, taking her arm in his. With a smile to each other they began the walk to the waiting groom, Niamh's bridesmaids, each in a plain white shift with green and white matching bouquets falling in line behind.

Oisin thought his heart would burst with love and pride as he watched his bride-to-be start towards him. He turned to Sean.

"There's dozens of them," he said.

"Don't worry. You're only marrying one of them."

"Am I supposed to do anything?" he asked Sean.

"Just keep smiling Oisin," he replied, pretty sure Oisin was going to anyway.

The crowd's cheers rose to a roar as Niamh and Manannan made their way to the stage, reaching a crescendo as they arrived. Manannan smiled at Oisin, took Niamh's hand and offered it to the young man.

"This is my only daughter, Oisin, a precious gift. I'm trusting you to care for her and love her as she deserves," he said.

"Of that you can be certain Manannan," said Oisin, taking Niamh's hand.

"Then let's get you married," said the King.

Niamh and Oisin sat side by side as Manannan walked around the table and stood still, ready to address the crowd – as soon as they quietened.

Eventually the throng realised the ceremony was about to start and fell silent.

"First," said Manannan in a voice that boomed around the stadium, "Thank you for coming."

That brought a huge cheer once again. They needed no thanks but were glad of it anyway.

"I know that many of you have travelled for days to join us today so, please, be assured of a very warm welcome on this very special day for us.

"It's not every day on this island we get the chance to see a princess being married. For Fand and myself, today is filled with joy – and just a tiny piece of sadness. Sadness that our little girl is a woman now. But joy that she has found, truly, the man of her dreams."

And while there were few on the island unaware of Niamh's trip to the Well of Dreams and then the mainland to find Oisin, Manannan felt it only right to retell the story to add to the magic of the occasion.

"And so," he said, "that's how we came to have this fine young man here with us today.

"He may not have been born here but Oisin has all the attributes you'd expect in a Tiran. He has courage. He's strong. He's loyal. He'll put his shoulder to the mill.

"Most of all, though, he loves our Princess. I'm sure that my daughter could be in no safer hands than his.

"For her part, I've never seen Niamh so happy.

"I'm sure they'll look after each other for the long lives we expect them to have here, in happiness, in Tir na nOg.

"So, as tradition has it, is there anyone here today who has any good reason why this couple should not make their promises to each other and leave here as man and wife?"

Silence filled the stadium. No-one dared so much as cough for fear of spoiling the proceedings.

"Right," said Manannan. "I'll ask Niamh and Oisin to stand for The Promise."

The bride and groom rose from their seats and turned to face each other.

"Have you rings?" asked Manannan.

They both nodded. Sean produced a plain gold band from his pocket and laid it on the table in front of Oisin. Kaitlin, who had been keeping Niamh's ring safe on here own little finger, fist tightly clenched, slipped it off and placed it in front of Niamh.

"Now," said Manannan. "Let us ask our wedding couple to demonstrate their love for each other.

Manannan produced a quaiche, a silver cup decorated with sparkling emeralds. Perfectly round, it had two handles, so two could drink from different sides of the same cup.

"We used this very quaiche when Fand and I were married," Manannan told the couple.

He produced a flask from another pocket and poured a measure of liquor into the cup before handing it to Niamh.

She took the cup in both hands, raised it to her lips, looked into Oisin's eyes and said: "Always and forever."

She sipped the fiery liquid and swallowed, feeling it burn as it slid down her throat, and handed the cup to Oisin.

He held the cup and looked at Niamh.

"Always and forever," he said before draining the cup and holding it high for all to see it was empty.

An almighty, appreciative cheer went up as Oisin placed the cup back on the table.

Then Manannan asked for calm.

"Now, Oisin. Do you promise to love Niamh as long as you live, to place her above all others, to be true to her love and make her health, wealth and happiness your first and most important goal in life and does this ring represent that promise?"

"I do," said Oisin, "and it does."

"Then give her the ring."

Oisin duly did so, slipping it onto the third finger of her left hand.

Manannan turned to Niamh and asked her to make the same promise, which she did, slipping an almost identical ring onto Oisin's finger.

Manannan's voice boomed around the stadium once again as he declared: "My friends – they are married."

And they kissed for the first time as man and wife.

Oisin had never heard a noise so great as the roar that rose from the crowd in that stadium. They were both taken by surprise by the genuine outpouring of affection their wedding had sparked.

"I reckon they can hear that on the mainland," Oisin shouted in Niamh's ear.

"Pardon?" shouted Niamh, giggling.

And they both laughed long and happily. It was a new beginning and the party was just starting.

TRUE TO FORM, as soon as they were wed, they were separated: the bride and groom were whisked away and around the arena for much handshaking, back-slapping and general well-wishing.

It was only to be expected. Many hundreds of Tireans had travelled from afar with wedding gifts and congratulations. They all had to be met and thanked for their kindness and generosity.

Oisin gave up trying to count how many bands were playing. Seemed everyone with a fiddle, pipe or drum had brought it. And those without an instrument sang.

Niamh floated through the throng, revelling in her big day. She delighted in the mass outpouring of love for her and her husband, even if she sometimes wondered where in the grounds he was.

Tireans didn't need much of an excuse for a party but when they had one they threw everything into it. The food just kept on coming, the music played on and the beer and wine flowed as rivers.

Oisin had decided early on that he'd enjoy a few sociable beers with his new friends and family but he wanted to be in good shape when the time came for him and Niamh finally to retire to their new home and spend their first night together as a married couple.

When the light began to fade and the torches began to be lit, Oisin went looking for his wife.

"I think we can leave these good people to the party, don't you?" he said.

It was true. The Tireans were set to party till dawn.

"Time we started the rest of our lives, then," said Niamh, taking Oisin's hand.

They slipped away, avoiding any more fanfare. The Tireans could have their party. Finally, Niamh and Oisin had each other.

SETTLING down to married life proved pretty straightforward for them both. In truth little had changed apart from their address. Niamh revelled in her new status as a married woman and Oisin was a fully fledged member of Tir na nOg's first family but most meals were still taken in the Great Hall and the days' routines remained intact.

Oisin was allowed to find his own place in society. He was acknowledged as the island's foremost hunter, chiefly because of his success, and no-one begrudged him the status as there was never a shortage of fresh meat on the table.

He was unofficially in charge of defence, training the lads – and lasses - in the arts of swordplay, archery, fist-fighting and battle tactics.

He'd lend his hand to any task – and there were many. Crops needed sowing, tending and harvesting. Cattle needed herding, fences needed mending… Oisin became a very handy man to have around.

Little changed in Niamh's routine. By day she helped in the running of the castle. Tirean women might be feisty creatures but they had their roles and the men had theirs. Women were seldom seen behind a plough and men seldom over a hot stove. It did happen, when needs must. Just not very often.

In truth, Niamh was happier than she'd ever been. She had her friends and family around her in a magical world and every evening she went home to a man she loved entirely and who loved her right back.

Oisin picked up his pencil again, spending some time each evening writing the stories he knew so well and the poems he'd never shown to anyone on the mainland for fear of ridicule. He wrote the story of meeting his wife, the story of their wedding, the stories he heard told as he lived in Tir na nOg.

And he wrote the stories he remembered from another time: before Niamh. He wrote about hunting expeditions, clan disputes, adventures in the far-flung reaches of the mainland.

Niamh loved that Oisin wrote and she loved what he wrote. Tir na nOg had a long history but the stories were never written. They were passed from generation to generation over open fires of an evening when the elders would tell tales of great adventures to youngsters at their knee. With so many fabulous storytellers, it was no surprise the island had so many fabulous stories. And so many versions of each, depending on who was telling it.

Oisin was the first in Tir na nOg to put stories onto paper, that they may be read in generations to come and remain as they were originally meant, not altered to suit the mood of the teller.

And Niamh loved him all the more for it.

"You know," she said, "when I read your stories, I can almost hear you telling them.

"It's like I can hear your voice coming from the page."

"I just write down what I hear in my head," said Oisin. "Maybe that's why."

THE SEASONS came and went and little changed. It was cooler and wetter in the winter but that was to let the land recover for the sunnier and warmer growing season.

Tir na nOg offered Oisin a pleasant life and he knew he was loved and in love.

And yet…

The more Oisin wrote the more he found himself dragged to stories of bygone days simply because, pleasant as it was, very little happened in Tir na nOg. Each day was much the same as the previous one. And the more he wrote of his friends' and family's adventures on the mainland, the more he longed to know their fate.

He knew that, since time worked differently in Tir na nOg, generations would have passed at his old home. But still he ached to know that his father had faced down the Hooligans and that he had lived long and well and happy.

Niamh noticed Oisin's mood and she understood.

"I'm not sure I could have done what you did," she said. "Could I have walked away from all I have here to live with you in a strange land? We'll never know. But I do know the sacrifice, the choice you made to come here wasn't an easy one."

Oisin threw himself into Tirean life, working harder and longer than the others but the nagging thought of his earlier life wouldn't go away.

Eventually he told her.

"I have to know. So I have to go."

And, despite a cold, terrible fear in her heart, Niamh knew it too. He would never be settled without a final mission of discovery to the mainland.

THE PREPARATIONS were simple enough. The Silver Spur was readied for departure at daybreak. Oisin packed a bedroll and some provisions. He was used to travelling light.

Niamh went with him to the wharf in the morning. Sean was waiting.

"And what brings you here so early in the day Sean?" asked Oisin.

"D'you really think I'm letting you sail off to a land full of Hooligans on your own?" said Sean. "Anyway, it's quiet around here. Too quiet. I don't like it. I'm for a bit of adventure eh?"

Niamh sighed with relief. She hated the thought of Oisin leaving, even on a short trip, but was glad that he was in the company of a warrior friend.

They kissed and held each other before Oisin prepared to board the Spur. Before he did, however, Niamh had one last warning.

"Remember, Oisin, that your flesh cannot touch the soil. You are not a Tirean and these years on Tir na nOg are only borrowed years if you return to the mainland. Your boots, gloves and clothes will protect you and have no fear of floors or beds. But you can't touch the soil. If you do, all those years that work differently will come back to you and you will age in a moment."

Oisin looked long and hard at his wife.

"I'll take care. I'm not going to do anything that stops me coming back to you. A short trip to find out the truth and then I'll be home."

With that, they kissed once more and Oisin and Sean took their horses aboard the Spur and headed towards the rising sun and the mainland.

Niamh stood at the quay, watching until the ship was just a dot on the horizon. She had a bad feeling about this trip. She couldn't stop him.

But that didn't mean she had to like it.

THE PORT was bigger than they remembered. Much bigger. It had two quays now and the boats moored up were bigger too. There was a bustle about the place which had replaced the relaxed ease of the earlier way of life.

From the Spur Oisin and Sean watched as the shoremen handled ropes and pulled the catches from boats brimming with fish.

"Changed a bit," said Sean.

"Looks like it," said Oisin. He hadn't known what to expect. But bustle hadn't been on his list.

The Spur clearly didn't have a hold full of fish. She sat too high in the water and the shoremen knew. They also knew they hadn't seen this ship before.

One of them took charge and stepped forward.

"What's your business?" he bellowed from the quay.

"Two passengers to offload and re-embark in a few days," Oisin shouted back.

The shoreman pointed to a docking bay to the left and Finnegan began to maneouvre towards it.

"You can offload here," shouted the shoreman. "But you can't moor. There's more boats due in and we need the space. You'll have to anchor in the bay. And keep out of the way will ye?"

It wasn't exactly a welcome, but Oisin figured the man was too busy to be friendly.

Finnegan's lads threw the lines ashore and the shoremen helped them moor up, the gangway dropping to the quay as they touched land.

"Welcome to Coltoun", said the shoreman.

Oisin and Sean led their horses onto the quay.

"See you in a few days lads," said Oisin. "Try not to get into any bother, eh?"

The gangway swept up behind them and Finnegan did as he'd been told, pulling the Spur a few hundred yards offshore to allow the expected arrivals to dock. Then he dropped anchor and settled down to wait.

"What's your plan?" asked Sean as they surveyed the area.

"I figure if you ever want to know something you're best starting at an inn," said Oisin. "And there's one right there."

The Cannon stood where it always had, on the roadside opposite the waterfront, two great windows on either side of a door that seemed to offer a welcome. Sun streamed through the frames, showing a bar with a reasonable crowd taking their ease.

"As good a place as any," said Sean, hoping an ale or two would settle his stomach, still queasy from the crossing.

They tied Django and Shelbourne to a post outside the bar and strolled in, their eyes slowly adjusting to the changing light.

They'd been expected. The regulars had watched the strange ship dock and had watched the two travellers walk from the quay to the tavern. There was a mumble of curiosity as they approached the bar.

"Good day lads," said the barman, a great, balding bear of a man with a belly way too big for his height and a glass of his own beer firmly in his paw. "What can I get you?"

"We'll take a couple of whatever you recommend, thanks," said Oisin.

The barman poured them two black beers that Oisin remembered from long ago. It seemed to form a waterfall in the glass and settle completely black with a creamy, white layer on top.

"Have you come far?" asked the barman, placing the beers in front of the travellers.

"A fair distance," said Oisin. "We're here in search of a bit of history and figured your shop would be a good place to start."

In the corner a man the size of Sean, but a much older version, had been watching the pair since they stepped off the boat. He waited until they'd both taken a draught of their drink.

"D'you mind telling me lads," he piped up, "What's that flag your ship's flying."

"That," said Sean, wiping his lips clear of the white moustache his beer had left, "is the royal ensign of the island kingdom of Tir na nOg."

"So, that'll be the Silver Spur then?" asked the wizened little man, clearly the elder statesman of the tavern.

"It is," replied Sean, surprised. "How would you know that?"

"I take an interest in our country's folklore, young fella. Will you tell us your names?

Sean, unused to being called "young fella", answered quietly, on guard for any tricks.

"My name is Sean and this is Oisin," he said.

The old man cackled a laugh.

"I knew it!" he shouted. "I knew it.

"Adam," he shouted to the barman, "I'm buying these boys' drinks. It's not every day you run into living legends and that's exactly what these fellas are – Sean Maloney of Tir na nOg and Oisin McCool, formerly of this parish."

He stuck his hand out in welcome.

"Paddy McGinty," he said. "Nice to meet the pair of you, though I never, ever expected to."

The bar was now buzzing with questions. McGinty might have been a scholar of folklore but not many others were. They knew the name McCool from stories told long ago but that didn't explain the stranger in their midst.

McGinty delighted in holding court and explaining the story of how the Princess Niamh had come to the mainland and persuaded Oisin to leave for her island all those years ago. But that still didn't explain how Oisin could be standing shoulder to shoulder with Sean at the bar with a beer in his hand.

"Time works differently in Tir na nOg," said Oisin. "It's only been a few years since I arrived on the island but it's been hundreds since I left the mainland."

"So," said Paddy, "why have you come back?"

"I need to know how my family fared," said Oisin.

McGinty shook his head in sorrow.

"The family line of McCool became a legend long ago, Oisin. It passed a few generations after the Mighty Finn passed on. But I'll introduce you to someone I think you'd like to meet in a moment," he said, spotting a strapping lad on the street heading for the bar door.

The lad came in and was waved over by McGinty.

"Oisin, I'd like you to meet my grandson. The family name McCool disappeared many years ago when one generation failed to produce a son to continue the line.

"But one of your female ancestors refused to let the name die entirely and named her first son McCool.

"It's a tradition that's carried on ever since."

Oisin stuck his hand out to shake McGinty's grandson's hand.

"Oisin McCool," he said.

"Mac McGinty," said the man. "That 'Mac' is short for McCool."

Oisin grinned.

"Looks like I've come to the right place," he said.

"So Oisin," said McGinty. "What is it you've come all this way to find out?"

Oisin took a second then asked: "What happened after I got on the boat?"

"RIGHT LADS," shouted McCool as he caught his last sight of his son's back disappearing over the hill.

"We've got work do to and it needs done before nightfall so let's get to it. We've got Hooligans coming to call and we want to give them a proper McCool welcome."

They all set to. McCool gave the instructions and the lads, disappointed at not charging after the enemy, warmed to the task when they heard McCool's plan.

It was vital that the camp looked occupied when the Hooligans arrived. The horses had to be tethered, a fire blazing and allowed to die down through the night, the shelters looking occupied by sleeping, unsuspecting men and, most importantly, no sign of the real lads. They had to be fed, watered and completely hidden in the scrub around the camp. It would likely be a long wait in the dark of the night but it had to be done for McCool's trap to work and war be avoided.

As nightfall came the lads finished their meals, adjusted their camouflage, took their swords and crept off to take their places.

It was, indeed, a long wait. The Hooligans had no intention of giving up the element of surprise they thought they still had so they pulled their horses up in the darkness some distance from the glowing embers of a dying fire which pinpointed McCool's camp.

They remained there until just before dawn when they began their approach, dismounting and completing the last few hundred yards on foot, waiting for first light to show them where their targets lay.

Then, just as night began to turn a murky light, they attacked, storming the camp with fury, slashing and screaming as they went.

But in the gloom they didn't see each other fall victim. The best any of them could do was listen as screams of shock rang out from all around. And they weren't coming from McCool's men.

One by one the Hooligans felt their legs swept from beneath them and their feet hoisted skyward.

The gloom gave way to dawn and the eight Hooligans dangled from the trees McCool and the Gang had turned into snares. They bellowed and roared but the harder they struggled the tighter the knots binding their legs became.

It was an old trick for trapping large animals in a land far away. McCool had learned it from a pirate he'd befriended on an earlier adventure.

The Hooligans were livid and outraged and helpless as they swung upside down from the branches.

Only then did McCool's men reveal themselves. They rose from their positions and approached their captives who stared wildly as the armed gang approached.

It was then that McCool unleashed the most terrible and hurtful weapon he could possibly use on the Hooligans: laughter.

McCool himself started the laughter and the lads quickly joined in. It truly was an entertaining sight, eight Hooligans armed for battle strung up like puppets.

They laughed long and hard and spun the Hooligans in their snares, making the absolute most of the moment.

"So," said McCool eventually, "this is you Hooligans' idea of a surprise dawn raid, is it?"

And they all laughed again for a while until McCool decided to get serious.

"Be very grateful you Hooligans that I didn't decide to slit every single one of your throats. You came here with murder in mind, determined to maim me, my son, my men and the Princess Niamh of Tir na nOg.

"The only reason I'm letting you live is I pity you. Pity for you being so ugly. Pity for you being so mean spirited. But mostly pity for you being so stupid. And stupid you are. What's more I'm going to make sure the name Hooligan means 'idiot' in every part of this country."

The Hooligans calmed when they realised McCool was going to let them live. They weren't exactly comfortable but then, neither were they dead.

"Right lads," called McCool again. "That's another adventure we've got to tell the people. Let's get this camp broken up and get into Myleen. Start spreading the news. We're leaving today.

"Gather up all these eejits' weapons. We're taking them with us. And someone go and scatter their horses. They probably don't like Hooligans any more than we do but make sure they head for the hills when you let them go.

"And check all those ropes are good and fast. Don't want any of these eejits slipping and bumping his head, do we?"

It was a cheery bunch that began work as McCool directed. They wanted to get into town as soon as they could. Half the fun of an adventure with McCool was bragging about it afterwards.

THE TAVERN at Myleen was only just opening for the day when McCool's men bundled into town amid much joking and arm-punching, clearly in high spirits

"Morning to you McCool," said Michael Ross, the landlord, surprised at such custom so early in the day. "What brings you in from the hunt?"

"We're celebrating," said McCool. "We're celebrating a fine victory over a vicious enemy and the betrothal of my only son, Oisin."

"Oisin?" said Michael. "Oisin's getting married? I didn't know he even he was courting. All a bit sudden isn't it? And where is he?"

"Michael, he's run off with a princess," said McCool, causing the lads to erupt in laughter again. "It's a long story but we're surely going to tell it so you'd better start pouring beer my friend. And keep it coming. By the time you've served the rest of the lads, I'll be waiting for another. And then so will they.

"This is as close as I'm going to get to my boy's wedding and I'm going to enjoy myself. And we've a lovely little story to tell you about some Hooligans we've just run into."

"I'm all ears," said Michael, pulling the first of what he reckoned would be many, many pints that day.

As most of the lads queued for their first beer, two of them led laden horses to the blacksmiths. The Hooligans' swords were too big and heavy for normal men so they sold the lot to the blacksmith on the condition he melted them down and made horseshoes. It put the weapons beyond reach and paid for more beer. Good job all round, they thought.

Word spread rapidly through the town and soon the crowds were gathering to hear McCool's latest exploits. Oisin was a popular lad and everyone wanted to know about his wedding. And what was all this about dangling Hooligans from trees?

The bar was heaving with people when the door burst open and a giant strode in – a Hooligan.

"What have you done to my kinsmen, McCool?" he demanded from the doorway.

McCool barely looked up from his beer.

"Look lads," he said, "here's another one claiming to be an eejit."

Before the lads could laugh though, the Hooligan reached for his sword.

There was a loud, metallic swish as a score of swords were instantly drawn from the scabbards on McCool's men's hips.

"Looks like you're not just claiming to be an eejit, you seem determined to prove it," said McCool, rising and approaching the Hooligan.

"I've told the other eejits and now I'm telling you. I could have killed them but I didn't.

"They're hanging in the air a few miles north west. You'll doubtless hear them when you get close.

"Now you and your eejit family leave us alone. You haven't the brains to win a fight with us."

The Hooligan stared hard at McCool and, perhaps, decided he was right. What was clear was he wasn't going to win a fight in that bar. Without another word he spun on his heel and marched to his horse, off in search of his humiliated cousins, the sound of jeering in his ears.

McCool raised a tankard of beer above his head and called for quiet.

"Friends," he shouted. "I ask you to join me in a toast.

"Raise your glasses please and hail the joyous wedding of Oisin McCool and Princess Niamh of Tir na nOg."

And to a man, they did.

"IT WASN'T the last time your dad had a run in with the Hooligans," said McGinty. "In fact, he never missed a chance to wind them up, to make them look stupid. But they were smart enough to know they were beaten and didn't try anything as rash again."

"How long did he live?" asked Oisin.

"Difficult to tell, really. There's dozens of stories about his exploits and adventures but no telling how long he took to do them. It's fair to say he reached a good age, though, and lived happily enough even although he never really got over losing his son. He never had another one."

"Where's he buried?" asked Oisin.

"Again, no-one knows exactly," said McGinty. "Seems he chose a spot in a field and only told a few of his men where he wanted buried. He didn't want any Hooligans interfering with his grave when he couldn't fight back. When the time came, his friends laid him to rest in peace in his own part of the country."

"But I know where the field is," said Mac, out of the blue.

"And how the blazes would you know such a thing?" demanded McGinty.

"The name McCool may be no more, but there's a line of family, mainly the women, determined not to forget where we came from," said Mac. "Every generation has passed on the secret to one of the next. It was my Mum who told me, in case, one day, Oisin came back."

Oisin, Sean and McGinty stared at him in silence. It seemed McCool's legacy survived after all.

"Can you tell me where he lies, Mac?" asked Oisin.

"No, I can't. But I can take you there."

"And will you?"

"Of course. It's why I was told, after all. We can leave in the morning."

"Fine by me," said Oisin. "Gives us time for another few ales, don't you think, Sean?"

"Surely does," said Sean. "If I'm going scampering all over the mainland I might as well enjoy the company."

And so the tales began to flow, McGinty retelling everything he could remember of the life and times of Finn McCool.

Oisin took notes. He didn't know if he'd happen this way again but he was making sure he wouldn't forget his father's escapades.

One of these days, he was going to write them down.

THE TRIP to McCool's resting place was a day and a half's ride away and Oisin was pretty sure he'd know it when he saw it – the hills and valleys couldn't have changed much, even in 300 years.

Mac had given his mother an oath that he'd never pass the secret of the location on to anyone other than the next generation, which was why he was honour-bound to show Oisin the site, rather than simply point him in the right direction.

Of course, Mac also revelled in the privilege of time spent with Oisin and Sean. As Paddy said, you don't meet living legends every day and, what was more, he was related to one of them, however remotely. Moreover, they shared a name. Mac would have used any excuse to show Oisin where Finn McCool lay.

The heads were groggy in the morning but a fine day had dawned and the mission was clear so there was little point in delaying departure.

They'd slept in a room at The Cannon and Adam served them a fine breakfast before they tended the horses and headed out of the port towards the hills.

They chatted idly as they rode at a steady pace. Mac was keen to know all there was to know about Tir na nOg but it didn't take long for Oisin to run out of stories to tell. Not much happened on the island, he explained.

But still Mac had questions and Oisin and Sean were happy to answer. They had, after all, spent hours the day before asking question after question of McGinty and anyone else who had a tale to tell of Finn McCool.

They were over the hills and into the valleys when the day drew to a close. Mac revealed that they'd find the field over the next hill and on a bit in the morning, so they camped for the night, Oisin careful to ensure he had a shelter which would prevent him touching the ground should he roll over in his sleep.

They woke to a fine, hazy morning. The sun was low but aiming higher and the day was shaping up to be a cracker, which was all that Oisin could ask for.

Mac's word was good. From the top of the hill they could see a valley with a glinting silver river snaking through it, winding gently through woods and open grassland.

"It's there," said Mac, pointing. "Just where the river bends before entering that wood.

"The story goes that Finn knew he was nearing the end, took his bow and fired an arrow from that point into the field. He asked to be buried where it landed."

The trio descended the hill and crossed the river at a shallow ford, reaching the other side and following the bank to the point where the river turned towards the trees. It was as pretty a spot as anyone could imagine. The sun had burned off the haze and everything seemed to sparkle, from the river to the leaves on the trees.

"You can see why he picked the spot Oisin," said Sean "Wouldn't mind being laid here myself. As long as it's not any time soon, like."

Oisin laughed and they dismounted.

"I think we'll camp here," said Oisin. "No rush to get back over that river today, is there?"

Sean shook his head.

"No rush at all Oisin. You take your time."

Sean and Mac began setting up camp and preparing a fire. They'd brought food for the dinner and Sean had secretly brought beer and liquor. He figured the least they could do for McCool was throw a wake at his graveside.

Oisin walked into the field, taking in the view. He didn't expect to find a grave that had lain unmarked for 300 years but he knew he was close to his father's resting place.

And yet, he felt no sorrow at his passing. Oisin had long ago come to terms with the fact that his father was very long dead.

But he mourned that he hadn't been around to share the many adventures McCool had had in his absence. And that his father had died with no heir. Perhaps if Oisin had stayed, the name McCool would have lived on.

He mourned that he had been unable to bury his father himself.

But as he walked through the dozens of shades of green, with the sun on his back and the ripple of the river in his ears, Oisin came to be content. It was almost as if Finn McCool was speaking to him.

McCool had lived long and happily, a life full of fun and adventure. He'd been surrounded by good friends who had stood by his shoulder, whatever the threat, and who had tended to his passing with as much care as Oisin would have done.

There may have been no mound of earth but Oisin felt he was near. McCool, he realised, had accepted his son having to leave. There had been no option. It was Oisin's turn to come to terms with his own future.

He had all the answers he needed now.

It was time to get on with life.

It was time to go home to Niamh.

THE TRIO woke wearily, having spent the night drinking toast after toast to the late Finn McCool, draining most of the beer and liquor Sean had carried with him from Coulton.

Oisin slept particularly well, and not just because of the drink. For the first time in years he had nothing nagging at his mind in the middle of the night. He'd laid the memory of his father to rest.

And he knew that in just a few days he'd be home with Niamh.

Another fine morning brought the promise of fine travelling weather, so they broke camp and headed back.

On reaching the ford in the river, though, they found their passage blocked. Actually, they could still have crossed but a cart was stuck in the middle of the ford, a man struggling in front of it, shoving desperately at a large rock. The cart's wheel was snagged on it and his donkey couldn't pull it free. The cart wouldn't go either backwards or forwards. The man was stuck.

"Looks like you've got a bit of bother there my friend," said Sean, eyeing the situation. It was clearly a job for more than one man and a donkey.

"You'll never shift that on your own, man," said Mac, climbing from his horse. Sean followed suit but Oisin stayed in his saddle. He remembered

Niamh's warning and decided that clambering about in a river pushing rocks was perhaps a little too risky.

Mac, Sean and the stranger pushed the rock as hard as they could but they couldn't get a proper grip and the weight beat them. It seemed buried in the riverbed.

The stranger shook his head.

"Donkeys aren't as easy to guide as horses," he said.

"Not as strong either," said Oisin, patting Django's neck. "Have you a rope?"

The stranger went on to his cart and produced a length of strong rope which he held up for Oisin to see.

"That'll do," said Oisin. "Get it strapped round that rock so it doesn't slip then throw me the other end. You three pull from the side of the cart and me and Django will tow it out. If that doesn't do it, the cart will have to come apart."

Sean did the tying of the rope. Somehow the stranger didn't seem the most practical of travellers.

Oisin grabbed the other end and tied it to Django's saddle.

Right fellas," said Oisin. "Whenever you're ready"

"On the count of three then," said Mac.

"One, two, threeeeee….."

They all heaved, straining at the boulder.

And it shifted: tugged and hauled from under the cart's wheel.

But just as the cheer went up, Django's saddle strap snapped. The strain had proved too much. And as the saddle slipped sideways, so did Oisin, falling to the ground.

As he fell he turned and landed, his shoulders taking the impact. His shoulders, covered by his leather jacket, posed no threat. His head, though….

Oisin's head cracked the ground hard and fast, enough to knock him senseless.

Which was just as well because, as Oisin lay unconscious on that river bank, Sean, Mac and the stranger watched him wither like a plant hit by the first icy blast of winter. In the course of just a few seconds Oisin, son of Finn McCool and Prince of Tir na nOg, took on 300 years of mainland time, shrivelling and wrinkling before their eyes.

They ran to him but dared not touch him at first, terrified that a touch might break him.

It was the stranger who leaned forward first, lifting Oisin's head gently from the ground, searching for signs of life.

"He's breathing," he said. "No blood. Looks like just a bump on the head. But what a bump, eh?"

He looked up at Sean and Mac.

"Can either of you explain to me just what happened here?" he asked.

"After we tend to him," said Sean. "We need to get him comfortable and then figure out what to do."

The stranger went back to his cart and led the donkey across the ford and onto the far bank. He then prepared the back of the cart as a makeshift bed with clothing and mats as a mattress.

Sean and Mac considered the still unconscious Oisin, a fraction of his former self.

"The Princess is going to kill me for this," said Sean to no-one in particular.

"She doesn't sound that type, Sean," said Mac. "And we've enough to deal with right now without worrying about Princess Niamh's reaction."

Sean gave himself a shake.

"You're right. Do you think you can lift him?" he said. Even at around 325 years old, Oisin was still going to be too heavy for Sean to carry.

"No problem," said Mac. "Let's get him on that cart."

"NOW what?" asked Mac, Oisin resting, out cold, on the cart.

"No idea," said Sean. "This is well outside my experience. I'm stumped."

"You're stumped?" said the stranger. "I'm utterly mystified. Will one of you, please, tell me what is going on here? Because I can assure you it's not normal."

A whole world of weariness seemed to settle on Sean's shoulders. He had travelled to the mainland with one aim – to protect his friend Oisin. And he'd failed.

Whatever the creature lying in the cart was, it wasn't Oisin.

Sean was a man of few words so he attempted to sum the situation up for the stranger as briefly as he could.

"I'm from an island called Tir na nOg. Time works differently there. Our princess, Princess Niamh, had a dream about a man in trouble – this man – and we came to the mainland to find him. Niamh took him home but he missed his family and friends. So we came back to the mainland to find out how they had fared.

"But because time works differently in Tir na nOg, Oisin's family died and faded away while he lived and loved our Princess. Now, because he's made the contact with the earth he was born to, the years have come back to him. He's now over 300 years old. And unconscious."

Sean paused. He could have gone on but he figured he'd said everything that needed saying.

"So who are you to get a daft wee donkey cart stuck in a stream?" he asked.

The stranger looked at Sean and then at Mac, drew a breath and said: "My name is Patrick and I've come to this country to spread the word of God. There is a God who created the entire universe: the world, the sun, the moon and the stars. He created you and me and we should all worship him for that.

"He saw we had lost our way and sent his only son to us to teach us how to love and respect all of humanity. Some bad people killed him and sent him back to his father, who forgave us for our sins, proving His love for us.

"And now I travel the land to persuade mankind to devote themselves to God, who created everything, and to love Him as He loves us."

There was a long pause before Sean turned to Mac.

"You know Mac, I thought my story was ridiculous, but this fella's got me beat hands down in the story-telling game."

He turned to Patrick.

"Good luck wi' that," he said.

Patrick shrugged.

"Not everyone gets it," he said. "However, I do have a suggestion as to what we do with your Oisin."

"And what's that?" asked Sean.

"If he really is over 300 years old, I suggest you get him home to die in peace with his wife instead of in the back of my cart."

Sean sighed. Patrick might be mad but he was also right. He had to get Oisin back to Tir na nOg.

"The Princess is going to kill me for this," he said.

OF COURSE, Sean knew that both Mac and Patrick were right. Princess Niamh wouldn't hold him responsible for Oisin's condition. And he had to get her husband back to Tir na nOg.

"It's going to take a while to get him back to the boat in that cart," he said.

"Can't see an option," said Mac. "He's out cold so can't sit on a horse. Don't know if he's going to come round either, so we'd probably be better getting on with it than hanging about here, eh?"

"Agreed," said Sean. "Patrick, it looks like we're going to have to borrow your donkey and cart for a while."

"That's no problem," said Patrick.

"I've devoted myself to serving The Lord by helping others."

Sean hesitated for a moment before replying. Patrick was clearly mad but he was Oisin's only hope.

"Well," he said eventually. "I'm very grateful for that."

They set off with the donkey at walking pace. And since Hoatie – the name Patrick had been told the donkey answered to, on the few occasions it answered to anything – would be unable to pull the loaded cart over hills, they'd have to go round. Neither Shelbourne nor Mac's mount Reilly would fit the harness or the yoke. They'd look for a better way of carrying Oisin at the first town they reached.

It was a painstaking afternoon and they didn't make much headway. Hoatie seemed more interested in scenery than progress. It seemed to Sean that'd hardly covered any distance when dusk came upon them and they decided to camp.

They built shelters and erected a cover over the cart to avoid moving Oisin.

It was when Sean was strapping the shelter over the cart that Oisin showed new signs of life. He moaned and raised his hand to his head, then slowly opened his eyes.

"What happened?" he asked in a voice that sounded every one of his 320 years old.

"You fell Oisin. Touched the soil. And it looks like all those years you missed while you were on Tir na nOg have come back to you."

Oisin tried to sit up but failed. He lay back on the cart and raised his arm, his elderly eyes looking at the frail limb with its wrinkled, paper-like skin. His head fell back onto his pillow.

Oisin realised his life had changed forever. He'd lost his family, his friends and now his youth. He'd undoubtedly lost his beautiful Niamh too. Even if he could live to see her again, she wouldn't recognise the shell of a man he was now as her husband.

Oisin wept.

SEAN TRIED to console Oisin but he had no words for the circumstances. Oisin wanted to be left alone. Apart from having taken on a great age, Oisin had also taken a bad knock to his now elderly head.

Sean reckoned the best he could do was let Oisin rest and get some sleep himself. They all faced a hard, long day on the hoof in the morning.

When they woke, Patrick set about tending to Oisin. He made him as comfortable as was possible and persuaded him to take water and some bread he'd soaked so Oisin would be able to swallow it. He promised to make soup first chance he had. Oisin needed to keep up whatever strength he had left.

"What's the plan then Sean?" croaked Oisin from the cart once they were under way.

"It's not much of a plan Oisin, to be truthful," said Sean.

"Right now we're heading back to the Silver Spur to get you back across to Tir na nOg and the Princess. It might not be brilliant, but it's the best idea we've got at the minute. Unless you can think of anything better."

"I'm afraid not Sean," he said. "I've no idea how much longer I'm likely to last and I'd love to see Niamh one last time before I pass away."

"Well," said Patrick, "it might not be as bad as you think, you know. You don't seem to be ill. Just old."

Oisin looked at Patrick from the bed of the cart.

"Thanks for your help," he said. "I'm sure you'd rather not have got mixed up in all these shenanigans."

"Not at all Oisin," said Patrick. "This is my calling. I believe I was meant to be here, doing what I can to help."

Oisin raised himself onto a fragile elbow to look Sean in the eye.

"Is this fella serious?" he asked.

"You haven't heard the half of it," said Sean. "But, since we've got time on our hands, I'm sure you will. He's looking for converts."

"Converts?" said Oisin, his voice beginning to regain some power.

Sean looked over the cart to Patrick, tending Hoatie's reins.

"Why don't you tell him Patrick? The lad needs cheering up and a good laugh might help."

With good grace, Patrick told Oisin the story of his god and his mission to spread the word.

It took some time.

When he was finished, Oisin considered what he'd just been told,

"Aye," he said. "Good luck wi' that."

THEY'D been trekking for a few hours when they rounded a headland and spotted a small farm, smoke billowing from the farmhouse chimney and windmill turning gently in the breeze.

The sight stirred a startling response from the donkey, which began a loud, angry-sounding braying, as if shouting at the farm, pawing the ground as if preparing to charge. It almost reared but was held in place by the cart's yoke.

"What's got into that beast?" asked Sean as Patrick did his best to keep the donkey on track.

"Bizarre," said Patrick. "I've had him for a month now and he's done nothing but plod along and now, this. The fella who sold him to me did warn me about something, though."

Patrick thought for a moment.

"That's it," he said. "He said: 'That donkey, Hoatie, doesn't like windmills'."

"Well you'd better steer him away from that farm, then," said Mac.

"I was hoping to get some vegetables to make Oisin some soup, though," said Patrick.

"I'll go see the farmer," said Mac. "You keep heading straight and I'll catch you up. Not that that's going to be hard work the pace we're setting."

Mac rode to the farm and persuaded the farmer's wife – the farmer was tending the land and out of sight – to part with a bag of root vegetables for Patrick's soup.

He rejoined the group and they stopped earlier than planned so they could camp and cook. They were all concerned that Oisin should get as much nutrition as he could swallow.

It took a while but the soup was good and Oisin took it readily. So did Sean and Mac. It was the first hot meal they'd had for some time.

Patrick had made enough soup to last a few days and Oisin took more before they turned in for the night and again before they set off in the morning, Hoatie once again refusing to break into anything more than a light walk.

After another full day traipsing through the greenery they camped again, hoping they'd make the port the following day and meet up with the crew of the Silver Spur.

But there were others with other ideas.

WHEN THEY set off in the morning the port was on the horizon. In fact, they could see the main mast of the Spur in the distance. They'd have been aboard in jig time if they weren't relying on a donkey to get them there.

Oisin was persuaded to take more soup before the little group saddled up and headed out. He knew how close he was to the boat and that meant he was getting closer to Niamh. He didn't, though, realise how far away he was.

They set off early, hoping to make the dock that day. It was not to be.

Before they'd made any distance at all they found their way blocked. In their tracks stood three huge men astride three large horses.

"Why do I get the feeling there's trouble ahead?" asked Sean.

"Because they're Hooligans," said Mac. "You seldom run into Hooligans without some kind of trouble. It's like it's been bred into them."

They approached the Hooligans slowly. Actually, they had no option.

"Hah!" shouted the biggest of the Hooligans. "Looks like it's our lucky day lads. I reckon that's Oisin McCool and Sean of Tir na nOg."

He turned to Mac, looked him in the eye and said: "We heard you'd come back to the mainland McCool. Homesick were ye?"

There was a moment's confused silence as Sean and Mac worked out the Hooligans' error. They were ignoring the ancient bag of bones in the cart.

The Hooligans thought Mac was Oisin.

"McCool's the name, right enough," said Mac honestly. "Have you three a good reason for standing there making our beautiful country look ugly?"

The Hooligans snarled and stepped forward menacingly.

"You and your little band are prisoners now," growled the leader. "Unless you feel like fighting for yer freedom."

"But that's....." started Patrick, completely unaware of what was going on.

"That's fine by us," jumped in Sean. He knew they couldn't fight with Oisin's condition. And he knew he had a little weapon in the Hooligans' case of mistaken identity. Sean wanted to keep that in reserve until he had a chance to figure out how to raise help.

"We're not looking for trouble," he said.

"That's a shame," growled the Hooligan. "Because you've surely found it."

THE HOOLIGANS marched the little group at swordpoint to their camp. They'd set up just a few hours from the port. Experience had taught them they weren't welcome in Coltoun and they preferred their own company. Seemed Coltoun preferred them to keep their own company too.

Sean cursed their luck: another few hours would have seen them safe onto the boat. Instead Mac was now trussed arms and legs apart between two trees in the shape of an 'X'. Sean, who seemed less of a threat, was simply tied to a tree.

"Must think I'm less dangerous than you," Sean whispered to Mac when the Hooligans weren't listening.

"Well, they are idiots, after all," said Mac. "You've got to get back to that boat and get help, Sean. And it's not going to take these guys long to round up their country cousins. Then they'll wrap themselves around a few gallons of beer and we're probably in a whole new world of trouble."

"Once again Mac, it's not much of a plan, but it's the only one we've got," said Sean. "I'll have to get out of this rope but there's no point while they're still watching and it's light. If they find I'm gone you'll need to tell them I'm an old coward and a traitor. They'll understand that. I just hope I can bring back a gang in time."

Patrick and his daft donkey pulled the little cart with Oisin still in the back to a little cluster of trees which offered shelter. The Hooligans weren't bothered that they were apart from the other captives. They were harmless and clearly going nowhere in a hurry.

When they had settled and Patrick had rigged a shelter he turned to Oisin.

"What on earth are you boys working on?" he said. He was a good man, unused to badness or treachery. He had never thrown a punch, unlike anyone now around him. He was truly out of his depth.

"These are bad people, Patrick," said Oisin. "They're stupid but they're also bad. They have fought the people of Tir na nOg for many centuries and have never won. They hate that.

"Right now, they think Mac is me. They haven't killed him or Sean, which means they might be waiting for somebody more important to kill him. Or me, if you follow.

"But more likely, they're going to hold me – or Mac – hostage. They're likely wanting to pick a fight with Manannan – a fight they lost a long, long time ago and want to fight again."

Oisin looked at Patrick who was still looking puzzled.

"Sorry Patrick," he said. "It's a bit confusing."

"Not half as confusing as this thing with time," said Patrick, none the wiser.

"I can't explain the time thing. Don't understand it all but I know it works. The fight between me and these Hooligans I understand well enough though," he said, inching himself to the edge of the cart.

Oisin slowly swung his legs over the side and began to reach for the ground. His feet touched down. He tried to stand. But his muscles were too aged and weak to hold the weight. He began to fall.

"Whoa, there," said Patrick. "It was touching the ground that got you into all this bother in the first place Oisin. You need to take it easy my friend."

"Useless," hissed Oisin, enraged at his impotence." "Absolutely useless. Mac and Sean tied like hogs and me free to do absolutely nothing to help. Useless. How did it come to this?"

"God works in mysterious ways," said Patrick.

"If this is the work of your god, I want a word with him" said Oisin. "And it's not a nice one."

THE HOOLIGANS sent a rider out to let their cousins know the news. He'd be back the following day with as many Hooligans as he could find. There would likely be a few of them. It wasn't every day they captured Oisin McCool, after all. It was time for a celebration.

Mac and Sean had been stripped of their swords and bows but the Hooligans had missed Sean's two little throwing daggers he kept hidden in his boots. There was little point in breaking loose until nightfall, though.

In the meantime, Sean had to sit still as the two remaining Hooligans took it in turns to poke, pinch and punch Mac whenever the notion took them. They were having fun beating up on the wrong man.

Mac didn't do anything to help himself, right enough. He answered every punch, every kick, with a single word.

"Eejits," he'd say, knowing they hated it.

It only made them madder but the Hooligans weren't going to kill Mac – at least not yet. Still they managed to give him a good going over as his feet and hands were bound to trees.

Every now and then Sean would take a blow to the head or a kick to the ribs, just to make sure he was paying attention. Since the Hooligans were easily twice Sean's size, the blows hurt but he wasn't going to let them know that. An occasional grunt was all he allowed himself.

But Sean had learned many, many years ago that there was no point in fighting a lost battle today if you thought you could win the war tomorrow.

So he held his peace, such as it was.

The Hooligans finally fell flat from drinking and toying with their captives. Secure in the knowledge that Oisin – Mac – and Sean were tied tight and that Patrick and the bag of bones were going nowhere, they felt free to let down their guard.

Sean was bound tightly but he was a wiry wee guy and a few minutes of wriggling gave him enough slack to reach his throwing dagger. With that in his hand he was free in seconds.

He could easily have freed Mac, too but that would only set the Hooligans on the warpath, likely leading to a bloodbath. Sean's only hope was to reach help at the Spur. Even a few hands that could help overpower the small band of Hooligans and get Oisin back to the ship would be good.

"Remember Mac, as far as they're concerned, I'm a turncoat and I've just ratted out on you," he said. "I'll be back with as much help as I can get as quick as I can get it here."

"Good luck my friend."

"Don't stop to smell the flowers will ye?" said Mac. "It's getting kind of tense around here."

Sean scuttled off and found Shelbourne. He'd walk through the night rather than ask the horse to run in the dark. But he should make the port by daylight.

Then all he'd have to do was get the attention of the lads on the boat. And raise an army unit.

SHELBOURNE stood like a post as Sean approached, sensing that movement was probably a bad thing. Sean unhitched him – the Hooligans hadn't thought to secure him – and began the long, dark walk through the night.

The Hooligans had enough beer on board to allow Sean to leave unnoticed but, even with the moon in his favour, progress was slow. His eyes were adjusted to the dark but there was no way of seeing little dips in the ground that might trap and twist his ankle. Trees and bushes were no problem but holes in the ground?

He plodded long for a while, by then well out of the Hooligans' earshot before he felt a nudge in the back. Shelbourne had had enough of this inching about and he whinnied and gave Sean another shove to let him know.

Sean took the hint and mounted up.

Shelbourne, with eyesight far superior to Sean's in the dark, set off at a gentle trot. It wasn't racing, but it was better than plodding. Sean reckoned his horse would get him there on schedule.

He began to get things prepared in his mind.

He was prepared to hail the crew of the Spur and bring them to shore.

He was prepared to have them moor, mount their horses and launch a raiding party on the kidnappers.

He was prepared for the notion that he was leaving Spur defenceless if he took its tiny crew on a rescue mission.

He was prepared to raise his sword and charge the enemy with no regard for his own safety.

He was, however, completely unprepared for the sight that met him at dawn at Coltoun.

THE PRINCESS woke in the night again, but this time with a gasp. Deep in the night she knew, instantly, that Oisin was in trouble. Big trouble.

It was like a dagger to her heart and she bolted upright in her bed, arms clenched across her chest.

She had to go to him. And quickly.

NIAMH raised her tiny fist and was about to hammer on her parents' bedroom door when it opened.

Manannan stood in the doorway, dressed as if for the fields.

"Oisin's in trouble," gasped Niamh, struggling to breath through her panic.

"I know," said Manannan. "I felt it too."

"But…how…what…?" Niamh fumbled for words.

"We're very similar, you and I, Niamh. It's probably why we argue and fight so much. But we're cut from the same cloth and I know what you know and I feel what you feel. Oisin is family.

"That's why we're going to get him."

Niamh threw her arms around her father, pulling him close.

"Thanks Dad," she whispered, the tears not far away. Oisin might be in trouble but she knew her dad was going to fix it.

"Your mother's pulling on her gown. She'll be here in a minute. Wake Dimpna and get the kitchens open. We'll need to feed the lads before we get to work.

"I'm off to the quay to check on The Vantage and the tide. We'll talk about this when I get back."

With that Manannan marched off with a determined glint in his eye.

"Hooligans," he muttered to himself. There was no-one about to hear him anyway. "What's the matter with them, these eejits? Every two or three years they're at it, giving me more grief.

"I'm getting right scunnered with it. One more trip," he said. "One more trip and I'm going to sort these eejits good and proper, one last time."

He headed off into the dark, muttering.

"I'm getting too old for this stuff," he said.

FAND burst through the door, hair wild like she'd slept in a storm.

"This is no time for a nightdress Niamh," she snapped. "Get dressed like you're Oisin's wife."

Just then the castle bell rang out, deafening in the silence. It rang hard, loud and urgent, echoing round the stone walls and out to the grounds and the fields.

"That's your dad," said Fand. "I haven't seen him like this for years but I know when to keep my own counsel and let him be King of this place. He's in charge because he's the absolute best at this stuff so, for now, it's time to do what he says."

FOR MILES around the castle, men bolted from their beds, pulled on their boots and reached for their swords. The castle bell didn't ring in the night without good and serious reason.

Torches were lit. Horses were saddled. Tir na nOg's menfolk raced to the castle.

FLOYD MAYWEATHER heard the bell. He knew he'd have the King on his doorstep in minutes, so he snapped himself awake and dressed, ready with his answers. The Vantage was ready, as ever. Its cannon were shining, inside and out, its ammunition loaded and stacked, its powder dry and its crew just minutes away. They'd be on site within minutes of the first instruction: the sound of the bell of the castle of Tir na nOg.

Floyd peered through the gloom, expecting either the first crewman or the King. In the event it was, indeed, Manannan who got there first, muttering and cursing to himself in the dark.

"Manannan?" said Floyd. "You alright?"

"It's stupid o'clock, dark and I'm down at the quay checking out the warship Floyd. Do you think I'm even remotely close to alright?" barked Manannan. "How's the boat? And how's the tide?"

"The Vantage is fit for battle Manannan. The crew are on their way at the sound of the bell. Tide's out but we can sail around noon. We've got eight hours after that and then we'd have to wait for the next day.

"I can start loading men and horses in an hour."

"Good," said Manannan and spun on his heel, heading back to the castle. He had work to do.

But the King stopped, stood for a second, then turned back to Floyd.

"I'm sorry Floyd," he said. "I knew you'd be ready when we needed you. We need you now. When your crew arrive bring them up to the castle and I'll tell you why. You don't need breakfast. We'll have it waiting for you."

"No apology needed Manannan," said Floyd. "We'll be there. Armed and dangerous."

Manannan smiled at last.

"That's just what I needed to hear, Floyd. Thanks"

OISIN HAD trained them to fight. He'd given them a whole new set of skills and were fitter than they'd ever been. And they knew it. The men of Tir na nOg were going to be a handful for any band that crossed them.

But they were hopeless at assembly.

When Manannan got back to the castle there were hundreds of men, many on horses, milling around mystified. A bit of leadership was required, Manannan decided.

He stepped up to the dais at the far end of the courtyard which was by now well lit by torches. And he waited for hush.

Eventually it came. And then he spoke.

"My friends, it seems our Prince, Oisin, has run into a bit of bother on the mainland. It's not the kind of bother I can send a couple of lads in a wee boat over to fix, either. And worse than that, it's the kind of bother that could end up coming back here to Tir na nOg unless we stop it right in its tracks over there.

"So, we've got two missions: I'm going to get Oisin and bring him back; and I'm going to take those eejits who cause me bad dreams every couple of years and sort them out once and for all.

"I'm taking the Battle Battalion – you know who you are – and we're leaving as soon as we can get The Vantage loaded."

Manannan paused, letting his message sink in.

"Lads, this is full battle order. I can't guarantee we're all coming back.

"I'm not taking husbands or only sons but you'd better say what you have to say before you pull on your armour.

"If you're not coming, we still need you. If we fail, I need everyone on this island ready to defend it. If the next boat that comes up to that quay isn't flying our flag, I need every hand to hold a sword and know how to use it."

Manannan paused again.

"Right," he said. "The kitchens are open. Take breakfast, go home, saddle up and be at the quay by noon. And don't be bringing a sword that needs sharpening, eh?"

"OF COURSE I'M BLOODY GOING!"

Niamh yelled at Manannan with more vigour than she'd ever used before.

"That's my husband that's in trouble over there. What makes you think I'm sitting here waiting for you maybe to come back with him, maybe not?"

"I'm getting on that boat whether you're King or not because it's my husband we're going to get."

Manannan pulled his belt a little tighter then said quietly: "No you're not."

Niamh let out a scream filled with anger, anguish and helplessness.

"For a man who's supposed to be wise and lead our nation, you are remarkably stupid," she spat.

"That's not true, Niamh," said Fand, looking on. "Your dad's actually quite clever. But even clever people make mistakes, don't they Manannan?"

Being a king, Manannan chose to ignore his wife. That surely was a mistake.

Fand chose not to escalate the situation. Her shouting would only make Manannan dig his heels in further.

"Niamh, give me a few minutes alone with your father, will you?" she asked.

Niamh withdrew from the room, seething.

Manannan rummaged in a corner for his breastplate. He hadn't needed it for a few years. Hopefully it would still fit.

"Tell me, Manannan," began Fand, "how bad was this vision you had?"

"It wasn't a vision, Fand. It was a feeling. Overwhelming so it was. Almost a pain in the chest, so strong was it."

"And it was definitely Oisin?"

"It was. He's our Prince now so I figure that's why it touched me, as the King around here, something not everyone seems to remember."

"And he's definitely in bother?"

"Oh aye, big time. I've no idea if we can fix it or not but we've got to try."

Fand paused for a moment.

"Seems to me that you and Niamh had the same thing happen in the night Manannan," she said.

"Aye Fand. And that's double proof we need to go."

Fand paused again.

"Manannan, if I had that 'vision' about you, how do you think they would keep me off that boat?"

It took Manannan a moment to process Fand's words.

"I am not taking my daughter into that kind of danger," he said.

"Times have changed Manannan. She might still be your daughter but she's not your little girl any more. Niamh is a grown woman and she's as handy with a sword as plenty of your raiding party are.

"And she's right. She's married to our prince. It's her fight too."

"Manannan, I hate to say this but I have to. Niamh's place is not tending a field or a stove while you're off fighting for Oisin. She'd never forgive you.

"You've got to let her on that boat or risk losing her forever."

Manannan slumped into a chair. He marvelled how he thought himself so smart and how his wife and child could still run rings around him.

"And what," he said, "if this island loses a king, a prince and a princess in one day?"

"Then I'll help them elect another king," said Fand. "Oisin might already be gone for all we know. And princesses? They're 10-a-penny."

Manannan laughed at last and raised himself. He pulled his wife close.

"Ten-a-penny, eh?" he asked. "I'll not come home without her, though."

"Best you hadn't Manannan. Bring them both home."

NIAMH was striding the length of her room, backwards and forwards, arms folded tightly, face like thunder, when Fand entered.

She stared at her mother.

"There must be another boat I can take," she said.

"You don't need another boat," said Fand. "But you might need this."

Fand pulled the cover from the hanger she was holding.

"This is my armour," she said. "I never had to use it but was always ready to. It should fit.

"Your Dad says you've to be ready before noon to head to the quay with him."

Niamh stepped back, her face confused and hopeful.

"You mean, I can go?" she asked.

"You can go," said Fand.

Niamh ran to her mother and clutched her tightly.

"Thanks Mum. Thanks," she said.

"What, for sending you to battle? Maybe to your death? It's not thanks, I need, Niamh, it's forgiveness."

"You've got it Mum," said Niamh. "I couldn't watch them sail without me knowing I'd maybe never see Dad or Oisin again."

"Aye, but you'll let me stand at the quay and watch you sail will you?"

"Somebody's got to run the island while we're away Mum. That's the Queen's job, isn't it?"

"We'll be waiting for you, Niamh," said Fand. "Safe home."

RIDERS were dispatched to all corners of the island. All Tireans were to be on alert. There was no imminent threat to Tir na nOg but an attack couldn't be ruled out. If danger arose, they were to retreat to the castle. There was safety in numbers.

FLOYD HAD spent hours loading supplies. He'd no idea how long he'd have The Vantage at sea or moored away from home so he had laid in as much food and drink as the stores could push into the hold. The bulk of his space was reserved for men, horses and weapons though.

It was mid-morning when the crowds began to gather. It had been years since Tir na nOg had sent off a war party. Experience told them it might be the last time they saw some of the friends they would watch boarding the warship.

When they were ready, the expeditionary force gathered at the head of the quay, waiting for Manannan's order to board. They had said their farewells, just in case.

When Manannan mounted and stood Embarr at the castle gates to wait for Niamh his face was set: grim and determined.

When Niamh joined him, armour gleaming, helmet hiding her tied-up locks, she carried her father's bearing.

Manannan looked over at his daughter and she gave him a tiny nod.

She was ready.

"Let's go," said Manannan.

The path to the quay was lined with wellwishers. As they neared the pier, Niamh's friends stepped forward on either side, swords held high, offering her a guard of honour.

Niamh nodded to them all, too set on her mission to smile. But she liked the gesture. And she knew the girls would fight without her if they had to.

Floyd greeted them at The Vantage.

"Ready when you are Manannan," he said.

Manannan looked at the raiding party. They were 50 strong, plus a king, a princess and a fighting ship's crew. They were all steeled for action.

At the head of the column stood Andy Nicol, a fearless giant of a man. With his horse's reins in hand, he stepped forward.

He was officially head of the corps.

"Permission to board, Manannan?" he asked.

"Lead on Andy," said Manannan. "Let's get this job finished."

The party trooped on in single file, men and horses assuming their rehearsed positions on board.

When they were settled, Floyd's crew slipped loose the ropes and the sails dropped from the crossbeams, instantly filling with wind.

The Vantage sprung into action, bow lifting as she leapt towards the surf.

They were off.

SEAN made good, steady progress through the darkness and gradually picked up the pace as daylight approached. When dawn broke he saw her: the sails of The Vantage picked out against the rising sun.

"Manannan?" he said to himself. "How the Tir does he know to bring the warship to the mainland?"

Sean watched The Vantage sweep past The Silver Spur with a salute from the King to his fellow Tireans.

Finnegan had spotted The Vantage bearing down on Coltoun and weighed anchor and made way. He'd no idea what was going on but he wasn't standing in the way of the King of Tir na nOg when he was charging forth in his warship.

Finnegan and Mayweather were both master sailors but their skills lay with their own boats. Finnegan watched in admiration as Mayweather headed full tilt for the quay then spun the vessel like a toy just before impact.

The wash from The Vantage swamped the Coltoun quay as the warship edged up sideways. Mayweather's crew leapt ashore, dragging ropes to the capstans as the massive gangway crashed down from the ship's side and slapped onto the pier.

In seconds Manannan was ashore, ahead of a phalanx of men in armour leading horses. None of them looked in the mood for an argument. They marched up the quay to a band of alarmed townsfolk. Many had already fled but the curious remained, even if they did fear an invasion.

Manannan led the troops onto land, then addressed the locals.

"I'm looking for Oisin McCool," he called. "He came here with Sean Maloney of Tir na nOg on that boat in the bay. Who knows where I can find him?"

The townsfolk cowered back, unsure of the intentions of the new arrivals. And then a voice from the back rose up.

"Let me through, let me through," shouted Paddy McGinty shoving his way to the front.

"Tell me who you are, young fella," McGinty demanded.

Manannan had to smile at the greeting. It had been sometime since he'd been called "young fella".

"I'm Manannan, King of Tir na nOg. Have you seen Oisin McCool?"

"Seen him?" asked McGinty. "I got blind drunk with him and that Sean only a couple of nights ago. Didn't think it was going to cause all this bother, right enough.

"But that makes three living legends I've met in a week, Your Highness. It's a privilege and a pleasure to make your acquaintance. Paddy McGinty at your service," he said.

Manannan realised the local was friendly enough.

"Oisin's in trouble," he said. "Can you tell me where he is?"

"He's off with my grandson to find his father's grave," said McGinty. "Now if Oisin's in trouble, I figure that means both Sean and Mac are in trouble and I don't like the sound of that one wee bit. Who tells you they're in bother?"

"I do," said Manannan. "It came to me in the night. It was the same for my daughter."

At that, the men and horses who had surrounded Niamh broke ranks as the Princess walked her horse forward.

"Do you know where my husband is?" she asked.

McGinty tore his cap from his head and threw it in the air.

"Four!" he shouted. "Four living legends in less than a week. Unless I'm mistaken you're the Princess Niamh of Tir na nOg. This is unbelievable."

"Believe it," said Niamh. "Do you know where my husband is?"

"No, he doesn't," shouted a familiar voice from the back of the crowd. "But I do, Princess."

Sean had finally made the quay and had watched as his fellow islanders disembarked. He'd never seen a more welcome sight. He broke through the crowd and stood in front of his King and Princess.

"Why in the name of Tir is the Princess here Manannan?" he asked.

"I'm thinking that myself Sean, but there's only so many fights worth fighting."

"I don't suppose anyone thought to bring my armour, did they?" asked Sean.

"Took me ages to find it in that dingy wee hovel you call home Sean," said Manannan. "If we get out of this alive, I'm getting you a cleaner."

Manannan handed Sean his armour.

"Am I right in thinking we're going to need this kit?" he asked.

"More than likely," said Sean. "We've got a situation on our hands with some Hooligans. But it's worse than that."

Sean stopped and looked at Niamh.

"Princess, we stopped to help a man shift a cart in a river. Oisin's saddle strap snapped and he hit the ground. Your prediction was true. The years have come back to him."

Niamh showed no emotion. She was a princess on a mission.

"Where is he?" she asked.

"He's captured by Hooligans half a day away and they've got more on the way. But it's complicated. They've got the wrong man."

"You can tell us on the way Sean," said Manannan. "If there's going to be a fight I want to see the playground as soon as I can."

THE ROUTE was straightforward for Sean in daylight. The raiding party rode four abreast into the hills, Manannan, Sean, Niamh and Andy as the flag-bearer leading the way.

Sean explained how he and Oisin had met Paddy McGinty and Mac, how they'd gone to McCool's burial ground and paid their tribute. He told them about Patrick and his donkey and how Oisin had fallen and aged, how they'd been taken by just a handful of Hooligans.

They understood almost everything: the time that had come back to Oisin; the rudeness of the Hooligans; Mac's mistaken identity.

But Patrick stumped them.

Sean told them several times how Patrick planned to convince the world there was a single god who created everything and who deserved worship for everything, even if it was bad.

"Aye," said Manannan. "Good luck wi' that."

BY LATE-afternoon more than 20 Hooligans had gathered and were taking turns to goad Mac, still strapped between two trees.

"Help me to my feet," said Oisin. "I'm not having this."

"Settle, Oisin, settle," said Patrick. "What do you think you can do? You're in no shape to stand, never mind fight."

"I can tell them they've got the wrong man, Patrick," said Oisin. "I can't watch Mac take my kicking. It's me they think they're kicking and he's taking it. At this rate they'll kill him before long. And I'm already dead. I'm 320 years old and lost to my wife and family. I can tell them what's going on, Mac can live and I can do what I'm going to do anyway."

"I don't think so Oisin. If anything these fellas look like they'll kill you both and I can't see the point in that."

"There is no point at all, Patrick," said Oisin. "It's stupidity. But I can't let Mac die for me."

"The Son of God died for you so that you might live," said Patrick.

Oisin glared at Patrick from half-closed eyes.

"Will you give me my sword, please Patrick?" he said. "I swear I'm going to kill someone before I die, even if it's only you for being such an eejit."

SEAN CALLED the troops to a halt just before the crest of the hill. He dismounted and invited Manannan and Niamh to check the situation. From behind some shrubs they looked down on the Hooligans' camp.

It was wild.

The Hooligans were lining up to take turns punching or kicking the man they thought was Oisin. If they weren't queuing they were dancing and drinking. They'd caught themselves a living legend and planned to make him pay for their terrible history.

From the hilltop they could see the whole camp: horses tethered to the west; Mac bound to the trees at the northern edge and Oisin and Patrick unguarded to the south.

"Now," said Sean, "last I heard before I left was there's more Hooligans on their way, including Mawkit, who's the new boss Hooligan.

"I don't know what your plan is Manannan but we're up against it with 20 of these guys. If we don't fix it now we might be up against double their numbers later."

Manannan decided instantly.

"We'll hit them at dawn. It's nearly nightfall and these guys like to wrap themselves around lots of beer before it's dark so the rest won't be turning up tonight."

"I'm taking most of the lads and hitting them from the east and west. I'll head round to the far side and lead the first assault, with the second coming from the other side. That should cause enough of a stir to get their attention. I'll get a four-man squad to free Mac and I need one man to scatter their horses.

"Sean, keep Niamh out of the fight. Take her and two men and get Oisin and whatever his name is out of danger."

"You sure you don't want me with you Manannan?" said Sean

"You are with me Sean but we've all got jobs to do and these Hooligans are mine. I'm asking you to get my daughter and her husband to safety. That's a bigger job than mine and I can't think of anyone better for it."

Sean hadn't slept for a day and a half but Manannan's words rang true. If the King took the Battle Battalion, Sean could free the prisoners with relative ease.

"Best get to it, then" said Sean. "Will you make sure that lad Mac doesn't come to any more harm, eh? I've grown kind of fond of him."

Manannan was a giant compared to Sean.

"Give me your hand, Sean," he said.

When it was given, Manannan pulled his friend into his arms.

"Here we go again, my friend. Good guys against bad guys. Look after my wee girl will you?"

"With everything I've got Manannan."

IT TOOK Manannan several hours to get his troops into place but by dark they were ready. He knew time was important, that even more Hooligans were on the way. He needed to hit the camp before reinforcements arrived but he also needed surprise and he had to hold his position to guarantee that.

While the Tireans circled the Hooligans, the Hooligans continued their celebrations, revelling in having captured the Prince of Tir na nOg. And with every punch and kick Manannan saw them land on Mac, a man he'd never met, the more he resolved to finish things once and for all.

AT DAYBREAK, Manannan judged his troops were in place. With 20 men in his party there was no need for a signal. The Tireans were spread out in battle order.

Manannan simply spurred Embarr on and his men followed suit, building up speed as they neared the camp.

The first the Hooligans knew they were in danger was when the fire arrows fell from the skies, flaming and stinking and threatening. But they landed on the outskirts of the camp. And they kept coming, forming a blazing ring around the makeshift settlement.

When a full score of determined horsemen bore down on the Hooligans from the west, they were upon them before the enemy knew it.

But a wild, hungover Hooligan roused from his sleep is not to be underestimated. For a start, he knows no fear.

He's also enormous. And angry. And armed.

As the first wave of horsemen swarmed into the camp, the Hooligans instantly countered. They slashed wildly at the attackers.

But what they lacked in balance and reason, they made up for in sheer aggression and hatred. They were under attack and it didn't sit well. Attack was the best form of defence so they launched themselves at the invaders.

Too late they realised their horses were gone, scattered by Tireans intent on keeping the enemy on its feet and not on horseback.

Two Hooligans fell under the first wave, too slow, too drunk or too stupid to react to the assault.

The instant wave one tore through the other side of the camp, wave two arrived, ripping through the Hooligans still reeling from the first assault. Two more Hooligans fell as the Tireans burst through the other side of the camp.

As the second wave left another torrent of fiery arrows laid the camp to siege. The Hooligans could hardly see for smoke and flames and they had lost four men. Manannan had taken casualties but they were injured, not dead.

The Hooligans stumbled, blinded by smoke, befuddled by drink.

Manannan made them an offer: "Lay down your weapons and I will let you live."

He wasn't surprised when the Hooligans roared in anger and charged around looking for someone or something to stick their swords into.

"Round Two," called Manannan and another rain of fire fell on the camp's boundary followed by another battle charge from the west. Another two Hooligans fell in the smoke and heat.

Once again as the first wave left the scene, a second wave attacked, slashing and screaming through the Hooligans.

"Yield or die!" bellowed Manannan as quiet descended on the flaming, terrible settlement.

Manannan's men closed in on the camp. He counted 18 Hooligans surrounded by fire and horsemen.

One by one the Hooligans dropped their swords. One by one, they dropped to their knees, defeated.

"Who's your leader?" shouted Manannan.

There was no response.

"Who's in charge here?" he demanded.

Still nothing. The leader had either bolted for the coast to tell Mawkit what a clever Hooligan he was to have captured Oisin, or he'd fallen at the hands of Manannan's Tirean horsemen.

Whichever it was, these Hooligans were leaderless.

As the smoke began to clear, the Tireans rode gently through the dying flames and corralled the Hooligans together.

"Tie them up lads," ordered Manannan. "Tie them tight by the wrists behind their backs but loose at the feet. Then rope them together. I'll want to march them later."

Manannan surveyed the scene: four Hooligans killed; twelve Tireans injured enough to not to fight again that day.

They were losing three men to their one. He needed this plan to work.

MAC HAD truly had enough. He'd started the whole trick thinking he'd be out of the ropes in a few hours. But he'd hung there for much longer now and he'd been used as a kicking board by dozens of the biggest cowards he'd ever met.

And every time they hit him, he'd called them "eejits", which only seemed to make them madder, if that was possible.

He hung between the trees, the ropes just allowing his feet to touch the ground, every muscle beaten and strained beyond its capacity.

He was a puppet. And not a well one.

"Mac, we're here to help," said Dominic quietly amid the mayhem going on over his shoulder.

"Eejits," said Mac. It was the only word he'd said for over a day now.

"It's true, my friend," said Dominic. "We know what you did and we're here to get you out of it.

"Now, the lads are going to hold you and I'm going to cut the ropes. Then we'll get you seen to, alright?"

Mac gave a weak nod that Dominic had no option but to take as approval.

When they cut him down, Mac looked barely human after the beating he'd taken.

NIAMH and Sean inched their way to the shelter holding Oisin. The Hooligans had their hands full with the battle lighting up the air around them but still Niamh and Sean were on guard as they neared the shelter.

And then Niamh saw him – a bag of bones lying in the corner of a travelling tent. She knew in a heartbeat it was Oisin, being fed water by a stranger she assumed was Patrick.

"Oisin," she whispered, starting towards him

But the Hooligans had another idea. Almost all of the Hooligans had gone to the main camp to drink and beat up on the Prince of Tir na nOg. This Hooligan was guarding the prisoners, unimportant though they were. This Hooligan was left out of the celebration because this Hooligan was female. Part of the camp, she was dragged around the mainland and used and abused, mainly to cook for the menfolk.

But she was a loyal Hooligan and stood steady at her task. Spotting Niamh, Sean and another two Tireans advancing on her turf, she grabbed her sword and readied for battle.

Sean stepped forward, sword at the ready. But Niamh threw her hand across his chest to stop his advance.

"Sean," she said, "you can't hit a woman."

Sean stopped, unsure of his next move.

"I think you'll find that's my job," said Niamh.

She drew her silver and emerald sword and stepped forward.

She looked the Hooligan in the eye and, in a voice that started slow and low and rose to a threatening yell, she said: "Get away from him you BITCH!"

The Hooligan, for a second, was surprised. Then she looked around at the bag of bones being fed by a stranger.

"You came," she said, bemused, "for this?"

"That," hissed Niamh, "is my husband."

She paused and added: "And the father of the child I am carrying."

If Niamh thought her announcement would win any sympathy from the Hooligan, she was wrong.

The Hooligan thought for a moment as the significance of what Niamh had told her sank in.

She said: "Then he must die."

The Hooligan turned and made for the shelter, sword ready to kill.

Niamh leapt forward and drove her sword into the Hooligan's calf muscle, twisting twice before wresting it free.

The Hooligan howled and twirled, sword swirling in the air, but Niamh was too small and too quick to be caught by basic slashing.

As the Hooligan flayed about, Niamh drove her sword down into her enemy's massive sandal. She could feel it strike through bone, muscle and gristle as the Hooligan bellowed again with pain.

Niamh slipped away, sword poised, ready for a fatal strike.

The Hooligan was injured in both legs and couldn't fail to fall. She stared at Niamh and held her sword out in defiance.

"You are going to die," she shouted.

"Yes," said Niamh.

"But not today."

She leapt forward again and drove her sword into the Hooligan's other thigh. The Hooligan roared and reeled, trying not to fall but failing.

When she fell, the ground shook.

Winded, the Hooligan lay on her back, cursing, gasping for breath, blood streaming from her wounds and the crack on the head she'd taken in the fall.

In an instant Niamh was astride her, that emerald sword almost, but not quite, piercing the skin on the Hooligan's throat.

"Yield or die," whispered Niamh as she stared into the eyes of the woman who had planned to kill her husband. "Your choice."

It seemed to take the Hooligan minutes to decide but it was probably only a second or so before she dropped her sword and lay back, beaten.

"Remind me never to fall out with you," said Sean.

Niamh took a moment to gather her breath.

"That's not likely to happen Sean," she said. "I take it you had my back covered then?"

"Like I said to Oisin some time ago Niamh, it wasn't me that got the job done.

"Very nice, Princess. Very nice."

OISIN WATCHED, horrified, as his beautiful, tiny wife battled and bested the Hooligan woman. He knew he had taught her to fight but he'd never meant her to actually do it.

Incapable of interfering, he'd managed to raise himself from his cot enough to watch the entire episode. His misery was now complete: he was so utterly useless his wife had to fight for him.

And what should have been the happiest news since his marriage, that Niamh was carrying their child, was dashed by his certainty that he would never see his offspring born.

His heart, however, took a leap when the love of his life lifted herself from the stricken Hooligan, leaving her to the escort party to rope up, and began the short walk towards him.

Patrick, who had watched events from Oisin's side, said: "You must have done something right for that young woman to do this for you Oisin."

Niamh stood over Oisin, took his hand, still double the size of hers but now every bit as light, with skin she could see through, and said: "It's about time you came home, don't you think?"

"I thought I'd never seen you again Niamh," he croaked. "And now I have I wish you had never seen me like this. You should remember me as I was, not as this bag of bones."

Niamh gathered Oisin's head and held him close.

"Don't you remember what we said?" she asked. "Always and forever?"

Oisin sighed: "Aye, but it wasn't meant to be like this."

But they were where they were. Niamh had just one purpose now – to get Oisin back to Tir na nOg. Her father would need The Vantage for whatever he had in mind and for getting home. She'd have to take The Spur.

She looked up from her husband and met the stranger's eyes.

"I take it you're Patrick?" she said.

"Indeed," he replied. "I've done what I could to keep him comfortable but I'm afraid I've never seen anything like his condition before."

"And you're not likely to again," said Niamh. "But thank you."

"You're welcome Princess. But it's simply my calling," said Patrick.

"Aye," said Niamh. "Sean told me. Good luck wi' that."

"I seem to be getting wished a lot of luck by you Tireans. Perhaps I should take it as a sign."

"I shouldn't if I were you," said Niamh. "But I really am grateful for your help. And I do wish you luck."

The Princess paused for a moment.

"I came prepared for battle," she said, "so I've nothing to give you as a token of my thanks for your efforts. But this is a good luck charm my mother gave to me to take on my travels. I hope it brings you the luck you'll need."

Niamh held out her tiny purse for Patrick to take.

"What is it?" he asked.

"Plants. Leaves. We call it shamrock. It seems to have brought luck to Tir na nOg. It's probably just my mum being superstitious but it's meant well for you."

"What should I do with it?" asked Patrick.

"Just keep it with you," she said, then paused. "It might keep you safe from snakes, right enough. They seem to be scared of it. Maybe it's a smell or something."

"Think I'll get to planting the stuff," said Patrick. "I can't stand snakes."

"And what about all that 'all God's creatures under the sun' stuff, then?" asked Oisin, keen to show he could still join an argument.

"Well," he said, "that's the theory. But I'm only human and I draw the line at snakes. If this stuff keeps them away, I'll be planting it all over, believe me."

"Whatever you like," said Niamh. "But can we get Oisin back on the road? I'd like to get him to the port before we miss the next tide."

MANANNAN took one look at what used to be Oisin and instantly revised Niamh's plan.

"You've got to get that man home in a hurry, Lass. I'm not sure what good landing on the soil of Tir na nOg can do for him but he's not got much longer here."

"I'm old but I'm not deaf," said Oisin, wishing people would stop talking about him as if he wasn't there.

"Nevertheless Oisin, I figure there's no time to waste. Also, there's every likelihood that Floyd will have had to pull The Vantage away from the quay by now. You could get to the port and find the boats are offshore because of the tide."

Manannan turned to Niamh.

"There's no option. You'll have to take Embarr, riding two up."

Niamh instantly knew her dad was right. Embarr could easily beat even The Silver Spur back to the island. Embarr could run on water and, being a Tirean, would make a different sort of time on the way.

"But don't you need Embarr for dealing with the rest of the Hooligans?" she asked.

"I'll use Merlin. Straight swap. He'll be fine."

"He's never been in battle Dad. Embarr knows the score in a fight."

"He'll be fine, trust me."

IT TOOK three of the Tireans to get Oisin onto the saddle behind Niamh. He wasn't that heavy but they had to make every move for him, his muscles and joints had suffered so much.

Niamh held Embarr's reins tight in her fists. She'd known the horse for years and he her but she'd never left land on him.

For his part, Embarr stood steady, relaxed, as if knowing his task and knowing he was up to it.

Manannan made sure the couple were strapped securely. Embarr was likely to set quite a pace when he got going.

They were almost ready when Niamh turned to her father.

"Don't be going doing anything daft Dad, will you? Bring everyone home safe as soon as you can eh?"

"I told you, this time I'm putting this squabble to rest, once and for all. I've got a plan for these Hooligans when they make an appearance."

She turned to Sean.

"Safe home, Sean. All of you, eh?"

"We'll be fine, Princess. You look after my pal, will you?"

"And look after my horse too," said Manannan.

"Now go, before the Hooligans turn up or Oisin dies in front of us."

"Love you Dad," said Niamh.

"Love you back," said Manannan.

"Tell your Mum to have a good dinner ready tomorrow. We'll be famished."

He clapped Embarr on the neck.

"Go on, Boy. Take them home," he said.

Embarr turned without further instruction and began a walk, which broke into a trot and then stepped up to a steady gallop as he headed by the shortest route to the coast.

This time, he didn't need a pier.

SEAN TURNED to Manannan.

"So, Your Highness," he said, "We've got a dozen wounded, 18 prisoners, some wounded and a Hooligan war party on the way.

"What's your plan?"

"I'm taking those prisoners with us. But right now?

"We wait."

Patrick was enlisted to tend the wounded. Being a good man he tended to those with the worst injuries first, Tirean or Hooligan. He was no surgeon but treated those that could be treated and made comfortable those that couldn't. The Tireans would have to wait until they were home to be treated. Manannan would let the Hooligans who had started all this look after their own.

Mac, it turned out, was bloodied and bruised, but his injuries would heal with time and rest. The Hooligans might have been rough but they hadn't used weapons.

Manannan shook the man's hand.

"That took some nerve, my friend," he said. "And you didn't have to do it, so we're all grateful. Thank you."

"Ah, but I did have to do it," Mac mumbled through lips swollen and bleeding from blows. "Oisin's a living legend and I helped keep him living for a bit longer, that's all. And anyway, he's my cousin. Sort of."

Manannan laughed at the man who was squinting at him through eyes barely open through the swelling.

"Well, I'm still thanking you. You're welcome to join us on the boat when we head back, Mac. Tir na nOg can always use good men.

"And you'll live long and well."

"Aye," said Mac. "That's what your daughter said to my cousin and look what happened to him."

"Can't argue with that, Mac," shrugged Manannan. "But there's nothing can stop a man searching for a lost family if that's what he needs. Didn't have to be like that, though."

"Yes it did, Manannan. Oisin was always going to come back to trace the McCools. And I'm glad he did. He gave me a sense of place and purpose.

"It's been too long since this country had a McCool charging around making life a misery for Hooligans. They've been getting away with too much for too long. I'm going to put that to rights just as soon as I'm fit to get on a horse again. I know I owe a few of them a few slaps.

"As long as you're not planning to kill them all first, of course."

"That decision," said Manannan, "is mostly down to them."

MAWKIT Hooligan rounded the bend at a fair pace, his score or so of a party holding steady as a group just behind. Mawkit wanted to get his hands on Oisin McCool so badly he could almost taste it.

Mawkit wanted to go down in history.

Which he did.

Just not how he wanted to.

He knew – he'd been told by one of his own – that a small band of Hooligans had captured the son of Finn McCool.

What puzzled him when the camp came into view was the lighted torches. They surrounded the camp, forming, in the distance, an almost pretty circle.

It was bright daylight.

Undeterred, Mawkit bore down on the camp, determined to hold Oisin McCool to a sword and bring the Tireans ashore to meet his vengeance for 300 years of hurt.

"What's going on down there?" he wondered.

THE TIREANS had packed their wounded off, heading for The Spur and The Vantage. All those who remained were fit and ready, if needed, to join battle for the second time that day. One last push to finish the job.

They spotted the Hooligans at a distance and took up positions. The horses were tethered at a safe distance, under guard. Every man in the camp was on foot. And they all held a flaming torch.

As the Hooligans neared. Manannan mounted up. Sean joined him. The pair rode out without urgency. They planned to meet the visitors, not attack them.

Around 50 yards out, Manannan and Sean steadied their mounts and stood their ground, awaiting the party arriving at speed.

MAWKIT'S elation turned to dust as he neared the camp and realised it wasn't a Hooligan waiting to welcome him. In fact, it looked like his Hooligan cousins were corralled inside the flaming circle.

He slowed his approach. And as he got closer, he slowed again and then again, drawing to a halt just 20 yards from the two-strong welcoming committee.

Things didn't look like they were going to plan.

EMBARR picked up speed as he galloped onto the beach. The sea, he could see, was calm. The beach was flat. Not a single obstacle all the way to Tir na nOg. Time to break into a sweat.

He let loose a roaring whinny by way of warning to Niamh and Oisin: Hold on tight – it's going to be a bumpy ride.

"SEAN, I'M looking for a deal here but we might not get one," said Manannan, watching the Hooligans pull up in front of them. Stay close and ready, eh?"

"I've got a wee throwing dagger in my hand right now Manannan and it's itching to get between that eejit's eyes," said Sean.

Manannan turned his attention to the now-stationary Hooligans in front of him.

"Who are you and what's your business?" he demanded, staring straight at Mawkit, who looked over Manannan's shoulder, past the flaming torches and their smoke and regarded the gaggle of Hooligans tethered like cattle,

"What have you done to my kinsmen?" he growled.

"Kinsmen, eh?" asked Manannan. "You claim to be related to these thugs? These vermin who kidnap and beat up innocent travellers. These eejits who think they can hold decent folk for a ransom?

"You're related, are you?"

"You," said Mawkit, "are going to die."

"Correct," Said Manannan. "But, as my daughter would doubtless say 'not today'.

"You now have a choice.

"I'm taking my men back to our boats and I'm taking your eejit kinsmen with me. You can either watch me do that or watch your kinsmen die a terrible death.

"Every one of them is coated with the pitch we use to light the torches.

"It's coated on their jackets, their trousers. Even their boots.

"On my word – or if I fall – my lads will light your lads up."

EMBARR HIT the water and started to accelerate. He knew his mission was critical. He knew he couldn't just run over water today.

Today Embarr had to fly over it.

He upped the pace again.

Embarr flew.

"YOU WOULDN'T dare," said Mawkit, reaching for his sword.

Manannan raised his hand, wordless.

Behind him, four men raised their torches and walked towards the score of Hooligans on their knees in the centre of the clearing.

"If I drop my arm," said Manannan, "I'll show you a bonfire like nothing you've seen or heard before."

WEE JAMIE saw it first. Something on the horizon moving fast – very fast – towards the island.

Tir na nOg was on high alert.

Wee Jamie sounded the alarm.

From his look-out post above the quay he had a clear view for miles. His bell only needed to be heard for a few hundred yards.

Every hand reached for a weapon. Swords, knives, arrows, clubs.

If that was Hooligans approaching, Tir na nOg had a welcome for them.

"HOLD ON to me Oisin," shouted Niamh, clinging to the saddle herself. "This won't take long. Just stay with me."

Oisin felt like he imagined Mac must have felt - like being in a fight with your arms tied. And Oisin was 320 years old.

There was little point in him answering. His voice was too weak to be heard above the roar of the wind that Embarr was carving his way through and the surf he was clearing with every bound.

Oisin knew he'd be lucky to see this day out.

But at least he'd die knowing that, for one last time, he had his arms around Niamh's waist.

MAWKIT let his arm slip from his sword and back to the saddle. He'd have to kill Manannan later, he decided.

"We'll escort you to your boat," he said.

"I know," said Manannan. "In fact, I insist."

"On your feet you eejits," shouted Nicol. "We're going for a walk."

The now sober and thoroughly beaten Hooligans raised themselves. Their hands were still bound and they were bound to each other. The stench of the pitch that covered them from the neck down was almost overpowering.

Manannan figured he'd drive the Hooligans to the port well before nightfall. He didn't want to be hanging around on a pier for hours in a standoff with these Hooligans.

He knew he had just one shot at this. His trip could end in fire, death and eternal warfare if he didn't get this right.

THE DOT on the horizon grew larger as it approached but not by much.

Clearly it wasn't a boat, certainly not a big one. And it was travelling very, very fast.

"It's Embarr," thought Wee Jamie.

He turned and shouted: "IT'S EMBARR!"

MANANNAN led the way, the Hooligans strung out in a ramshackle, flammable chain with the Tireans on either side and Sean at the rear.

Sean had asked to bring up the rear, claiming his little throwing dagger was still itchy for Mawkit's eyebrows.

"You're dead," said Mawkit.

"You're an eejit," said Sean.

"I CAN see it, Oisin," said Niamh, screaming above the roar. "Nearly there."

Embarr was travelling so fast Niamh's eyes could barely pick out the horizon as the wind whipped at every part of them.

Oisin clung to his wife for what he thought might be the last time.

"GET BLANKETS, hot tea and buckets of water down here quick," shouted Fand. "And hot soup. Heat some soup in a hurry. Whoever's on that horse in going to be in a right state when it gets here."

THE TIDE was fine. Floyd had The Vantage moored but ready. His plan was only to drift into the bay if he was going to touch down. He'd have made a foolish warship captain whose ship ran aground as retreating troops needed to board. But the quay was deep and the tide was kind.

The Vantage remained ready and able. Her gangway rested on the quay for friendly boarders.

She also had 20 cannon fully loaded and ready to fire.

EVERY man and a few women and children in Coltoun turned out to see the spectacle. It wasn't often two score warriors on horseback rode into town with a score of shackled, stinking prisoners and a mounted band of 20 Hooligans bringing up the rear.

And no-one had seen so many torches lit in daylight.

"Get them aboard Andy," said Manannan and Nicol started with the least able, most of the wounded already aboard either The Silver Spur or The Vantage earlier in the day. The remaining warriors boarded without fuss.

The Hooligans, shackled, stinking and flammable, huddled at the quayhead, surrounded by four torch-carrying Tireans.

The torchbearers, Manannan and Sean were the last left on the mainland, their horses already on board.

Manannan stood on the quay and faced down Mawkit and his men, all livid and desperate for a chance to spill some Tirean blood.

"Right," shouted Manannan, "here's what's going to happen."

The townsfolk looked on, curious and nervous at once. Nobody wanted to be in the middle of someone else's battle.

"You," shouted Manannan at Mawkit, "will pledge your clan never to attack Tir na nOg or trouble a Tirean again. That pledge will extend to our extended family, which includes the clan McCool. And McGinty. You might start to see a few more of them in years to come.

"Now, Mawkit, because time works differently in Tir na nOg, your pledge is eternal. So your children and their children and so on will be bound by your vow."

Mawkit and his cohort stirred uncomfortably. None of them liked the sound of this. And yet they had no answer.

"You do have an option Mawkit," said Manannan.

"You can refuse that pledge and declare an eternal war on me, my family and my friends. And we can start that war right now.

"If you fail to pledge to peace, I'll take that as a declaration of war and I'll burn every Hooligan on this quay right now."

Mawkit was trapped. His options were few and he knew he was being beaten in front of a huge audience without even a fight.

"Get on your boat," he growled. "And don't come back."

Two flaming arrows dropped into the ground just feet from the tethered, pitch-covered prisoners. The lads on The Vantage knew their cue.

"Floyd," shouted Manannan, "give me two shots onto that hillside and train the rest of your cannon on this eejit I'm talking to."

The Vantage erupted into life as two of its cannon sent shells screaming into the hillside, erupting into blazing infernos. Startled by the sight of the flaming hillside, Mawkit turned back to look at The Vantage. He was staring straight down her other 8 starboard barrels.

"I need your word in front of these witnesses," said Manannan.

"You have my word," said Mawkit almost in a whisper.

"I heard that Manannan," shouted Mac through his split lips. "Plenty of us heard it. I'll make sure every man, woman and child in this land knows what he said. If he breaks that vow – or if another Hooligan in years to come does – they'll be known everywhere not just as eejits but lying, cheating eejits."

"Not even Hooligans want that as a reputation."

Mawkit slumped in his saddle.

"Leave now and never let me see you or your kin again, " he said.

"That," said Manannan, "is the only smart thing I've ever heard a Hooligan say.

EMBARR slowed to a gallop as he neared shore, then to a canter and a trot as he brought Niamh and Oisin back to the island.

Fand led the welcoming party.

"For the love of Tir, Niamh, what's going on?" she asked, alarm ringing in her voice. "And who's that you've got on the back there?"

"It's Oisin Mum. The years have come back to him. Help me get him home, please?"

There were enough hands around to bring Oisin to the ground. They lowered him onto the stretcher Fand had ordered.

"What about your father? And Sean and the rest of the lads?" asked Fand.

"Last I saw them, they'd beaten a band of Hooligans and taken only light casualties, Mum. Dad seemed to have a plan to fix this once and for all but I've no idea what it is. He did say you'd to get a good dinner on for tomorrow, though. Said they'd all be famished.

"They'll be home soon enough I hope. But Oisin's in a bad way and I

110

had to get him here in a hurry. Dad's got Merlin and he gave me Embarr."

Fand looked at the pitiful sight that used to be her son-in-law. There was little to be done for a man over 300 years old.

"Get them to the castle," she ordered. There were times an island needed a queen and this was one of them.

"We'll make him comfortable straight away Niamh. But I've no idea what else we can do."

"Getting him to his own bed will do Mum," said Niamh, grasping her husband's hand and walking beside the stretcher up the hill from the beach.

RIGHT Floyd," said Manannan, "have we got them all?"

"Everyone's here or on The Spur Manannan. We're ready when you are."

"Let's get these boats back where they belong then," said the King.

He looked back at the quay and the tethered Hooligans. Their kinsmen were drawing swords and slashing at their ropes, trying not to get themselves covered in the pitch which could so easily result in a fireball.

He turned to Sean: "I'm getting too old for this stuff, Sean."

"You're not alone Manannan," said his friend. "But when push comes to shove, somehow or other there's only a few of us come to the fore. If we don't do it when we have to, who will?"

"I had high hopes for Oisin, you know," said Manannan. "But it looks like he's six times my age now."

"You know she's having a baby, don't you?" asked Sean.

Manannan looked dumbstruck as the news sunk in.

"That's why she refused to leave him on the mainland.

"He's the father of her child," he said.

"How do you know? She kept it from me."

Sean told Manannan of the female Hooligan incident.

"Heh, heh, that's my girl," laughed Manannan. "But I'd have never put her on Embarr if I'd have known that."

He was still for a moment.

"We can't wait 25 years for Niamh's child to grow before we pick a new ruler, though," he said eventually. "And what if it's a girl? We can't ask our women to do our fighting for us."

"Niamh did it for Oisin," said Sean. "Pretty good at it too, she was."

"Ah well," said Manannan. "I'd been looking forward to spending more time with my horse and letting Oisin make the decisions. Seems I'm King for an awful lot longer. Unless the Tireans figure there's someone better for the job."

"You'll not have to worry about that, Manannan. They're as loyal as can be and they'll follow you anywhere, as they've just shown you.

"And you don't know what getting back to the island will do for Oisin."

"No, we don't," said Manannan. "But I can't see him riding fences in the morning.

MAC MIGHT have been in poor shape but he wasn't going to admit that to the Hooligans.

He stood on the quay watching The Vantage slip away then turned and shouted up the hill to Paddy McGinty, watching proceedings from the door of The Cannon, tankard in his hand.

"Grandad," he shouted. "Tell Adam I'm choking for a beer."

"A pleasure Mac," McGinty called. "I'll get it poured right away."

Mac pulled himself up to his full height.

"Haw Mawkit," he called. "You best start scrubbing these dirty eejits up. They're starting to stink the place up."

Mawkit was in no mood for banter but he'd been truly routed and had nowhere to hide from Mac's goading.

"Think they'll end up having to burn all those clothes they're wearing eh?" called Mac as he started the stroll to the bar. "Mind and tell the eejits to take them off first, though, eh?"

And the townfolk, still nervous from the standoff they'd witnessed, began to laugh.

And gradually the laughter grew until grown men were howling at the downfall of the Hooligans.

Mawkit's humiliation was complete.

NIAMH sat on the edge of the bed and cradled her husband in her arms. She had asked for help to change his clothes, wash him and lay him on their own mattress.

Then she'd asked for privacy. She had no idea how long Oisin might live but he was surely nearing the end and she wanted to tend to him herself and help him pass peacefully.

"Things have looked better, Niamh," said The Voice, talking inside her head, to no one else. Even Oisin couldn't hear her.

Niamh hardly stirred this time. Hearing The Voice in her head somehow seemed perfectly natural.

"Yes," she said. "We've had better times than this. There's nothing to be done now, other than to help him rest in comfort."

"Nothing to be done Niamh?" said The Voice, mildly surprised. "I thought you'd learned so much since we last had our little chat."

"Oh, I've learned," said Niamh. "I've learned to love. I've learned to fight. Now I'm learning how to lose."

"But you've a child on the way Niamh. Surely that must make you happy?"

"Of course," said Niamh. "Carrying Oisin's baby is a truly joyful thing. But loving Oisin and knowing he won't see his child is heartbreaking. It's so heartbreaking, I can't even let myself feel for now."

"The grieving can wait."

"You're not going to let him go without sipping from the Well of Dreams, are you?" asked The Voice. "The tiniest sip would help."

Niamh snorted.

"That's days away," she said. "And there isn't even a well to draw a drink from."

"You're a smart girl, Niamh," said The Voice. "I'm sure you'll work it out. And I'm sure we'll talk again.

"Good luck," said The Voice. And then it was gone.

Alone in the darkness, cradling her dying husband, knowing her child would never know his or her father, Niamh finally cracked.

She rocked gently, caressing Oisin's head, and began to weep.

Her sadness was all-consuming.

The tears poured from her eyes and she sniffed in her sorrow as they streamed down her cheeks.

And as her tears flowed, they fell on Oisin. On his face. On his lips.

As Niamh's tears wet his lips, Oisin licked them. The more she cried, the more Oisin sipped.

He sipped from the Well of Dreams.

It was tiny at first but Oisin began to move. His eyes awoke first. Then the fist clenched in Niamh's clenched back.

Gradually, Oisin began to grow strength.

Niamh sat and watched as her husband slowly began to throw off his years.

Oisin was recovering.

And then Niamh understood.

All this time she had carried the Well of Dreams with her. It was part of her, part of her very being.

Everyone she knew had a Well of Dreams inside them. It was a guide, a compass to tell them good from bad, right from wrong, love from hate. It was Niamh's Well of Dreams that made her who she was.

It made others too. Those who chose to ignore their dreams all too easily took the wrong turning, away from good.

As she watched Oisin grow right in front of her, she realised The Voice had meant Oisin to sip the tears from her Well of Dreams and to taste the pure love she and her unborn child felt for him.

And Niamh's husband came back to her.

"What's happening?" he asked.

"It's complicated," she said. "But I think you're going to be alright.

"Might need a bit of exercise and feeding up, right enough. But I think you're getting better. Welcome home."

She kissed him with love enough for the three of them.

And Oisin kissed her back.

STANDING on the deck of The Vantage, Sean bolted upright, as if he'd been struck by an arrow.

He looked at Manannan who stood at the helm with Floyd guiding them home. Manannan's face said it all: he'd felt it too.

"What was that?" asked Sean.

"You felt it too, then Sean?" asked Manannan. "I thought you didn't get dreams."

"I don't Manannan. And anyway, that wasn't a dream. I'm wide awake. What just happened?"

"It was a message, Sean. A feeling. And this is a good one."

"I've never known anything like that before, Manannan. It's really strange."

"Maybe you're one of the lucky ones Sean. Maybe you only get the good messages."

Sean stood, mystified, for a moment.

"Manannan," he said eventually. "I think Oisin's going to be alright."

"Me too," said Manannan, allowing himself a smile.

"Things just took a turn for the better, I think."

Sean remained flummoxed.

"But how?"

Manannan sighed.

"I've no idea Sean. Just because I'm the King around here – at least for the time being – doesn't mean I've got the answer for everything.

"All I can tell you is what you already know: time works differently in Tir na nOg."

ABOUT THE AUTHOR

Steve Brennan has been a writer and journalist most of his adult life,
sometimes even being paid for it. He lives in Coatbridge, Scotland, where
his wife Kate and daughter Niamh put up with him admirably.
He's pretty sociable so feel free to get in touch at

stevebrennan@europe.com

Printed in Great Britain
by Amazon